EAST BALI
Pages 100–123

LOMBOK
Pages 150–163

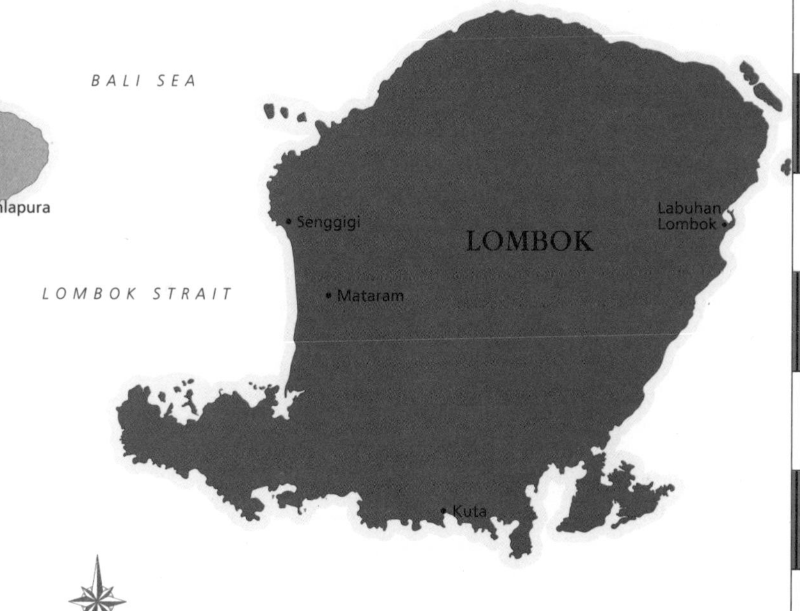

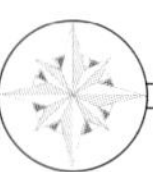

EYEWITNESS *TRAVEL GUIDES*

BALI & LOMBOK

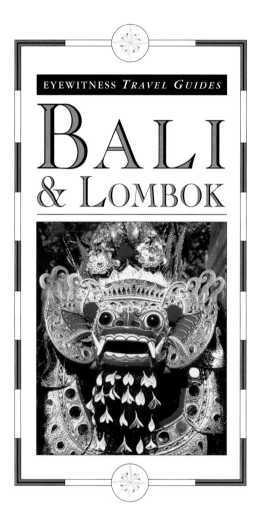

EYEWITNESS TRAVEL GUIDES
BALI
& LOMBOK
DK

LONDON, NEW YORK,
MELBOURNE, MUNICH AND DELHI
www.dk.com

Produced by Editions Didier Millet, Singapore
EDITORIAL DIRECTOR Timothy Auger
PROJECT EDITOR Choo Lip Sin
ART DIRECTOR Tan Seok Lui
EDITORS Samantha Hanna Ascui, Marilyn Seow
SENIOR DESIGNER Felicia Wong Yit Har
DESIGNERS Nelani Jinadasa, Norreha Sayuti, Annie Teo Ai Min

CONTRIBUTORS
Andy Barski, Albert Beaucourt, Bruce Carpenter, John Cooke,
Jean Couteau, Diana Darling, Sarah Dougherty,
Julia Goh, Lorca Lueras, Tim Stuart, Tony Tilford

MAPS
ERA-Maptech Ltd, Ireland

PHOTOGRAPHERS
John Cooke, Koes Karnadi,
Tim Stuart, Tony Tilford, Richard Watson

ILLUSTRATORS
Anuar bin Abdul Rahim, Denis Chai Kah Yune,
Chang Huai-Yan, Choong Fook San, Koon Wai Leong,
Lee Yoke Ling, Poo Lee Ming, Thomas Sui,
Peggy Tan, Yeap Kok Chien

Reproduced by Colourscan, Singapore
Printed and bound by South China Printing Co. Ltd., China.

First published in Great Britain in 2001
by Dorling Kindersley Limited
80 Strand, London WC2R 0RL

Reprinted with revisions 2005

A CIP CATALOGUE RECORD IS AVAILABLE FROM THE BRITISH LIBRARY.

ISBN 0 7513 6870 9

The information in this
Dorling Kindersley Travel Guide is checked regularly.
Every effort has been made to ensure that this book is as up-to-date as possible at the time of going to press. Some details, however, such as telephone numbers, opening hours, prices, gallery hanging arrangements and travel information are liable to change. The publishers cannot accept responsibility for any consequences arising from the use of this book, nor for any material on third party websites, and cannot guarantee that any website address in this book will be a suitable source of travel information. We value the views and suggestions of our readers very highly. Please write to: Publisher, DK Eyewitness Travel Guides, Dorling Kindersley, 80 Strand, London WC2R 0RL, Great Britain.

◁ **Pura Bukit Sari in the monkey forest at Sangeh, West Bali**

CONTENTS

Ganesha statue at Pura Luhur Uluwatu

INTRODUCING BALI AND LOMBOK

A pavilion in the grounds of Puri Agung Karangasem, Amlapura

Gunung Agung, the most sacred volcano on Bali and a prominent feature in the landscape

Bali and Lombok Area by Area

Freshly gilded temple parasols drying in the sun

Travellers' Needs

Nasi campur, "mixed rice", the most common Balinese dish

Survival Guide

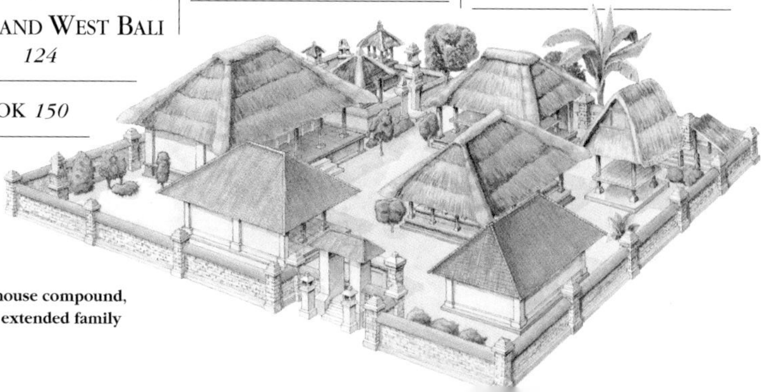

A Balinese house compound, home to an extended family

How to Use this Guide

THIS GUIDE helps you to get the most from your visit to Bali and Lombok. It provides detailed practical information and expert recommendations. *Introducing Bali and Lombok* maps the islands and sets them in their historical and cultural context. Features cover topics from festivals and music to wildlife and diving. Four chapters on Bali's regions, plus one on Lombok, describe sights of interest, using maps, photographs and illustrations. Restaurant and hotel recommendations can be found in *Travellers' Needs*. The *Survival Guide* has tips on everything from transport to safety.

Bali and Lombok Area by Area

The island of Bali is divided into four areas, each with its own chapter. A further chapter covers the island of Lombok. A map of these regions can be found inside the front cover of this book. All the sights are numbered and plotted on each chapter's *Pictorial Map*.

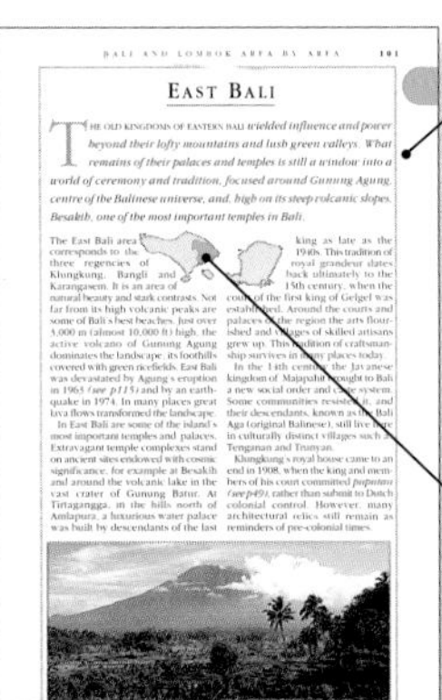

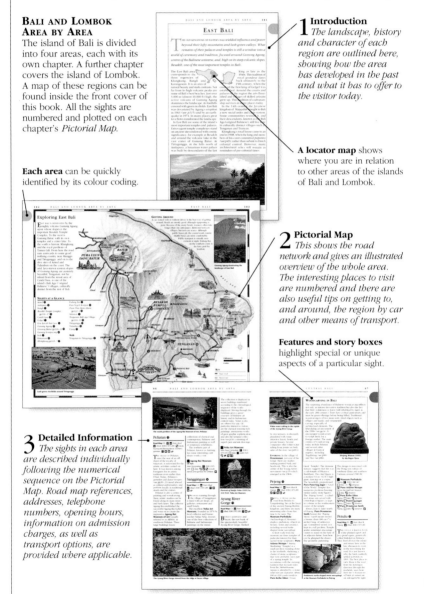

1 Introduction
The landscape, history and character of each region are outlined here, showing how the area has developed in the past and what it has to offer to the visitor today.

A locator map shows where you are in relation to other areas of the islands of Bali and Lombok.

Each area can be quickly identified by its colour coding.

2 Pictorial Map
This shows the road network and gives an illustrated overview of the whole area. The interesting places to visit are numbered and there are also useful tips on getting to, and around, the region by car and other means of transport.

Features and story boxes highlight special or unique aspects of a particular sight.

3 Detailed Information
The sights in each area are described individually following the numerical sequence on the Pictorial Map. Road map references, addresses, telephone numbers, opening hours, information on admission charges, as well as transport options, are provided where applicable.

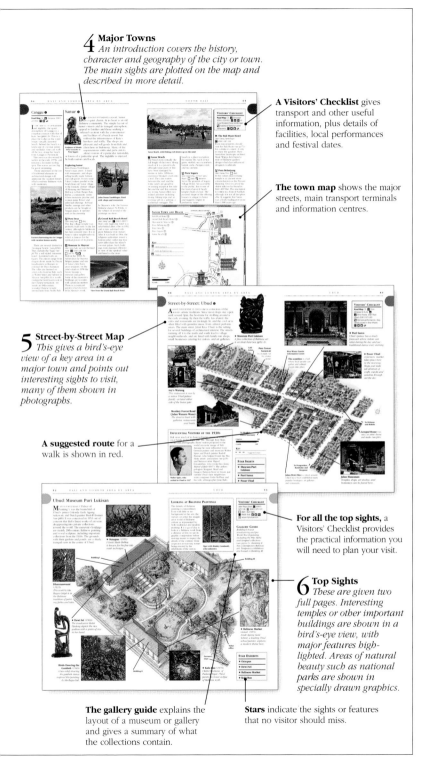

4 Major Towns
An introduction covers the history, character and geography of the city or town. The main sights are plotted on the map and described in more detail.

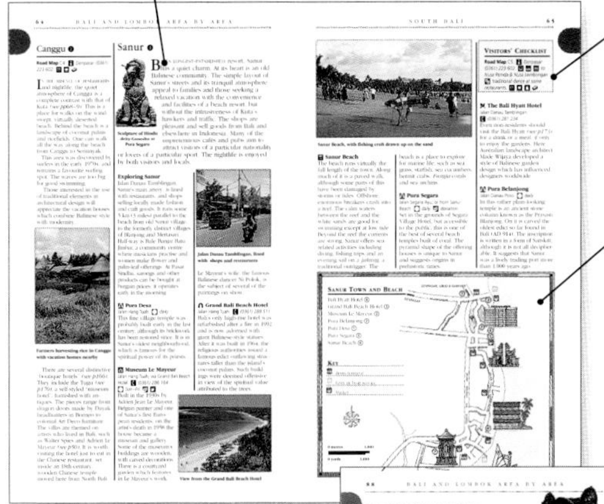

A Visitors' Checklist gives transport and other useful information, plus details of facilities, local performances and festival dates.

The town map shows the major streets, main transport terminals and information centres.

5 Street-by-Street Map
This gives a bird's-eye view of a key area in a major town and points out interesting sights to visit, many of them shown in photographs.

A suggested route for a walk is shown in red.

For all the top sights, a Visitors' Checklist provides the practical information you will need to plan your visit.

6 Top Sights
These are given two full pages. Interesting temples or other important buildings are shown in a bird's-eye view, with major features highlighted. Areas of natural beauty such as national parks are shown in specially drawn graphics.

The gallery guide explains the layout of a museum or gallery and gives a summary of what the collections contain.

Stars indicate the sights or features that no visitor should miss.

Introducing Bali & Lombok

Putting Bali and Lombok on the Map

THE ISLAND OF BALI lies east of Java, separated from it by the Bali Strait. Bali is 5,633 sq km (2,253 sq miles) in area. Lombok lies east of Bali, with an area of 5,435 sq km (2,098 sq miles). Bali (population 3 million) is more developed than Lombok (population 2 million). The main airport for both islands is Ngurah Rai International Airport near Denpasar in Bali; most onward travel to Lombok is by domestic flight, or by ferry from Padang Bai or Benoa Harbour. The road network reflects the islands' mountainous nature; many of the most important routes run along the coasts; roads across the islands follow the lie of the land.

KEY

- Airport
- Ferry and boat service
- Dual carriageway
- Major road
- Minor road
- Provincial boundary
- Regency boundary

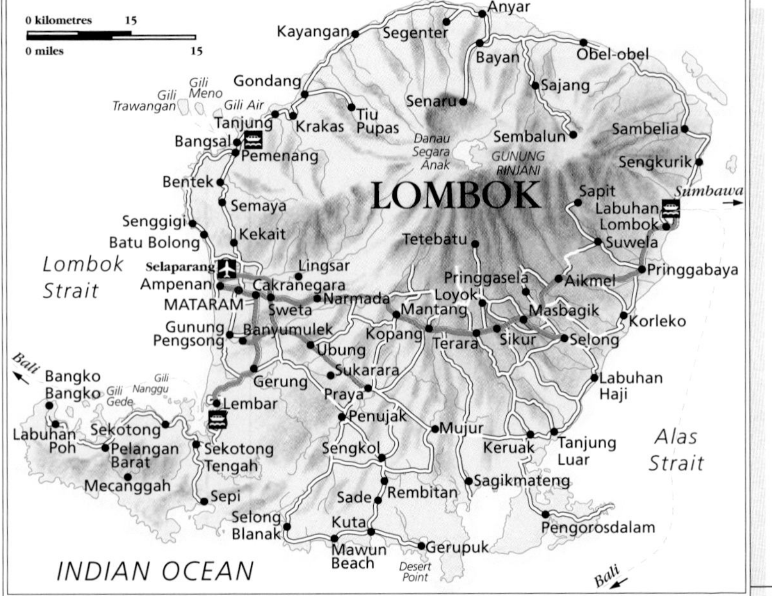

The Indonesian Archipelago

Bali and Lombok lie at the heart of the archipelago that makes up the Republic of Indonesia. The Balinese, however, with their Hindu tradition and rich artistic heritage, have a strong sense of distinctness from the rest of Indonesia.

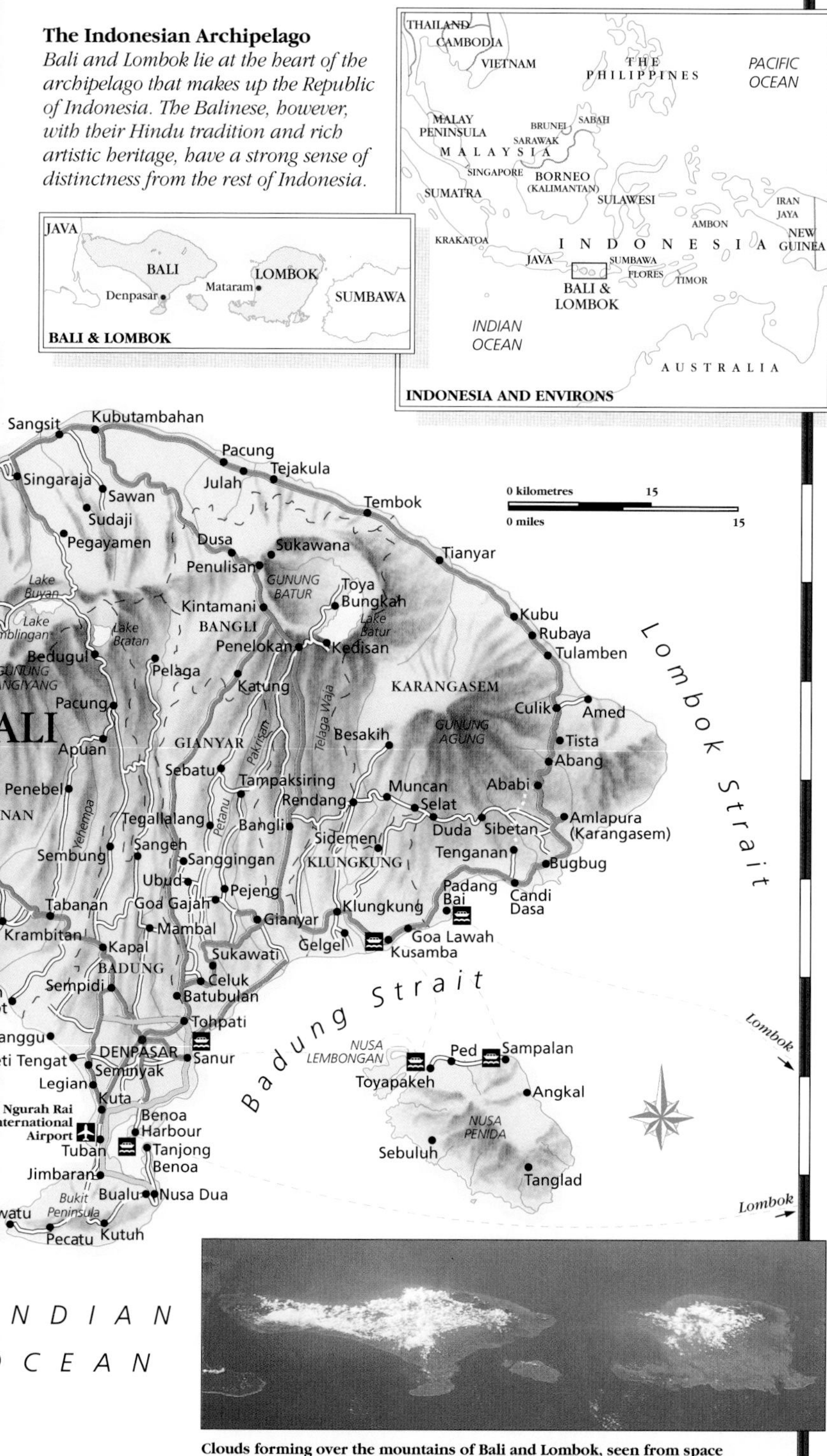

Clouds forming over the mountains of Bali and Lombok, seen from space

A Portrait of Bali and Lombok

The islands of Bali and Lombok are sufficiently close to be visible to each other on a clear day. They are both volcanic, are of similar size and have much else in common. However, they offer the visitor very different experiences. Bali – noisy, colourful, crowded and glamorous – is one of the world's most celebrated destinations; quiet Lombok was long a travellers' secret.

Geographically, Bali and Lombok are at the centre of the Indonesian Archipelago. This is a vast chain of islands stretching from the Indian Ocean to the Pacific. It lies across the ancient trade routes between Europe, the Middle East, India and China, and has absorbed influences from all these civilizations.

Bali is a province within the Republic of Indonesia, with its provincial capital at Denpasar. Lombok is part of the province of West Nusa Tenggara; Mataram, the provincial capital, is on the island. Both are mainly rural societies, despite the urbanization of southern Bali in the 1980s and 1990s.

Stone statue from Klungkung

Facilities such as electricity and television came to most places only in the last quarter of the 20th century (despite this, the internet is already widely used).

In daily life on Hindu Bali and mostly Muslim Lombok, great importance is attached to community matters, including social harmony. With Indonesia's move in the late 1990s from dictatorship to democracy, there is great awareness of the importance of religious tolerance, while at the same time each society takes pride in its own identity. Bali eagerly shares its flamboyant religious culture; the people of Lombok, however, are generally more reticent.

The Mayura Water Palace in Mataram, a legacy of Balinese rule in Lombok ***(see p155)***

◁ **A villager carrying her offering to an *odalan* (temple festival)**

A Balinese family group carrying holy water to their house temple

The Balinese Way of Life

At the core of Balinese society is the village, a cohesive religious community organized around a group of temples. Village members are required to take part in temple rituals and assist in the community's funerary rites.

Religious practice in Bali entails music, theatre and elaborate offerings. The labour-intensive nature of rituals requires a high degree of social organization, visible in the village layout. Family house compounds are usually laid out on a north-south axis. The village core is dominated by temples, market, civic structures and often *puri*, houses of the nobility.

Painting of rice terraces

On Lombok, most of the indigenous Sasak people are orthodox Muslims *(see p23)*, their social life organized around the family and village mosque.

A road-side food stall near Candi Dasa

Economic Development

Bali and Lombok were both prime rice-producers until land began to become scarce in the mid-20th century. Since then the government has encouraged crop diversification, particularly into commodity crops such as coffee, vanilla, cloves, tobacco and citrus fruits. Today, land is increasingly being used for tourism. There seem to be few alternatives. Marine and coastal resources have never been energetically developed, perhaps because of the more salubrious climate of the rice-growing regions; until the advent of tourism, the coasts produced little more than coconuts and salt. Fishing remains generally a poor man's occupation.

There has been little true industrialization. Some artisanal manufacturing has emerged in South Bali, particularly in the garment industry around Kuta; but although this does absorb some local labour, it also attracts workers from other, poorer islands who are willing to work for lower wages, compounding problems of unemployment with new social challenges.

On the other hand, cottage industry, in particular handicrafts, has allowed local economies within Bali and Lombok to shift away from agriculture without a great rural exodus.

Arts and Handicrafts

Handicrafts and the production of art objects for secular use have become a vigorous export industry in Bali. Styles of painting, wood sculpture, jewellery and textiles have been adapted for sale to visitors and to export markets *(see pp36–7)*, and this has opened up new creative opportunities.

A sizeable expatriate community in Kuta, Sanur and Ubud has played an important role in developing this sector together with local entrepreneurs. Recently, Bali has also become a marketplace for handicrafts, antiques and reproduction furniture from other islands of the Indonesian Archipelago.

Lombok has a venerable tradition of making low-fired domestic pottery *(see p154)*. The artisans are generally women, aided in the heavier chores and the marketing by their husbands. Lombok's hand-woven textiles and shapely rattan baskets have also found an eager international market. There are great hopes that tourism will further strengthen the island's local economy.

A beach in South Bali, the tourist centre of the island

Tourism

Tourism came to Bali much earlier than to Lombok *(see p51)* and is far more developed here. On both islands there is awareness of its economic importance. On Bali, it has created an almost urban density in Kuta and Sanur; this is increasingly the situation in Ubud too, and density of road traffic is also now a problem. On Lombok, tourism is concentrated on the fertile west coast around Senggigi and the unspoilt Gili Isles *(see p156)*. The south coast of Lombok has splendid beaches that are still relatively pristine, although extensive development there is planned around the village also called Kuta *(see p162)*, where tourism is still on a small scale. For most travellers, even from outside Indonesia, access to Lombok is mainly by way of Bali.

Despite sporadic internal disturbances associated with broader political changes in Indonesia, Bali and Lombok remain places where social harmony is greatly prized and visitors are regarded as welcome guests.

The rural landscape of Central Bali

The Volcanoes of Bali and Lombok

Bali and Lombok lie in one of the geologically most active regions on earth, part of the Pacific Rim's great "ring of fire". They are two in a chain of volcanic islands which stretches some 3,500 km (2,200 miles) from Sumatra to Flores, and which marks the point where the Australian tectonic plate is being forced beneath the Eurasian plate at a rate of 6 cm (2 inches) each year. The volcanoes of Bali and Lombok have influenced the way human societies on the islands have developed, and still play a very important role in the culture of the islands' inhabitants.

Gunung Agung (see p114), *at 3,142 m (10,308 ft), is Bali's highest and most sacred volcano.*

The peak of Gunung Batur*, seen here from the air, and nearby Lake Batur are set in a spectacular caldera, created about a million years ago, when the top of the mountain was explosively blown off by the pressure of accumulated magma.*

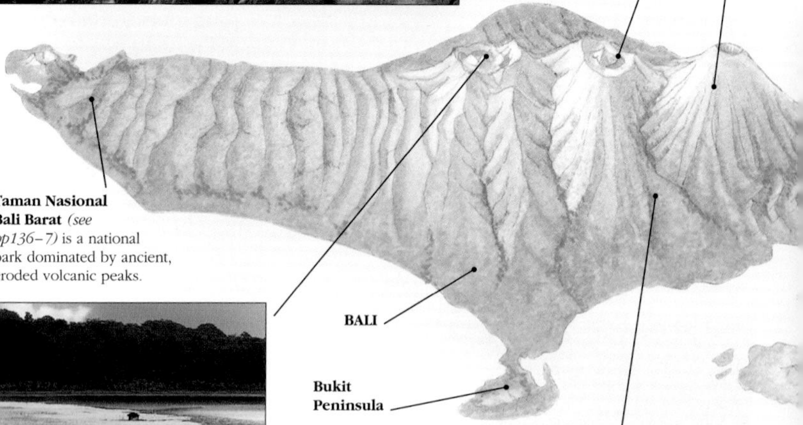

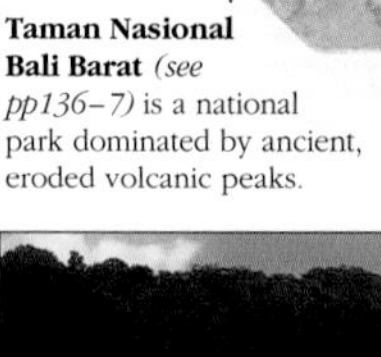

Taman Nasional Bali Barat *(see pp136–7)* is a national park dominated by ancient, eroded volcanic peaks.

BALI

Bukit Peninsula

Lake Tamblingan (see pp140–41) *lies in an ancient caldera. Volcanoes, such as Gunung Lesong, have grown within the caldera since its formation, hiding all traces of the southern rim.*

Deep gorges and steep ridges *run north and south from the higher peaks, making east-west travel difficult. This is why traditional Balinese society developed along river valleys and on the coastal plains.*

Volcanic Eruptions

Volcanic activity, including the deposition of magma, can cause changes in the landscape. These drawings show the rapid changes in the peaks of Gunung Batur during the major eruption of 1926. Today the volcano is still active and it enjoys small, regular eruptions. The last one in 2000 created a small cone, which is visible from Kintamani. Other major eruptions in recent years include that of Gunung Rinjani in 1994 and that of Gunung Agung in 1963. The latter caused widespread devastation and hardship *(see p115)*.

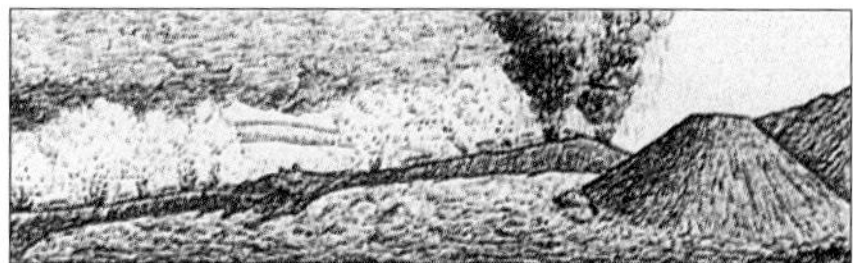

An early stage in the very destructive eruption of Gunung Batur which took place in 1926

The landscape a few days later than the view in the upper drawing, showing significant changes

The Volcanic Landscape

The line of volcanic peaks running along Bali and Lombok is the islands' most conspicuous physical feature. One mountain or another is visible from almost any location. The combination of volcanic soil and rainfall has created a richly fertile environment for agriculture.

Gunung Rinjani (see pp158–9)*, at 3,726 m (12,224 ft), is Indonesia's second-highest mountain. Within its caldera is the small but still active volcano Gunung Baru, and a beautiful crater lake, Danau Segara Anak.*

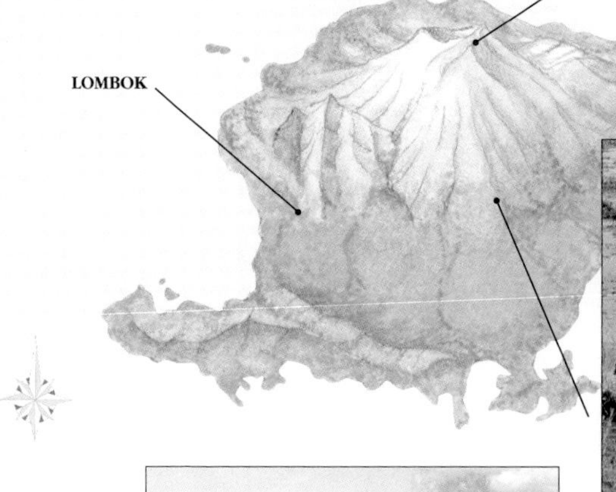

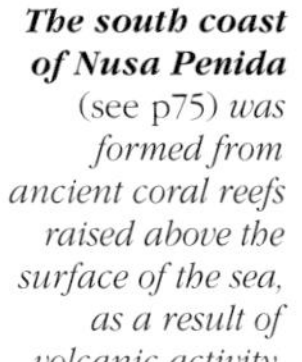

The south coast of Nusa Penida (see p75) *was formed from ancient coral reefs raised above the surface of the sea, as a result of volcanic activity.*

Fertile ricefields *are irrigated by the streams flowing down Gunung Rinjani. The soil is rich in tephrites and silica.*

Landscape and Wildlife of Bali and Lombok

Tree frog, common in Lombok

Bali and Lombok have a rich flora and fauna. Human activity, including agriculture and (more recently) tourism, has caused some loss of habitat diversity. Nevertheless, large areas are still unspoilt, and some are officially protected. There are few places better for the nature-lover than Bali and Lombok, where conditions for walking and exploring range from arid mountain slopes and high natural forests to the margins of rivers and ricefields and the seashore.

Giant golden orb weaver, common in lowland areas

Forests

Much of Bali and Lombok was once covered in forest, including large areas of lowland rainforest. Much has been destroyed; causes include volcanic eruptions, coffee and coconut cultivation and collection of firewood. Lush forests still grow on Bali's southern and western mountain slopes. On the drier, northern slopes the forest is deciduous.

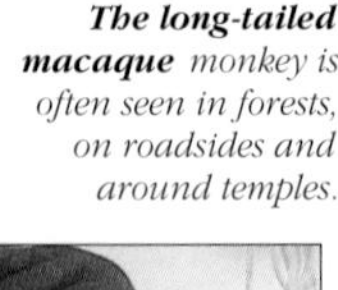

***The long-tailed macaque** monkey is often seen in forests, on roadsides and around temples.*

***The black-winged starling** is an endangered species that lives in the deciduous forests of northwest Bali, as well as in open grasslands.*

Volcanic Peaks

After volcanic ash is deposited by an eruption, centuries pass before the formation of soil capable of sustaining a rich plant life. However, the slopes are soon colonized by mosses, grasses and ferns, and there is a diverse bird life. On the arid northern and eastern slopes grows a grassland vegetation often punctuated by lontar palms.

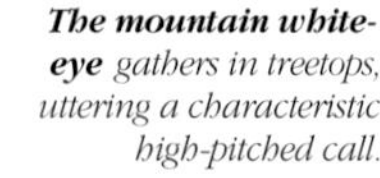

***The mountain white-eye** gathers in treetops, uttering a characteristic high-pitched call.*

***The helmeted friar bird** inhabits the arid mountain areas of Lombok.*

***The senduduk flower**, with its exotic pink petals, is found in mountain scrub.*

Wallace's Line

Alfred Russel Wallace (1823–1913), a British naturalist, noted differences between the wildlife of the former tectonic landmasses of Asia and Australia – marked by a line that passes between Bali and Lombok at its southern extremity. The Australian group includes birds of paradise, and species such as the orange-banded thrush, which is seen in Lombok but not in Bali. The Asian group includes monkeys and the tiger (the latter last seen in Bali in the 1930s). Another example is the fulvous-breasted woodpecker, more often seen in Bali than in Lombok.

Orange-banded thrush

Wallace's Line

Rivers and Ricefields

Some 150 rivers flow through the gorges of Bali and Lombok, assisting irrigation of the rice crops. Here birds, frogs, toads and spiders can live on planthoppers and other small pests which cause damage to the rice itself. The birds include egrets, herons, ducks and small finches.

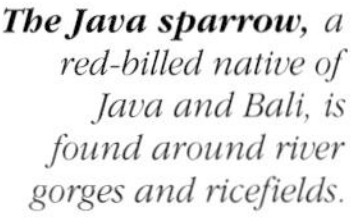

The Java sparrow, *a red-billed native of Java and Bali, is found around river gorges and ricefields.*

Toads *live in damp habitats such as ricefields; here they survive on a diet of insects, including grasshoppers, beetles and crickets.*

Coastlines

The beaches, coral reefs and shallow waters around these islands support a huge variety of marine life, even in developed areas such as Sanur. Although little true mangrove forest remains, mangroves still absorb the force of waves, helping to reduce coastal erosion.

The lionfish*, while visually attractive, is poisonous to touch. It lives in waters off the smaller islands around Bali.*

The green turtle *is endangered; it is hunted for its meat, sometimes used in Balinese ritual.*

Rice Cultivation

Rice goddess

THE MOUNTAIN LAKES, the gentle climate and the volcano-enriched soils of Bali and Lombok are ideally suited for the growing of rice (*Oryza sativa*). Although some of the islands' rice-farming land is being converted to other uses, terraced ricefields are still the dominant feature of the rural landscape, and the cult and cultivation of rice remain much as they were in Neolithic times. Steep terrain makes mechanization difficult and poses a particular problem for "wet rice farming" – water flows far below the arable land, in deep river gorges. The Balinese solution, which dates from as early as the 9th century AD, is an ingenious and complex network of irrigation channels, tunnels and aqueducts that diverts water from sources high up in the mountains to water-sharing communities known as *subak*.

Padi Bali *is the generic term for several strains of traditionally grown rice, a tall, strong plant with a growing cycle of 210 days.*

The paddy field *is a basin of packed earth reinforced with intertwining grassroots. Irrigation water is let in and out of each field individually through a small gap in the earthen wall that can be opened or closed with a hoe. The water is drained off through channels that empty into rivers.*

Rice plants nearing full growth

RICEFIELD CEREMONIES

Across the island of Bali and among traditional farmers in Lombok, offerings are made in the ricefields at significant stages of the rice-growing cycle. These rituals reflect the central importance of rice cultivation in the traditional life of the islands. The most elaborate ricefield ceremony takes place when the rice grain begins to form on the stalk. A small shrine to honour Dewi Sri, the rice goddess *(see p25)*, is built by the farmers in a corner of their ricefields and decorated with handmade palm-leaf festoons.

Bamboo shrines where offerings are given to the rice goddess

***The rice barn**, once a common feature of houses in Lombok and Bali, is where sheaves of the older strains of rice are stored. The grain is threshed by hand as needed. These buildings are less frequently seen than in the past.*

Coconut, banana and bamboo grow along high ridges above the river valleys, concealing small village communities

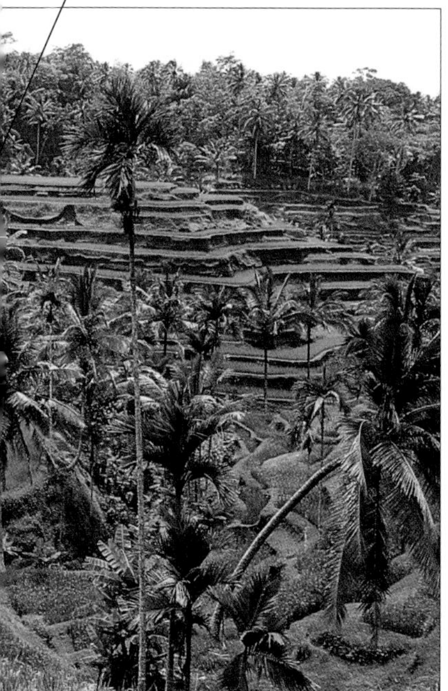

RICE TERRACES

Bali's terraced ricefields have been described as an "engineered landscape", a collaboration between nature and human beings. Terracing allows rice to be planted on steep slopes and protects the land from erosion. Each terrace is irrigated by a complex series of channels, controlled by small dams.

River gorges can often be seen below rice terraces.

THE RICE-GROWING CYCLE

*1. **Rice seed** is planted in a protected bed. While the seedlings mature, farmers prepare the fields.*

*2. **The planting basin** is prepared by flooding, ploughing and levelling the field.*

*3. **Seedlings are transplanted** into flooded fields by hand. As the plants mature, the fields are alternately flooded and dried at specific stages to maximize growth, and they are periodically weeded.*

*4. **Harvesting** is done by women, who cut the stalks with a small knife concealed in their palms so as not to frighten the rice goddess.*

*5. **High-yield varieties of rice** are threshed directly in the fields and put in bags to be taken to a rice mill. Older strains of rice are kept on the cut stalks and gathered into bundles to be stored in a rice barn until needed.*

*6. **After harvest**, fields are burned off, producing a soil-protecting alkaline ash.*

The Islands' Religions

THE MAJORITY OF THE BALINESE are Hindu. Most of the Sasaks, the indigenous people of Lombok, practise orthodox Islam. However, permeating religious practice on Bali and Lombok are animistic beliefs and a sense of the supernatural *(see p24)*. Ancient agricultural and mountain cults are reflected in temple and village architecture, and in rural rituals. There are Muslim and Christian minorities in Bali's towns and coastal areas and a smaller number of Buddhists.

Temple offerings *are a prominent aspect of Hindu observance in Bali* (see pp38–9).

Traces of Ancient Cults

In architecture and ritual practice, the forms and beliefs of prehistoric Indonesian societies are still visible today in modern Hindu Bali and the traditions of rural Lombok.

Spirit house

A temple *in stepped-pyramid form suggests that a site predates Hindu times.*

Rice cult image made from palm leaves

A shrine *at the grave of folk hero Jayaprana, near Labuhan Lalang* (see p138), *draws petitioners for supernatural favours.*

Hinduism

Balinese Hinduism has elements not only of the Shivaite cult, but also of animism and Buddhism. Deities are believed to visit the human realm on ritual occasions. Temples hold *odalan* (anniversary festivals), during which gods are honoured with offerings, music and dance *(see pp38–9)*.

Holy water*, the medium of the gods, is sprinkled on offerings and distributed along with rice grains to worshippers after prayers.*

Villagers carrying a temple effigy in a portable "ancestral spirit house" during a temple festival

ISLAM

Most people on Lombok are Muslims. Like the majority of Indonesians, they follow a traditional form of Islam which often incorporates underlying folk traditions. In some of the more isolated parts of the island, the Sasaks adhere to a form of Islam known as Wetu Telu, mixing Islamic beliefs with pre-Islamic, indigenous and Hindu-Buddhist elements. Like Balinese Hinduism, Wetu Telu ascribes great powers to the spirits that dwell within nature.

A village mosque in Lombok

Many Muslims *in Bali and Lombok can be seen wearing the traditional* peci *cap, particularly on Friday, the day of prayer.*

BUDDHISM

Although certain Buddhist cults flourished in Bali at around AD 1000, it was not until late in the 20th century that mainstream Buddhism gained any significant presence here. Buddhists are still a small minority.

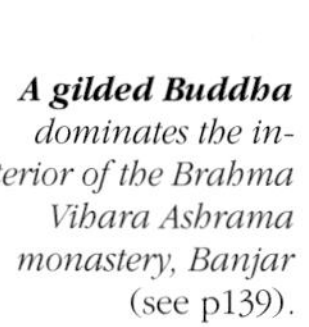

A gilded Buddha *dominates the interior of the Brahma Vihara Ashrama monastery, Banjar* (see p139).

CHRISTIANITY

Small communities of Protestants and Catholics are to be found in West Bali, where they resettled after conversion by missionaries in the early 20th century. Many Balinese people of Chinese descent are Christian.

The Catholic cathedral *at Palasari has architectural features which echo Balinese temples.*

RELIGION IN COMMUNITY RITUALS

In Bali and Lombok religion plays a part in rituals such as weddings, funerals and coming-of-age ceremonies, which require the participation of an entire village *(see pp28–9).* In Muslim Lombok, the most festive rituals are circumcision rites, undergone by boys around the age of eleven.

A gilded offering bowl holds ritual implements.

Hindu high priests *conduct a ceremony as part of the preparation for a royal cremation.*

This palanquin (ceremonial litter) is in the form of a painted lion.

At a circumcision rite, *a Sasak Muslim boy is paraded through the streets.*

Traditional Beliefs

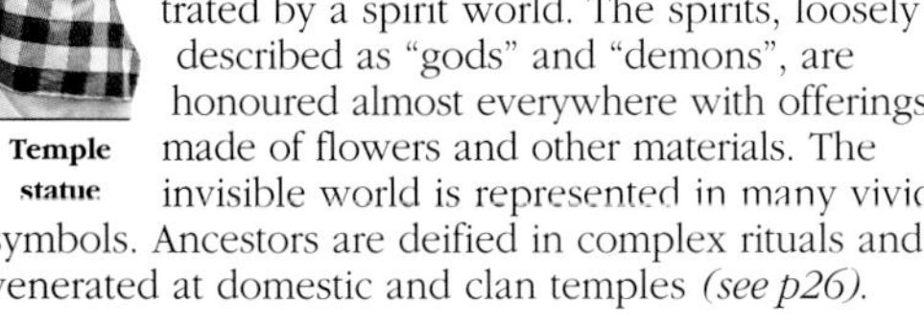

Temple statue

ANIMISM AND ANCESTOR WORSHIP are a strong undercurrent in Balinese life, even in local Hindu observance. The Balinese term *sekala niskala* ("visible-invisible") sums up the idea that the physical world is penetrated by a spirit world. The spirits, loosely described as "gods" and "demons", are honoured almost everywhere with offerings made of flowers and other materials. The invisible world is represented in many vivid symbols. Ancestors are deified in complex rituals and venerated at domestic and clan temples *(see p26)*.

Figure of Rangda at Puri Saren, Ubud's royal palace *(see p90)*

Animism

Large stones, trees and other powerful-looking natural objects are believed to be favoured dwellings for invisible beings. To keep these spirits content, a shrine or small temple may be erected for them. *Buta kala* (ground spirits) are demonic energies that cluster at crossroads, graveyards, rivers, in certain trees, or wherever there is an important life event such as a birth, a death or an accident. They are appeased with offerings that contain meat or strong drink.

***Keris* (dagger)**

***Objects** such as daggers and consecrated masks are seen as imbued with great spiritual power, and can give rise to trance possession.*

Parasols indicate that a deity is present.

The effigy of the god is presented with offerings.

Guardian spirits reside in demonic statues.

A shrine by a sacred tree, decorated on holy days when holy water and offerings are placed here

Magic

Fear of the supernatural feeds a widespread fear of witchcraft. Practitioners of Balinese "black" and "white" magic may engage invisible powers such as *buta kala* (ground spirits) to heal or harm. Household offerings are made to the spirits daily.

Daily flower offerings known as *canang*

A *tumbal*, a type of magical drawing often prepared by a witch doctor, is shown as protecting a man against the influence of a *buta*, or spirit.

***Tumbal (Magical Amulet)* (1938) by Anak Agung Gede Sobrat, Ubud**

THE RICE GODDESS

The Hindu goddess of prosperity, Dewi Sri, became identified in Bali with the rice spirit of local belief, and she is honoured in the fields, the granary and the rice basket. Her image in offerings and textiles is known as the *cili* motif. According to tradition, after the daily meal has been cooked, tiny rice offerings must be set out before food can be consumed.

Wooden ornament with *cili* motif representing the head of the rice goddess

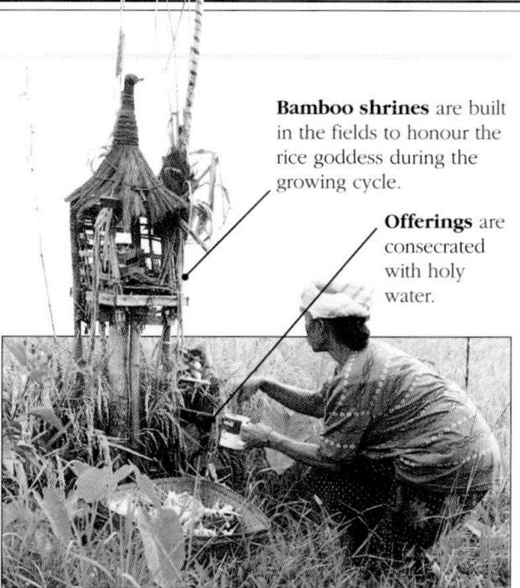

Bamboo shrines are built in the fields to honour the rice goddess during the growing cycle.

Offerings are consecrated with holy water.

BARONG AND RANGDA

The dragon-like Barong (representing order, harmony and health) and his demonic counterpart Rangda (associated with chaos, illness and harm) are guardian effigies. They are periodically "awakened" to restore the spiritual balance of a village by means of a ritual battle culminating in wild trance. Devotees of the Barong attack Rangda with their *keris* daggers. Rangda's power turns the daggers against the attackers; the Barong's power prevents the blades from piercing their bare skin.

Rangda, identifiable by her fangs, striped breasts and necklace of entrails

The Barong's beard is made of human hair.

The magical power *of the Barong and Rangda is concentrated in their masks, which are kept in a village temple and given offerings.*

"HIGH" AND "LOW" SPIRITS

The Balinese believe that human beings can help keep "high" and "low" spirits in balance through making ritual offerings to both. For the Balinese, the universe is dualistic in nature, a play of ever-shifting opposites. This opposition is symbolized by the black-and-white checked textile known as *poleng*, in which statues and other objects thought to be magically charged are often wrapped.

The ubiquitous *poleng* cloth

Guardian statues wrapped in *poleng* cloths, as often seen in Balinese temple forecourts

Balinese Temple Architecture

A BALINESE *PURA* (public temple) is a holy enclosure where Hindu deities are periodically invited to descend into *pratima* (effigies) kept in shrines. During *odalan* (festivals), temples are alive with music, dance and offerings *(see p38)*. Otherwise they are rather quiet. Temples include the *kahyangan tiga* (the three village temples – *see pp28–9*), clan temples, market temples, irrigation temples, temples to nature deities, and "state" temples of former kingdoms. Temples are usually open to visitors during daylight hours.

***The* padmasana shrine** *("lotus throne"), in the most sacred corner of the temple, has an empty seat at the top open to the sky, signifying the Supreme God.*

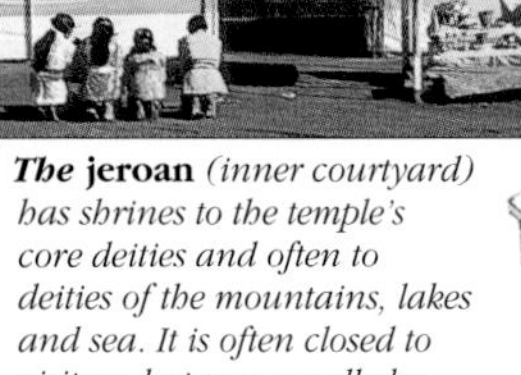

***The* jeroan** *(inner courtyard) has shrines to the temple's core deities and often to deities of the mountains, lakes and sea. It is often closed to visitors, but can usually be viewed from outside the walls.*

Pelinggih *are shrines or "seats" of the gods. The dark fibre used for the roof, which resembles human hair, is a product of the sugar palm.*

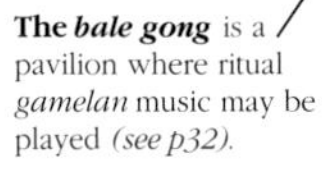

The *bale gong* is a pavilion where ritual *gamelan* music may be played *(see p32)*.

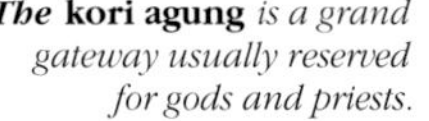

***The* kori agung** *is a grand gateway usually reserved for gods and priests.*

The *bale agung* is the village council pavilion.

TEMPLE LAYOUT

The arrangement of Balinese temples follows a generally consistent pattern, with individual structures orientated along a mountain-sea axis. Degrees of sacredness are reflected in proximity to the mountain.

***The* meru** *shrine has 3, 5, 7, 9 or 11 tiers, depending on the importance of its deity. It symbolizes the Hindu holy Mount Meru, but can also represent other sacred peaks.*

BALI'S MAIN TEMPLES

There are tens of thousands of temples on Bali, perhaps 200,000 including house temples. The locations of the most important ones are shown here. Visitors should observe temple etiquette *(see p219)*.

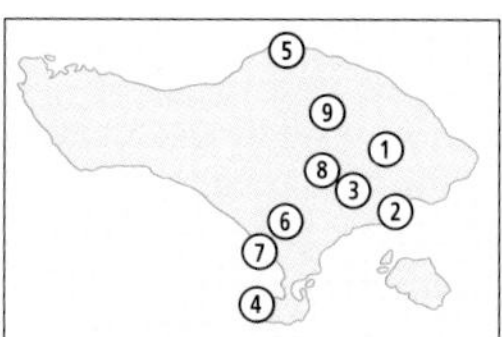

WHERE TO FIND THE PRINCIPAL TEMPLES

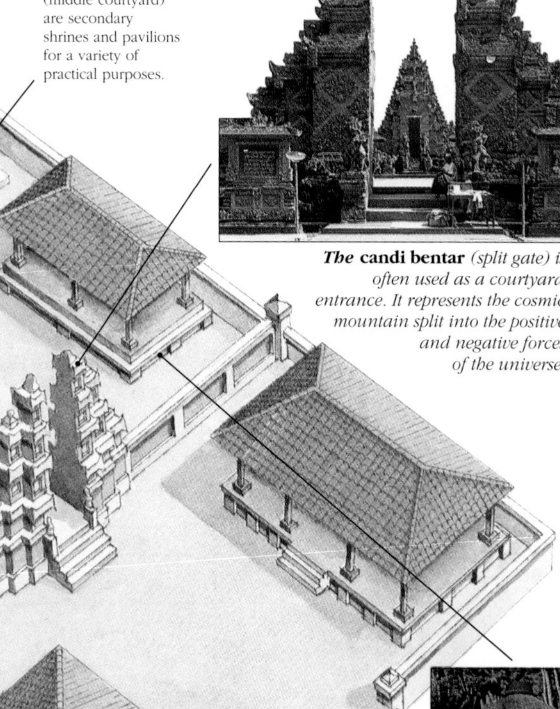

In the *jaba tengah* (middle courtyard) are secondary shrines and pavilions for a variety of practical purposes.

***The* candi bentar** *(split gate) is often used as a courtyard entrance. It represents the cosmic mountain split into the positive and negative forces of the universe.*

The *kulkul* is a watchtower with a drum which is struck when deities are thought to descend to the temple.

Entrance

***The* bale piasan** *is a sacred pavilion for placing religious offerings.*

Village Life

THE BALINESE VILLAGE is one of the island's most visually distinctive features. It is essentially a religious community, organized around a core of temples. Village land is considered a bequest of the founding ancestors, who are worshipped as local deities. Private life is largely ruled by *adat* (village customary law). Every married couple is obliged to belong to the *banjar* (community association); among the *banjar's* duties are funerary rites for village members. Not to belong to a *banjar* is to risk perdition in the afterlife.

Funerary rites *involve all village members, who will congregate in the spirit of* banjar suka duka *("together in happiness and woe").*

Village streets *are usually aligned with the mountain and the sea, an arrangement which the Balinese call* kaja-kelod *(mountainward-seaward).*

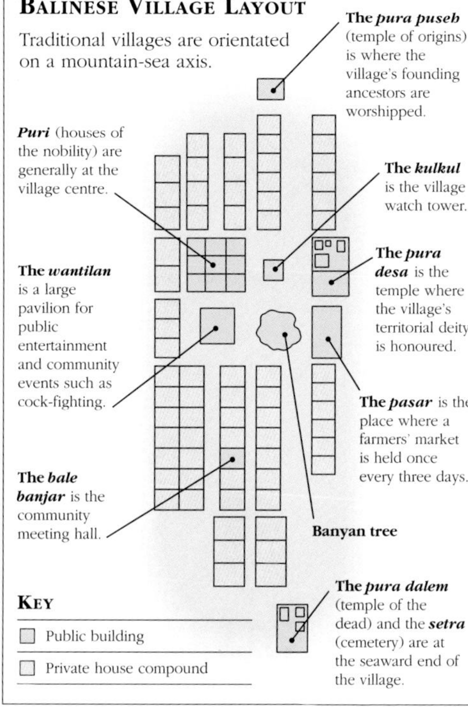

BALINESE VILLAGE LAYOUT
Traditional villages are orientated on a mountain-sea axis.
The *pura puseh* (temple of origins) is where the village's founding ancestors are worshipped.
Puri (houses of the nobility) are generally at the village centre.
The *kulkul* is the village watch tower.
The *pura desa* is the temple where the village's territorial deity is honoured.
The *wantilan* is a large pavilion for public entertainment and community events such as cock-fighting.
The *pasar* is the place where a farmers' market is held once every three days.
The *bale banjar* is the community meeting hall.
Banyan tree
The *pura dalem* (temple of the dead) and the *setra* (cemetery) are at the seaward end of the village.
KEY
Public building
Private house compound

The slit-log drum *in the* kulkul *tower summons* banjar *members to village duty, announces a death, and serves traditionally as a general alarm bell.*

The **warung**, *a family-run coffee-stall-cum-mini-shop, is at the heart of village social life, although it has no special location.*

A Village House Compound

Village land is divided into uniform residential plots or compounds enclosed on all sides by a wall of clay or brick. Living quarters are enclosed pavilions for sleeping and storage, with large verandahs for work and socializing. The courtyards are generally floored with packed earth, and kept free of vegetation except perhaps for a few ornamental flowers or a decorative tree. Most compounds house extended families of the male line. They may not be sold. Upon the death of the occupant, if there is no heir the property reverts to the village.

A courtyard wall built of clay and capped with bamboo.

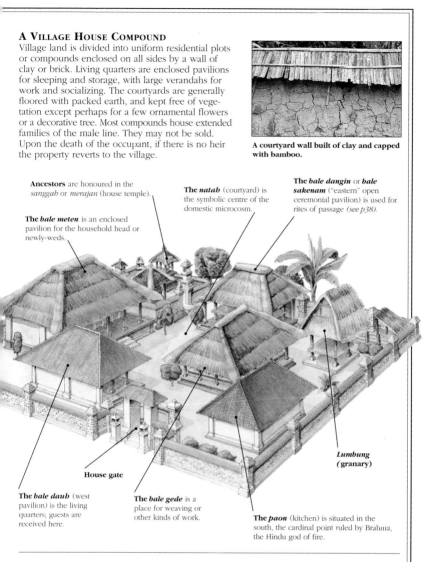

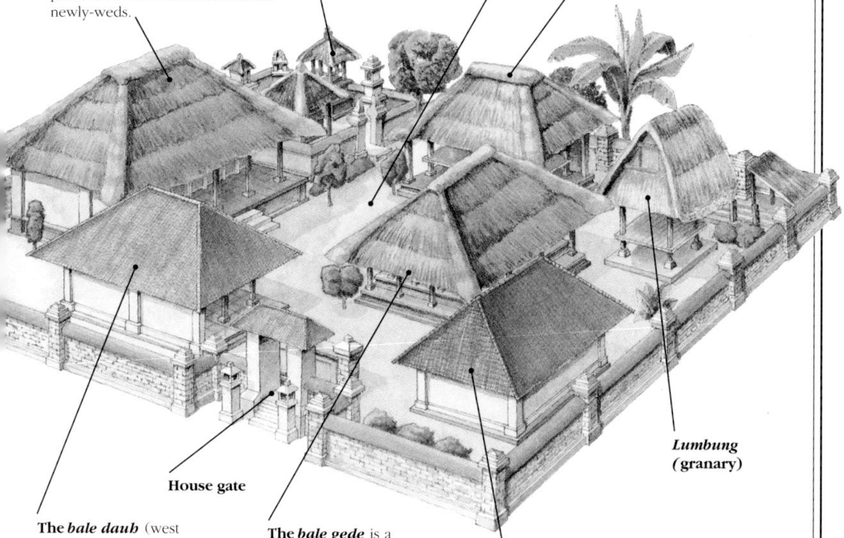

Ancestors are honoured in the *sanggah* or *merajan* (house temple).

The *natab* (courtyard) is the symbolic centre of the domestic microcosm.

The *bale dangin* or ***bale sakenam*** ("eastern" open ceremonial pavilion) is used for rites of passage *(see p38).*

The *bale meten* is an enclosed pavilion for the household head or newly-weds.

***Lumbung* (granary)**

House gate

The *bale daub* (west pavilion) is the living quarters; guests are received here.

The *bale gede* is a place for weaving or other kinds of work.

The *paon* (kitchen) is situated in the south, the cardinal point ruled by Brahma, the Hindu god of fire.

House Gates

The range of gates lining the narrow streets is one of the most striking features of a Balinese village. The gate is traditionally positioned towards the *kelod* (seaward, or downhill) end of the house compound. The degree of architectural elaboration generally reflects the material status of the family living in the house.

Simple house gate with *alang alang* grass thatch

Gate with tiled roof and minimal decoration

Gate with decorated roof and brickwork

Traditional Dance and Drama

Wayang kulit **shadow puppet**

THE ROOTS OF Balinese dance are trance ritual and the Javanese theatrical forms known as *wayang*. Various performances take place at religious ceremonies, often late at night and several hours long. Shorter versions are put on for visitors in more convenient circumstances. In Lombok, the dances of the Sasak are ritual performances, often involving men in competition or combat. Islam has favoured literary rather than performing arts, one reason why dance is less common in Lombok than in Bali.

Arja *is a dance-opera in which choreography, music, costume and singing styles are strictly defined for twelve core character roles.*

THEATRICAL PERFORMANCE

Various forms of dance and drama can be seen at the annual Bali Arts Festival *(see p41)*. Some tell a story; some are non-representational. New genres such as *sendratari* often contain elements of older traditions.

The oleg tambulilingan, *a dance created in the 1950s, is performed to the accompaniment of the Gong Kebyar* gamelan *orchestra* (see p32).

Sendratari *was devised in the 1960s as an art form without ritual function. The name is a contraction of the words for "art", "drama", and "dance".*

RITUAL AND TRANCE

Ritual-based performances range from dances performed for temple deities to complex dramas. They often contain elements of trance *(see p24)*. Even trance dances for visitors require ritual offerings.

Baris gede *is an old ritual dance performed by a regiment of soldiers to protect the deities.*

Kecak *is based on a* sanghyang *(trance) chorus formerly used in times of epidemic.*

MASK AND PUPPET THEATRE

Bali evolved its own style of the Javanese *wayang kulit* puppet theatre and *wayang wong* masked dance drama. Both are vehicles for the Indian epics *Mahabharata* and *Ramayana*. In *topeng*, the performer changes masks and costumes to show different characters.

Wayang kulit *(shadow puppet theatre) uses flat leather puppets which cast shadows on a screen. The puppet master manipulates the puppets with sticks.*

Masks are often carved by the dancer.

Servant-clowns interpret the Kawi (Old Javanese) speech of "high characters".

Topeng ***dancers*** *recount genealogical histories of dynasties through a series of masks. Players may be a troupe of three or more, or may perform solo.*

Servant-clowns *in* topeng *amuse the audience and make moral commentaries.*

Wayang wong *characters wear masks and move like puppets. This is Garuda, a mythical bird.*

Wayang kulit *characters are distinguished by headdress and manner of speech. These are the "prince" and the "demon".*

Puspawresti *is a modern creation inspired by* rejang. *A dance addressed to the gods,* rejang *is performed by females, usually either young or past child-bearing age.*

SASAK DANCES

In Lombok, the performing arts reflect both indigenous Sasak rites and Balinese traditions. Dances in Lombok are very often accompanied by drums; they often consist of a sequence of energetic movements alternating with slower actions and graceful poses. *Peresehan*, a dance which is often performed for festivals, is the ritual enactment of a duel between two Sasak warriors.

***Peresehan*, a traditional fight using poles and shields made of rattan.**

Musical Instruments of Bali and Lombok

Cengceng cymbals

IN BALI AND PARTS OF LOMBOK, traditional music is performed by a *gamelan* orchestra. This is a percussion ensemble consisting largely of bronze metallophones (instruments with tuned metal keys), led by drums; there are a few wind and stringed instruments. The music is based on rhythmic and melodic cycles punctuated by gongs. Many orchestras play for tourists. Most villages in Bali own at least one set of *gamelan* instruments for ritual occasions. Some sets are considered sacred and are played only during religious ceremonies.

***The* gamelan tingklik**, *with bamboo keys, accompanies traditional dances.*

Instruments of the Gamelan

Most of the orchestra is made up of pairs of metallophones, which are tuned to a very slight but precise dissonance which gives the *gamelan* its piercing, shimmering sound. Each *gamelan* has its own unique internal tuning; instruments are not interchangeable between orchestras.

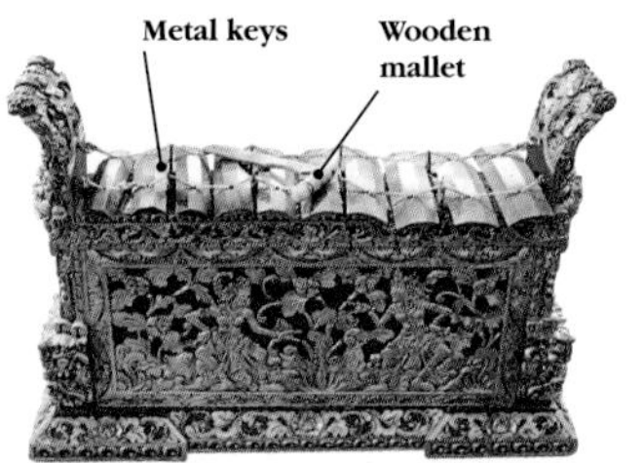

Gangsa, *which are keyed metallophones of various sizes, are played in syncopation to create a complex melodic texture.*

***A pair** of "male" and "female"* kendang *(drums) conduct the orchestra.*

Bamboo resonators amplify sounds made by the bronze keys.

Carved *pelawah* (instrument stands) are custom-designed for each orchestra.

Bronze material is recycled from old gongs to make new ones.

Gongs

Bronze gongs of various sizes form the heart of the *gamelan* orchestra. They are struck with padded mallets or sticks to produce resonant sounds which punctuate the melodies made by keyed instruments.

Kemong gong ***Kempur*** ***Kempli*** ***Gong Ageng***

Balaganjur, *a walking orchestra of cymbals and drums, has an exciting, crashing sound intended to scare off evil spirits in its path.*

The *terompong* is a series of inverted kettle gongs played by a single musician.

The *reyong* is a row of small gongs played by a group of two, three or four musicians.

THE GAMELAN ORCHESTRA

The Gong Kebyar is Bali's newest, most popular and most complex form of *gamelan*. Its sound has been described as a "cascade of blazing gold".

Large bamboo musical instruments *are used by* gamelan jegog *orchestras, a type of ensemble associated particularly with West Bali.*

DRUMS IN LOMBOK

Drums play an important role in the music of Lombok. The island's main musical traditions reflect Hindu-Buddhist forms which originated in Java and Bali, and others which developed from the traditions of Islam.

Kendang beleq **("big drum") at a cultural festival in Lombok**

Celebration of a special occasion with the aid of drums

The use of drums and ceremonial dress at a wedding

Suling *are bamboo flutes of various degrees of thickness and length. The players use a special breathing technique to produce a continuous stream of sound.*

Balinese Painting

BALINESE ART is a rich tradition very much alive today, especially in the villages of the Ubud-Mas-Batuan area of Central Bali. During the 20th century the influence of Westerners *(see p88)* was a factor in Balinese painting. However, themes and images still show traces of Bali's Javanese heritage, including Indian themes which predate the arrival of Islam in Java *(see p45)*. In the late 20th century, when some artists were educated in academies, what is known generally as "modern art" began to appear.

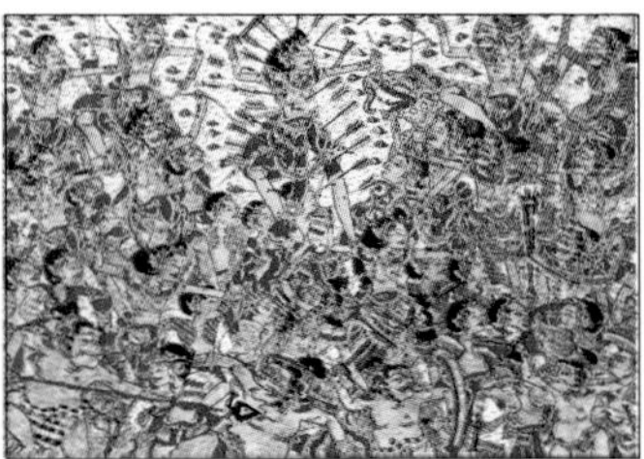

***The "wayang" style** dominated pre-colonial painting; this anonymous canvas from Kamasan dates from the 19th century.*

***One of the most gifted** Balinese artists of the mid-20th century was I Gusti Nyoman Lempad, who created expressive and stylized works such as* The Tantri Stories *(1939). Lempad took the art of drawing in Bali to new heights.*

Garuda, the mythical bird

A busy market scene

THE IDIOT BELOG WHO BECAME KING

The Batuan style, as in this work painted by Ida Bagus Made Togog in 1932, is typical of much Balinese painting in its full occupation of the canvas, repetition of patterned iconographic elements, fine detail and slightly monochromatic quality. Balinese painters often tell a story by showing scenes of everyday life. The basis of this story is not known.

REGIONAL STYLES

The Pita Maha association, which was centred around Ubud, led to the creation of the "Ubud Style". This stimulated the emergence of other local styles, such as that of Sanur in the south. The villages of Pengosekan and Penestanan, though both in the Ubud area, also developed distinct artistic identities.

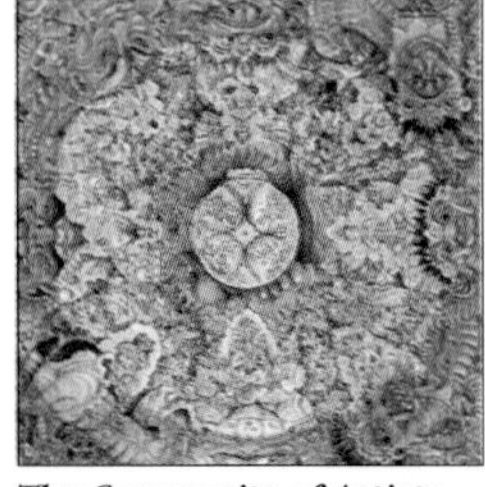

***The Community of Artists** in Pengosekan uses subtle colours, as in I Dewa Nyoman Batuan's* Cosmic Circle *(1975).*

***The Sanur School** flourished in the 1930s.* Fighting Horses *(undated) by I Gusti Ketut Rundu is essentially decorative rather than narrative in nature.*

Modern Art in Bali

Academic art education has introduced a new, more analytical approach to Balinese art. Some painters have opted for academic realism; others have chosen a modernist look. I Nyoman Gunarsa combines the free brush-strokes of American Expressionism with exotic Balinese themes, such as traditional dancers and *wayang* figures. Painters such as Made Wianta and Nyoman Erawan have also produced art which is modern yet at the same time strongly Balinese in feeling.

***Three Dancers* (1981) by I Nyoman Gunarsa**

A battle scene provides a sharp contrast to the peaceful scenes of daily life shown in the rest of the painting.

The river at the centre of the painting gives it a strong graphic structure.

Farmers are shown working with their cows in the ricefields.

The Pita Maha *association was founded in 1936 by Cokorda Gede Agung Sukawati and European painters Walter Spies and Rudolf Bonnet. It encouraged local artists to create non-religious art using their own imaginative resources.*

The Ubud Style*, as in* Balinese Stone-Craftsmen Working *(1957) by I Nyoman Madia, is characterized by themes of daily life and a way of showing anatomy influenced by Rudolf Bonnet.*

The Young Artists School *of Penestanan, influenced by Dutch artist Arie Smit, typically uses bright colours, as seen here in* Jayaprana Ceremony *(1972) by I Nyoman Kerip.*

Crafts and Textiles

GOLD- AND SILVERSMITHING, stone carving, woodcarving and weaving are crafts that have survived from the age of Bali's opulent kingdoms. Today, a thriving handicraft industry produces goods mainly for tourism and export. Crafts are generally practised in specialist villages, and Bali is an important market for goods made on other islands. Lombok has a long tradition of domestic pottery, and produces colourful handwoven textiles *(see p161)*.

Garudas (mythical birds) carved in wood and painted in the villages around Ubud

Carved Architectural Elements

The virtuoso carving of architectural elements, still practised today in Bali, blurs the distinction between crafts and fine arts. The works of craftsmen can be seen adorning many temples, palaces and houses; an industry has also developed producing items for general decoration.

Wall ornamentation *such as this example from Pura Tirta Empul* (see p99) *is carved from volcanic stone* (paras).

Chinese-inspired motifs *decorate this door in Puri Agung* (see p112), *the work of Chinese artisans in the 19th century.*

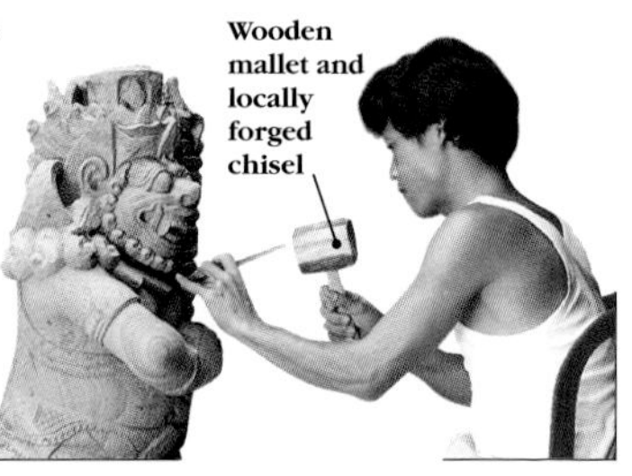

Wooden mallet and locally forged chisel

Stone sculpture *is a thriving industry as a consequence of strong local demand in the restoration of Bali's temples.*

Lombok Pottery

Renowned for its simple designs and fine craftsmanship, Lombok pottery is made using simple, age-old techniques and fired in straw on open ground. Sasak women have been making pottery since the 14th century, when the skill was probably introduced by Majapahit migrants. Among Lombok's most prominent pottery villages are Penujak *(see p161)*, Banyumulek *(see p154)* and Masbagik Timur.

Forms are built by hand.

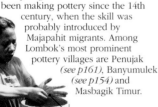

Clay material comes from local riverbeds.

Domestic pottery, *such as this water jar, is widely used in Lombok households for storage, cooking and bathing.*

Lombok pottery range from a terracotta colour to rich reddish-brown and black

Artshop Ware

A large cottage industry has grown up in Bali, based on craft work. It provides employment to thousands of rural families who can no longer make a living by farming. The level of skill demonstrated by a sizeable part of the Balinese population is remarkable. Some craftsmen have an "artshop" in their home.

Painted wooden trinkets

Lacquer-painted baskets woven in Bali

Basketware *is widely made in Lombok using rattan, grass, bamboo and lontar. Designs vary between villages. Sometimes palm leaves are used for smaller boxes.*

Gold and silver *are imported to Bali from other islands and worked by members of the metal-smithing Pande clan.*

Traditional Handwoven Textiles

The most common textiles are *endek* or warp *ikat* (made by dyeing the threads before weaving) and the more costly *songket* (gold tapestries). The Balinese are the only weavers in Southeast Asia to master double *ikat*, in the form of *geringsing* made in the village of Tenganan *(see pp110–11)*. Most of this work is woven on simple backstrap looms in the home.

The traditional hand-operated loom *is supported by the weaver who leans back to maintain the tension of the threads. Very complex pieces can take years to complete.*

Silk sarong made in North Bali in the 19th century, showing a mythological story enacted by shadow puppets

Detail of flower motif, part of a *geringsing* from Tenganan

***Prada*, a gold-painted fabric made in Bali**

The rich design of *songket*, with a pattern of gold or silver thread

Festivals and Holy Days

BALI'S HOLY DAYS, often the occasion for extravagant celebrations, are calculated according to either a lunar calendar or the 210-day Balinese calendar. *Odalan* (temple festivals) are the anniversary celebrations of particular temples. There is almost always a temple festival taking place somewhere. Rites of passage and other religious holidays are mostly celebrated with guests at home in the family temple. Outsiders may watch more public occasions such as *odalan* and even cremations, provided they show due respect.

The ingredients *of offerings include palm leaves, flowers, fruit and other foodstuffs.*

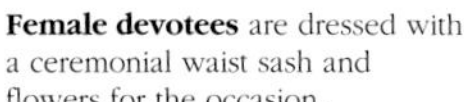

Female devotees are dressed with a ceremonial waist sash and flowers for the occasion.

Offerings *are made by the women in the household. This skill is passed from mother to daughter. Older women are highly respected as* tukang banten *(offerings experts).*

Male devotees, shown here praying, wear a white formal costume which includes a white headcloth.

Temple Festivals

At an *odalan*, the deities of a temple are honoured with offerings, prayers, and entertainment. Temples sometimes strike the visitor as rather quiet places, but they come alive during temple festivals, which generally last three days. The whole occasion has a carnival atmosphere, and demands elaborate preparations. All village members contribute labour and materials.

In a Balinese cremation, *the corpse is placed in an animal-shaped sarcophagus.*

Balinese Rites of Passage

Rites of passage ease a soul along the cycle which runs from before birth to after death. A person's *oton* is his or her birthdate on the Balinese calendar, and so occurs once every 210 days. A child's first and third *oton* are usually lavish occasions. A tooth-filing ceremony, in which the front teeth are filed even, marks the coming-of-age of an adolescent. A wedding ceremony takes place in the family home of the groom, where a high priest conducts prayers; a ritual bath is followed by a feast. A ritual cremation usually involves elaborate preparations by the community.

***This guardian statue** has been elaborately decorated with flowers, cloth and offerings in preparation for a temple festival.*

Offerings are brought by worshippers from home and placed on a special platform.

Decorated bamboo poles *known as* penjor *adorn Bali's village streets at Galungan.*

GALUNGAN AND KUNINGAN

Galungan occurs every 210 days, in the 11th week of the cycle. This holiday celebrates the creation of the universe. A period of festivity culminates ten days later in Kuningan, the Balinese "All Saints' Day".

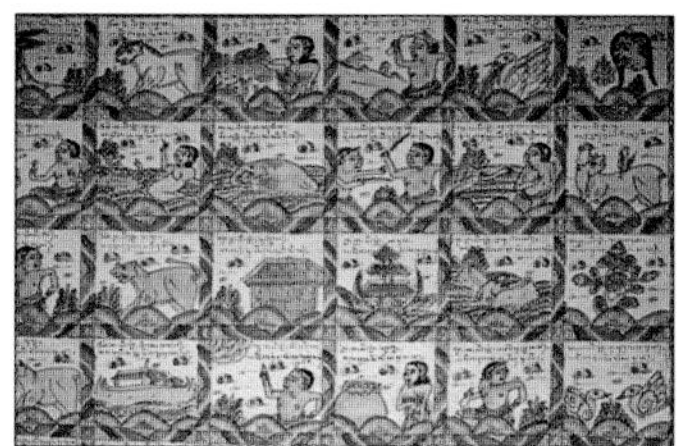

The Balinese Calendar, each day represented by an appropriate image

THE BALINESE CALENDAR

Certain Balinese holy days are calculated according to the complex 210-day *pawukon* calendar. This is made up of 30 seven-day *wuku* (weeks), along with nine other overlapping *wewaran* (cycles) of different lengths. The most common *wewaran* are the three-day "market" cycle, the five-day cycle and the seven-day cycle. Many festivals fall when these cycles cross.

Saraswati and Renewal of the Cycle: On the last day of the 210-day cycle, Saraswati, the goddess of learning, is worshipped. Books are honoured with offerings laid on them and sprinkled with holy water. Children make offerings at school while adults bring gifts to healers and traditional teachers.

Banyu Penaruh: The first day of the 210-day cycle is one of ritual cleansing with holy water, usually at a spring temple or at the house of a high priest.

Pagerwesi: This is a day for spiritual strengthening; it is celebrated elaborately in North Bali with *penjor* and feasting as at Galungan. The name means literally "fence of iron".

Tumpek: Once every 35 days, offerings are made to specific categories of valued things, such as metal objects, trees, books, musical instruments, livestock and *wayang* puppets; in modern Bali, motorcycles, cars, computers and refrigerators may be included. There are six Tumpek days in the 210-day calendrical cycle.

Devotees receiving holy water during a religious festival

Bali and Lombok Through the Year

The seasons in North Bali, South Bali and Lombok do not coincide precisely. In very broad terms the coastal areas are generally drier than those at higher altitudes. Any particular day can often differ from place to place: the situation in Ubud may well be different from that in Sanur. For precise dates of religious holidays and cultural festivals, visitors should check with tourist information offices or consult the internet – and be prepared for slight discrepancies. Many temples have festivals on the *purnama* (full moon). A few are mentioned below. Besides the high season in July and August, the long weekends around Chinese New Year, Easter, Christmas and New Year are particularly crowded. If you plan to travel then, book well in advance and expect to pay higher rates for accommodation.

Buffalo racing in Negara, at its best from July to October

***Ogoh-ogoh* (demonic effigies) in a Nyepi procession in spring**

Dry season

From April to October, occasional rain is normal. July and August are relatively cool and pleasant months, and nights in the highlands can even be chilly.

April

Nyepi *(Mar/Apr).* Falls on the day after the ninth new moon. At midday on the eve of Nyepi, massive offerings are set out at major crossroads; they are believed to have the power to exorcise evil spirits. That evening, there are noisy torchlit processions of huge *ogoh-ogoh* (demonic effigies). These are created each year by village youth groups, who compete to make them as frightening, funny or outrageous as they can. At the end of the festivities, the effigies are burned.

On Nyepi itself, the Day of Silence, no one is allowed to go out on the street and no lights may be lit, until 6am the following day.

The growing impact of tourism and modern lifestyle on religious culture has caused some Balinese to become increasingly scrupulous about keeping the Day of Silence. Visitors are expected to observe these restrictions and remain indoors in their hotels. Special arrangements are made to look after guests, and sometimes to include them in the festivities on the eve of Nyepi. During this 24-hour period airline travel is suspended. Travellers should check for details ahead of time.

Purnama Kedasa *(two weeks after Nyepi).* To mark this, the full moon of the tenth month, there are large festivals at important Balinese temples, especially at Besakih *(see pp116–17)*, Pura Ulun Danu Batur *(see pp122–3)* and Pura Samuan Tiga *(see p87)*. These are opportunities to see offerings, music and sacred dance in their full cultural context.

May

Waisak *(Apr/May).* The small Buddhist community of Bali visits the few Buddhist temples of the island on this holiday, which takes place on the day of the full moon

Balinese worshippers at a temple festival at Pura Taman Ayun

Sunshine Chart
The island of Lombok typically receives about an hour less sunshine each day compared to Bali. Daylight hours are fairly constant throughout the year on both islands as they are close to the equator. Days and nights are about the same length.

The annual Bali Kite Festival in South Bali

usually in May, according to the Buddhist lunar calendar.
Purnama Desta *(full moon).* Hindu temple festival held at Pura Maospahit in Denpasar *(see p61),* and Pura Segara, near Ampenan on Lombok.

June

Pesta Kesenian Bali (Bali Arts Festival) *(mid-June to mid-July)*, Denpasar. The height of Bali's secular cultural calendar, this is a two-to-four-week jamboree of mostly Balinese (but increasingly international) dance, theatre, music and cultural events at the Taman Werdhi Budaya (Bali Arts Centre) *(see p61)*. The dates and duration vary somewhat from year to year. The opening-day parade is a spectacular procession in which the participating troupes perform as they move through the city streets, sometimes even going into a state of trance.

July and August

This is the high season for visitors from Europe and North America. It is also thought to be an auspicious time for cremations.
Bali Kite Festival *(date variable)*, South Bali. An annual, international event which draws participants from all over Southeast Asia and Japan, the Bali Kite Festival takes place at the time of year when winds are most suitable for kite-flying. The festival inspires children throughout the countryside; they construct kites from plastic bags or any other materials they can find, and fly them from drying rice fields and village streets.
Indonesia's Independence Day *(17 Aug)*. In the week leading up to Independence Day, which is marked by events throughout Indonesia, Bali's traffic may be held up by ranks of schoolchildren marching along the roads, in preparation for the military-inspired ceremonies held on the big day itself in the provincial capital, Denpasar.
Mekepung *(Jul–Oct, dates variable)*. Buffalo races held in Negara *(see p134)*. A more modest version is put on for visitors all year round.

September

Nusa Dua festival showcases traditional music and dance from all over Indonesia.
Purnama Katiga *(full moon)*. Temple festival at the Gunung Kawi Royal Monuments at Tampaksiring in Central Bali *(see p99)*.

October

Purnama Kapat *(full moon)*. Festivals at many major temples, including Besakih *(see pp116–17)*, Pura Ulun Danu Batur *(see pp122–3)*, Pura Tirta Empul *(see p99)*, Pura Pulaki *(see p138)* and Pura Tegeh Koripan *(see p115)*.
Hari Raya Sumpah Pemuda *(28 Oct)*. A working day commemorating the independence movement. It has come to be associated with political reform in Bali and elsewhere in Indonesia.

Kuta Beach during the high season in July and August

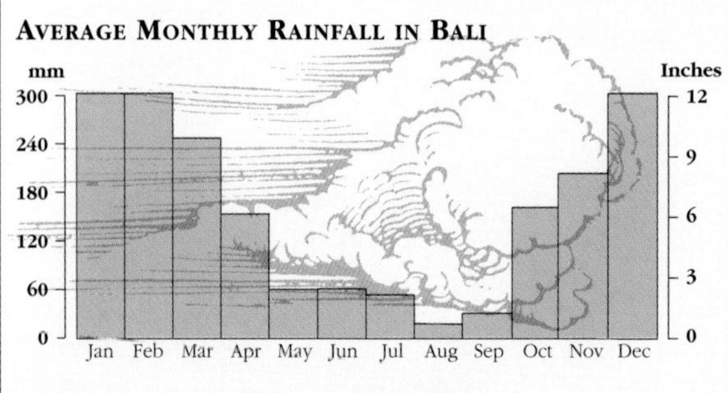

Rainfall Chart
The dry and rainy seasons fall in the same part of the year in both Bali and Lombok, although Bali experiences greater fluctuations in the amount of rainfall. The rainfall pattern has been somewhat distorted by the El Niño phenomenon in recent years.

Raindrops falling on an irrigated ricefield

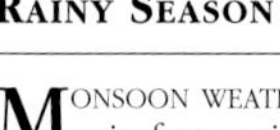

Rainy Season

Monsoon weather brings rain from mid-October to mid-March, the wettest months being December and January. Several days of uninterrupted rain may be followed by a week without any rain at all. Rain normally begins at midday and lasts until late afternoon. These are also the warmest months at the equator and rain brings relief from the heat. Sunny days during this period are hot and humid.

Bali and Lombok are not subject to typhoons, but in February there are normally a week or two of southwesterly wind and rain before the monsoon shifts direction and brings in cooler, drier weather from the northeast.

November to December

Purnama Kalima *(Nov).* The full moon of the fifth month of the Hindu calendar is the occasion when Pura Kehen in Bangli *(see p104)* holds its temple festival.

The height of the rainy season comes in December and January, when, according to local belief, people are at their most susceptible to illness. During this period many villages hold *melasti* processions, carrying statues of gods to the sea or to holy springs.

Purnama Kenam *(Dec).* On the full moon of the sixth month, the temple festival takes place at Pura Lingsar in Lombok.

Siwa Latri *(Dec).* "Shiva's Rite" is celebrated by Balinese Hindus two weeks after Purnama Kenam, on the night before the seventh dark moon (*Tilem Kapitu*). It involves a 24-hour vigil, usually held in a temple.

February to March

Chinese New Year *(Jan/Feb).* Crowds of Chinese come to Bali from Singapore and Jakarta. Following liberalization of government policy towards Indonesia's religious minorities, this holiday has become increasingly characterized by Chinese ritual ceremonies. Like the Eve of Nyepi *(see p40),* the Chinese New Year is celebrated with great fanfare, particularly in Denpasar.

Bau Nyale *(Feb).* Sasak courtship rites take place on Kuta beach *(see p162)* in South Lombok, on the appearance of the *nyale* sea-worm, a traditional symbol of fertility.

Purnama Kesanga *(Feb/Mar).* The temple festival of Pura Penataran Sasih in Pejeng *(see p97),* near Ubud, takes place on the day of the full moon.

A street procession at a Muslim festival

Hindus praying during a temple festival at Pura Taman Pule in Mas

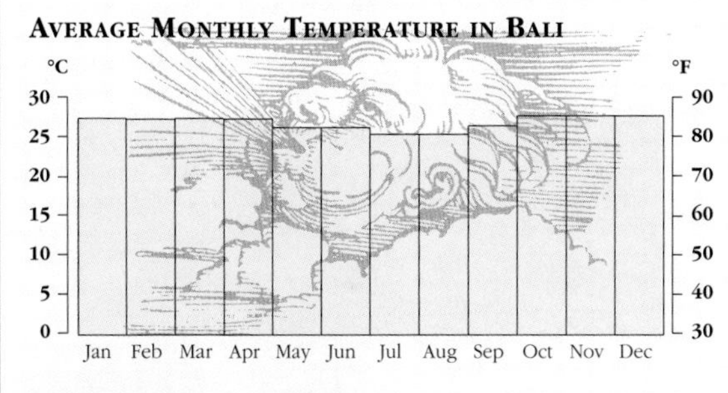

Temperature Chart
Bali has an average temperature which is higher than Lombok by about one degree Celsius. Temperatures on Bali and Lombok fluctuate only marginally throughout the year, but it is generally cooler in the hill regions than in the areas near the coast.

Moving a musical gong in preparation for celebrating Galungan in Ubud

BALINESE HOLY DAYS

BETWEEN THE major religious holidays and annual temple festivals, the 12-month lunar calendar is the framework for regular ritual celebrations and religious observance.

On the *tilem* (new moon) and *purnama* (full moon) of each month, special offerings are prepared and presented within the household and at local public temples.

The monthly celebration of *purnama* is particularly lively at certain "state" temples, such as the Pura Jagatnatha in Denpasar, Pura Kehen in Bangli and other regional capitals. It is marked by shadow puppet theatre and readings of sacred poetry.

Other festivals are based on the 210-day Balinese Calendar *(see p39)*. The most important of these is Galungan, which occurs in the 11th week. The whole of Bali is festively decorated, and people dress up in their best finery. Kuningan follows ten days after Galungan, on a Saturday, and marks the end of the holiday period. The day after Kuningan is Manis Kuningan, a big day for temple festivals at Pura Sakenan on Pulau Serangan, and Pura Taman Pule in Mas.

RAMADAN – MUSLIM MONTH OF FASTING

DURING RAMADAN, the ninth month of the Islamic calendar, Muslims refrain from eating, drinking and smoking from dawn to dusk. Visitors to Lombok should avoid these activities in public in Ramadan.

At the end of Ramadan is **Idul Fitri**, a two-day holiday. Most Muslims return to their villages, causing massive air, sea and land traffic throughout the country.

Greeting cards for the Muslim festival of Idul Fitri

PUBLIC HOLIDAYS

New Year's Day (1 Jan)
Nyepi (Hindu New Year; 11 Mar 2005, 30 Mar 2006, 19 Mar 2007)
Hari Paskah (25–27 Mar 2005, 14-16 Apr 2006, 6–8 Apr 2007)
Hari Waisak (Buddhist holy day; 24 May 2005, 13 May 2006, 31 May 2007)
Ascension of Christ (5 May 2005, 25 May 2006, 17 May 2007)
Hari Proklamasi Kemerdekaan (Independence Day; 17 Aug)
Christmas Day (25 Dec)

Hindu holidays based on Balinese 210-day calendar:

Galungan (9 Mar and 5 Oct 2005, 3 May and 29 Nov 2006, 27 Jun 2007)
Kuningan (10 days later)
Saraswati (23 Jul 2005, 18 Feb and 16 Sep 2006, 14 Apr and 10 Nov 2007)

Muslim holidays based on Islamic 354- or 355-day calendar:

Idul Adha (21 Jan 2005, 10 Jan and 20 Dec 2006)
Maulid Nabi Muhammed (21 Apr 2005, 11 Apr 2006, 31 May 2007)
Isra Miraj Nabi Muhammed (1 Sep 2005, 22 Aug 2006, 11 Aug 2007)
Idul Fitri (3 Nov 2005, 24 Oct 2006, 13 Oct 2007)

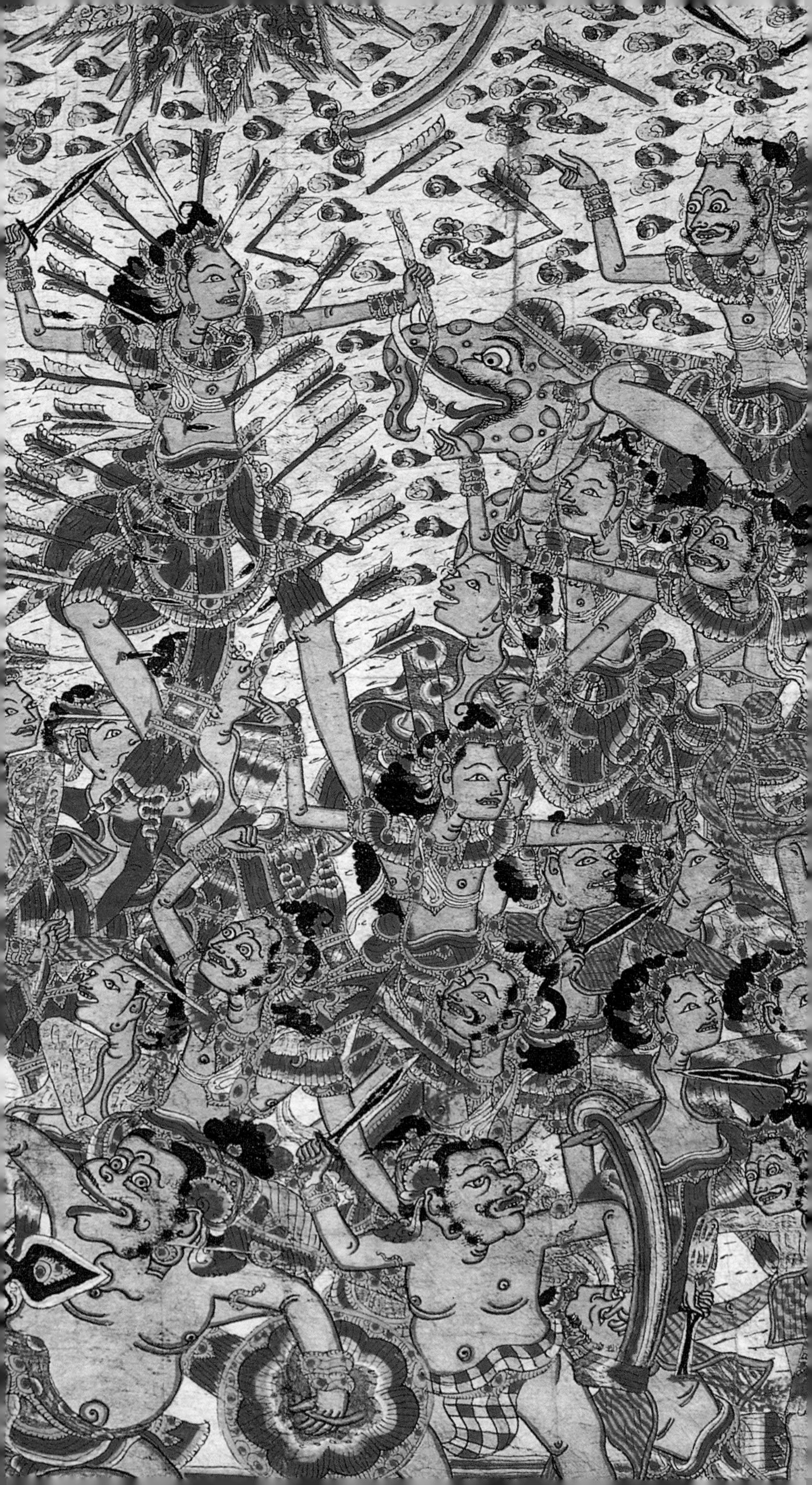

The History of Bali and Lombok

HILLTOPS AND MOUNTAIN GODS *are both prominent in Balinese legend. The landscape of the islands has deeply influenced their cultural, political and economic life for thousands of years. Old traditions have persisted remarkably, despite the successive impacts of colonialism, political strife and the travel industry.*

The Balinese, and the Sasaks (the indigenous people of Lombok), are thought to be descendants of migrants from southern China who arrived around 2000 BC. Their legacy is believed to include the growing of rice as a staple crop, the craft of metal-working and the prevalance of mountain cults. These cultural traits, still clearly observable in traditional Balinese life today, suggest broad affinities with other peoples of Southeast Asia and the Pacific Ocean.

Keris (dagger) handle

Early Kingdoms

There are few written records of Bali and Lombok before the 20th century, and none of Lombok before 1365; but ancient artifacts tell of Hindu kingdoms and the continuous influence of Java. An inscribed pillar in Belanjong, Sanur, dated to AD 914, implies that relations had been established before that date between Bali and the Buddhist Sanjaya dynasty of Central Java. In Central Bali there are relics of a Hindu-Buddhist kingdom, dating from the 10th–13th centuries, whose seat was near today's Pejeng and Bedulu. During the 11th century, the Gunung Kawi Royal Monuments *(see p99)* were built in order to commemorate the king Anak Wungsu and his queen Betari Mandul. This king's edicts have been found in Sangsit on the north coast and as far as Klungkung in the south, implying that he was ruler of the entire island. Pura Tegeh Koripan *(see p115)* may have been built to venerate him. Anak Wungsu's reign, which began around 1025, was a period of close contact with Java. His mother was a Javanese princess; his father was the Balinese king Udayana; and his older brother was the great Airlangga, who ruled a large kingdom in East Java.

A contemporary of Anak Wungsu, Mpu Kuturan, is thought to have established the three-temple system common in Balinese villages *(see p28)*: the *pura puseh* (temple of origins), the *pura desa* (village temple), and the *pura dalem* (temple of the dead).

There was substantial Chinese influence in early Bali. *Kepeng* (Chinese coins) were in circulation from the 7th century onwards; the dragon-like Barong effigy *(see p25)* is thought to be of Chinese origin; and King Jayapangus of Bali married a Chinese princess in the 12th century.

Timeline

250,000–10,000 BC Upper Pleistocene era

Ancient pillar in Pura Belanjong, Sanur

AD 914 First written inscription, on a pillar in Pura Belanjong, of a Balinese royal name

250,000 BC	10,000 BC	2,000 BC	1,000 BC	AD 1	AD 1000

2000 BC Migrations from China to Indonesia

Prehistoric bronze spearheads

AD 960 Holy spring temple of Pura Tirta Empul built

◁ ***The Death of Abhimayu*, from the epic *Mahabharata*; late 19th century, Kamasan style (detail; artist unknown)**

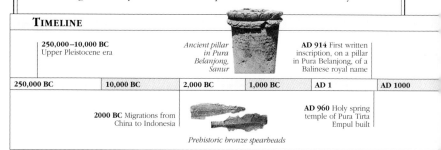

Shrine in Denpasar's Pura Maospahit, a temple established in the Majapahit era *(see p61)*

MAJAPAHIT BALI

Bali maintained its independence from the kingdoms of East Java until 1284. In that year the Singasari king Kertanegara sent an expedition to Bali, and as a consequence brought the island into the Javanese political sphere.

Kertanegara's successor in East Java, Raden Wijaya, founded the kingdom of Majapahit, which over the next two centuries became the largest empire ever in Southeast Asia. Bali was not truly subjugated by Majapahit until 1343, when the Javanese prime minister, Gajah Mada, defeated the king in Bedulu. Majapahit sovereignty was eventually established at Gelgel.

The Gelgel kings ruled with the help of local chieftains under a Majapahit lord. The people of some villages declined to adopt Majapahit's religious and social customs. These people, now known as the Bali Aga ("original Balinese"), remained isolated in their village settlements, and became a culturally distinct minority *(see p121)*. Majapahit shaped the culture that has survived in Bali to the present day, including architectural, dance and theatrical forms; literature written in Kawi script; and painting and relief sculpture influenced by *wayang* puppet theatre *(see p31)*. However, with time the imported culture gradually took on certain features of the more rustic Bali.

Majapahit also ruled Lombok. A 1365 Javanese chronicle mentions Lombok as a dependency. Lombok histories tell of Majapahit princes being sent to Bali, Lombok and Bima (present-day Sumbawa). The old Hindu-Buddhist elements in Lombok's culture can be traced to this period.

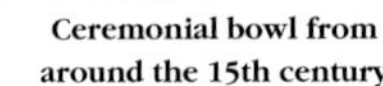

Ceremonial bowl from around the 15th century

BALI'S GOLDEN AGE

By the end of the 15th century Bali had recovered its independence. Majapahit was seriously foundering, a decline accelerated by the rise of Islam in Java. The Balinese kingdom of Gelgel flourished in the mid-16th century under King Waturenggong, who extended it westward to Java, and over Lombok to Bima. Some Hindu Javanese nobles migrated to Gelgel, bringing a fresh infusion of Majapahit court culture. Waturenggong's reign was a time of rebirth in the Hindu arts, literature and religion.

Around the 1540s, two new streams of religious thought spread eastward from Java: Islam, which was never to become widely established in Bali; and a Hindu reformation movement led by Waturenggong's priest, Dang Hyang Nirartha. This Javanese brahman was a poet, architect and

TIMELINE

1050–1078 Reign of Anak Wungsu

1284 King Kertanegara of Kediri, Java attacks Bali

14th century coin from the Majapahit empire

1100 | 1200 | 1300 | 1400

An edict written in old Balinese, 10th to 11th century

1294 Raden Wijaya founds Majapahit kingdom in East Java

1343 Majapahit invasion of Bali by Gajah Mada

religious teacher. Among his reforms was the introduction of the *padmasana* shrine *(see p26)*, an altar to the Supreme God. He established, inspired or renovated many temples in Bali, including Pura Tanah Lot *(see p128)*. He preached in Lombok; and he is considered to be the ancestor of Bali's Brahmana Siwa clan, the island's main priestly kinship group.

Meanwhile, from the 16th century Lombok was embracing Islam. Two of the most important figures in the process were Sunan Prapen, a disciple of the Islamic saint Sunan Giri; and the possibly mythical Javanese prince, Pangeran Sangupati, whom the Sasaks consider founder of the mystical Islamic sect Wetu Telu *(see p23)*.

Kukul tower at Pura Taman Ayun, built in Mengwi around 1740

Rise of New Powers

By 1597, which saw the first recorded visit to Bali by Europeans, the court at Gelgel was decadently rich. The dynasty was soon displaced by a new branch, founded around 1650 at Klungkung, the kings taking the title Dewa Agung ("great lord"). Soon, the Klungkung dynasty began to break into smaller kingdoms. Over the next 250 years, warfare and intermarriage created a complex political landscape.

The 18th and 19th centuries saw the rise of other kingdoms that foreshadowed the regencies of Bali today. These were Klungkung, Karangasem, Buleleng, Jembrana, Bangli, Badung, Gianyar, Tabanan and Mengwi. Buleleng became a major power under Panji Sakti, who ruled from 1660 to 1704; in the 18th century it was rivalled by Mengwi and Karangasem. Mengwi was split up among its enemies in the late 1890s, but a trace of its former glory remains at the royal temple complex Pura Taman Ayun *(see pp130–31)*. Although the territory ruled by Klungkung was smaller than the other great kingdoms, the Dewa Agungs retained prestige because their realm included the important temple at Besakih *(see pp116–17)*.

The kingdom of Karangasem in eastern Bali occupied Lombok in 1740; Balinese settlers lived in the western part of the island. There was resistance in the centre and the east from the Sasak nobility and Bugis migrants *(see p135)*. Conversely, contacts with Islam increased in Bali itself. By the end of the 18th century all of the kings on Bali had hired Muslim mercenaries. This is why many "Balinese-Muslim" villages still exist near what were formerly important court centres.

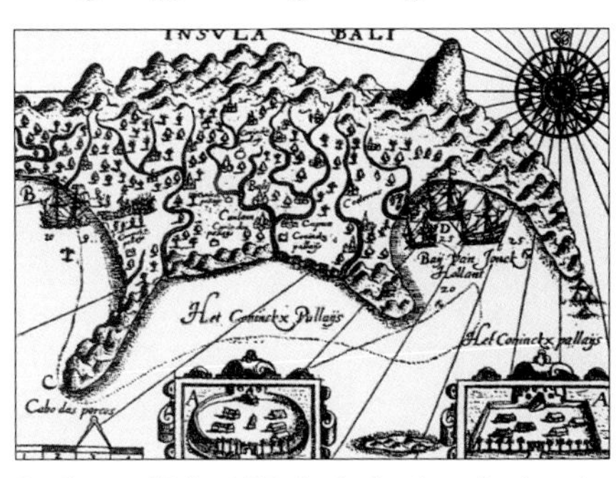

Dutch map of Bali, c.1597, clearly showing volcanic peaks

Puri Agung, grand palace of the 18th-century Karangasem dynasty

c.1540 Sunan Prapen sent as a Muslim missionary to Bali and Lombok

c.1550–70 Reign of Waturenggong in Gelgel – Bali's Golden Age

1619 Founding of Batavia in West Java

c.1650 Establishment of Klungkung dynasty

1740 Karangasem conquers Lombok

1500 | 1600 | 1700 | 1800

c.1540 Hindu reformer Nirartha reaches Bali

1597 First recorded visit of Europeans to Bali

1602 Founding of the United East India Company (VOC) *(see p48)*

c.1660–1704 Rise of Buleleng

c.1680 Rise of Karangasem

c.1700 Rise of Mengwi

1800 VOC is dissolved; Dutch colonial government installed

Arrival of the Europeans

The 17th century saw a new player on the scene. The Dutch set up the United East India Company (VOC) in 1602, a trading company succeeded in 1800 by the Dutch East Indies colonial administration.

Until the mid-19th century, Dutch colonial attention was concentrated in Batavia (now Jakarta), on the island of Java. Bali had little contact with the Dutch, except for trade in opium and slaves. Balinese kings sold debtors and prisoners of war; the Dutch sold opium.

The raja of Buleleng, mid-19th century

A Tumultuous Century

The 19th century brought enormous suffering to Bali and Lombok, as a consequence of volcanic eruption, famine, disease and war. There were military incursions by the Dutch and petty wars between the kingdoms. Thomas Stamford Raffles (later the founder of Singapore) showed some interest in Bali during the British interregnum in Java (1811–16), a consequence of the Napoleonic Wars – this caused some concern to the Dutch. The Dutch were to become far more militant after their victory over the Javanese, who were led by the prince Dipanagara, in the Java War of 1825–30. They also found themselves in conflict with Balinese kings over salvage from shipwrecks: the kings regarded cargo as a just reward for saving ship and crew. One such dispute with the king of Buleleng in 1845 led to the landing of Dutch troops on Balinese soil. The Balinese, led by the brilliant tactician Gusti Jelantik, resisted three military expeditions before they were finally defeated in 1849 at Jagaraga; Jelantik fled to Karangasem where he was killed in a palace intrigue.

The Dutch now had direct control of the northern Balinese kingdoms of Buleleng and Jembrana. Rivalry prevented a lasting alliance among the

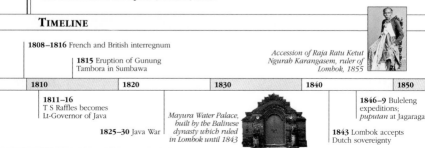

View of the harbour of Ampenan, Lombok, c.1850

Timeline

1808–1816 French and British interregnum

1815 Eruption of Gunung Tambora in Sumbawa

Accession of Raja Ratu Ketut Ngurah Karangasem, ruler of Lombok, 1855

1810 | **1820** | **1830** | **1840** | **1850**

1811–16 T S Raffles becomes Lt-Governor of Java

1825–30 Java War

Mayura Water Palace, built by the Balinese dynasty which ruled in Lombok until 1843

1843 Lombok accepts Dutch sovereignty

1846–9 Buleleng expeditions; *puputan* at Jagaraga

Dutch cavalry in Lombok, 1894

other kingdoms; most aspired to Dutch help against their neighbours. The Balinese ruler in Lombok during this time had accepted Dutch sovereignty in 1843. In 1849 he sided with the Dutch against Buleleng by attacking Buleleng's ally Karangasem, his own ancestral home. Thus Karangasem became a vassal of Lombok.

The Fall of Bali's Old Kingdoms

Dutch control over Lombok was not fully asserted until the end of the 19th century. In 1894, seizing the pretext of a Sasak revolt against their Balinese masters, the Dutch attacked and subdued the whole island, in the process acquiring Karangasem as well. In 1900, Gianyar put itself under Dutch control, while Bangli hesitated. Three kingdoms remained independent – Badung, Tabanan and Klungkung.

The occasion for the next and decisive Dutch attack was another dispute over a shipwreck – the pillage of a small Dutch ship which had run aground off Sanur. The matter escalated and became a political stand-off. In September 1906, a large Dutch fleet arrived. In Denpasar, kings, princes and brahmans dressed in white and had their ritual weapons blessed. As the Dutch advanced towards the town, they were met by hundreds of men, women and children emerging from the Denpasar palace. The Balinese ran towards the Dutch guns and were mown down. The survivors turned their weapons on themselves in an orgy of suicide. That afternoon a similar tragedy took place at the nearby Pemecutan palace. The king of Tabanan surrendered with his son; two days later they committed suicide in their cell. In Klungkung, the Dewa Agung and his court were shot down in another *puputan* in 1908. Bali was then wholly incorporated into the Dutch East Indies.

Colonial Rule

Royal houses were stripped of property and power as the Dutch recruited surviving "rajas", as junior personnel, into their bureaucracy. With a *modus vivendi* established, The Netherlands were to conserve Bali as a "living museum" of classical culture, a show

Interior of the Karangasem royal palace, built c.1900

The Ruins of Denpasar *(1906)* *by W O J Nieuwenkamp*

1860–88 Epidemics and plagues in Bali

1860	1870	1880	1890	1900

1882–1900 Inter-kingdom wars in Bali

1888 Major earthquake in Bali and Lombok

1894 Dutch conquest of Lombok

1906 Dutch expedition against Badung; *puputan* in Denpasar; Tabanan falls case for enlightened Dutch colonialism. The restoration of the role of the rajas as custodians of ritual matters gave the appearance of cultural continuity.

At the same time the Dutch used compulsory labour, formerly a royal prerogative, to improve irrigation and build a network of roads across the island. They streamlined village laws and class structure; new taxes rewarded loyal nobility but impoverished the peasantry, and were especially harsh on Lombok. These actions created tensions that were to erupt later, when post-colonial governments raised popular expectations but were not able to resolve certain fundamental social problems.

King and visitor at the gateway of Puri Gianyar, 1910

Photograph of Balinese women, taken by G P Lewis in the 1920s and coloured for publication

The Last Paradise

To visitors from abroad, however, Bali was a paradise. Early images by Dutch illustrator W O J Nieuwenkamp, and German photographer Gregor Krause, inspired Westerners to visit the island. The Dutch cautiously encouraged tourism. Some visitors stayed on more permanently, settling mainly in Ubud and Sanur, and presented to the outside world an image of Bali as "the island of the gods" where "everyone is an artist".

Meanwhile, a modern bureaucracy was growing, whose members soon constituted, with Chinese, Arab and Muslim traders, the core of a new urban intelligentsia. Together with other Indonesians from Java, Sumatra and the eastern islands, they formed the pan-archipelago political networks which later gave rise to Indonesian nationalism. In 1928, the *lingua franca* of the archipelago, Malay, was declared the official language of the Dutch East Indies, Bahasa Indonesia.

War and Independence

In 1942 Japan invaded and occupied the Dutch East Indies. Requisition of crops led to deprivation. Non-Indonesians were imprisoned by the Japanese or deported. The occupation spurred on the forces of nationalism. Leading the nationalists was Javanese intellectual Sukarno, who proclaimed independence on 17 August 1945, two days after the Japanese surrender.

However, the Dutch returned to reclaim their colonies. They met fierce resistance. In Bali they achieved a

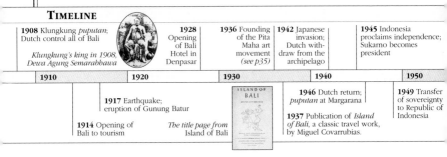

Timeline

1908 Klungkung *puputan*; Dutch control all of Bali

Klungkung's king in 1908, Dewa Agung Semarabhawa

1928 Opening of Bali Hotel in Denpasar

1936 Founding of the Pita Maha art movement *(see p35)*

1942 Japanese invasion; Dutch withdraw from the archipelago

1945 Indonesia proclaims independence; Sukarno becomes president

1910 | 1920 | 1930 | 1940 | 1950

1914 Opening of Bali to tourism

1917 Earthquake; eruption of Gunung Batur

The title page from Island of Bali

1937 Publication of *Island of Bali*, a classic travel work, by Miguel Covarrubias.

1946 Dutch return; *puputan* at Margarana

1949 Transfer of sovereignty to Republic of Indonesia

Balinese judges under the colonial regime, 1935

political foothold amongst the former nobility. Pro-republican youths waged guerrilla war until November 1946, when a band of 94 freedom-fighters, led by Gusti Ngurah Rai, died in a *puputan* at Marga *(see p132)*. Despite this victory, the Dutch were in an unsustainable position. Three years later they withdrew from Indonesia, transferring sovereignty on 27 December 1949.

The prosperity promised by independence did not materialize for many years. Guerrilla bands roamed the islands of the archipelago. Successive governments, powerless or over-nationalistic, deterred foreign investors. Thought to be extinct, Bali's highest volcano Gunung Agung erupted in 1963, killing thousands of people, devastating East Bali and causing famine. Political polarization worsened.

Suharto in Bali, 1979

Autocracy and Reform

On 30 September 1965, an alleged coup attempt took place in Jakarta. Sukarno was displaced by the little-known general Suharto, who then led a "cleansing" campaign in which thousands of communists and suspected communist sympathizers were murdered, and countless internal conflicts brutally settled. Suharto's "New Order" eventually brought prosperity to Bali with the resurgence of tourism.

The first modern tourists were travellers on the "hippie trail" of the late 1960s and 1970s. The Australians discovered Bali as a nearby holiday destination. The coconut groves of Kuta were gradually replaced by "art-shops" and small hotels. In the 1980s and 1990s, South Bali was transformed by a building boom. There were just a few hundred hotel rooms in 1965, and 30,000 by 1999.

In the Suharto era, development took place at the expense of civil liberties, a trade-off destroyed by the financial crisis of 1997. In May 1998, Suharto was forced to resign. Suppressed social pressures erupted.

Pro-democracy banner, 1999

In Bali, after the 1999 elections, some public buildings were burned down. Later, Lombok suffered unrest, apparently provoked by outsiders; tourists were unharmed. Megawati Sukarnoputri, favoured by the majority of Balinese as presidential candidate, became vice-president. With the new millennium came the promise of a slow but real economic recovery. But, on 12 October 2002 a terrorist bomb in Kuta killed over 180 people.

1965 30 September coup attempt; Anti-Communist purges begin

1966 Bali Beach Hotel is opened

1983 Opening of Nusa Dua Beach Hotel, part of a 5-star resort complex

Nusa Dua Beach Hotel

1960	1970	1980	1990	2000

1967–98 Suharto's New Order; rise of tourism

1999 PDI-P party led by Megawati Sukarnoputri wins 80 per cent of vote in Bali; Abdurrahman Wahid becomes president of Indonesia

1963 Eruption of Gunung Agung

Bali & Lombok Area by Area

Bali and Lombok at a Glance

The attractions of Bali and Lombok are varied, appealing to visitors with an interest in cultural heritage, natural beauty, and sports. South Bali has the greatest concentration of beach resorts and nightlife; Central and East Bali are particularly rich in history and artistic interest. Throughout both islands there is wonderful scenery, from volcanic peaks and lakes to rice terraces and a beautiful coastline, in many areas quite undeveloped.

Pura Meduwe Karang (see pp148–9) *is a temple noted for its stone sculptures, wall carvings and reliefs.*

Bali Bird Park (see pp84–5) *is home to more than 1,500 birds of over 250 species displayed in a fine tropical garden.*

Singaraja *(see pp146–7)* retains the atmosphere of an old port and colonial capital.

Ubud *(see pp88–95)* and the nearby villages are at the heart of Bali's cultural life.

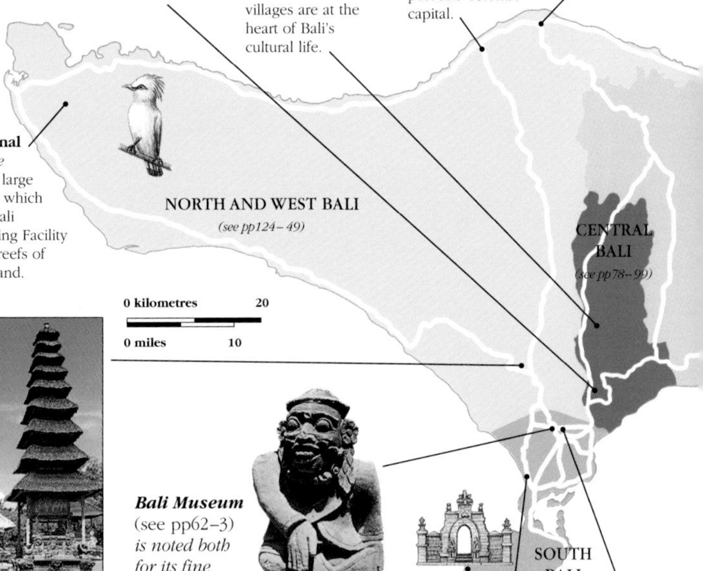

Taman Nasional Bali Barat *(see pp136–7)* is a large nature reserve which includes the Bali Starling Breeding Facility and the coral reefs of Menjangan Island.

NORTH AND WEST BALI
(see pp124–49)

CENTRAL BALI
(see pp78–99)

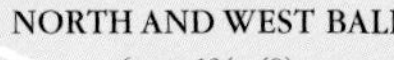

Pura Taman Ayun (see pp130–31) *is a royal temple with an inner and an outer moat.*

Bali Museum (see pp62–3) *is noted both for its fine collection of artifacts and for its architecture.*

SOUTH BALI
(see pp56–77)

Denpasar *(see pp60–61)* is Bali's administrative capital and commercial centre.

Kuta *(see pp66–9),* the most developed tourist centre in Bali, is crowded with hotels, shops, bars and restaurants.

Pura Luhur Uluwatu (see pp76–7) *is set high on the edge of a cliff at the end of South Bali's Bukit Peninsula.*

Taman Nasional Gunung Rinjani (see pp158–9) *is a national park and trekking area encompassing Lombok's highest volcano and the crater lake Danau Segara Anak.*

Gunung Batur (see pp120–21), *an active volcano, and Lake Batur are enclosed within a spectacular caldera within which are several historic temples and some trekking routes.*

Besakih Temple Complex *(see pp116–17)* contains 22 temples built on the lower slopes of the sacred volcano Gunung Agung.

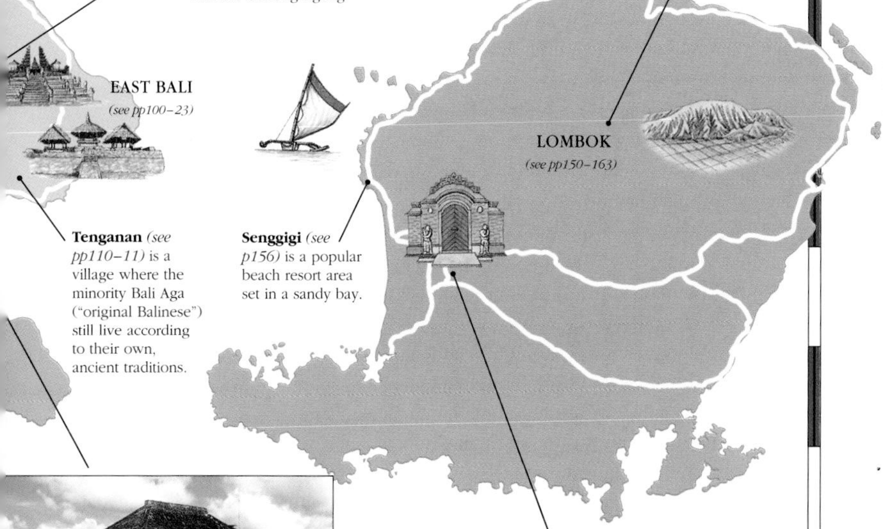

EAST BALI
(see pp100–23)

LOMBOK
(see pp150–163)

Tenganan *(see pp110–11)* is a village where the minority Bali Aga ("original Balinese") still live according to their own, ancient traditions.

Senggigi *(see p156)* is a popular beach resort area set in a sandy bay.

Taman Gili (see pp106–107) *is a royal compound with beautiful ceiling paintings in its two main pavilions.*

Pura Lingsar (see p154) *in Sweta is a temple with 300 years of history. Apart from the temple's importance to worshippers, the lotus ponds in the precincts give pleasure to local children.*

South Bali

A BLEND OF HISTORY, CULTURE AND TOURISM, *South Bali offers many contrasts. Budget travellers have flocked to the beaches here since surfers first arrived decades ago; at the other extreme, lavish hotels and resorts have created a more glamorous and exotic version of Bali. Meanwhile, despite modern development, temples and village communities still maintain their cultural and artistic traditions.*

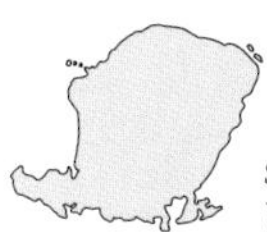

At the heart of South Bali is Denpasar, the island's provincial capital since 1958 and today a busy, modernizing city, Bali's administrative and commercial hub. Denpasar used to be a royal capital – the kingdom of Badung dominated the southern part of Bali from the late 18th to the beginning of the 20th century, and its heritage is to be seen in several of its older buildings. Two important cultural centres are here: the Bali Museum *(see pp62–3)* and Taman Werdhi Budaya (Bali Arts Centre) *(see p61)*.

The city lies within Bali's most important tourist area, a triangle formed by the beach resorts of Kuta, Legian, Seminyak and Canggu on the west coast, Sanur on the east coast, and Nusa Dua to the south.

Kuta is Bali's leading tourist centre. The beaches are famous. There are hotels of every standard, exciting restaurants and clubs, water sports, pulsating night life and shops to suit every budget. Sanur has many of the attractions of Kuta, but in a gentler, less raucous style. Nusa Dua, a development planned specially for visitors, offers the manicured gardens of a 5-star resort-hotel complex complete with an 18-hole golf course.

The highland peninsula of Bukit in the far south is arid and stands in stark contrast to the verdant gardens and rice terraces that enriched the rajas of old. One of Bali's holiest temples, Pura Luhur Uluwatu, is set high on a cliff at the Bukit's southwest extremity, with a spectacular view of the ocean.

The sea is never far away in South Bali. Surfers come for the waves, divers and snorkellers for the reefs and underwater life. Everyone comes for the beach life, which has few rivals in Asia or further afield.

Fishermen off the South Bali coast in their light outrigger boat

◁ **Woodcarving of a Garuda (a mythical bird), an example of the craft work typical of South Bali**

Exploring South Bali

Most visitors arrive at Denpasar's airport at the centre of South Bali. The most important resort areas, with their beaches and nightlife, are only a short taxi ride away. Some people feel no need to venture further afield, but communications are good to other parts of Bali, and to Lombok. South Bali is therefore a good base for further exploration; it is easy to make all the practical arrangements here. This is the least mountainous part of the island, but much of the landscape is lush with gardens and ricefields, and the Bukit Peninsula in the south offers a more rugged contrast. Offshore to the east lie the islands of Nusa Lembongan and Nusa Penida, usually reached from Benoa Harbour.

Sights at a Glance

Benoa Harbour 7
Canggu 2
Denpasar pp60–61 1
Jimbaran 11
Kuta and Legian pp66–9 4
Nusa Dua 10
Nusa Lembongan 13
Nusa Penida 14
Pulau Serangan 8
Pura Luhur Uluwatu pp76–7 12
Sanur 3
Seminyak 5
Tanjung Benoa 9
Tuban 6

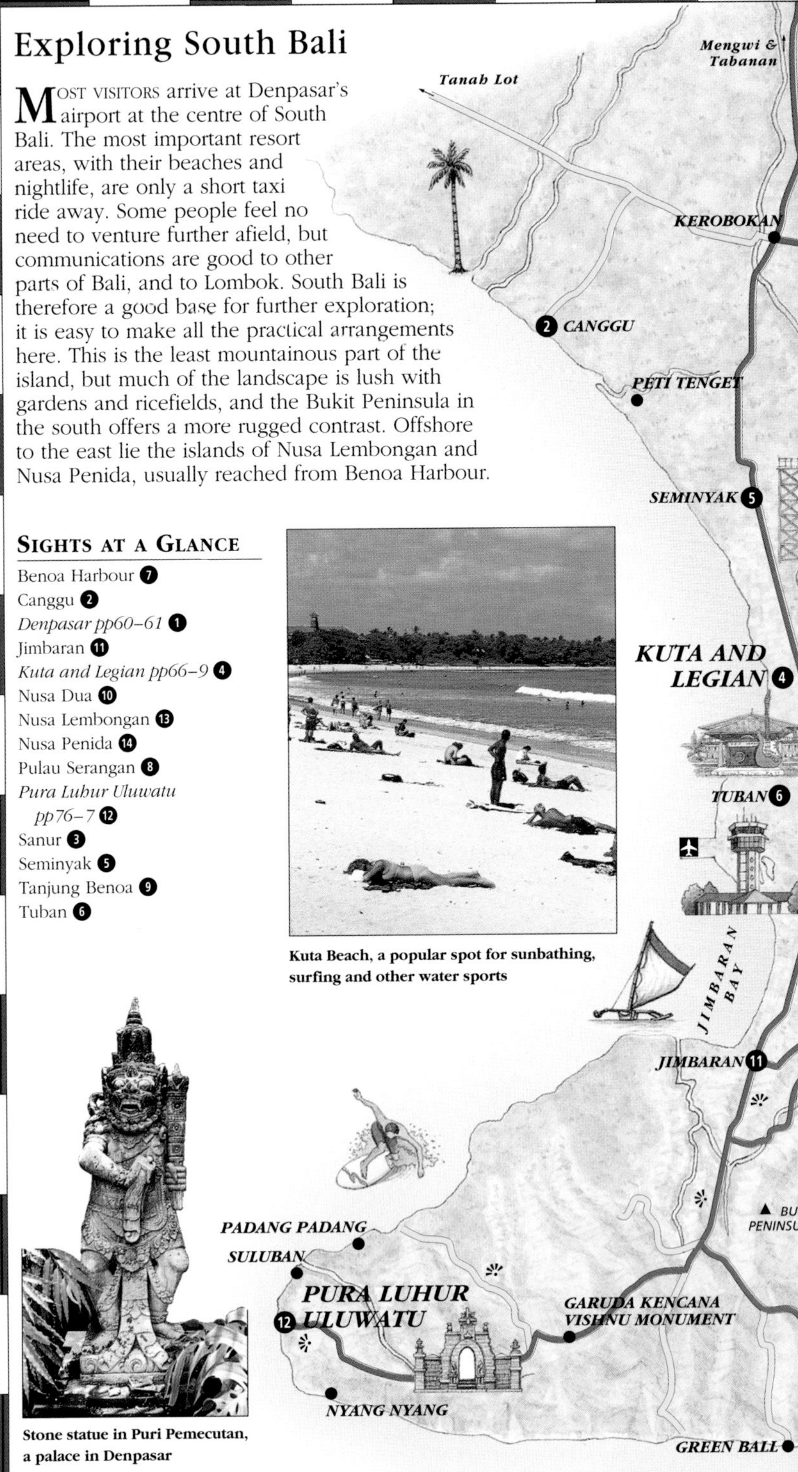

Kuta Beach, a popular spot for sunbathing, surfing and other water sports

Stone statue in Puri Pemecutan, a palace in Denpasar

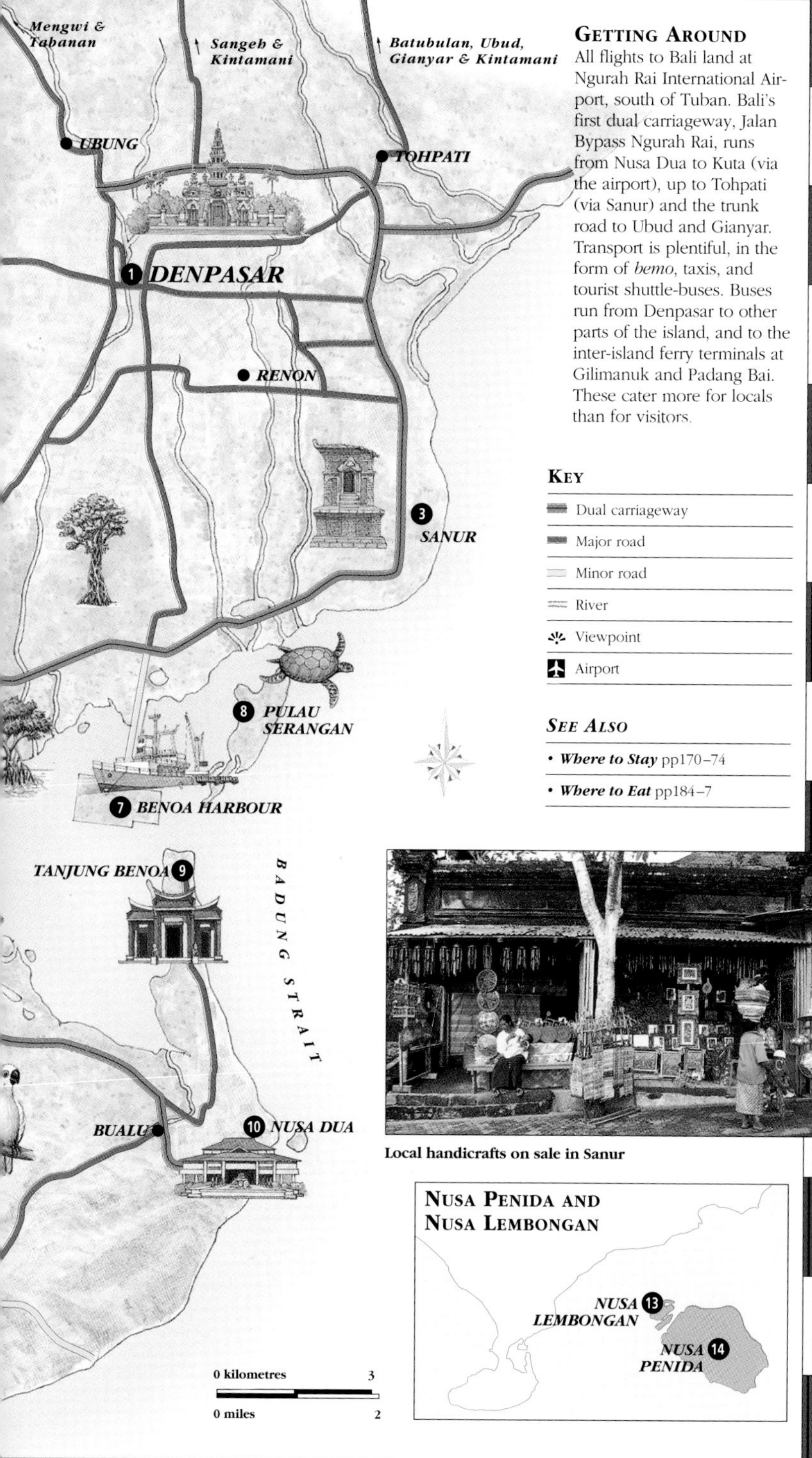

Getting Around

All flights to Bali land at Ngurah Rai International Airport, south of Tuban. Bali's first dual carriageway, Jalan Bypass Ngurah Rai, runs from Nusa Dua to Kuta (via the airport), up to Tohpati (via Sanur) and the trunk road to Ubud and Gianyar. Transport is plentiful, in the form of *bemo*, taxis, and tourist shuttle-buses. Buses run from Denpasar to other parts of the island, and to the inter-island ferry terminals at Gilimanuk and Padang Bai. These cater more for locals than for visitors.

Key

- Dual carriageway
- Major road
- Minor road
- River
- Viewpoint
- Airport

See Also

• ***Where to Stay*** pp170–74

• ***Where to Eat*** pp184–7

Local handicrafts on sale in Sanur

Denpasar ❶

Detail of wall carving

DENPASAR IS Bali's bustling provincial capital. Some older buildings predate the Dutch invasion of 1906 *(see p49)*, and there are still some white-walled, red-tiled structures dating from colonial times. On the streets can be seen several statues commemorating heroes of Indonesia's struggle for independence. Around the main street, Jalan Gajah Mada, are shophouses built by Chinese, Arab and Indian traders. Shopkeepers from all over Bali buy wholesale here.

Bronze statues in Taman Puputan commemorating *puputan* heroes of 1906

Pasar Badung

Jalan Gajah Mada. daily.

This is a lively market full of colour and excitement. The extensive flower section is not to be missed – exotic blossoms used in religious offerings *(see p38)* are a major commodity on Bali.

The fruit, vegetable and fish market is full of spectacular tropical harvests. Bargains can be found among the textiles, baskets, mats and traditional dancers' costumes.

Jalan Hasanuddin

Gold jewellery in Balinese, Indonesian and Western designs is sold here.

Jalan Sulawesi

This three-block stretch houses a myriad of fabrics and textiles. Everything from cheap batiks to imported silks and brocades can be found here. This is where the Balinese come to buy their temple clothing, and the delicate lace used for *kebaya* (a traditional tight-fitting ladies' blouse).

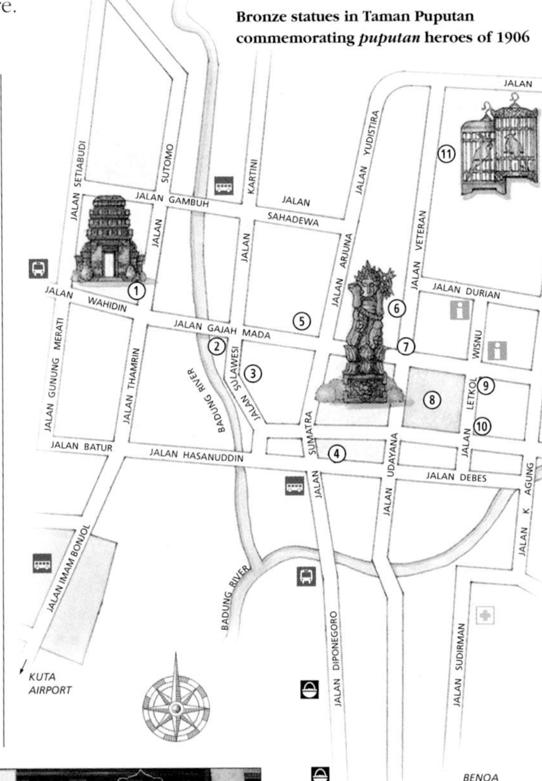

Colourful textiles for sale on Jalan Sulawesi

Jalan Gajah Mada

Several interesting Chinese apothecaries with an array of herbal medicines can be found on this busy street. One of the largest is Toko Saudara. Other stores sell electronics, sporting goods, handicrafts, batik and *ikat* textiles. Many traders of Arab and Indian descent have businesses here.

Taman Puputan

Jalan Udayana and Jalan Surapati.

A bronze statue in this large square (once the site of Denpasar's palace) commemorates the *puputan* of 1906 *(see p49)*.

Catur Muka

Northwest corner of Taman Puputan.

Wisnu, the four-headed Hindu god, is shown in the form of a stone statue 20 m (65 ft) tall, dating from the 1970s. The name means "four faces".

Bali Hotel

Jalan Veteran 3. *(0361) 225 681.*

Built in 1928, and once the only luxury hotel in Bali, the Bali Hotel has welcomed famous guests including Charlie Chaplin and Noel Coward. The open pavilion on the opposite side of Jalan Veteran was built to stage dances for guests. Seen here were many great performers who helped to make Balinese dance world-famous.

Statue of Ngurah Rai ***(see p51)***

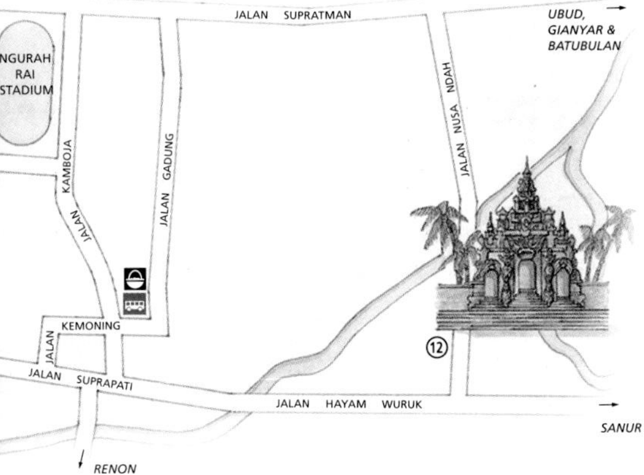

0 metres 500

0 yards 500

Denpasar

Bali Hotel ⑥
Bali Museum ⑩
Catur Muka ⑦
Jalan Gajah Mada ⑤
Jalan Hasanuddin ④
Jalan Sulawesi ③
Pasar Badung ②
Pasar Burung ⑪
Pura Jagatnatha ⑨
Pura Maospahit ①
Taman Puputan ⑧
Taman Werdhi Budaya ⑫

Key

- Tourist information
- Bus terminal
- *Bemo* terminal
- Hospital
- Market

Pura Jagatnatha

Taman Puputan, Jalan Letkol Wisnu.
daily. donation.

This temple was built in the 1970s for the worship of Sang Hyang Widhi Wasa, the Supreme God. It is crowded on the full and new moons, and on Kajeng Kliwon, which falls every 15 days in the Balinese calendar *(see p39)*. It has a very tall *padmasana* shrine *(see p26)*.

Bali Museum

Jalan Letkol Wisnu. *See pp62–3.*

Pasar Burung

Off Jalan Veteran. *daily.*

At this lively bird market many species of birds and other animals can be seen. The Balinese love song-birds and those with exceptional voices can sell for very high prices. There is also trade in dogs, tropical fish, fighting crickets and fighting cocks.

Visitors' Checklist

Road Map C4. *from Kuta, Sanur & Nusa Dua.*
Jalan Surapati 7, (0361) 234 569. Bali Arts Festival: Taman Werdhi Budaya, Jun – Jul (see p41).

Taman Werdhi Budaya

Jalan Nusa Indah. *(0361) 227 176.*
FAX *(0361) 247722. daily.*
public hols.

Also known as the Bali Arts Centre, this is an attractive if under-used complex with extensive gardens, an art museum, several indoor theatres and an outdoor amphitheatre. There are frequent dance and music performances, but no set programme.

The centre is a good place to come to during the heat of the day. The permanent collection of sculptures and paintings reflects the art world of the 1970s and 1980s. More recent works are shown in rotating exhibitions.

Information can be found in the *Bali Post* newspaper and tourist magazines.

Pura Maospahit, one of Bali's oldest temples

Pura Maospahit

Jalan Sutomo, Grenceng.
to public.

This temple dates from the time between the 13th and the 15th centuries, when the Majapahit ruled over Bali *(see p46)*. The style of the statuary and brickwork developed at that period. The restrained ornamentation is delightful. Although the temple is closed to visitors, the architecture can be seen from outside.

Denpasar: Bali Museum

Ritual Bronze Age axe

THE BALI MUSEUM houses one of the world's best collections of Balinese art. Completed and opened in 1931 by architect P J Moojen, its attraction is not only the items on show but also the buildings and setting. The exterior walls, gates and courtyards were executed in the manner of an old Denpasar royal palace, while the Tabanan, Karangasem and Buleleng *gedung* (pavilions) are built in the style of the regions after which they are named.

Ceremonial Gate
Fine brickwork without mortar is combined with volcanic-stone reliefs.

Carved Palace Doors
On display are these carved, gilded doors from the 19th century.

★ Stone Sculptures
Lining the verandah of the pavilion are stone statues from the 16th to the 19th centuries. The one shown here depicts motherhood.

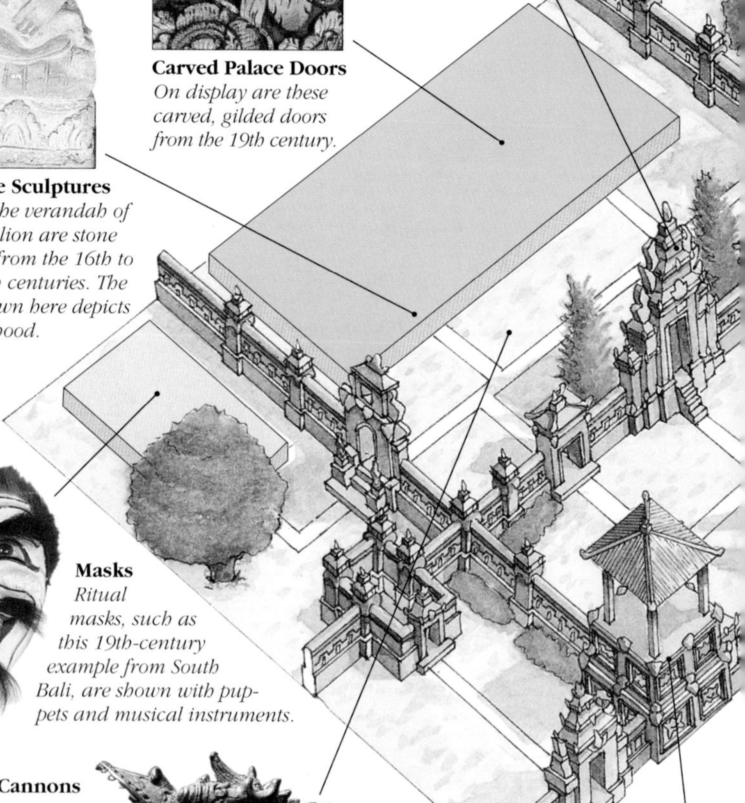

Masks
Ritual masks, such as this 19th-century example from South Bali, are shown with puppets and musical instruments.

Bronze Cannons
This 17th-century gun, with monster-head muzzle, is one of a pair made for a Denpasar prince.

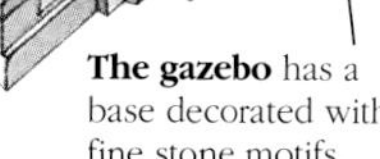

The gazebo has a base decorated with fine stone motifs.

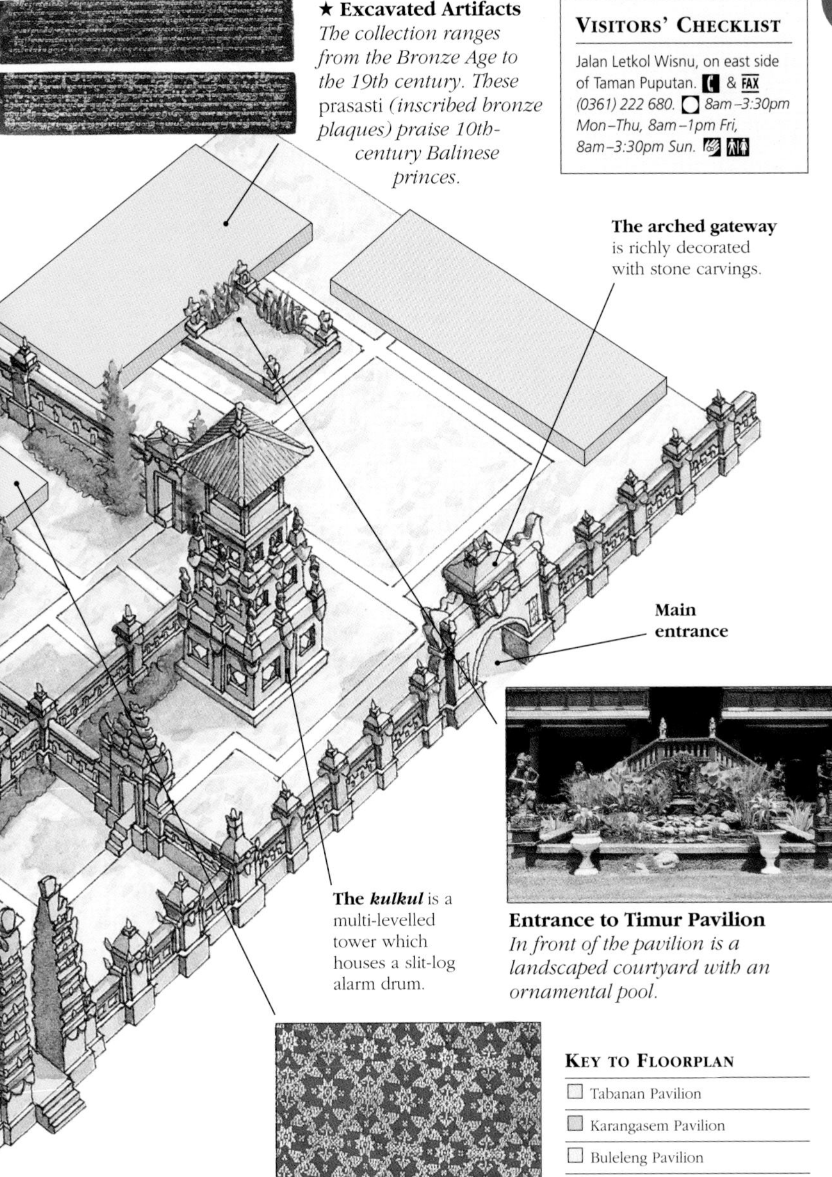

★ Excavated Artifacts
The collection ranges from the Bronze Age to the 19th century. These prasasti *(inscribed bronze plaques) praise 10th-century Balinese princes.*

Visitors' Checklist

Jalan Letkol Wisnu, on east side of Taman Puputan. ☎ & FAX *(0361) 222 680.* ◯ *8am–3:30pm Mon–Thu, 8am–1pm Fri, 8am–3:30pm Sun.*

The arched gateway is richly decorated with stone carvings.

Main entrance

The *kulkul* is a multi-levelled tower which houses a slit-log alarm drum.

Entrance to Timur Pavilion
In front of the pavilion is a landscaped courtyard with an ornamental pool.

Key to Floorplan

- Tabanan Pavilion
- Karangasem Pavilion
- Buleleng Pavilion
- Timur Pavilion
- Library

Gallery Guide
The collections are housed in four pavilions: Tabanan is noted for its theatrical masks and musical instruments; Karangasem has a display of sculptures, woodcarvings and paintings; Buleleng has a collection of textiles; Timur contains prehistoric finds and, upstairs, some antique woodcarvings.

★ Textiles
The collection contains pieces woven in the Bali Aga villages (see pp110–11)*, such as this gold brocade from North Bali, and examples of* geringsing *double* ikat *from Tenganan.*

Star Exhibits

- ★ **Stone Sculptures**
- ★ **Excavated Artifacts**
- ★ **Textiles**

Canggu ❷

Road Map C4. *Denpasar (0361) 756 175.*

IN THE ABSENCE OF restaurants and nightlife, the quiet atmosphere of Canggu is a complete contrast with that of Kuta *(see pp68–9)*. This is a place for walks on the wind-swept, virtually deserted beach. Behind the beach is a landscape of coconut palms and ricefields. One can walk all the way along the beach from Canggu to Seminyak.

This area was discovered by surfers in the early 1970s, and remains a favourite surfing spot. The waves are too big for good swimming.

Those interested in the use of traditional elements in architectural design will appreciate the vacation houses, which combine Balinese style with modernity.

Farmers harvesting rice in Canggu with vacation homes nearby

There are several distinctive "boutique hotels" *(see p166)*. They include the Tugu *(see p170)*, a self-styled "museum hotel", furnished with antiques. The pieces range from dragon doors made by Dayak headhunters in Borneo to colonial Art Deco furniture. The villas are themed on artists who lived in Bali, such as Walter Spies and Adrien Le Mayeur *(see p50)*. It is worth visiting the hotel just to eat in the Chinese restaurant, set inside an 18th-century, wooden Chinese temple moved here from North Bali.

Sanur ❸

Sculpture of Hindu deity Ganesha at Pura Segara

BALI'S LONGEST-ESTABLISHED resort, Sanur has a quiet charm. At its heart is an old Balinese community. The simple layout of Sanur's streets and its tranquil atmosphere appeal to families and those seeking a relaxed vacation with the convenience and facilities of a beach resort, but without the intrusiveness of Kuta's hawkers and traffic. The shops are pleasant and sell goods from Bali and elsewhere in Indonesia. Many of the unpretentious cafés and pubs aim to attract visitors of a particular nationality or lovers of a particular sport. The nightlife is enjoyed by both visitors and locals.

Exploring Sanur

Jalan Danau Tamblingan, Sanur's main artery, is lined with restaurants, and shops selling locally made fashion and craft goods. It runs some 5 km (3 miles) parallel to the beach from old Sanur village, to the formerly distinct villages of Blanjong and Mertasari. Half-way is Bale Banjar Batu Jimbar, a community centre where musicians practise and women make flower and palm-leaf offerings. At Pasar Sindhu, sarongs and other products can be bought at bargain prices; it operates early in the morning.

Pura Desa

Jalan Hang Tuah. *daily.*

This fine village temple was probably built early in the last century, although its brickwork has been restored since. It is in Sanur's oldest neighbourhood, which is famous for the spiritual power of its priests.

Museum Le Mayeur

Jalan Hang Tuah, via Grand Bali Beach Hotel. *(0361) 286 164.* *Sun–Fri.*

Built in the 1930s by Adrien Jean Le Mayeur, Belgian painter and one of Sanur's first European residents, on the artist's death in 1958 the house became a museum and gallery, which has seen better days. Some of the buildings are wooden, with carved decorations. The courtyard garden features in Le Mayeur's work. Le Mayeur's wife, the famous Balinese dancer Ni Polok, is the subject of several paintings on show.

Jalan Danau Tamblingan, lined with shops and restaurants

Grand Bali Beach Hotel

Jalan Hang Tuah. *(0361) 288 511.* www.grand-balibeach.com

Bali's only high-rise hotel was refurbished after a fire in 1992 and is now adorned with giant Balinese-style statues. After it was built in 1964, the religious authorities issued a famous edict outlawing structures taller than coconut palms. Such buildings were deemed offensive due to the spiritual value attributed to the trees.

View from the Grand Bali Beach Hotel

Sanur Beach, with fishing craft drawn up on the sand

Sanur Beach

The beach runs virtually the full length of the town. Along much of it is a paved walk, although some parts of this have been damaged by storms or tides. Offshore, enormous breakers crash into a reef. The calm waters between the reef and the white sands are good for swimming except at low tide. Beyond the reef the currents are strong. Sanur offers sea-related activities including diving, fishing trips and an evening sail on a *jukung*, a traditional outrigger. The beach is a place to explore for marine life, such as sea grass, starfish, sea cucumbers, hermit crabs, *Fungia* corals and sea urchins.

Pura Segara

Jalan Segara Ayu, or from Sanur Beach. *daily.* *donation.*

Set in the grounds of Segara Village Hotel, but accessible to the public, this is one of the best of several beach temples built of coral. The pyramid shape of the offering houses is unique to Sanur, and suggests origins in prehistoric times.

Visitors' Checklist

Road Map C5. *Denpasar (0361) 756 175.* *to Nusa Penida & Nusa Lembongan.* *traditional dance at some restaurants.*

The Bali Hyatt Hotel

Jalan Danau Tamblingan. *(0361) 281 234.* www.bali.resort.hyatt.com

Even non-residents should visit the Bali Hyatt *(see p173)* for a drink or a meal, if only to enjoy the gardens. Here Australian landscape architect Made Wijaya developed a style of Balinese garden design which has influenced designers worldwide.

Pura Belanjong

Jalan Danau Poso. *daily.* *donation.*

In this plain-looking temple is an ancient stone column, the Prasasti Blanjong. On it is carved the oldest edict so far found in Bali (AD 914). The inscription is written in a form of Sanskrit, although it is not all decipherable. It suggests Sanur was a lively trading port more than 1,000 years ago.

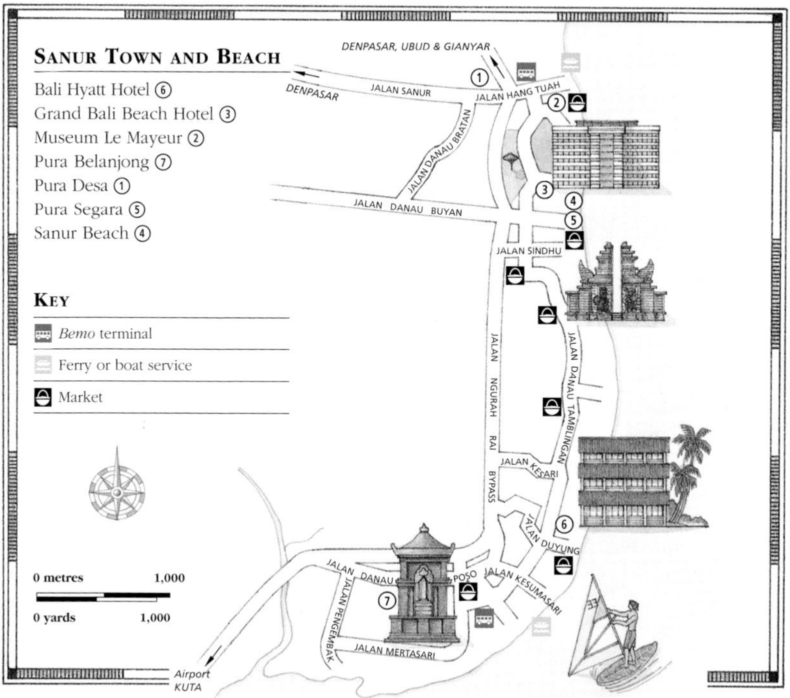

Sanur Town and Beach

- Bali Hyatt Hotel ⑥
- Grand Bali Beach Hotel ③
- Museum Le Mayeur ②
- Pura Belanjong ⑦
- Pura Desa ①
- Pura Segara ⑤
- Sanur Beach ④

Key

- *Bemo* terminal
- Ferry or boat service
- Market

0 metres 1,000
0 yards 1,000

DENPASAR, UBUD & GIANYAR
DENPASAR
JALAN SANUR
JALAN HANG TUAH
JALAN DANAU BRATAN
JALAN DANAU BUYAN
JALAN SINDHU
JALAN NGURAH RAI BYPASS
JALAN DANAU TAMBLINGAN
JALAN KESARI
JALAN DUYUNG
JALAN DANAU POSO
JALAN KESUMASARI
JALAN PENGEMBAK
JALAN MERTASARI
Airport
KUTA

Kuta and Legian ❹

THE BEACH at Kuta is long and sandy. However, the dollar-a-night homestays which attracted young backpackers and surfers in the 1970s have been replaced by a resort strip which is now world-famous *(see Street-by-Street, pp68–9)*. Besides the beach and water sports, the principal attractions are shopping and nightlife. Development has spread beyond the original Kuta Beach, including Legian, and has now enveloped Tuban in the south and Seminyak in the north.

Surfers at Kuta Beach, a location suitable for all levels of ability

Exploring Kuta and Legian
As Bali's main tourist hub, Kuta is a good base for relaxation and organizing trips to other parts of Bali. Off the beach, shopping is perhaps the most tempting activity; there are no major cultural or historic sights in Kuta or Legian. A good rest-stop is Made's Warung *(see p184)*, casual and cool, and one of Kuta's most famous restaurants. Legian and Seminyak are now as built-up as Kuta proper. However, its labyrinth of back streets offers low-priced accommodation.

Locals and visitors alike relaxing in the evening on Kuta Beach

Kuta Beach
The beach is flat and sandy, and stretches for over 3 km (2 miles), backed by some sizeable hotels. Hawkers sell their wares and refreshments are available all day long. Surfboards can be rented – this is a good place for the novice surfer, although one should watch out for the rip tides. Because of currents, swimmers should stay between the safety flags. Kuta Beach becomes Legian Beach north of Jalan Melasti. Legian Beach's famous nightspots are Kama Sutra, Gado Gado and Club Double Six.

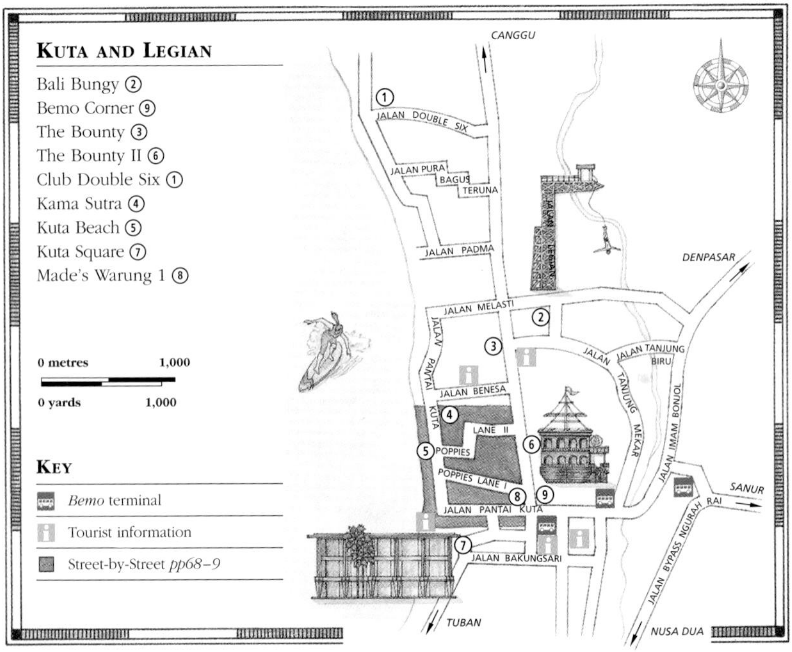

KUTA AND LEGIAN

Bali Bungy ②
Bemo Corner ⑨
The Bounty ③
The Bounty II ⑥
Club Double Six ①
Kama Sutra ④
Kuta Beach ⑤
Kuta Square ⑦
Made's Warung 1 ⑧

0 metres 1,000
0 yards 1,000

KEY

Bemo terminal
Tourist information
Street-by-Street *pp68–9*

Poppies Lanes I & II

These two narrow lanes are lined with small shops, stalls, hotels and bars. One of the first hotels was Poppies, from which the lanes took their name. The network of alleys in this part of Kuta offers a refuge from the traffic, pollution and noise of the main streets.

Jalan Legian

This is the commercial artery of Kuta, running parallel with the beach. At the southern end is Bemo Corner, a busy intersection. Jalan Legian is the place to find banks, travel agencies, car-rental outlets and the like. Pubs, bars and nightclubs proliferate – some, such as The Bounty and The Bounty II, are landmarks in themselves. Thrill-seekers will find Bali Bungy *(see p207)* close by. Near Jalan Melasti, the memorial to the 202 victims of the Kuta bomb blast of October 2002 is located.

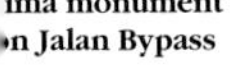

ima monument
on Jalan Bypass

Environs: On the outskirts of Kuta, on Jalan Bypass Ngurah Rai at Simpang Siur roundabout, is an ornate modern statue of Bima, hero of the Hindu *Mahabharata* epic. It is one of several public monuments recently erected by the authorities for the benefit of visitors.

Shop in Jalan Legian, selling craft goods from Bali and elsewhere

Pool volleyball at the Waterbom Park & Spa, Tuban

Seminyak 5

Road Map C5. *from Kuta.* *Kuta, (0361) 756 176.*

Seminyak extends north of Kuta and Legian. The further northward one goes, the more peaceful the atmosphere becomes, although Seminyak is now an important tourist centre. Some good fashion boutiques can be found here, selling inexpensive but stylish clothes made in the region.

The luxurious **Oberoi Hotel** *(see p173)* has very attractive gardens overlooking the beach. Further north still, development on the palm-lined beach has been less aggressive, although this is likely to change with time.

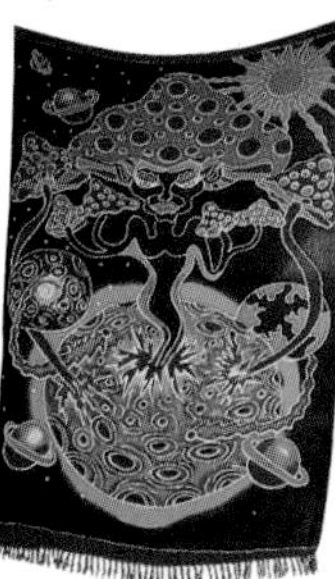

Colourful scarf for sale in Seminyak

Environs: A short walk up the beach north of Seminyak is the **Pura Peti Tenget** ("magic chest") temple, raised some 8 m (26 ft) above road level. Founded by the 16th-century priest, Dang Hyang Nirartha *(see pp46–7)*, it is considered one of Bali's most mystically charged temples.

The area from Seminyak to Kerobokan, 5 km (3 miles) to its north, is a furniture-making centre *(see p194)*. Galleries line the main road.

Pura Peti Tengat

Jalan Kayu Aya. *daily.* *donation.*

Tuban 6

Road Map C5. *from Kuta.* *Kuta, (0361) 756 176.*

It is hard to know where Kuta ends and Tuban begins. However, the streets of Tuban are laid out on a slightly larger scale, and the effect is a sense of greater order than in Kuta. By the beach is a series of large luxury hotels with spacious gardens. Shopping in Tuban has an international feel. Some people may find it a welcome respite from the bustle that often accompanies shopping in Bali. The northern limit of Tuban is the Matahari department store, selling a huge range of practical items, T-shirts and handicraft goods.

Near the Matahari store it is possible to take a ride on a *dokar*, one of the colourful carts pulled by small, hardy horses originally brought in from Sumba Island.

A very popular attraction for visitors in search of entertainment is the **Waterbom** Park and Spa *(see p201)* which has an array of slides and pools. It is also a good place to relax and eat.

Tuban is one of the departure points for surfers making their way to the break at Kuta Reef, off Jimbaran *(see p74)*. Fishermen with motorized outriggers can be chartered for the trip.

Street-by-Street: Kuta

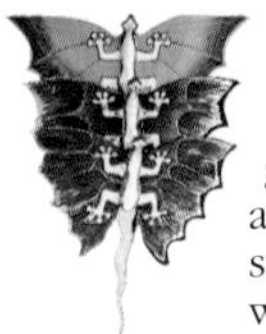

Kite for sale on the beach

KUTA IS THE most developed visitor destination in Bali. Thirty years ago the beach was set against coconut groves and banana plantations. It is still a great attraction today; however, a few steps away, there are now streets lined with businesses catering for visitors – bars, restaurants, hotels, nightclubs and department stores. Packed along the narrow lanes are shops and stalls selling many kinds of product likely to appeal to travellers from around the world, as well as *losmen* offering budget accommodation *(see p166)*. Commercialized Kuta may be, but it is a vibrant place, and caters for all budgets.

Signboards on Jalan Legian ***(see p67)*** **advertising pubs and cafés**

★ Poppies Lane II
Along this narrow alley are shops, stalls, restaurants and reasonably priced accommodation.

JALA
POPPIES LANE II
To Legian
JALAN PANTAI KUTA

★ Kuta Beach
The sandy beach, which stretches northwards towards Seminyak and beyond, is a place to surf, swim, and relax in the sun.

STAR SIGHTS

- ★ Poppies Lanes I & II
- ★ Kuta Beach
- ★ Kuta Square

★ Poppies Lane I
Named after Poppies Restaurant, one of Kuta's oldest eating establishments, this is a good area for casual dining.

Bemo Corner
Busy shopping streets radiate from this intersection, which is Kuta's central hub.

Visitors' Checklist

Road Map C5. *Jalan Bunesari 36B,* FAX *(0361) 756 175,* @ dipardabadung@go.id W www.badung.go.id*; Jalan Pantai Kuta 2, (0361) 756 176.*

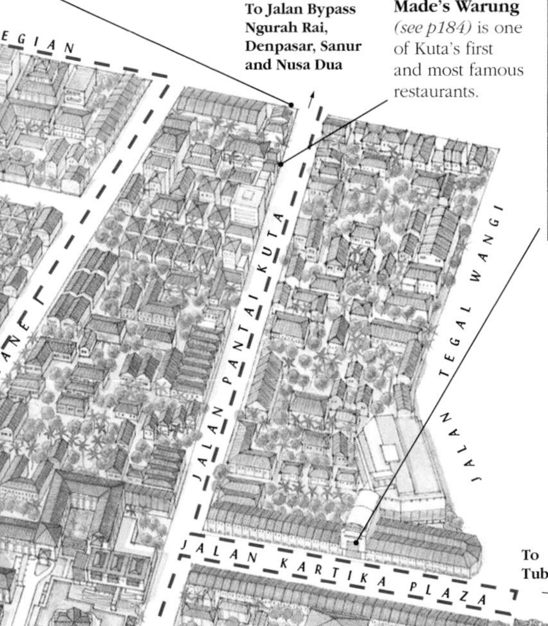

Made's Warung *(see p184)* is one of Kuta's first and most famous restaurants.

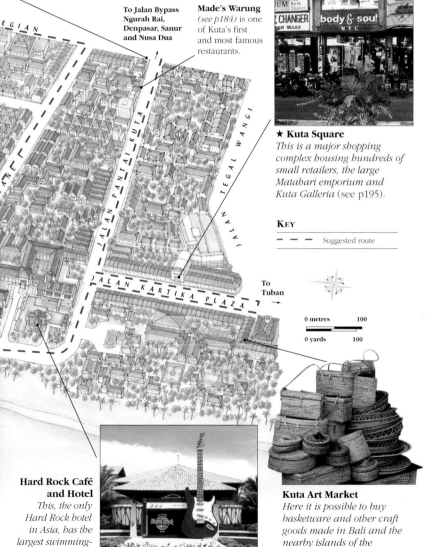

★ Kuta Square
This is a major shopping complex housing hundreds of small retailers, the large Matahari emporium and Kuta Galleria (see p195).

Key

– – – Suggested route

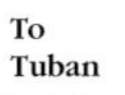

0 metres 100
0 yards 100

Hard Rock Café and Hotel
This, the only Hard Rock hotel in Asia, has the largest swimming-pool in Bali.

Kuta Art Market
Here it is possible to buy basketware and other craft goods made in Bali and the nearby islands of the Indonesian Archipelago.

Cruise vessels in Benoa Harbour

Benoa Harbour ❼

Road Map C5. *from Denpasar (shuttle bus services available to Benoa from hotels).* *to Lembar on Lombok.*

BENOA HARBOUR will appeal to boat-lovers. Among the commercial and privately owned vessels, there is often an interesting variety of traditional craft from the Indonesian Archipelago. These include *pinisi*, broad-beamed sailing cargo boats from South Sulawesi; and brightly coloured fishing boats from Madura, off north-east Java. There is a multitude of boat-charters and tours on offer. Day trips to Nusa Lembongan *(see p74)* are recommended. A yacht or traditional Bugis ship can be hired for a day-trip; longer trips go as far as Komodo and the Lesser Sunda Islands.

Nearby, on the Jalan Bypass Ngurah Rai, is the Mangrove Information Centre (0361 728 966), which aims to preserve the 15 species of coastal mangrove in its natural forest.

Pulau Serangan ❽

Road Map C5.

THE ISLAND OF SERANGAN is separated from the southern curve of Sanur beach by a mangrove area known as Suwungwas. The name "Turtle Island" is sometimes used, because of the sea turtles that used to lay their eggs here. The island has been greatly extended by reclamation during construction works for a hotel. A bridge now links it to mainland Bali. Local people maintain an unofficial guard post, and charge visitors a small fee for access to the island. Besides the Balinese, there is an old Bugis community *(see p135)*; their ancestors migrated from South Sulawesi, in the 1600s.

Here also is one of the six most sacred temples in Bali, **Pura Sakenan**, said by some to have been founded by the 16th-century reformist priest Dang Hyang Nirartha *(see pp46–7)*. Others believe the temple was founded in the 11th century by the Javanese Buddhist priest Mpu Kuturan. Within the inner courtyard is a stepped pyramid built of white coral, reminiscent of temples in Polynesia. During Manis Kuningan *(see p43)*, a vibrant festival takes place here marking the temple's anniversary.

The island is a good vantage point from which to watch vessels returning to Benoa Harbour at the end of the day. There are views of the islands and great sunsets.

Pura Sakenan

Pulau Serangan. *daily.* *donation.* *Manis Kuningan.*

Wall motif in a mosque in Tanjung Benoa

Tanjung Benoa ❾

Road Map C5. *from Nusa Dua.* *Badung, (0361) 756 175.*

TANJUNG (meaning "Cape") Benoa is a long, narrow, sandy spit, with a small fishing village built on it. The cape is separated from Benoa Harbour by a narrow stretch of water. The village was once a trading port, and some Chinese and Bugis as well as Balinese still live here. There are some Balinese temples built of carved limestone, as well as a mosque. At an ancient Chinese temple built by sailors and traders, fishermen of all religions consult with the fortune-teller in the hope of finding a good catch.

There is now a modern road leading to the tip of the peninsula from Nusa Dua. Hotels, spas and restaurants specializing in grilled seafood have grown up along both sides of the road. One quirky landmark is the stone pine-apple motif marking the entrance to the Novotel.

Despite development, Tanjung Benoa still attracts those in search of a relaxing beach off the beaten track. There are facilities for water sports, such as water-skiing, banana-boat rides, fishing and paragliding. Cruise operators offer trips out to sea for snorkelling in waters rich in corals and tropical fish.

An ancient Chinese temple on Tanjung Benoa

◁ **The *kecak* dance, in which a chorus of men chant an accompaniment as the *Ramayana* story is enacted**

The world-renowned Bali Golf and Country Club, and beyond it the resorts of Nusa Dua and the sea

Nusa Dua ⑩

Road Map C5. Denpasar (0361) 223 602.

THE NUSA DUA (literally "Two Islands") area is named after the two peninsulas along its coast. It consists primarily of luxury resorts run by major hotel chains. The beaches are sandy and clean. The entrance road is lined with rows of statues; it leads through a large *candi bentar* (split gate), on each side of which carvings of frogs serve as guardian figures.

Split gate at the entrance garden of the Nusa Dua Beach Hotel

Inside, there is an air of gentility and order. The hotels are built on a big scale. Their grandiose entrances have been described as "Bali Baroque" or "expanded traditional" in style – they are of interest to architecture enthusiasts. Young visitors will love the fish ponds of the Hilton Hotel, with thousands of brightly-coloured *koi* (a type of carp first bred in Japan) swimming among water lilies.

The Bali Golf and Country Club *(see p204)* has a championship course over three types of terrain (highland, coconut grove and coastal). Other facilities at Nusa Dua include the Bali International Convention Centre and the Galleria complex. The latter has shops, restaurants, galleries, a supermarket and a performance theatre. There are regular dance and other cultural activities here.

ENVIRONS: Bualu is a bustling village outside the gates of the Nusa Dua complex. Several streets are lined with restaurants offering fresh fish and shops selling handicrafts.

Between the Sheraton and Grand Hyatt hotels a headland with native flora and several Balinese shrines juts out into the sea. The views are good from here. Camel safaris through the arid hills are offered at the Nikko Hotel. One beach near the Nikko is a favourite haunt of surfers.

Beautiful beaches line the southern coast. Most require a hike or climb; many are popular surfing spots, but they can be dangerous for beginners, with big waves and strong currents.

West of Nusa Dua, on the road to Uluwatu, is the **GWK** (Garuda Wisnu Kencana, or "Golden Garuda Vishnu") cultural centre. The main feature will be a statue of the mythological bird Garuda and the Hindu god Vishnu. This will be taller than New York's Statue of Liberty. Its impact on the landcape has been controversial and plans for completion are unclear. Exhibitions and performances can already be seen here.

GWK
Jalan Raya Uluwatu, Bukit Ungasan, Jimbaran. (0361) 703 603. daily. www.gwk-bali.com

The Amanusa, a boutique hotel overlooking the golf course at Nusa Dua

Access to Jimbaran beach where the freshly cooked seafood is delicious

Jimbaran ⓫

Road Map C5. Kuta, (0361) 756 175. www.badung.go.id

JIMBARAN is a large village consisting of many family compounds laid out on traditional Balinese lines *(see pp28–9)*. There are no individual buildings of great interest to visit, but Jimbaran is a good place for those who like to see scenes of local everyday life. Several of Bali's most luxurious resorts have been built nearby. The most famous is the Four Seasons Resort *(see p170)*.

There is a very attractive beach, from which the sunsets and the views are spectacular. On a clear day the profiles of all Bali's volcanoes and hills are visible from here, including the three peaks of Gunung Batukau to the west *(see p133)*, and Gunung Batur *(see p120–21)*, Gunung Agung *(see p114)*, Gunung Abang *(see p121)* and Gunung Seraya *(see p103)* to the east. On the beach itself, it is possible to rent sailing-boats and take part in other water activities.

Jimbaran is a good place to eat. The beach is lined with thatch-roofed eating places, where customers choose their fresh seafood which is then grilled over coconut husks and delivered to the table.

There is a large fishing settlement here, consisting of simple huts built near the waterfront. Many of the fishermen are not of Balinese origin, but migrants from the islands of Java and Madura. The brightly painted boats with their impressive bows and sterns can be seen all day long bobbing at anchor in the surf off the coast. As the sun begins to set, the fishing craft set off into the dusk with lamps burning – it is an unforgettable sight.

Surfing at Kuta Reef, off the west coast of South Bali

ENVIRONS: Kuta Reef is one of Bali's famous surfing points. The reef break which lies off the coast of Tuban is one of the surfing spots in the sea around the Ngurah Rai International Airport. It can be reached by paddling for some time, or chartering an outrigger at Tuban *(see p69)* or at Jimbaran.

The **Bukit Peninsula** is the southernmost part of Bali, making up most of the area south of Jimbaran. Much of the coast is a series of inhospitable limestone cliffs. The Bukit is an arid place, but still attractive to those in search of some solitude.

Pura Luhur Uluwatu ⓬

See pp76–7.

Nusa Lembongan ⓭

Road Map E4. *from Sanur, Kusamba & Padang Bai.* *Klungkung, (0366) 21 448.*

THIS SMALL ISLAND has pristine beaches for sunlovers and good coral reefs for divers and snorkellers. Bird-lovers will find a variety of species.

Day trips to the island have been available since the early 1990s. In operation now are several jet catamarans, the best-known of them being the *Bali Hai (see p207)*; as a consequence the island is visited by larger groups than hitherto. Trips to the island are also offered by some local boat owners. The boats include *pinisi*, a type of Indonesian sailing vessel originating in the island of Sulawesi to the northeast.

Most boat-operators rent water-sport equipment, and snorkelling and diving gear.

On the island is an extensive underground house, known as the "**Cavehouse**". It was dug by a Balinese priest after he was instructed in dreams to live in the belly of Mother Earth. He has passed away but the cave remains a popular curiosity.

For those who like pristine islands with no cars, Nusa Lembongan is a good place to stay a night or two. There are some good homestays for budget travellers. After the daytrippers go, silence reigns; only some overnighters and the locals remain.

Ideal conditions for snorkelling off Nusa Lembongan

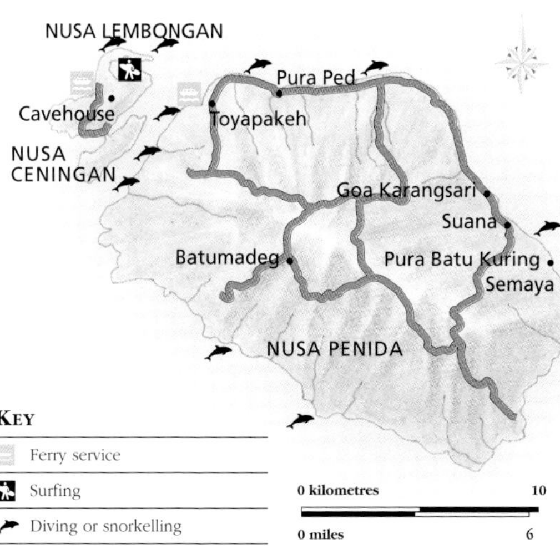

The coastal temple Pura Batu Kuning, on Nusa Penida

Nusa Penida ⓮

Road Map E5 & F5. *from Sanur, Kusamba & Padang Bai.*
Klungkung, (0366) 21 448.

THIS QUIET, UNDEVELOPED island, once the penal colony of the Raja of Klungkung, appeals mainly to hardy adventurers. Here, Balinese language and art have been less subject to change than on the mainland. The island is the legendary home of Ratu Gede Mecaling, the Balinese "King of Magical Powers". It is somewhat feared by many Balinese.

In general the landscape is dry, even arid, resembling the limestone hills of the Bukit Peninsula. Towards the south coast, with its tall white cliffs, there are a few lusher hills. Some cotton is grown here. From it is woven the *cepuk*, a form of *ikat* textile *(see p37)* thought to have magical, protective powers. Other local occupations include seaweed farming.

There are several interesting temples here. One is the **Pura Ped**, in the village of Toyapakeh. The temple is built on an island in a large lotus pond. Among the carvings in **Pura Batu Kuning**, near Semaya, are some explicitly erotic reliefs. The *pura desa*, or village temple, of the inland village of **Batumadeg** also has some interesting decorative reliefs. They show a number of sea creatures, including crabs and a variety of shellfish. The main gate is especially imposing.

Stone sculpture at Pura Ped

A short distance south of Suana there is a sacred limestone cave, **Goa Karangsari**.

In general there are few facilities of any kind on Nusa Penida. Visitors must take even basic supplies with them. Simple homestays are the only accommodation. The roads are not good. The best way to get about is by motorcycle or on foot. It is also possible to rent a car with a driver or take a *bemo*.

The waters off the coast of Nusa Penida are crystal-clear, although the currents are often strong. Here experienced divers will be able to see to see many large and rare species of underwater life. There are fine coral formations, especially off the south coast, where the sea is also famous for its rare but spectacular concentrations of giant sunfish *(see pp210–11)*; in December and January they float in the water like large hot-air balloons. Sailfish and the whale shark can occasionally be seen. Off the northern half of the island the waters, while also clear, are shallower and calmer, especially in the strait between Nusa Penida and Nusa Lembongan. Most people who dive off these islands make their arrangements with operators in Sanur.

For those who want to explore Nusa Lembongan there is a ferry which runs from Toyapakeh.

Diving off the coast of Nusa Penida

Pura Luhur Uluwatu ⓬

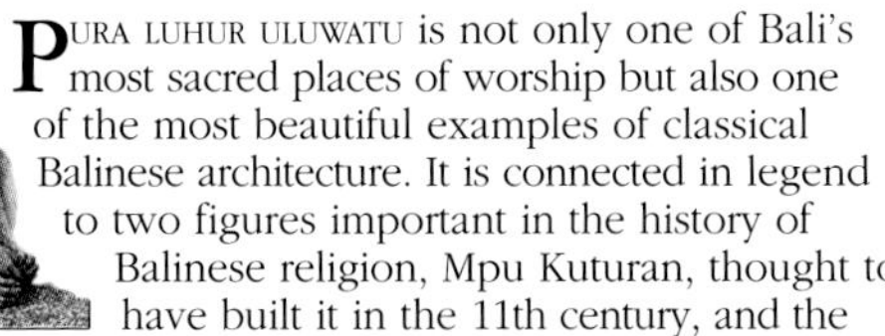

Local monkeys

PURA LUHUR ULUWATU is not only one of Bali's most sacred places of worship but also one of the most beautiful examples of classical Balinese architecture. It is connected in legend to two figures important in the history of Balinese religion, Mpu Kuturan, thought to have built it in the 11th century, and the reformer priest Dang Hyang Nirartha (later deified as Betara Sakti Wawu Rauh) *(see pp46–7)*, who rebuilt it some 500 years later. Until the beginning of the 20th century only the princes of Denpasar were allowed to worship here. It is best to visit during the late afternoon when the sea breezes rise, and then enjoy the sunset.

★ Three-tiered Meru
The pagoda is dedicated to Nirartha who achieved enlightenment here.

This courtyard is reserved for worshippers.

View of the Temple
From several points the temple can be seen in its full glory as the surf crashes onto the rocks below. It is sometimes possible to see turtles and dolphins in the sea.

Stairways
These stepped paths along the cliff rise 200 m (600 ft) above the sea.

STAR FEATURES

- ★ **Three-tiered Meru**
- ★ **Main Gate**
- ★ **Candi Bentar**

★ Main Gate
The unusual arched doorway has the shape of Meru, the Cosmic Mountain of Hinduism. Surmounting it are three finials and a kala *head – this is a fanged demon with bulging eyes, thought to ward off evil spirits.*

VISITORS' CHECKLIST

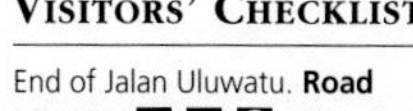

End of Jalan Uluwatu. **Road Map** B5. *8am–7pm daily.* *for festivals.* Kecak dance: 6pm daily. *temple anniversary (based on Balinese calendar).*

Guardian Statues
These Ganesha, elephant-headed guardian statues, wearing a belt with a clasp in the form of a cyclops, are masterpieces of Balinese sculpture.

★ Candi Bentar
At the top of the stairs leading to the temple is a candi bentar *(split gate) decorated with elaborate carvings.*

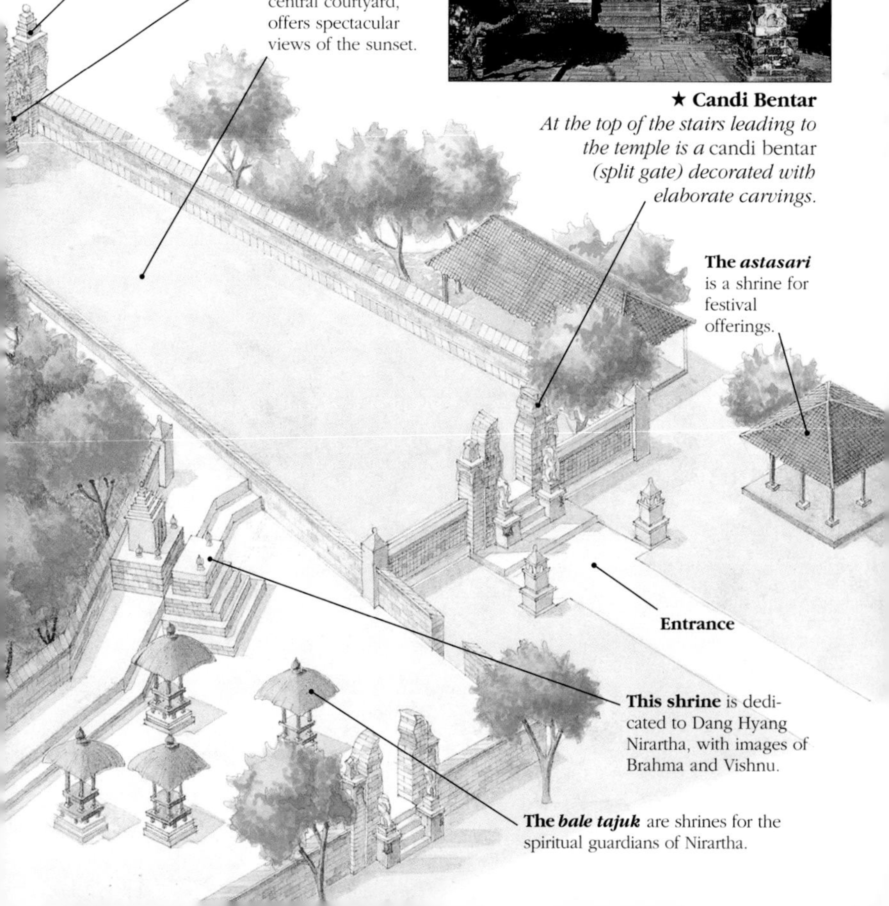

The *jero tengah*, or central courtyard, offers spectacular views of the sunset.

The *astasari* is a shrine for festival offerings.

Entrance

This shrine is dedicated to Dang Hyang Nirartha, with images of Brahma and Vishnu.

The *bale tajuk* are shrines for the spiritual guardians of Nirartha.

CENTRAL BALI

BALI'S BROAD SOUTHERN SLOPES, *with their terraced ricefields and hundreds of villages, were the cradle of traditional Balinese society. This area coincides with the regency (and former kingdom) of Gianyar, made up of many* puri *(noble houses) whose former glory lives on in the courtly arts of sculpture, painting, gold- and silversmithing, music, dance and theatrical performance.*

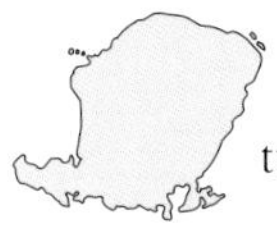

Gianyar is bounded on its western side by the tumultuous Ayung River and to the east by the Melangit River. A number of other rivers slice through the intervening landscape. Between the Petanu and Pakrisan Rivers are the remains of one of Bali's oldest civilizations. Here is the village of Ubud, a cultural centre and former kingdom, which attracts many visitors today.

From the 9th to the 11th century, Bali was ruled by Hindu-Buddhist kingdoms centred near present-day Pejeng and Bedulu, a short distance from Ubud. After the Majapahit conquest in the 14th century, power shifted to Klungkung but it returned here in the 18th century. At that time branches of the Klungkung dynasty grew into rival kingdoms, two of which were based in Sukawati and Gianyar. Satellite *puri* competed in architectural and ritual display. Inter-kingdom warfare at the end of the 19th century gave Ubud much of Gianyar's land. Politically, Puri Gianyar remained on top, partly because of its early incorporation into the Dutch colonial regime.

Ubud became internationally famous as a gateway into Bali's cultural heartland, when several Western artists and intellectuals settled here in the 1930s. Today, many farmers are turning to tourism and handicrafts for economic reasons. Local cultural traditions are being preserved as a consequence.

The climate of Central Bali cools noticeably as one ascends from the coastal region into the foothills, and can be chilly north of Tegallalang.

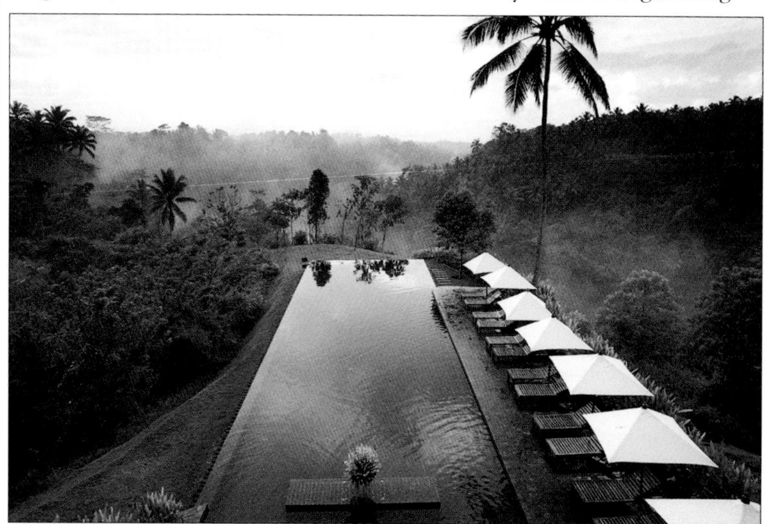

View across the Ayung River valley from the Chedi hillside resort, near Ubud

◁ **Densely carved temple gate of the Pura Desa (village temple) in Peliatan**

Exploring Central Bali

CENTRAL BALI, RICH IN HISTORY, is famous for craft production and the performing arts. Ubud is an important artistic centre, and a good base for exploring the area. Many other villages and monuments of historic and cultural interest are located on the roads running between the coastal plain and the slopes of Gunung Batur. The river gorges, separated by ridges and rice terraces, provide beautiful landscapes, and exciting white-water rafting. Near Singapadu are the attractively laid-out Bali Bird Park and Bali Reptile Park.

Pura Pengastulan, a temple in Bedulu

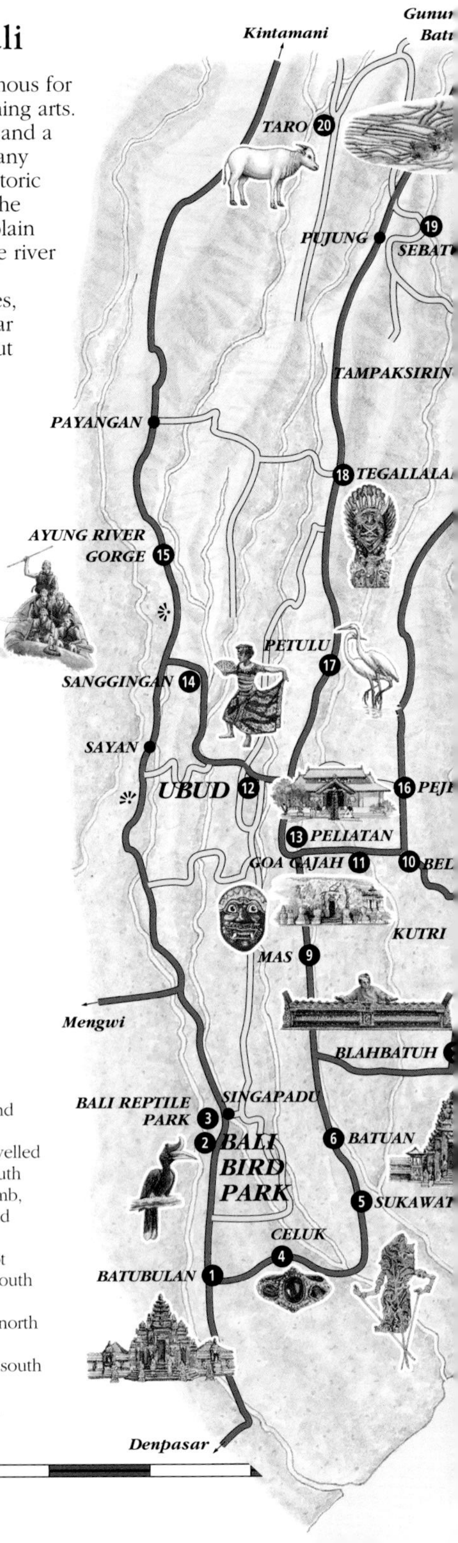

GETTING AROUND

The main route through Central Bali leads through several arts and crafts villages: Batubulan, Celuk, Sukawati, Batuan, Mas and Ubud. A parallel, more westerly road runs through Singapadu. These roads can be travelled by *bemo*. Taxis are not as frequent as in South Bali. North of Ubud three parallel roads climb, via the villages of Payangan, Tegallalang and Tampaksiring towards Gunung Batur and Kintamani. Bicycles and motorcycles are not pleasant ways of travelling on main roads south of Ubud, because of the density of traffic, although they are more satisfactory further north and on back roads. Public buses between Denpasar and Singaraja ply the main north-south route; however, tourist shuttle buses run frequently between South Bali's resorts and Ubud, and are much more comfortable.

Kintamani
TARO 20
PUJUNG
TAMPAKSIRING
PAYANGAN
AYUNG RIVER GORGE 15
PETULU 17
SANGGINGAN 14
SAYAN
UBUD 12
13 PELIATAN
GOA GAJAH 11
KUTRI
MAS 9
Mengwi
BLAHBATUH
BALI REPTILE PARK 3
SINGAPADU
2 BALI BIRD PARK
6 BATUAN
CELUK 4
BATUBULAN 1
Denpasar

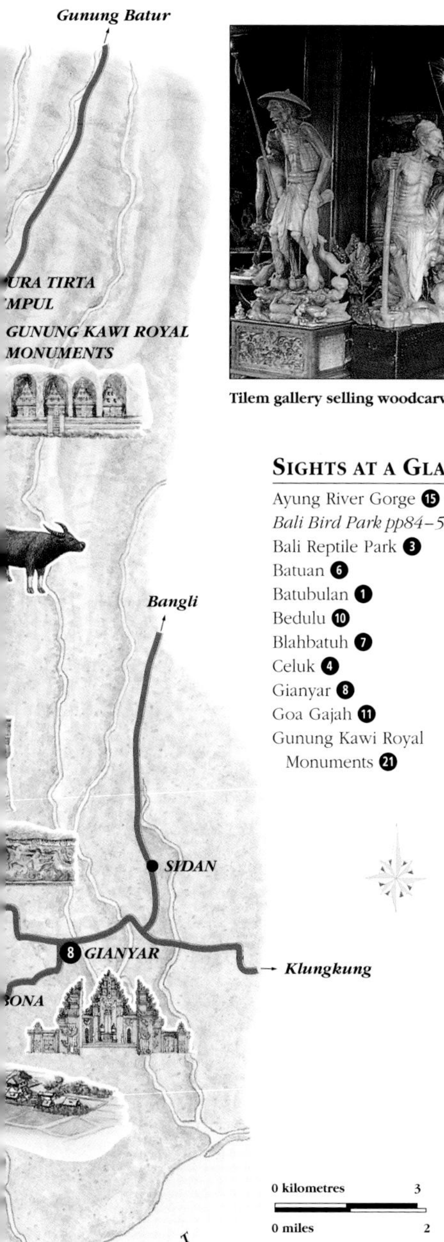

Gunung Batur

PURA TIRTA EMPUL

GUNUNG KAWI ROYAL MONUMENTS

Bangli

SIDAN

8 GIANYAR

Klungkung

Tilem gallery selling woodcarvings in the village of Mas

Sights at a Glance

Ayung River Gorge 15
Bali Bird Park pp84–5 2
Bali Reptile Park 3
Batuan 6
Batubulan 1
Bedulu 10
Blahbatuh 7
Celuk 4
Gianyar 8
Goa Gajah 11
Gunung Kawi Royal Monuments 21
Mas 9
Pejeng 16
Peliatan 13
Petulu 17
Pura Tirta Empul 22
Sanggingan 14
Sebatu 19
Sukawati 5
Taro 20
Tegallalang 18
Ubud pp88–95 12

See Also

• ***Where to Stay*** pp174–6

• ***Where to Eat*** pp187–9

0 kilometres 3

0 miles 2

BADUNG STRAIT

Key

Major road

Minor road

River

Viewpoint

Coconuts being collected near Ubud

Keris **trance, one of the energetic ritual dance performances which can be seen in Batubulan**

Batubulan ❶

Road Map C4. *Denpasar, (0361) 223 602.*

ALTHOUGH DENPASAR'S urban sprawl is enveloping Batubulan and the main road is now lined with shops selling "antique" furniture, this large village is still a centre of traditional stone carving. Craftsmen can be seen in countless workshops sculpting mythological and religious figures or highly imaginative modern forms, apparently oblivious to the heavy traffic passing by on the main road.

The village temple, **Pura Puseh**, is a good example of the use of *paras*, Bali's ubiquitous grey stone, which is in fact volcanic tuff, quarried from river gorges. *Paras* is used both for sculpture and as a building material. Its soft texture makes it very easy to carve.

Batubulan is also home to several venerable Barong and Keris dance theatre troupes. During alternate weeks the Pura Puseh is the pleasant venue of a daily Barong and Keris dance performance by the celebrated **Denjalan** troupe; in intervening weeks the location is Batubulan's *bale banjar*, or community pavilion. A few other troupes perform at around the same time. Daytime performances were developed in the 1930s, in response to the desire of visitors to take photographs. However, this exorcistic drama still has ritual significance.

Pura Puseh
Main Road, Batubulan. *daily.* *donation.*

Denjalan
(0361) 298 038 or (0361) 298 282. Performances: 9:30am daily.

Bali Bird Park ❷

See pp84–5.

Bali Reptile Park ❸

Jalan Serma Cok Ngurah Gambir, Singapadu. Next to Bali Bird Park. **Road Map** D4. *(0361) 299 344.* *daily.* *Nyepi.*

A VISIT TO THE Bali Reptile Park (Rimba Reptil) is easily combined with a visit to the Bali Bird Park nearby. The two are conceived in a similar style. Although somewhat smaller in area than the Bird Park, the Reptile Park is also set in lush, botanically interesting gardens. The landscaping concept is that of an ancient archaeological site, excavated and restored to its former glory. All the significant reptile species of Indonesia can be seen in the collection. They include Komodo dragons, four species of crocodiles, and what is claimed to be the largest known python in captivity. Many venomous snakes from around the world are well displayed in glass cages. Among them are a king cobra, a Malayan pit viper and a death adder.

Celuk ❹

Road Map D4. *Gianyar, (0361) 943 401.*

THE VILLAGE OF CELUK is devoted almost entirely to gold- and silversmithing. Much of the jewellery sold in Bali originates here. The workers belong to the caste clan of Pande Mas, traditionally practitioners of various metal crafts. Grand jewellery shops line the main road; smaller ones selling cheaper goods occupy the narrow side streets. Several studios produce traditional and modern designs of ornamental jewellery as well as *keris* daggers and religious items. Jewellery can be made to order. Buyers should be aware that at the larger outlets, prices may include a commission (often 40–60 per cent) passed on to tour guides.

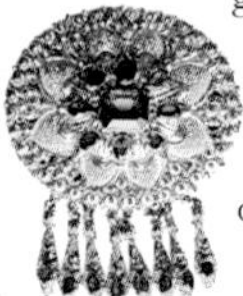

Silver earrings from Celuk

Sukawati ❺

Road Map D4. *Gianyar, (0361) 943 401.*

SUKAWATI IS worth visiting primarily as a handicrafts centre. Opposite the farmers' market on the east side of the main road through the town is the **Pasar Seni** ("Art Market"). It is housed in a complex of two-storey buildings packed with stalls selling craft goods. Behind it is a market selling woodcarvings, open until 10am daily.

To the people of Bali, Sukawati is important as the ancestral seat of many of the region's *puri* (noble houses), and as a centre of the sacred shadow puppet theatre, *wayang kulit (see p31).* In the early 1700s an off-shoot of the royal house of Klungkung was established here. The palace, on the northeast corner of the main intersection, is now much reduced; and the temples, further north on the main road and nestling in side streets to the east, are not generally open to visitors.

Stone sculptures of mythological figures in a shop at Sukawati

Batuan ❻

Road Map D4. *Gianyar, (0366) 93 401.*

THE HISTORY OF Batuan goes back almost 1,000 years. The population contains more nobility than commoners; and it is celebrated for its artistic excellence in the fields of not only dance but also painting and architecture. Painters' studios are prominent in the village. The Batuan school of painting is known for its dense graphics, dramatically restricted colour palette and astute observation of human life *(see pp34–5).*

The **Pura Puseh**, the magnificent village temple, welcomes visitors. Extensively renovated in 1992, its opulent shrines and carvings are proof that Bali's traditional building arts are thriving. *Gambuh* performances are held at the temple on the 1st and 15th of each month, a rare opportunity to see this ancient court dance. Among the dance troupes of Batuan are practitioners also of *topeng* and *wayang wong (see p31).* These are, like *gambuh,* performed to traditional music during temple festivals.

Giant baby statue near Blahbatuh

Pura Puseh
daily. donation. Gambuh *dance: 7–9pm, 1st & 15th monthly.*

Blahbatuh ❼

Road Map D4. *Gianyar, (0361) 943 401.*

THIS VILLAGE IS MARKED by a huge stone statue of a baby, erected in the early 1990s, said by some to be the village giant Kebo Iwo as an infant. Others whisper that the women of a nearby village urged their husbands to build the statue to placate a demon who was claiming the lives of children.

Vihara Amurva Bhumi Blahbatuh, a large Chinese temple (*klenteng*) with Buddhist and Hindu elements which underwent grand expansion in 1999, is a little-known centre of worship for Chinese Buddhists from throughout South Bali.

ENVIRONS: On the main north-south road between Blahbatuh and the Bedulu road is the large workshop and showroom of the **Sidha Karya Gong Foundry**, established by the renowned gongsmith I Made Gabeleran. A full array of traditional musical instruments and dance costumes is on sale here.

At **Kutri**, 3 km (2 miles) north of Blahbatuh, is a hill at the base of which is the temple complex **Pura Bukit Dharma Kutri**. On the hilltop, from which there are good views, is a shrine that houses a partly effaced, but still fine, relief carving of the goddess Durga killing a bull. It is thought to be a portrait statue of an 11th-century Balinese queen.

Kemenuh, 1.5 km (1 mile) west of Blahbatuh, is a woodcarving centre. Also here is **Sua Bali**, a modest eco-friendly resort, where courses are offered in local languages, crafts and cuisine, as well as cultural study programmes.

Vihara Amurva Bhumi Blahbatuh
Blahbatuh. *daily.*

Sidha Karya
Jalan Raya Getas-Buruan, Blahbatuh.
(0361) 942 798.

Pura Bukit Dharma Kutri
Kutri. *daily.*

Sua Bali
Kemenuh. *(0361) 941 050.*
suabali@indosat.net.id

Pura Bukit Dharma Kutri, a temple

Bali Bird Park ❷

Edward's fig parrot

BUILT ON WHAT WAS until 1995 an expanse of ricefields, Bali Bird Park, or Taman Burung, is a place where visitors can see a profusion of exotic wildlife at close quarters. There are more than 1,500 birds here, many of them in big, walk-in aviaries. There are 250 species not only from Bali and Lombok, but also from the rest of Indonesia, Africa, Australia and the Americas. Many of the birds are rare and endangered, and some of these are bred here. Among the inhabitants is Bali's only endemic bird, the Bali starling *(see p137)*. Besides the birds, there are more than 300 exotic trees and plants on display in a beautifully landscaped setting.

★ Birds of Paradise
The lesser bird of paradise, from New Guinea, has been hunted close to extinction.

Irian Jaya Forest Aviary

★ Rainforest Habitat
This huge, walk-in aviary has a raised walkway. The birds here include many birds of paradise, the toco toucan, and sun conures from South America.

Hornbills
The Asian pied hornbill has a very distinct, loud, raucous call.

Australian Pelican
This large waterbird sometimes wanders as far as Indonesia.

INDONESIAN OWLS

These nocturnal birds can rarely be seen in the wild and the buffy fish owl and the barred or Sumatran eagle owl are therefore a highlight of the Bali Bird Park. They are both large and feed on rodents. In all there are 38 recognised species of Indonesian owl – many of them found only on small islands. Their secretive nature and, in some cases, preference for inhospitable habitats are reasons why little is known about them.

Buffy fish-owl

Crowned Pigeon
This aviary has one of the three crowned pigeon species from New Guinea; also the Nicorbar pigeon; the pink-necked pigeon; and the great argus pheasant.

Komodo Dragons
These carnivorous creatures are the world's largest lizards, endemic to Komodo in Indonesia.

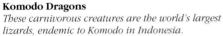

VISITORS' CHECKLIST

Jalan Serma Cok Ngurah Gambir, Singapadu, Batubulan. **Road Map** D4. *(0361) 299 352.* *8am – 6pm daily.* *Nyepi.* *No pets.* www.bali-birdpark.com

KEY

- Parking
- Souvenir shop
- Wheelchair access
- Café
- Toilet
- Tourist information point

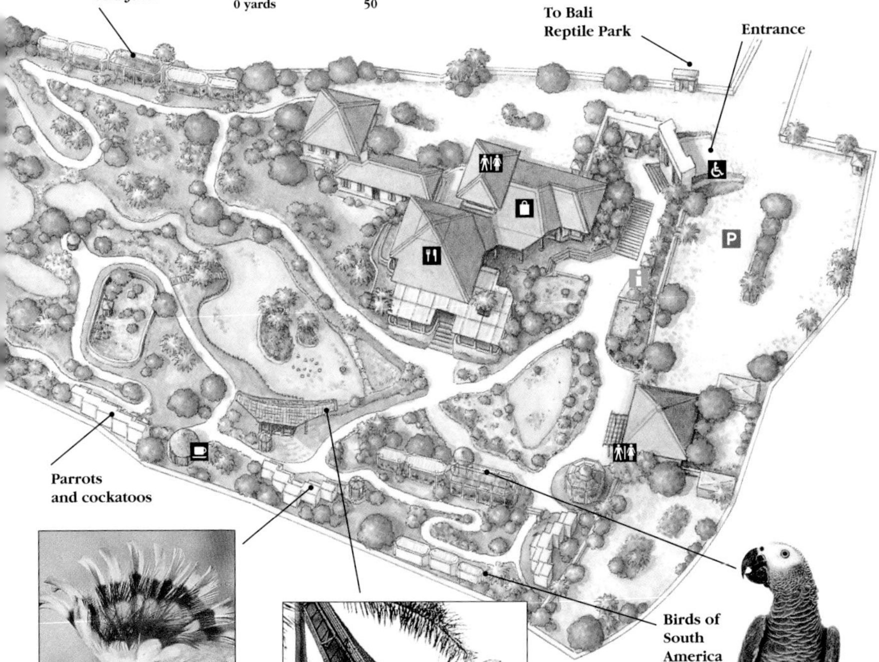

0 metres 50
0 yards 50

Birds of Bali and Java

To Bali Reptile Park

Entrance

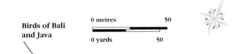

Parrots and cockatoos

Birds of South America

Major Mitchell's Cockatoo
Apart from this species from Australia, several parrots and cockatoos native to Indonesia (of which there are over 75 species) are bred in this bird park.

★ Toraja House
This typical house from Sulawesi is nearly 100 years old. It was dismantled, moved and re-assembled here.

The African Grey Parrot
This species can often be trained to mimic.

STAR FEATURES

- ★ **Birds of Paradise**
- ★ **Rainforest Habitat**
- ★ **Toraja House**

Puri Gianyar, a palace of the royal family of the former kingdom of Gianyar, restored to its past glory

Gianyar 8

Road Map D4. *Jalan Ngurah Rai 21, (0361) 943 401.*

THIS TOWN is a centre of administration rather than of the tourist industry. The people of Bali shop here for farm produce, household appliances and paraphernalia for ceremonies; there is also a large market (with food stalls in the evening). This is a good place to buy jewellery and hand-woven and hand-dyed textiles, many of them made locally. During the day, there are food stalls at the Bale Banjar Teges (community association meeting hall) at the town centre; the *babi guling* (roast pig) is famous.

On the north side of the town square is the impressive **Puri Gianyar**. Although the palace is closed to visitors, its grand outer walls and gates give a sense of the power of the former kingdoms. After damage by an earthquake in 1917, the *puri* was restored as a replica of the original 17th-century construction.

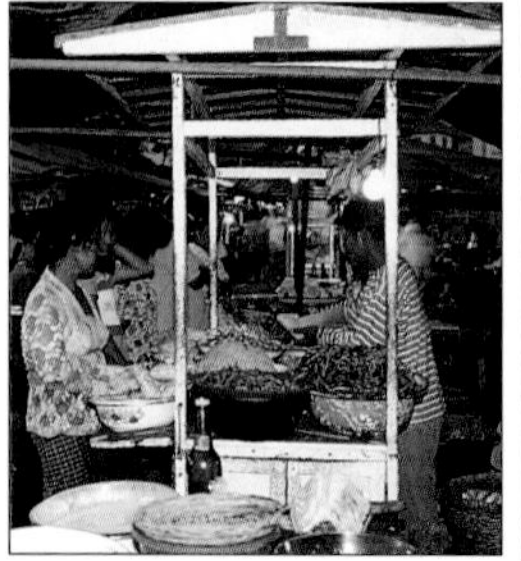

Local food stalls at the night market in Gianyar

ENVIRONS: Southwest of Gianyar are several villages whose livelihood is increasingly based on craft products from plant materials. Although these are sold for export and in shops around Bali, visitors can buy for better prices at source. **Bona**, 3 km (2 miles) southwest of Gianyar, specializes in hand-woven objects made from the leaves of the lontar palm. About 2 km (1 mile) southwest of Bona is the village of **Blega**, which is a centre for the production of bamboo furniture.

Mas 9

Road Map D4. *Gianyar, (0361) 943 401.*

THE VILLAGE OF MAS is most famous not for teak furniture, as the number of roadside shops selling it might suggest, but for fine wood sculpture and *topeng* masks *(see p31)*. The brahmans of Mas have been master-carvers for many generations; sculpture has been produced for the art market since the 1930s *(see pp36–7)*. Among the best-established studio-galleries are Siadja & Son, the Njana Tilem Gallery and Adil Artshop. Tantra Gallery and I B Anom (for masks) are well-known. Brahmans come to Mas from all over Bali every Manis Kuningan festival *(see p39)* to honour their ancestor, the Hindu priest Dang Hyang Nirartha (also known as Dwijendra) at the temple **Pura Taman Pule**. The large old tree in the temple is regarded as holy. According to local belief, a gold flower once grew from it. The tree is dressed up in ceremonial colours during the festival. On the evening of the festivities there is usually a ritual performance of *wayang wong* *(see p31)*.

Elaborately carved gateway at Pura Taman Pule, Mas

Pura Taman Pule

daily. wayang wong*: during festivals.* *Kuningan (lasts for three days).*

Bedulu ⑩

Road Map D3. *Gianyar, (0361) 943 401.*

THIS LARGE, quiet village was at the centre of the Pejeng kingdom of the 10–13th centuries. The monumental relief carvings on a large rock wall at the **Yeh Pulu** spring, south of the village, are thought to date from the mid-14th-century Majapahit conquest *(see p46)*. The carvings – about 25 m (80 ft) long with an average height of 2 m (6 ft) – are thought to be the work of a single artist. Myth attributes the work to the legendary 14th-century giant Kebo Iwo. The stories can be "read" by looking at the vigorously carved images from left to right. Among them are heroic scenes showing humans fighting demonic beasts.

The large **Pura Pengastulan** temple *(see p80)* has grand gates built in the art-deco style made fashionable by the artist I Gusti Nyoman Lempad *(see p34)*, who was born in Bedulu.

Lempad's style may be seen also in the nearby **Pura Samuan Tiga**. This name derives from a legend. In the 11th century, a meeting (*samuan*) is said to have been held here among the gods of three (*tiga*) warring religious sects after they had defeated the demon king Mayadanawa.

The annual festival around Purnama Kedasa *(see p40)* is a brilliant 11-day celebration; but even when empty, Pura Samuan Tiga has a great, quiet strength. The grand inner gate by Lempad is particularly impressive, as is the cockfighting pit on the east side of the first courtyard.

The village of Bedulu decorated for the Galungan festival

Carved rocks at the entrance to Goa Gajah, the "Elephant Cave"

Yeh Pulu
daily. donation.
Pura Pengastulan
daily.
Pura Samuan Tiga
daily. donation. Perang Sampian: 1pm during festival.
Purnama Kedasa (Apr, variable).

Goa Gajah ⑪

Bedulu. **Road Map** D3.
Gianyar, (0361) 943 401.
daily.

THE GOA GAJAH ("Elephant Cave") became known to Westerners only in 1923. It is thought to date from the 11th century. Steps lead down to the temple and other monuments, about 15 m (50 ft) below road level. The large springs, excavated in 1954, were intended probably for bathing and as a source of holy water. The cave itself, with a large face in the exuberantly carved surrounding rock, is a small, rather airless, T-shaped chamber in which are niches containing Shivite and Buddhist statues.

Outside the cave is a shrine to the Buddhist child-protector Hariti, depicted as the Balinese Men Brayut, a poor woman with too many children. In a ravine a little to the south are a spring and more shrines.

THE LEGEND OF BEDAULU

The name Bedulu comes from the 14th-century sorcerer-king Bedaulu, who was said to remove his head (*hulu*) to achieve more efficient meditation. One day he was disturbed in this practice and hastily took the head of a passing pig (*beda* means "different"). Thereafter it was forbidden to look at the king, lest his ugly secret be discovered, and he ruled from a tower, raised above eye level. However, the Majapahit general Gajah Mada tricked him during a feast. As Gajah Mada tipped back his head to drink, he looked up, glimpsed the king's true nature and so was able to overpower him.

The King of Bedulu in his Tower (1934) by I Tomblos

Street-by-Street: Ubud ⓬

ALMOST EVERYWHERE IN UBUD one is conscious of the town's artistic traditions. Since most shops stay open until around 9pm, the best time for strolling around is the early evening. By then the traffic has abated, the cafés and restaurants are invitingly lit, and the cool air is often filled with *gamelan* music from cultural performances. The main street, Jalan Raya Ubud, is the setting for several buildings of architectural interest. The streets running off it to the north and south lead to village neighbourhoods, and are lined with family-run shops, small businesses catering for visitors, and art galleries.

★ Museum Puri Lukisan
A fine collection of Balinese art is on show here (see pp92–3).

Ary's Warung
This restaurant is run by a minor Ubud palace family, on land either side of the house gate.

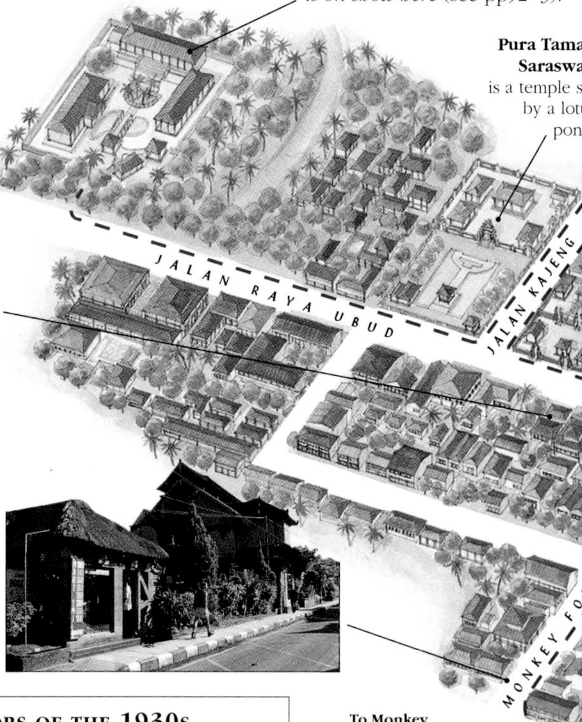

Pura Tama Saraswa
is a temple se by a lotu ponc

Monkey Forest Road (Jalan Wanara Wana)
The street is lined with galleries, restaurants and hotels.

To Monkey Forest Sanctuary

0 metres 100

0 yards 100

KEY

Suggested route

INFLUENTIAL VISITORS OF THE 1930S

Bali owes much of its fame to foreign guests of Ubud's royal family in the 1920s and '30s. Through their films, books and photographs, these visitors projected to the world an exotic image of Bali. Among the most influential were German painter and musician Walter Spies and Dutch painter Rudolf Bonnet, who helped found the Pita Maha artists' association *(see p35)*; and Mexican artist Miguel Covarrubias, who wrote the classic *Island of Bali* (1937). The anthropologists Margaret Mead and Gregory Bateson lived in Sayan, just outside Ubud; their neighbours were composer Colin McPhee and his wife, ethnographer Jane Belo.

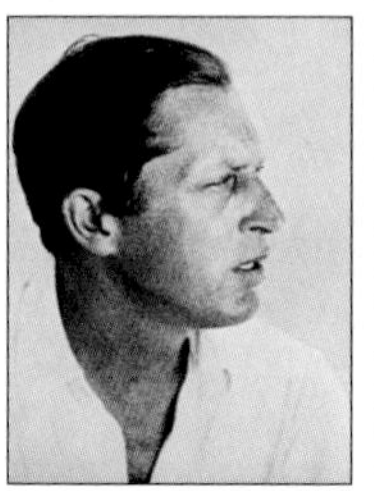

Walter Spies, who settled in Ubud in 1927

STAR SIGHTS

- ★ **Museum Puri Lukisan**
- ★ **Puri Saren**
- ★ **Pasar Ubud**

VISITORS' CHECKLIST

Road Map C3. *from Denpasar & Kuta.* *Ubud Tourist Information, Jalan Raya Ubud, (0361) 973 285.* *Balinese performances: daily, details posted at Ubud* .

★ Puri Saren
Ubud's palace has a shady forecourt where visitors can relax during the day and see traditional dance every evening.

Ubud Tourist Information Centre

The *wantilan* is a hall where local people can gather and cultural events take place.

★ Pasar Ubud
A farmers' market takes place here in the morning. Shops and stalls sell all kinds of crafts, snacks and sundries throughout the day.

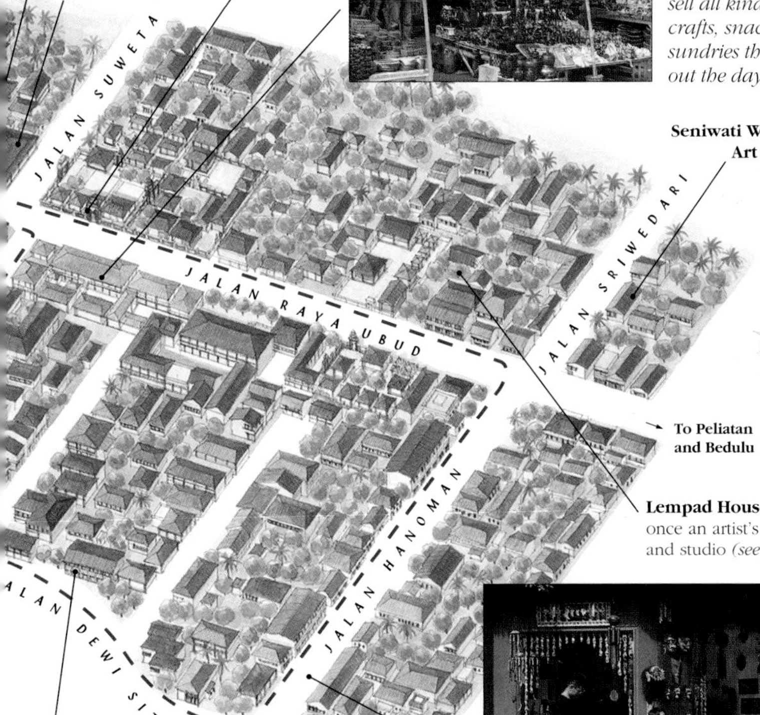

JALAN SUWETA

JALAN RAYA UBUD

JALAN SRIWEDARI

Seniwati Women's Art Gallery

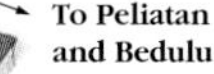

To Peliatan and Bedulu

Lempad House was once an artist's home and studio *(see p90).*

JALAN HANOMAN

JALAN DEWI SITA

To Pengosekan, Batubulan and Denpasar

Jalan Dewi Sita is a street around which have been established many popular boutiques, art galleries and restaurants.

Jalan Hanoman
Temples, shops, art studios, and homestays can be found here.

Exploring Ubud

Rangda mask

UBUD HAS LONG BEEN known as the "village of painters". In the 1930s, the encouragement of the *puri* (royal family) attracted foreign artists and intellectuals seeking the "real Bali", and so the village's international reputation was born. A peaceful hamlet until the 1980s, Ubud developed rapidly into a village of "cultural tourism". Now it is a small town, packed with galleries, craft-shops, restaurants, bars and hotels. However, Ubud spends much of its new prosperity on ritual ceremonies and conservation of traditional art forms.

Ubud Tourist Information Centre

Jalan Raya Ubud. (0361) 973 285. *daily.*

The centre is a reliable source of information about tours, transport, dance performances, and current cultural events. It provides information about local ceremonies and encourages foreigners to observe dress etiquette when visiting temples or rituals *(see p218).*

Seniwati Gallery Art by Women

Jalan Sriwedari 2B. (0361) 975 485. *Tue–Sun.*
www.seniwatigallery.com
Pondok Pekak Jalan Monkey Forest. (0361) 976194.

This is the only gallery exhibiting women's art in Asia. They work with 72 mostly Balinese artists, who paint in modern and traditional styles.

Their library and bookshop, **Pondok Pekak Library and Learning Centre**, offer language and arts classes.

Pura Taman Saraswati

Jalan Raya Ubud. *daily.*

This temple was built in the 1950s by I Gusti Nyoman Lempad at the command of Ubud's prince, in honour of Saraswati, the deity of learning and the arts. It is set in a water garden, with a lotus pond as the centrepiece. The temple has fine carvings by Lempad: a 3-m (10-ft) statue of the demon Jero Gede Mecaling; and the *padma - sana* shrine in the northeast corner, dedicated to the Supreme God *(see p26).* The temple is normally closed, but admission may be gained via the adjacent Café Lotus.

Museum Puri Lukisan

see pp92–3.

Pasar Ubud

Jalan Raya Ubud. *daily.*

At the huge Pasar Ubud (Ubud Market) there are sellers of agricultural produce and dry goods on the ground floor and between the buildings. The main attraction for visitors is the all-day handicraft market. The food Market is held every three days on *pasah.*

Pura Taman Saraswati facing Café Lotus across an ornamental pond

A palace gate in Puri Saren

Puri Saren

Jalan Raya Ubud. (0361) 975 057.
Traditional dances 7:30pm daily.
www.ubudvillage.com

The grandeur of Ubud's royal palace dates from the 1890s, the time of warlord Cokorda Gede Sukawati. The present walls and resplendent gates are largely the work of master artist I Gusti Nyoman Lempad *(see p34).* The *puri,* which owns several hotels, remains influential in Ubud's religious and cultural life, and spends lavishly on local ceremonies.

A group of woodcarvers at work near the Lempad House

Lempad House

Jalan Raya Ubud. (0361) 975 052. *daily.*

This is the family compound of I Gusti Nyoman Lempad *(see p34),* perhaps Bali's most celebrated artist. It is open to visitors and contains an art shop selling the works of local painters. Some works by Lempad are on display in the courtyard. Lempad was also an architect and builder in the traditional style, and the handsome north and east pavilions of the house were designed by him.

Monkey Forest Sanctuary

Monkey Forest Road (Jalan Wana Wanara). daily.

At the end of a long street known as Monkey Forest Road, this forest is a protected sanctuary for three troupes of long-tailed monkeys *(Macaca fascicularis)*. It is advisable to heed the warnings against feeding the monkeys – they are mischievous and can become aggressive. In the forest, there is an important temple complex and a graveyard. The large temple, **Pura Dalem Agung**, is a "temple of the dead"; its carved decorations are appropriately frightening. Down a short flight of steps between the roots of tall trees is a spring temple, renovated in the 1990s with the addition of some carvings.

A long-tail macaque in the Monkey Forest Sanctuary

Coconut palms surrounding rice plantations in the valley west of Ubud

Environs: To the west, Jalan Raya descends into the valley known as **Campuhan**, where two rivers meet (*campuh*). This has been a foreigners' residential neighbourhood since the 1930s when Walter Spies *(see p88)* built his house at what is now the Tjampuhan Hotel and Spa. A bridge built by the colonial Dutch survives next to the modern traffic bridge. From it can be seen the spring temple **Pura Gunung Lebah** (Pura Campuhan), which was founded in the 8th century.

Padang Tegal, on the southern outskirts of Ubud, is a large village notable for its full "set" of Balinese social classes and many painters and intellectuals, as well as its homestays. South of Padang Tegal is the small village of **Pengosekan**, home to many painters and woodcarvers. In the village of **Tebesaya**, east of Padang Tegal, there are many good places to eat, shop and stay. West of Pengosekan is **Nyuh Kuning**, the centre of woodcarving in the area.

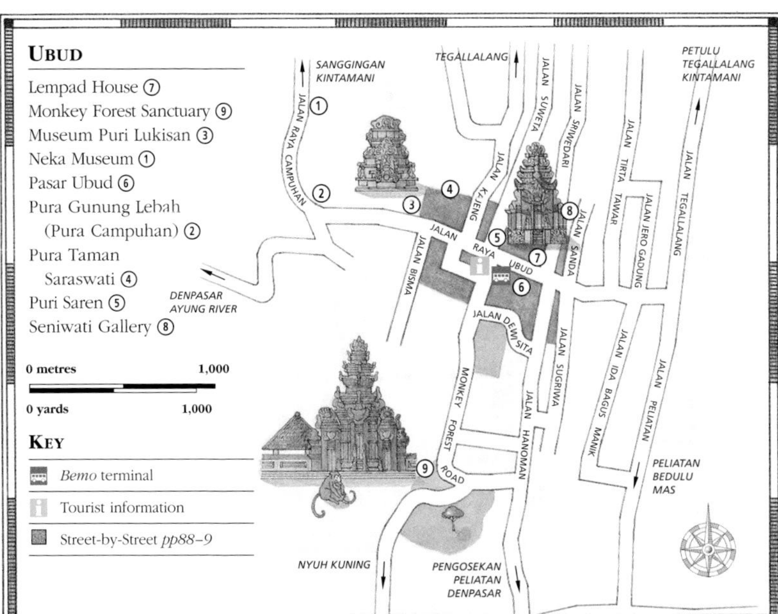

Ubud: Museum Puri Lukisan

Museum Puri Lukisan ("Palace of Painting"), was the brainchild of Ubud's prince Cokorda Gede Agung Sukawati, and Dutch painter Rudolf Bonnet *(see p88)*. It was conceived in 1953 out of concern that Bali's finest works of art were disappearing into private collections around the world. The museum's holdings are mainly 20th-century Balinese painting and wood sculpture, including important collections from the 1930s. The grounds, with their gardens and ponds, are a shady, tranquil oasis in the centre of Ubud.

★ **Octopus** *(1955)*
I Gusti Made Deblog is known for his fine ink-wash technique.

Building I

Dharmaswami *(1935)*
This work by Ida Bagus Gelgel is in the Balinese tradition of painting fables and tales.

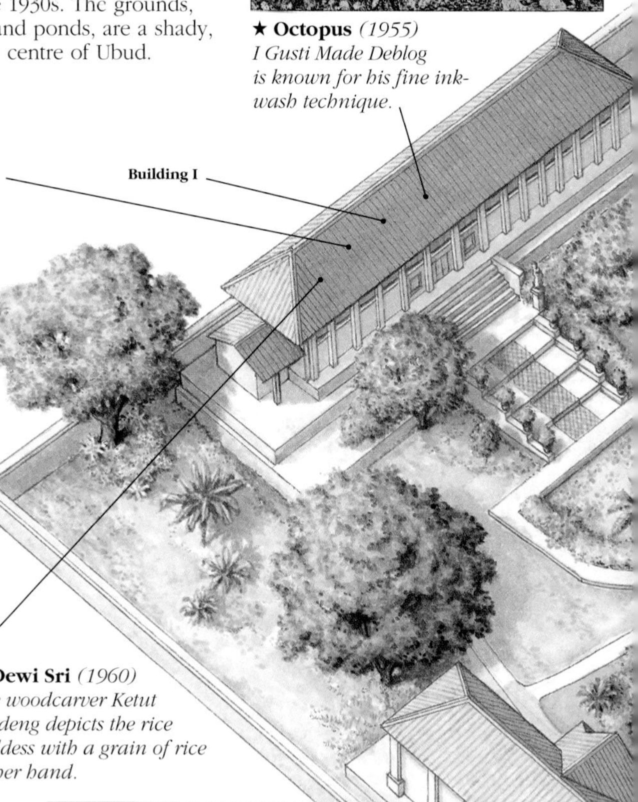

★ **Dewi Sri** *(1960)*
The woodcarver Ketut Djedeng depicts the rice goddess with a grain of rice in her hand.

Birds Dancing the Gambuh *(1940)*
A bas-relief showing the gambuh *dance inspired this painting by Ida Bagus Sali.*

Building II

Looking at Balinese Paintings

The density of Balinese painting is extraordinary. Even with little or no background in the arts, the viewer can enter the imaginative world of Balinese culture as represented by both traditional and modern painting. It is a good idea to look at a Balinese work from a distance at first, to see its graphic composition before moving nearer to inspect the details of the content. Close inspection reveals tiny scenes being enacted by the inhabitants of the canvas.

***Tiger with Monkey* (undated), artist unknown**

Visitors' Checklist

Jalan Raya Ubud. (0361) 975 136. FAX (0361) 975 137.
8am – 4pm daily.
Public hols.
www.mpl-ubud.com

Gallery Guide

Building I houses woodcarving and pre-World War II painting, including the Pita Maha and Lempad collections (see pp34–5). *Building II has contemporary Balinese art. Temporary exhibitions are housed in Building III.*

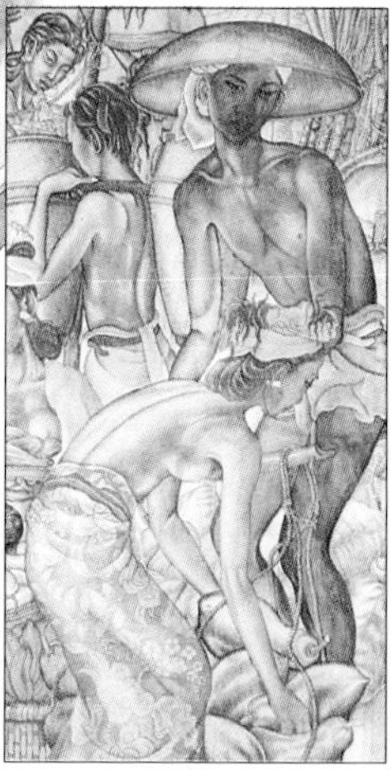

Building III

★ Balinese Market *(detail, 1955)*
Anak Agung Gede Sobrat, a leading Ubud school painter, explores a modern theme here.

Ticket office

Entrance steps

★ Kala Rau *(1974)*
I Ketut Budiana, of Padang Tegal, Ubud, paints the lunar eclipse of Balinese myth.

Star Exhibits

- **★ Octopus**
- **★ Dewi Sri**
- **★ Balinese Market**
- **★ Kala Rau**

A Walk in the Ubud Countryside

Lacewing butterfly

THE RICEFIELDS AND RIDGES around Ubud are very suitable for walking. Two routes are shown here. They can be followed separately, or one after the other forming a longer route. The ricefield walk is 6 km (4 miles) long but can be shortened to 4 km (nearly 3 miles) by omitting the northern loop. The 5-km (3-mile) ridge walk runs between two rivers, the Wos Timur and the Wos Barat. Walkers may cross ricefields provided they behave with due consideration. Wildlife sightings may include the iridescent blue Java kingfisher among other birds, the golden orb weaver spider, and a colourful variety of butterflies.

View from Pura Ulun Sui

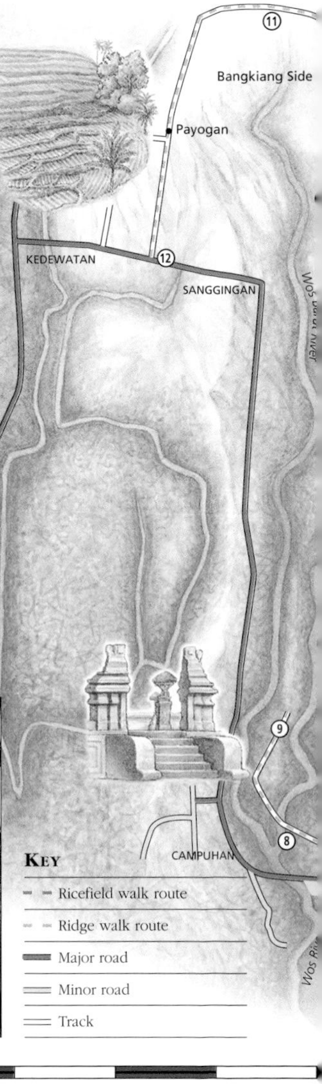

Jalan Raya Sanggingan ⑫
On this busy road, *bemo* transport can be found back into central Ubud.

Bridge ⑪
Near the bottom of the gorge, a bridge crosses the river to a steep road leading up to the village of Payogan.

Warung in Artists' Settlement ⑩
A small, isolated community of painters lives in this village, from which there are dramatic views along the Wos River gorges. Further north the landscape opens up to reveal ricefields.

Alang Alang Grass ⑨
After Pura Campuhan, a setting for some important religious ceremonies, the path continues through alang alang, a grass used for thatching roofs.

Large Banyan Tree ⑧
The ridge walk starts near the Ibah Luxury Villas, leading past an old banyan tree to a footbridge hanging over the river gorge.

Ayung River
Bangkiang Side
Payogan
KEDEWATAN
SANGGINGAN
CAMPUHAN

KEY

- Ricefield walk route
- Ridge walk route
- Major road
- Minor road
- Track

Rice Harvest ⑤
According to the season, rice farmers may be planting or harvesting. Across a narrow bridge carrying irrigation water is an attractive *subak* temple *(see pp20–21).*

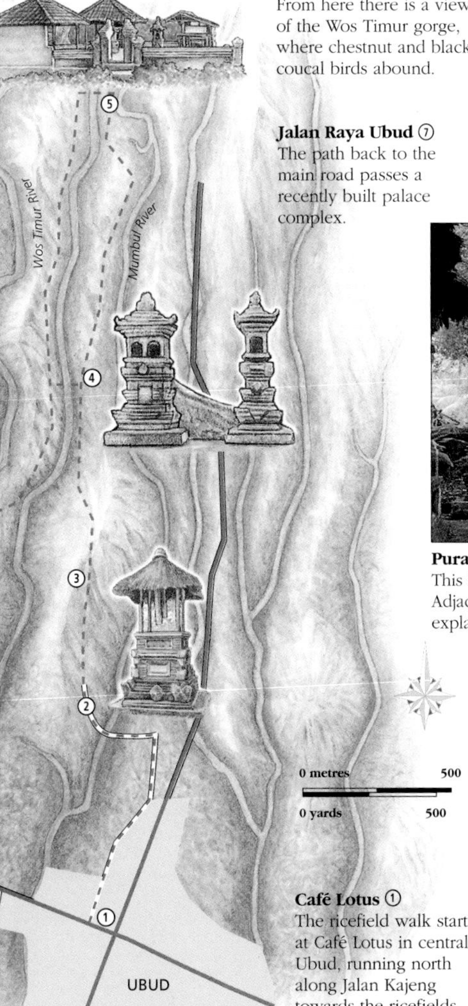

Pura Ulun Carik ⑥
From here there is a view of the Wos Timur gorge, where chestnut and black coucal birds abound.

Jalan Raya Ubud ⑦
The path back to the main road passes a recently built palace complex.

Café Lotus ①
The ricefield walk starts at Café Lotus in central Ubud, running north along Jalan Kajeng towards the ricefields.

Pura Pejenenang ④
Crossing the Wos Timur river to this temple cuts off the northern part of the walk, creating an optional shorter route.

Ricefield Shrines ③
Offerings are placed at these shrines to the rice goddess, who will bless the growing crops.

Pura Ulun Sui ②
This is also known as Juwukmanis Temple. Adjacent to it is a *subak* office with a map explaining the irrigation system of Bali.

Tips for Walkers

Start point: *Café Lotus, in Ubud.*
End point: *Jalan Raya Sanggingan.*
When to go: *All year, but in the wet season, trails can be slippery.*
Precautions: *River gorges are prone to flash flooding and should be crossed by the bridges. Do not descend into gorges without an experienced guide. Avoid the small trails down to the stone quarries in the Wos River gorge – they are slippery and prone to landslides. Care should be taken walking along the edges of ricefields. Walking shoes and sneakers are suitable footwear.*

The south pavilion of the Agung Rai Museum of Art, Peliatan

Peliatan ⓭

Road Map D3. *from Ubud.* *Ubud, (0361) 973 285.* kecak, *legong and Barong dance; women's* gamelan.

THE VILLAGE OF Peliatan, once the seat of an offshoot of the royalty of Sukawati, is renowned for artistic activities. It was known among foreigners for its artistic traditions even earlier than Ubud. Today, Peliatan's *gamelan* and dance troupes *(see pp30–33)* travel abroad as cultural ambassadors, and perform locally in traditional rituals and for visitors.

Peliatan is also a centre of painting and woodcarving. Many artists' studios can be found along its main street and back lanes. The collector Agung Rai established the successful Agung Rai Gallery and went on to create the impressive **Agung Rai Museum of Art** (usually referred to as ARMA), in southwest Peliatan. Three large buildings house collections of classical and contemporary Balinese and Indonesian painting as well as temporary exhibitions. The Rudana Museum houses an extensive painting collection.

The northern part of Peliatan, known as Andong, has some interesting craft shops.

ARMA
Jalan Pengosekan. *(0361) 975 449.* *daily.*

Rudana Museum
Jalan Cok Rai Pudak 44. *daily.*

Sanggingan ⓮

Road Map C3. *from Ubud.* *Ubud, (0361) 973 285.*

THE ROAD running through the village of Sanggingan is lined with art shops, art galleries, restaurants and small hotels.

The excellent **Neka Art Museum**, founded in 1976 by local collector and former teacher Sutéja Neka, houses one of the best collections of Balinese and Indonesian paintings on the island. The collection is displayed in seven buildings numbered according to the chronological sequence of the works displayed. Moving through the buildings gives a good overview of Balinese art history and its Indonesian context today. Some works are offered for sale. Of particular interest to visitors are the classical *wayang*-style paintings, anonymous works of great graphic sophistication; and also the Lempad collection *(see p34)*, consisting of superb pen-and-ink drawings.

Neka Art Museum
Jalan Raya Campuhan. *(0361) 975 074.* *daily.* *public hols.*

Portrait of Sutéja Neka **(1991) by Arie Smit, Neka Art Museum**

Ayung River Gorge ⓯

Road Map C3. *from Ubud.* *Ubud, (0361) 973 285.*

BETWEEN KEDEWATAN and Sayan, the east bank of the spectacularly beautiful Ayung River Gorge, flanked

The Ayung River Gorge viewed from the ridge at Sayan village

White-water rafting in the rapids of the Ayung River Gorge

by rice terraces, is discreetly populated with some attractive luxury hotels and private houses. Several companies offer white-water rafting from points on both sides of the river *(see p203)*.

ENVIRONS: In the village of **Penestanan**, just east of the Gorge, there are studios making painted batik and beadwork. This is also the centre of the Young Artists movement *(see p35)* which emerged in the 1960s.

WOODCARVING IN BALI

The surprising abundance of Balinese woodcarving reflects not only an intense decorative tradition but also the fact that Bali's wilderness is forest (still inhabited by tigers in the early 20th century). Trees have a ritual anniversary and must be given offerings before being felled. Traditional woodcarving is of two main sorts: ritual objects such as effigies and masks; and ornamental carving, especially of architectural elements. The liberalizing art movement of the 1930s *(see pp34–5)* encouraged woodcarvers to sculpt freely for a foreign market. The main centres of woodcarving today include Peliatan and several other villages in Gianyar regency, including Tegallalang *(see p98)* and Mas *(see p86)*.

***Sleeping Woman* (1956), by Ida Bagus Njana**

Pejeng ⑯

Road Map D3. *from Ubud & Gianyar.* *Ubud, (0361) 973 285.*

PEJENG, A VILLAGE on the road from Bedulu to Tampaksiring, lies at the heart of the ancient Pejeng-Bedulu kingdom, and there are many interesting relics from that time to be seen. The **Museum Purbakala** (Archaeological Museum) displays prehistoric objects in bronze, stone and ceramics, including several turtle-shaped stone sarcophagi.

A short walk from the museum are three temples of particular interest for their sacred stone sculptures. **Pura Arjuna Metapa** ("Arjuna Meditating" Temple) is a small pavilion standing alone in the ricefields, sheltering a cluster of stone sculptures that were probably once part of a spring temple. In accordance with the *wayang* tradition that recounts tales from the *Mahabharata*, Arjuna is attended by a stone-relief servant character. About 100 m (110 yards) north is **Pura Kebo Edan** ("Crazy Giant" Temple). The demonic statuary suggests that this was a cult-temple of Bhairava Buddhism. The chief figure is a masked 3.6-m- (12-ft-) high giant, dancing on a corpse. The beautifully proportioned **Pura Pusering Jagat** ("Navel of the World" Temple) has numerous pavilions housing similar tantric stone figures. The "Pejeng Vessel", a cylindrical stone urn carved with cosmological figures, is kept in a shrine in the southeastern corner of the temple.

About 2 km (1 mile) north of Pejeng, **Pura Penataran Sasih** houses the "Pejeng Moon" (*sasih* means moon), a bronze drum 186 cm (74 inches) long, of unknown age. Considered sacred, it is kept in a tall pavilion. Temple guides sometimes encourage visitors to stand on the base of an adjacent shrine; from here can be glimpsed the drum's fine geometric patterning. The design is associated with the Dong-son culture of southern China and northern Vietnam around 1500 BC.

Prehistoric turtle-shaped stone sarcophagi at the Museum Purbakala in Pejeng

Museum Purbakala
Pejeng. *(0361) 942 347.*
Mon–Fri. *donation.*

Pura Arjuna Metapa
Across the road from Museum.
daily. *donation.*

Pura Kebo Edan
Pejeng. *daily.* *donation.*

Pura Pusering Jagat
Pejeng. *daily.* *donation.*

Pura Penataran Sasih
Pejeng. *daily.* *donation.*

Petulu ⑰

Road Map D3. *from Ubud & Pujung.* *Ubud, (0361) 973 285.*

THIS VILLAGE is known for its white-plumed egrets and Java pond egrets, generically called *kokokan* in Balinese. They feed all over the island and return here in the late afternoon to roost in the trees lining the road. It is not known why the birds suddenly settled in Petulu in 1965. The best place to view them is the road from the Junungan direction through the ricefields; seen from here the V-formations of birds at sunset are an unforgettable sight.

Woodcarver at work in Kenderan, a village near Tegallalang

Tegallalang ⑱

Road Map D3. *from Ubud.* *Ubud, (0361) 973 285.*

PLAIN-LOOKING Tegallalang village, once the seat of a kingdom, is interesting as a centre of the woodcarving industry. As in most of the villages along this road, many people are engaged in producing cottage-craft wood products wholesale, retail, "antique" and made-to-order.

ENVIRONS: **Kebon** is a pretty village on a steep side road 3 km (2 miles) north of Tegallalang. At the junction with the main road is the excellent Kampung Kafe *(see p188)*. **Kenderan**, also on a back road, is a former micro-kingdom with several small *puri* (houses of the nobility).

The small village of **Manuaba**, about 4 km (2 miles) north of Kenderan, is notable for the important Brahman temple **Pura Griya Sakti**, renovated and modernized in the late 1990s, with a refurbished *wantilan* performance pavilion. A visit to see the huge intertwined trees behind the inner courtyard requires permission of the temple attendant.

There is an interesting holy spring, **Telaga Waja**, in Kapitu, 1 km (half a mile) south of Kenderan. Access is by way of a 200-m (220-yard) footpath and a long, steep flight of steps. At the site itself, traces of meditation niches suggest that Telaga Waja was a Buddhist retreat; it is possibly over 1,000 years old.

Pura Griya Sakti
Manuaba. *daily.* *donation.*

Stone sculpture in Pura Gunung Kawi

Sebatu ⑲

Road Map D3. *from Ubud.* *Ubud, (0361) 973 285.*

SEBATU VILLAGE, part of a larger area of the same name, is highly regarded among the Balinese not only for its painted wood sculpture but also for its dance, music and classical dance costumes. Easily explored on foot, the village is laid out on a grid of three north south streets, with the temples and *bale banjar* (community pavilion) at the northern end. The western-most street is lined with studios making woodcarvings for sale to visitors.

In a little valley on the western outskirts of Sebatu itself is the lovely spring temple **Pura Gunung Kawi**, not to be confused with the royal monuments of the same name near Tampaksiring *(see p99)*. The bathing springs are worth seeing (but should not be photographed if they are in use), as is the carp-filled spring pool in the northwest corner. In the centre of the pool is a handsome shrine. There are some interesting sculptures, some of them new and some old, among the small, colourfully painted pavilions in the central courtyard.

Pura Gunung Kawi
daily.

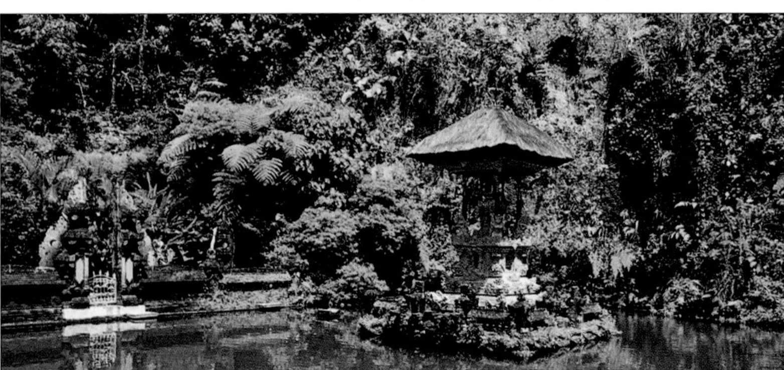

Pura Gunung Kawi, Sebatu's tranquil spring temple

Taro ⓴

Road Map D3. *Ubud, (0361) 973 285*

On a well-marked (but often rough) road to the west of Pujung is Taro, said to be one of the earliest settlements in Bali.

At the village centre is the large temple **Pura Gunung Raung**. Over its walls it is possible to admire the long *bale agung* pavilion, and a glowering three-tier *meru* pagoda. The latter represents the East Javanese mountain Gunung Raung; from here the legendary sage Rsi Markandya and his followers set out in the 8th century on a mission to Bali. Taro is the source of Bali's albino cattle; these animals are valued for their importance in large rituals. Formerly they were sacrificed; today they are merely borrowed for the ceremony and then returned. The herd has multiplied greatly in recent years and wanders freely in the forest south of the village.

An albino cow, revered in Bali

The well-run **Elephant Safari Park** *(see p206)*, created in the late 1990s, enables visitors to view the landscape from the back of a Sumatran elephant. Attractions include elephants that have been trained to paint, a museum of elephants and their history, and a large restaurant.

Gunung Kawi Royal Monuments ㉑

Tampaksiring. **Road Map** D3. *from Bedulu & Gianyar.* *Ubud, (0361) 973 285.* *daily.*

To the east of the small town of Tampaksiring, bordering the Pakrisan River, is a valley into the sides of which are carved nine immense monuments. They are shaped like *candi* (Buddhist-Hindu shrines), and are carved into niches in a natural rock wall in the hill. At their heart are a temple and a holy spring. A flight of stairs leads to the monument complex, which straddles the river. Commonly called "tombs", these are in fact memorial shrines, associated with the legendary 11th-century king Anak Wungsu *(see p45)* and his wives. To the south of the main complex are the "Second Cloisters" on the east bank, and the "Third Cloisters", which are believed to be monuments dedicated to the queens of Anak Wungsu or his descendents. The "Tenth Tomb", to the west, is reached by a walk along the edges of some ricefields.

On the steps leading to the tombs, craftsmen from Tampaksiring sell their wares, including some exquisite bone carvings.

Gunung Kawi Royal Monuments, *candi* shrines set in natural rock walls

Pura Tirta Empul ㉒

Manukaya. **Road Map** D3. *from Bedulu & Gianyar.* *Ubud, (0361) 973 285.* *daily.*

This sacred spring temple, near the source of the river Pakrisan, is a major tourist stop, but it is a pleasant place to visit. The main feature is a series of courtyards containing rectangular bathing-pools. The spouts dispense specific kinds of holy water, which devotees request with elaborate ritual offerings. The temple is thought to date from the 10th century; the present walls are recent. The pavilions are in an on-going state of restoration, an indication of the temple's importance. People come from all over the island for holy water and ritual ablutions, particularly on the day of the full moon (*purnama*).

Pura Tirta Empul, a spring temple and source of holy water

EAST BALI

THE OLD KINGDOMS OF EASTERN BALI *wielded influence and power beyond their lofty mountains and lush green valleys. What remains of their palaces and temples is still a window into a world of ceremony and tradition, focused around Gunung Agung, centre of the Balinese universe, and, high on its steep volcanic slopes, Besakih, one of the most important temples in Bali.*

The East Bali area corresponds to the three regencies of Klungkung, Bangli and Karangasem. It is an area of natural beauty and stark contrasts. Not far from its high volcanic peaks are some of Bali's best beaches. Just over 3,000 m (almost 10,000 ft) high, the active volcano of Gunung Agung dominates the landscape, its foothills covered with green ricefields. East Bali was devastated by Agung's eruption in 1963 *(see p115)* and by an earthquake in 1974. In many places great lava flows transformed the landscape.

In East Bali are some of the island's most important temples and palaces. Extravagant temple complexes stand on ancient sites endowed with cosmic significance, for example at Besakih and around the volcanic lake in the vast crater of Gunung Batur. At Tirtagangga, in the hills north of Amlapura, a luxurious water palace was built by descendants of the last king as late as the 1940s. This tradition of royal grandeur dates back ultimately to the 15th century, when the court of the first king of Gelgel was established. Around the courts and palaces of the region the arts flourished and villages of skilled artisans grew up. This tradition of craftsmanship survives in many places today.

In the 14th century the Javanese kingdom of Majapahit brought to Bali a new social order and caste system. Some communities resisted it, and their descendants, known as the Bali Aga (original Balinese), still live here in culturally distinct villages such as Tenganan and Trunyan.

Klungkung's royal house came to an end in 1908, when the king and members of his court committed *puputan (see p49)*, rather than submit to Dutch colonial control. However, many architectural relics still remain as reminders of pre-colonial times.

Ricefields of East Bali overlooked by the sacred volcano, Gunung Agung

◁ **Using the process of evaporation, traditional salt production on Bali's east coast**

Exploring East Bali

EAST BALI IS DOMINATED by the mighty volcano Gunung Agung, upon whose slopes is the important Besakih Temple Complex. To the west is Gunung Batur, with its own temples and a crater lake. To the south is historic Klungkung, and the royal pavilions of Taman Gili. From here the road runs eastwards to some good trekking country near Manggis and Tirtagangga, and on to the dive sites of Amed and Tulamben on the coast. The arid, lava-strewn eastern slopes of Gunung Agung are austerely beautiful. Tenganan, not far inland from the resort area of Candi Dasa, is one of the island's Bali Aga ("original Balinese") villages, culturally distinct from the rest of Bali.

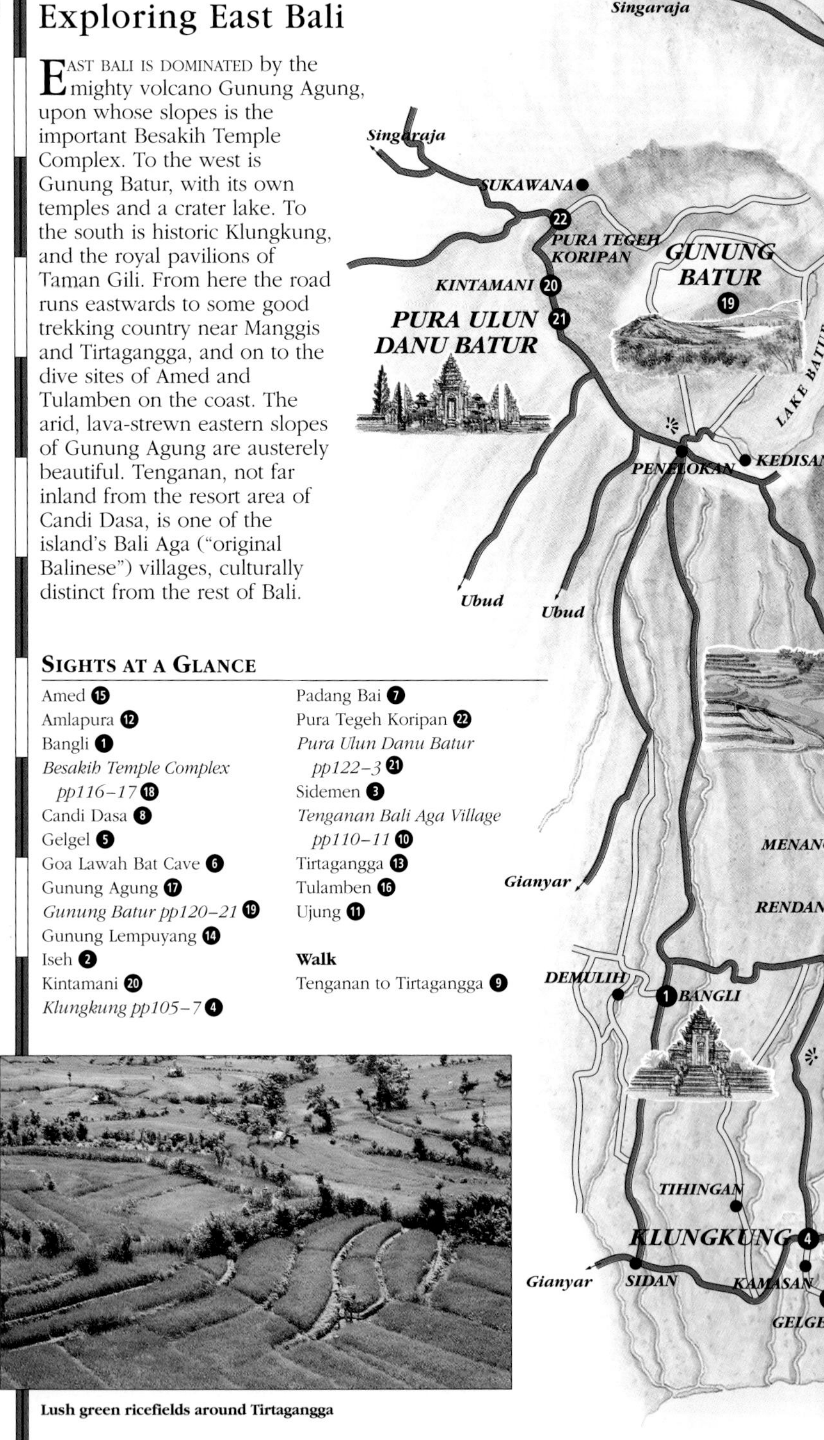

SIGHTS AT A GLANCE

Amed 15
Amlapura 12
Bangli 1
Besakih Temple Complex pp116–17 18
Candi Dasa 8
Gelgel 5
Goa Lawah Bat Cave 6
Gunung Agung 17
Gunung Batur pp120–21 19
Gunung Lempuyang 14
Iseh 2
Kintamani 20
Klungkung pp105–7 4
Padang Bai 7
Pura Tegeh Koripan 22
Pura Ulun Danu Batur pp122–3 21
Sidemen 3
Tenganan Bali Aga Village pp110–11 10
Tirtagangga 13
Tulamben 16
Ujung 11

Walk

Tenganan to Tirtagangga 9

Lush green ricefields around Tirtagangga

Getting Around

A car, rented with or without driver, is the best way of getting around. Roads are mostly good, although signposting is poor. Because of the many bends, journeys often take longer than one anticipates. *Bemo* run between villages, but taxis are scarce. Although public buses ply the coastal roads, tourist shuttle buses are more comfortable. Public transport is virtually non-existent at night. Padang Bai, on the southern coast, is the ferry port for Lombok.

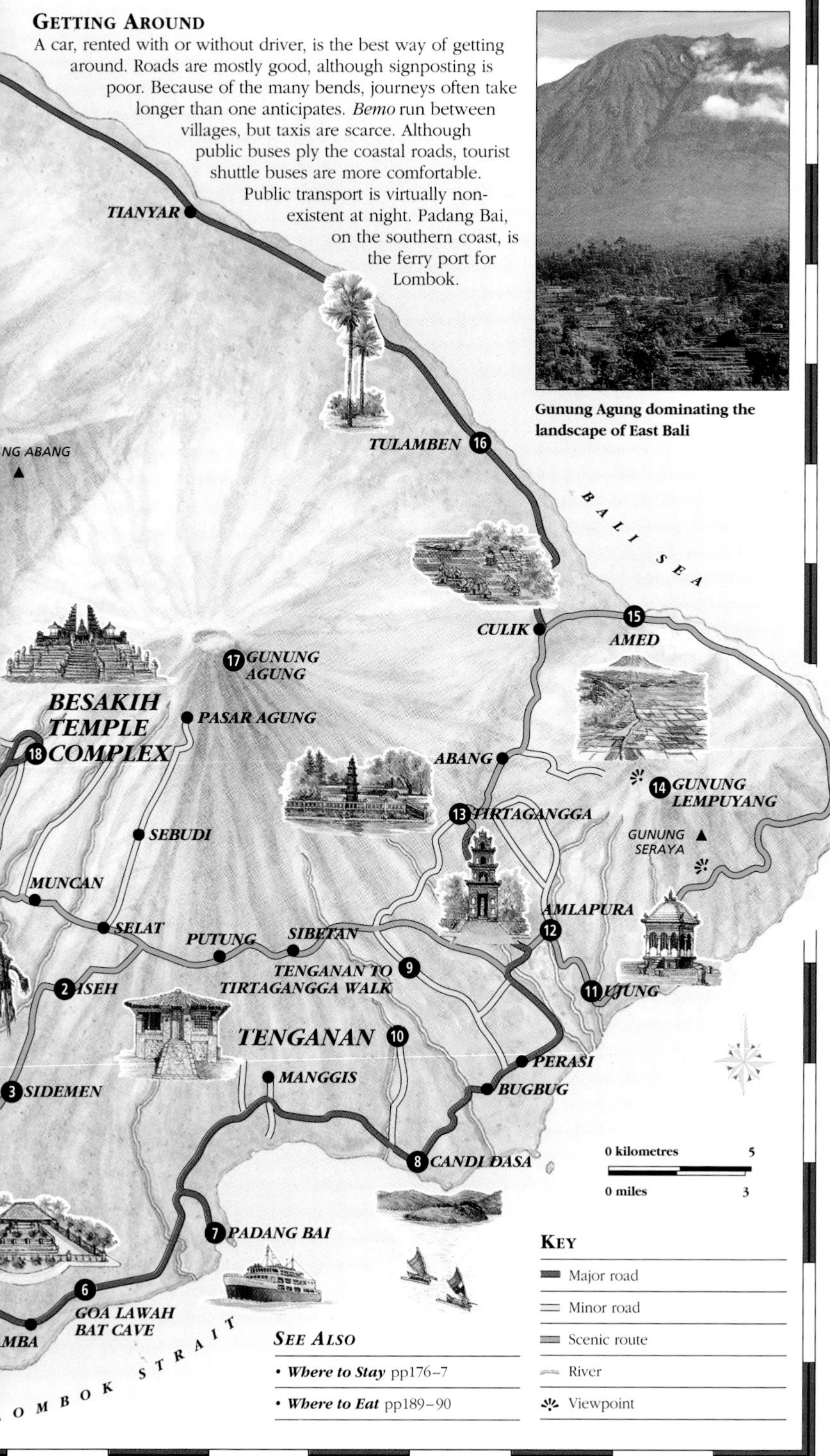

Gunung Agung dominating the landscape of East Bali

Key

- Major road
- Minor road
- Scenic route
- River
- Viewpoint

See Also

- ***Where to Stay*** pp176–7
- ***Where to Eat*** pp189–90

Bangli ❶

Road Map D3. *Jalan Brigjen Ngurah Rai 30, (0366) 91 537.*

A ROYAL COURT CITY from the 14th to the 19th century, Bangli is one of Bali's oldest towns, a small, well-ordered and tidy community. Set some way up the hills towards Gunung Batur, the town is ideal for a walk in the cool mountain air.

Pura Kehen, a place of worship since the 12th century, steps impressively up a hillside in a series of eight terraces, enclosing a huge banyan tree in the first courtyard of the complex. High in the banyan's branches is an almost invisible *kulkul* with an alarm drum. Fine statuary lines the steps leading to the *padmasana* shrine *(see p26)* with a multi-tiered *meru* roof in the inner sanctuary. The shrine is covered with elaborate ornamentation. The gold-painted doors of the temple are beautiful.

Pura Penyimpenan ("the temple for keeping things") contains three ancient bronze inscriptions which imply that the area was considered holy long before the present temple complex was built.

Images of heaven and hell, the latter imaginatively grim, cover the walls of **Pura Dalem Pengungekan**, a temple dedicated to the dead, and inside are shrines to Brahma, Shiva and Vishnu.

Mythological figure in Pura Dalem Penungekan, a temple of the dead

Pura Kehen
Jalan Sri Wijaya. *daily.* *donation.* *Pagerwesi (27 Jul 2005, 22 Feb & 20 Sep 2006, 18 Apr & 14 Nov 2007).*

Pura Penyimpenan
Jalan Sri Wijaya. *daily.* *for ceremonies.* *donation.*

Pura Dalem Pengungekan
Jalan Merdeka. *daily.* *for ceremonies.*

ENVIRONS: From the wooded **Bukit Demulih**, some 4 km (2 miles) west of Bangli, there are glorious views of Gunung Agung, and, on a clear day, as far as Nusa Penida and Sanur. At Bunutin, 7 km (4 miles) south of Bangli, **Pura Penataran Agung** has two small shrines on islands in a lake filled with water lilies.

Iseh ❷

Road Map E3. *from Bangli and Klungkung.* *Amlapura, (0363) 21 196.*

THE AREA AROUND Iseh is remarkable for glorious landscapes. Some of the best can be seen on the road eastward from Bangli via Muncan and Duda, which carves its way east through great volcanic valleys. The terraced ricefields are lush and green. Iseh itself is a small village with little in the way of tourist facilities. Walter Spies *(see p88)* once had a house here, and it was this location that inspired some of his most beautiful paintings.

ENVIRONS: At **Putung**, 6 km (4 miles) east of Iseh, there are some great lookout points and a couple of homestays *(see pp166–7)*. A further 4 km (2 miles) to the east is the the village of **Sibetan**, the best place to buy *salak (see p183)*, a small, crisp, tart-tasting fruit with a scaly exterior that looks rather like snakeskin.

Ricefields and coconut groves at Iseh, a good setting for a walk

Sidemen ❸

Road Map E3. *from Bangli and Klungkung.* *Amlapura, (0363) 21 196.*

SIDEMEN IS SET in some of the most beautiful country in East Bali. The views from the slopes of Gunung Agung stretch out like a green patchwork with an impressive mountain backdrop. The town is a retreat from the hustle and bustle elsewhere, and there are some good homestays *(see pp166–7)* overlooking ricefields. In Sidemen one can visit workshops making *songket*. This work is historically the preserve of higher castes, and still implies high social status.

Street corner in the town centre of Klungkung

Klungkung ❹

Road Map D4. *Jalan Untung Surapati 3, (0366) 21 448.*

KLUNGKUNG, also known as Semarapura, is a district capital and an important trading point on the road to the east of Bali.

The most important historic sight in Klungkung is a pair of pavilions set in an ornamental moat, known as **Taman Gili** *(see pp106–7)*. These are relics of the palace of the once-powerful rajas (kings) of the Gelgel dynasty. Adjacent to Taman Gili is the small **Museum Daerah Semarapura** in which can be seen a collection of bronze and marble sculptures, and paintings by Italian modernist Emilio Ambron, as well as photographs of the royal family and the palace dating back to the early 1900s.

***Wayang*-style painting by an artist from Kamasan village**

On the south side of Taman Gili is a large gateway, which is thought to be the entrance to the inner courtyard of the old palace from the outer courtyard. Legend has it that these massive wooden doors have remained stuck together since the *puputan* of 1908, when 200 members of Klungkung's royal court committed ritual suicide *(see p49)*. This event is marked by the **Puputan Monument** across the road from Taman Gili. The last raja died in 1965, bearing the scars of wounds received during the *puputan*. At the same road junction, a large indoor market sells temple and ritual paraphernalia, local handicrafts and food. It is one of Bali's best markets for textiles.

The Puputan Monument in Klungkung

ENVIRONS: Less than 1 km (half a mile) south of Klungkung is the "artists' village" of **Kamasan**; here painters can be seen at work. The artists of Kamasan have largely defined the style of traditional Balinese art *(see pp34–5)*. About the same distance to the northeast is the temple of **Pura Taman Sari**. In the temple's large, uncluttered compound is an eleven-roofed *meru* tower built on a stone turtle surrounded by a moat.

TEXTILES OF EAST BALI

In Bali great importance is attached to textiles and their making, and nowhere more so than in East Bali. This area is famous for a type of double *ikat* weave called *geringsing*, produced only in the Bali Aga village of Tenganan *(see pp110–11)*. *Geringsing* cloths are credited by the Balinese with protective spiritual powers. In Sidemen, complex, decorative motifs in gold and silver threads are woven into cloth to create a rich brocade textile known as *songket*. This is often worn by the Balinese at religious or social events, and as part of the costume of traditional dancers.

***Songket* fabrics woven in a Sidemen workshop**

Klungkung: Taman Gili

Built originally in the early 18th century, Taman Gili ("moated garden") is what remains of Klungkung's royal palace, most of which was destroyed in 1908 during the Dutch conquest. The main features are two raised, open meeting halls, or *bale*, with intricately painted ceilings. The paintings have undergone restoration and repainting several times in the last hundred years, but remain fine examples of the *wayang* style *(see p35)*, in which the figures resemble shadow puppets. The Kerta Gosa was originally the setting for the royal "high court". The present structure of the Bale Kambang dates from the 1940s.

The Moat
The surrounding moat gave the Bale Kambang its name, meaning "floating pavilion".

★ Kerta Gosa Ceiling Paintings
There are 267 painted panels arranged in several tiers. At the apex is a carved lotus flower surrounded by gilded doves, representing the goals of enlightenment and salvation.

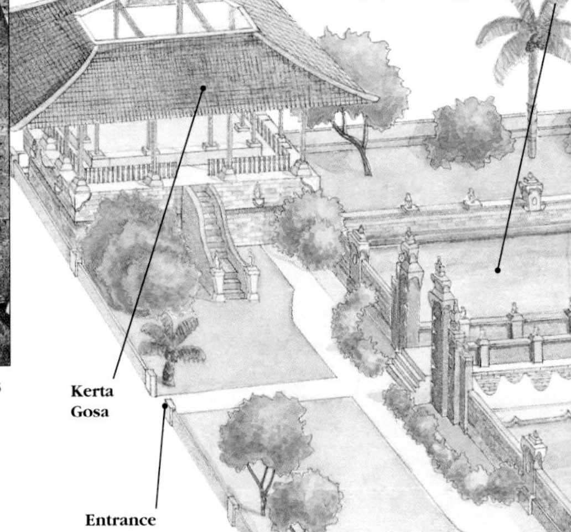

Kerta Gosa Ceiling Paintings

The main series shows part of the *Bhima Swarga* narrative, which was incorporated into Balinese tradition from the Indian *Mahabharata* epic. There are also scenes from the *Tantri* stories (a Balinese version of a series of Indian moral fables), and some based on an astrological calendar, showing earthquakes and eruptions.

The demon Wirosa pursuing sinners

A scene from the *Tantri* stories

A stage in the ascent to enlightenment and salvation

Visitors' Checklist

Puri Semarapura, corner of Jalan Surapati and Jalan Puputan, Klungkung. ◯ *7am – 6pm daily.* ● *public hols.*

★ Bale Kambang Ceiling Paintings
These depict scenes from Balinese myths, including the story of Sutasoma, a Buddhist saint symbolizing strength without aggression.

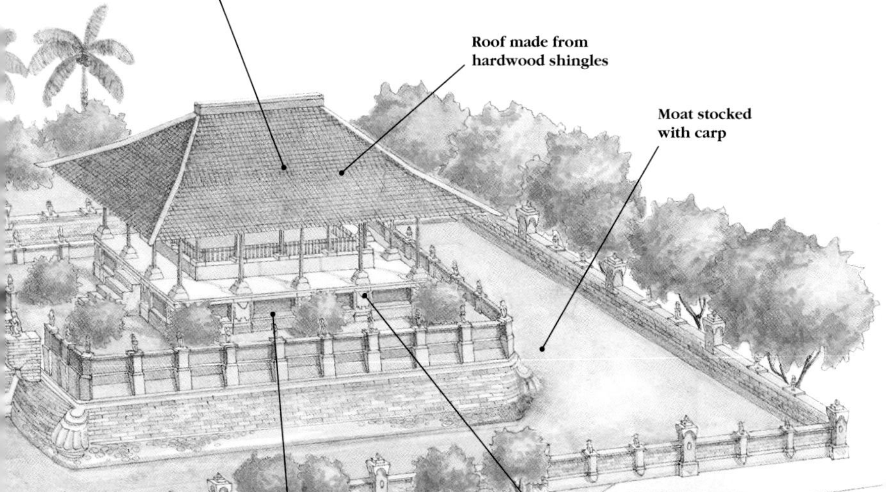

Roof made from hardwood shingles

Moat stocked with carp

Bale Kambang

Carved Stone Wall Relief
The building is decorated with carved reliefs of mythical creatures.

Museum Daerah Semarajaya
West of the Bale Kambang, the museum (see p105) has objects relating to the dynasties of Klungkung and Gelgel.

Star Features

- ★ **Kerta Gosa Ceiling Paintings**
- ★ **Bale Kambang Ceiling Paintings**

Temple entrance at the Goa Lawah Bat Cave

Gelgel 5

Road Map E4. *from Klungkung.* *Klungkung, (0366) 21 448.* *Purnama Kapat (Oct).*

THE ROYAL COURT of the Majapahit rulers of Bali *(see p46)* was established in Gelgel in the 14th century by Dewa Ketut Ngulesir, son of Bali's first Majapahit king. A reminder of the former kingdom is Gelgel's very ancient royal temple of **Pura Dasar**, with its large outer courtyard, and several tall *meru* towers.

The **Pura Penataran** is one of a number of other temples that can can be seen along the village's broad streets.

Goa Lawah Bat Cave 6

Road Map E4. *Klungkung, (0366) 21 448.* *daily.* *temple anniversary (29 Mar & 25 Oct 2005, 23 May & 19 Dec 2006).*

THOUGHT TO BE more than 1,000 years old, Goa Lawah is important to temple rituals pertaining to the after-life. The main feature of the temple is a cave inhabited by tens of thousands of fruit bats. Local legend has it that the cave stretches 30 km (19 miles) back into the mountain, as far as Besakih, *(see pp116–17)* and is the home of a giant dragon-like snake called Basuki who feasts on bats.

For visitors there are some good eateries outside the cave that have fine views over the ocean towards Nusa Penida and Lombok. However, it is also renowned for hawkers.

ENVIRONS: Kusamba, 4 km (3 miles) southwest of Goa Lawah, is a busy little fishing village with a black-sand beach. *Jukung* (outrigger fishing craft) line the shore, and are available for chartered day trips to nearby islands. The boats can feel vulnerable as the ocean swell picks up. Salt production pans can be seen on the coast here.

Colourful *jukung* (outriggers) on the black-sand beach at Kusamba

Padang Bai 7

Road Map E4. *to Nusa Lembongan, Nusa Penida & Lembar, Lombok.* *Amlapura, (0363) 21 196.*

THIS IS A RELAXED beach resort, a good base for the exploration of East Bali. It is also the main port for ferries to Lombok, and therefore the traffic from Denpasar is quite heavy. In the village are numerous restaurants, hotels, guesthouses, bars, tour guides and dive shops.

ENVIRONS: Within walking distance to the west of Padang Bai is **Biastugal**, an unspoiled white-sand bay where sunworshippers gather. A little further along the coast one can rent outriggers for diving and snorkelling. At the eastern end of the bay, a 20-minute walk away, there are several temples. They include **Pura Silayukti**, associated with Mpu Kuturan, who introduced the three-temple system to Balinese villages in the 11th century *(see p28)*.

Pura Silayukti

daily. *temple anniversary (Apr & Nov 2005, Jun 2006, Jan & Aug 2007).*

Candi Dasa 8

Road Map E4. *Jalan Candi Dasa, (0366) 41 204.*

ORIGINALLY a fishing village, Candi Dasa has now grown into a popular resort. However, since the reef which once lay offshore was largely destroyed by exploitation as a raw material, the beach has been almost completely eroded. Candi Dasa is still a good base for exploring the region, and for diving and snorkelling. There are some reputable diving schools, and good dive sites near the offshore islands. There is a wide range of *losmen* and other accommodation, restaurants and bars. The local dish is *bebek betutu*, succulent duck cooked with herbs and spices *(see p182)*.

The name Candi Dasa is said to be derived from the Balinese "Cilidasa", which means "ten children". In the centre of the village, overlooking a lagoon with water lilies, is **Pura Candi Dasa**, a temple dedicated to Hariti, the goddess of fertility.

Pura Candi Dasa

Jalan Candi Dasa. *daily.*

ENVIRONS: About 2 km (1 mile) east of Candi Dasa and up a steep flight of steps, is **Pura Gomang**, from which there are great views of the coast. A little further east is **Pasir Putih**, a secluded bay hemmed in on one side by a sheer rock face, and used as a harbour by *jukung* outriggers.

Walk from Tenganan to Tirtagangga ❾

The walk from Tenganan to Tirtagangga reveals some of the most scenic terrain of Bali's interior, and many glimpses of traditional Balinese life along the way. The 6-km (4-mile) walk takes about three hours. From the higher points there are impressive views of Bali's mountains; the route passes also through terraced ricefields and peaceful hillside villages. This is a good way to see village temples, local schools, tiny mountain *warung* (shops) and weavers of basketware. In the early morning vendors sell *tuak*, a sour-tasting alcoholic drink made from the flower of the *jaka* palm tree. These trees can be recognized by the enormous grape-like buds jutting from their trunks.

Ricefield toad

Budakling ⑥
North of the main road is this metalsmithing village, before one arrives at a lava trail.

Tirtagangga ⑦
The country road to Tirtagangga *(see p112)* offers good views of ricefields with the sea beyond.

Kastala ⑤
Across the river, the trail leads to this village near the main road. To cut short the walk, transport can be taken from Bebandem.

Hillside Warung ④
A small café stands on the slope overlooking the rice terraces. The trail leads on to an irrigation dam and a ricefield shrine before crossing a shallow river.

Pura Puseh ③
At the Pura Puseh temple is revealed a view to the far east of Bali; ricefields can be seen at various stages of cultivation. Gunung Lempuyang and Gunung Seraya are in the distance.

Gumung Kaja ②
In the village of Gumung Kaja, baskets and mats are woven with the stems of the *ata*, a kind of palm tree.

Ababi
Babandem
Bungaya
Tenganan

Key

- Major road
- Minor road
- Lava trail
- Walking route

0 kilometres 2
0 miles 1

Tenganan Village Gate ①
From the village, a stone-paved path leads to a temple complex and then to the edge of the forest. Here a wall marks the beginning of a half-hour climb to the primary school at Gumung.

Tips for Walkers

Start point: *Tenganan.*
End point: *Tirtagangga*
Getting there: *Bemo to Candi Dasa, then own transport.*
When to go: *Any time, but trails are slippery in rainy season.*
Walking time: *3 hours.*

Tenganan Bali Aga Village ⑩

Wall motif in clay

THE BALI AGA, "original Balinese" *(see p46)*, maintain a distinct cosmology and social organization. For example, villagers must marry in the community or leave the village. They make fine basketware, and this is the only place in Southeast Asia where *geringsing* double-*ikat* textiles *(see p37)* are made. Tenganan is the best preserved of the Bali Aga villages. It is closed to outsiders after dark.

Detail of double-*ikat geringsing* textile

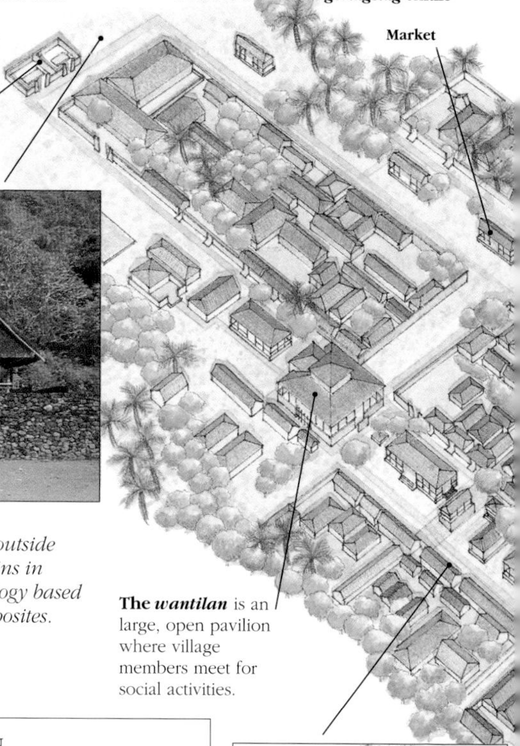

Market

Public baths

Village Temple

In the village's "temple of origins", outside the village walls, the community joins in rituals reflecting a dualistic cosmology based on principles of complementary opposites.

0 metres 30

0 yards 30

The *wantilan* is an large, open pavilion where village members meet for social activities.

THE LEGEND OF TENGANAN

It is said that in the 14th century, King Bedaulu, the ruler of Bali, lost his favourite horse and offered a reward for its return. The horse was eventually found dead near Tenganan and the villagers asked to be granted land as a reward. The King sent his minister to draw the boundaries of the area to be given to them, instructing the minister to include all of the land where he could smell the dead horse. Accompanied by the village chief, who had hidden some of the rotting horse meat in his clothes, the minister performed his duties and drew generous boundaries which remain today.

Land at Tenganan, owned communally according to Bali Aga tradition

Village Houses

A short flight of steps leads up to each house which also has a small courtyard.

STAR FEATURES

★ Bale Petemu

★ Main Street

Visitors' Checklist

Road Map F3. *from Candi Dasa.* *Amlapura, (0363) 21 196.* *daylight hours.* *donation.* *Usaba Sambah and Mekare-kare (stick fight) (Jun–Jul).*

★ Bale Petemu
This is the meeting hall of one of three associations of unmarried village men.

★ Main Street
The main streets are partly cobbled and rise in tiers, connected by ramps.

Fighting Cocks
Birds are often kept in cages in front of the houses; most fights take place outside the village.

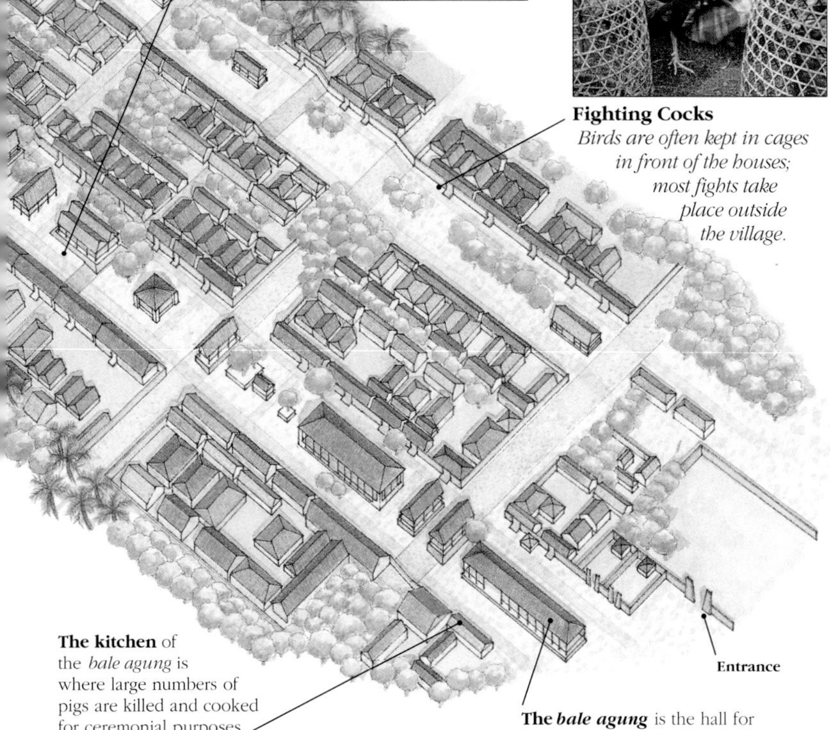

The kitchen of the *bale agung* is where large numbers of pigs are killed and cooked for ceremonial purposes.

Entrance

The *bale agung* is the hall for meetings of the village council, composed of all the married couples.

Ujung ⓫

Road Map F3. *from Amlapura.* *Amlapura, (0363) 21 196.*

UJUNG, meaning literally "at the end", is an appropriate name given the remote location of this fishing village. The **Puri Taman Ujung** is a water palace built in 1921 by the last raja of Karangasem, I Gusti Bagus Djelantik. The buildings were all but destroyed in the earthquake of 1974. But renovation in 2004 has restored it to its former grandeur.

ENVIRONS: The narrow road winding east from Ujung around the eastern tip of Bali is very scenic, with spectacular views of the ocean and Gunung Seraya. Before taking this road, one should check its condition with the locals.

Puri Taman Ujung
daily. *donation.*

Puri Taman Ujung, the royal water palace before renovation

Amlapura ⓬

Road Map F3. *Jalan Diponegoro, (0363) 21 196.*

THE SMALL BUT BUSY trading town of Amlapura is a district capital with an active market serving the area. The town was given its present name after reconstruction in the aftermath of the 1963 eruption of Gunung Agung. It is still often referred to by its former name, Karangasem.

Karangasem became an important power in the late 17th century. The royal families of Karangasem had strong political links with the nearby island of Lombok. In the mid-18th century they ousted the powerful kings of Sulawesi from Lombok and then divided the island up amongst themselves.

The Maskerdam Building, a royal residence furnished in Dutch style

The Balinese of Karangasem remained in power in western Lombok until 1894, although facing continuous challenges from the Sasak nobles. Karangasem became a vassal of Lombok in 1849, when the Lombok king attacked his own ancestral land. It placed itself under Dutch rule in 1894, after the Dutch conquest of Lombok.

Puri Agung, a royal palace of the kings of Karangasem, was built at the turn of the 20th century. It was the birthplace of the last king. The palace compound is no longer inhabited, descendants of the royal family preferring to live in the palaces of Puri Gede and Puri Kertasurahe across the road (unlike Puri Agung, they are not open to the public). Architecturally, Puri Agung is an eclectic mix of European and Balinese styles. It has a particularly impressive entrance gateway.

The main attraction is the **Maskerdam Building**, so-called as a tribute to the Dutch ("Amsterdam" as pronounced by the locals). Behind its carved doors are pieces of furniture donated by Queen Wilhelmina of the Dutch royal family. Another building in the compound is known as the Bale London, as some of its furniture bears the British royal family's coat-of-arms. There are two *bale* (open halls) beside ornamental ponds in front of the Maskerdam Building. These were used for ceremonies and meetings.

Over one of the *bale* entrances is a photograph of the raja, taken in 1939 when the district was granted limited self-rule by the Dutch.

Puri Agung
Jalan Gajah Mada. *daily.*

Tirtagangga ⓭

Ababi. **Road Map** F3.
Amlapura, (0363) 21 196.
daily.

TIRTAGANGGA (meaning "holy water from the Ganges") is the best surviving example of Bali's royal water palaces. It was built in 1947 by Anak Agung Anglurah Ketut, the last king of Karangasem, and restored after damage sustained in the 1963 eruption of Gunung Agung. The complex consists of a sacred spring, a cold spring-fed pool and several other ponds. Bathing is permitted in the pools. A small fee is charged at the spring-fed pool, which has simple changing rooms. The pools and fountains are set in well-maintained gardens.

Tirtagangga has a cool climate, and is a good base for walks in the area. There are several homestays here.

Gardens surrounding the bathing pools in Tirtagangga

Plantations beside the scenic route around Gunung Lempuyang

Gunung Lempuyang ⓮

Drive through villages of Tista, Abang and Ngis Tista. **Road Map** F3. *Amlapura, (0363) 21 196.*

At just over 1,000 m (3,300 ft), Gunung Lempuyang is worth a full day's trip, especially when there is a temple ceremony. Getting there is part of the attraction – the road from Tirtagangga runs northeast along a valley, with Gunung Agung to the west and Gunung Lempuyang to the east, carving its way through lush ricefields. The mountain itself is then reached via a side road.

At the top stands **Pura Lempuyang Luhur**. There has probably been a temple on this remote and sacred site since pre-Hindu times. The temple is important to Balinese today because of its location – at the top of the island's easternmost mountain. The temple is not large; there is just a single courtyard with a few simple *bale* (pavilions). The views of Gunung Agung are spectacular. Reaching the temple involves a two-hour climb up 1,700 stone steps, passing the smaller temple of Pura Telagamas at the bottom. There are several strategically located resting places along the way.

Pura Lempuyang Luhur
daily. temple anniversary festival (Manis Galungan, 10 Mar & 6 Oct 2005, 4 May & 30 Nov 2006)

Amed ⓯

Road Map F2. *Amlapura, (0363) 21 196.*

A sleepy little fishing-town, Amed is of interest for its dive sites and salt-production. In a simple evaporation process little changed for generations, salt is made from brine poured into wooden frames, gathered in sacks and laid out by the road for sale.

Divers come to this area, and in particular to the bay at Jemeluk to the east of Amed, to enjoy underwater views of colourful coral gardens and a spectacular variety of fish.

The east coast round Amed is hot, dry and economically rather poor. Barren hills pinned with thirsty-looking *lontar* palms stand in stark contrast to the green mountain slopes behind. The arid, harsh landscape is distinctly different from the lushness of most of East Bali.

Environs: Some 5 km (3 miles) east of Amed is the quiet coastal village of **Lipah**, where tourist facilities are being rapidly developed, happily in reasonable taste and at reasonable prices.

Boats for diving or snorkelling trips off the coast around Amed

Lontar palms in the coastal region of Tulamben

Tulamben ⓰

Road Map F2. *from Amlapura & Singaraja. Amlapura, (0363) 21 196.*

Tulamben is a nondescript little town, but it is of interest as the location of the wreck of the American cargo ship *Liberty*, 120 m (396 ft) long and torpedoed south-west of Lombok during World War II. It lies 40 m (44 yards) offshore and, at its deepest point, some 60 m (198 ft) down. The water provides great diving and snorkelling. Day trips off Tulamben can be arranged with dive operations *(see p202)*. Boats can be rented locally.

Gunung Agung ⓱

GUNUNG AGUNG IS A 3,142-m- (10,350-ft-) high, active volcano, the dominant feature of East Bali. It has a profound significance in the life of every Balinese. Communities orientate their houses, temples and even beds in relation to this sacred place, where the spirits of ancestors are believed to dwell. Visitors climbing the mountain should observe rules for temple dress *(see p218)* or risk offending local sensibilities.

From Besakih ①
This climb, the longer of the two routes, goes right to the top of the volcano, where there are spectacular views of Bali and Lombok when the weather is clear.

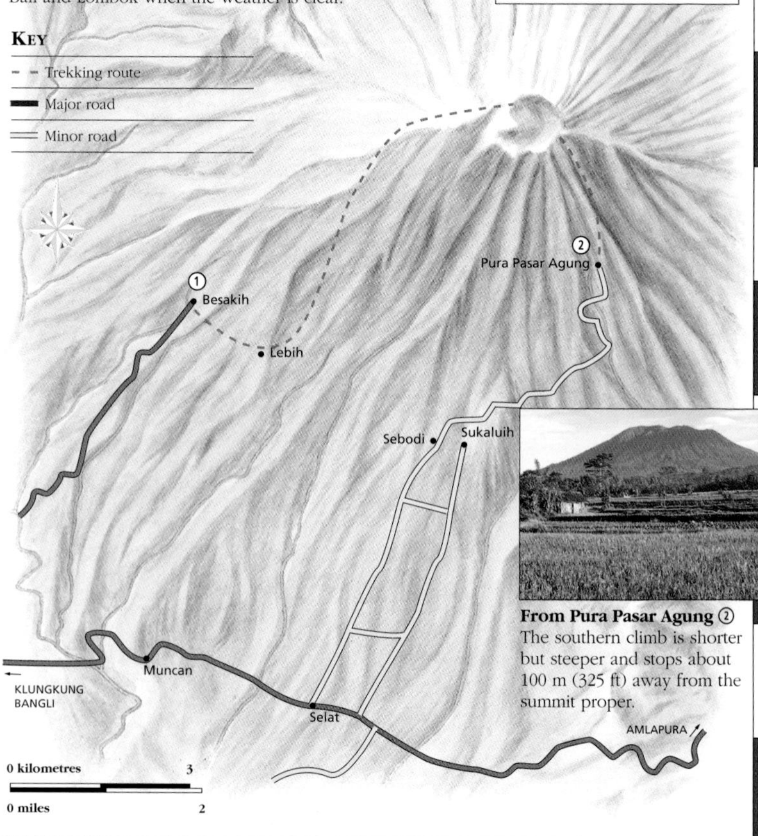

Tips for Climbers

Start point: *Either of two base camps: Besakih ①; and Pura Pasar Agung ②, north of Selat.*
Getting there: *Bus or* bemo *to Besakih from Denpasar, Gianyar and Amlapura. Own transport to Pura Pasar Agung.*
When to go: *Off-limits during the rainy season (Oct–May), when there are dangerous mud slides and swollen rivers, as well as ceremonies (Mar–Apr).*
Guide: *Visitors are strongly advised to engage a reliable guide* (see p205)*, because the climbs from both base camps are steep and require early-morning starts. The lower slopes are heavily forested. Changes in weather can be dramatic and sudden. Attitudes of local people to climbers may be unfriendly.*
Length of climb: *Six hours starting from Besakih; three hours from Pura Pasar Agung.*

Key

- - Trekking route
- Major road
- Minor road

Besakih ①
Lebih
Pura Pasar Agung ②
Sebodi
Sukaluih
Muncan
Selat
← KLUNGKUNG BANGLI
AMLAPURA ↗

0 kilometres 3
0 miles 2

From Pura Pasar Agung ②
The southern climb is shorter but steeper and stops about 100 m (325 ft) away from the summit proper.

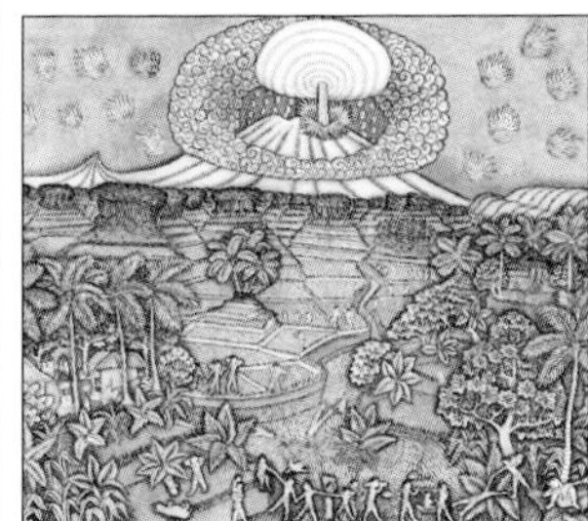

***Eruption of Gunung Agung* (1968) by Ida Bagus Nyoman Rai**

THE 1963 ERUPTION OF GUNUNG AGUNG

Although Gunung Agung had long been thought extinct, in 1963 it erupted dramatically, shooting boulders and ash high into the sky. In all, the event lasted six months. Whole villages were buried; nearly 2,000 people died; and much arable land was laid waste. The rock-filled rivers of East Bali and Agung's bare eastern flank still bear witness to the event. According to local belief the disaster happened because spiritual leaders wrongly timed the performance of Eka Dasa Rudra. This is a Hindu spiritual purification ceremony which takes place every hundred years. Ancient texts suggest that the ceremony should have taken place not in 1963, but in 1979.

Besakih Temple Complex ⓲

See pp116–17.

Gunung Batur ⓳

See pp120–21.

Kintamani ⓴

Road Map D2. *Penelokan, (0366) 51 370.*

ONE OF THE MOST popular destinations for visitors in Bali is Kintamani, notable above all for its view of a volcano within a caldera. The air here is fresh and the view from Kintamani into the caldera of Gunung Batur *(see pp120–21)* is perhaps the most famous on the island, as the tourist buses testify.

Kintamani is one of three small villages set high on Batur's caldera rim. Penelokan and Batur are the other two. It is hard to distinguish where one ends and the next begins, as they have now merged together to form a ribbon of development catering for the many visitors who come here. The whole road is transformed into a parking lot when the tour buses arrive. The hawkers can be particularly persistent.

However, people do not come to look at the village of Kintamani itself – they come to stand in awe of the view. It is worth stopping here just to get a real sense of the scale of the landscape from a high vantage-point; here it is easy to see the relative positions of Gunung Batur, the Bali Aga village of Trunyan *(see p121)* down on the shore of the lake, and Gunung Abang on the eastern side of the lake facing Gunung Batur.

There are many places to eat along most of the 10 km (6 miles) of the main road along the crater rim; most of them have good views. There is also a market selling fresh local produce.

Shop and *warung*, typical of those which line the road to Kintamani

Pura Ulun Danu Batur ㉑

See pp122–3.

Pura Tegeh Koripan ㉒

Road Map D1. *from Kintamani. Penelokan, (0366) 51 370. daily. during ceremonies. donation. temple festival (Oct).*

PURA TEGEH KORIPAN (also known as Pura Sukawana or Pura Penulisan) is one of the oldest temples in Bali, dating from the 11th century or earlier *(see p45)*. Set at more than 1,500 m (4,950 ft) on the side of Gunung Penulisan, it is certainly one of the highest *(see p120)*. It does not get very much tourist traffic and, therefore, has a peaceful atmosphere.

An ancient shrine in Pura Tegeh Koripan

It is in fact a complex of five temples. Its pyramidal structure, set on eleven levels of terraces along the slope, suggests that it dates from the pre-Hindu-Buddhist era, and is associated with the megalithic culture of Bali.

The main temple, Pura Panarajon, is over 300 steps up and at the highest position in the complex. Inside, there are some stone inscriptions and statues thought to date to the 10th century.

From the slopes of Gunung Penulisan there are good views: on clear days one can see as far as Java to the east, and the Bali Sea to the north.

Besakih Temple Complex ⓲

Stone wall carving

PURA BESAKIH is a grand complex of 22 temples spread over 3 sq km (1 sq mile) on the slopes of Gunung Agung *(see p114)*, where the Balinese believe the spirits of their ancestors live. Said to have been founded in the late 8th century by the Javanese sage, Rsi Markandya, it later came under the jurisdiction of the Klungkung kingdom. All but two shrines were destroyed in an earthquake of 1917, and it underwent several major renovations in the 20th century, escaping damage in the 1963 eruption of Gunung Agung. Now it is an important focus of modern Indonesian Hinduism.

★ Eleven-tiered Meru
The tall meru *(pagodas) are shrines for deified kings, ancestral spirits and nature gods.*

★ Main Courtyard
This is the main focus of worship at the temple. A padmasana tiga *(triple lotus shrine) is dedicated to Brahma, Shiva and Vishnu.*

Terraced Entrance
The terraces at the entrance to Pura Penataran Agung are an echo of the stepped pyramids of Indonesian prehistory.

Stairs
Only worshippers are allowed to use the entrance stairway.

Footpaths connect the temples in the complex.

Pura Ratu Pande
The roofs of this clan temple beside Pura Penataran Agung have been restored with black palm fibre and gilded roof caps.

Visitors' Checklist

Besakih. **Road Map** E2.
Amlapura, (0363) 21 196.
7am–6pm daily, but inner courtyards must be viewed from outside.
Betara Turun Kabeh (Apr); Purnama (full moons, throughout the year, particularly in Apr and Oct).

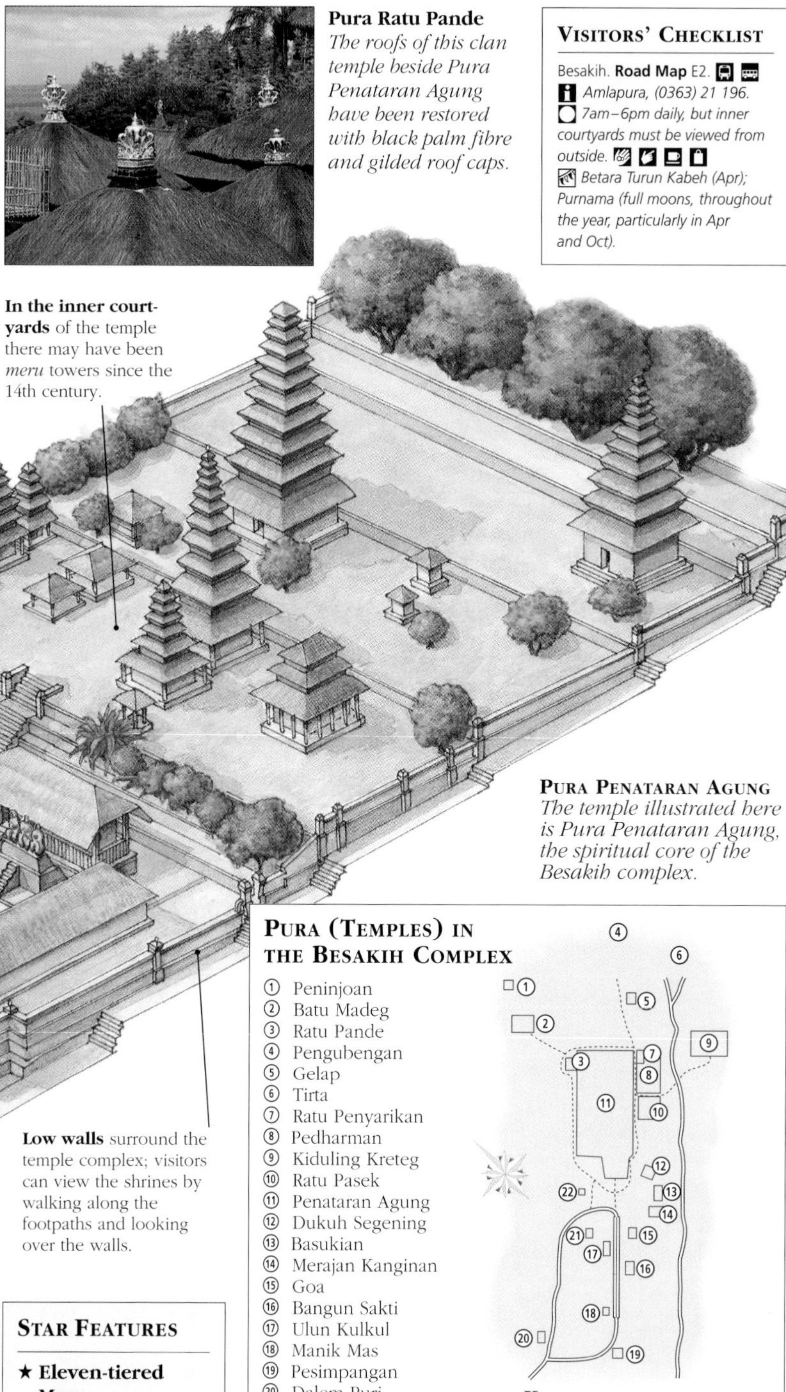

In the inner courtyards of the temple there may have been *meru* towers since the 14th century.

Pura Penataran Agung
The temple illustrated here is Pura Penataran Agung, the spiritual core of the Besakih complex.

Low walls surround the temple complex; visitors can view the shrines by walking along the footpaths and looking over the walls.

Pura (Temples) in the Besakih Complex

1. Peninjoan
2. Batu Madeg
3. Ratu Pande
4. Pengubengan
5. Gelap
6. Tirta
7. Ratu Penyarikan
8. Pedharman
9. Kiduling Kreteg
10. Ratu Pasek
11. Penataran Agung
12. Dukuh Segening
13. Basukian
14. Merajan Kanginan
15. Goa
16. Bangun Sakti
17. Ulun Kulkul
18. Manik Mas
19. Pesimpangan
20. Dalem Puri
21. Merajan Selonding
22. Jenggala

Key

--- Footpath

Star Features

★ **Eleven-tiered Meru**

★ **Main Courtyard**

Irrigated ricefield at Tirtagangga, with Gunung Agung in the distance ▷

Gunung Batur ⓳

Although Gunung Batur (Mount Batur) is not the largest volcano in Bali, it is the most active. It is surrounded by a spectacular caldera, which implies that it was once much larger than now, having blown off its top in an eruption. It has erupted on a large scale more than 20 times in the last 200 years. The most devastating occasion was in 1917 when more than 1,000 people died and over 2,000 temples were destroyed. Volcanic activity has made the slopes of Gunung Batur bare and dry, in contrast to the vegetation which covers the slopes of Gunung Abang, on the opposite side of Lake Batur.

Gunung Batur Eruptions
Minor but noisy eruptions occur frequently day and night, and can be watched from the road running through Kintamani.

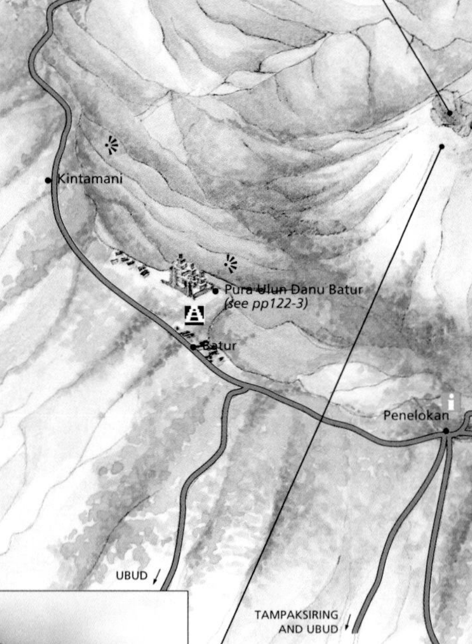

Tips for Walkers

*Walking up to one of the four craters of Gunung Batur takes an hour from **Serongga**, or three hours from **Kedisan**.*

*Guides are not necessary for day treks as the trails are easy to follow. It is important to keep to the trails. A small information centre is located at **Toya Bungkah**, where there is also losmen accommodation.*

The air can be quite chilly before daybreak, and warm clothing is highly recommended for night treks. Care should be taken to avoid the hot steam issuing from fissures in the rocks.

The slopes of the volcano are slippery and dangerous in the rainy season, and trekking is not recommended from October to April.

The Western Slopes of Gunung Batur
The area at the foot of the volcano is covered with lava deposited by old eruptions. The vegetation is sparse here.

0 kilometres 3

0 miles 2

Key

Major road

Footpath

Ferry/boat service

Temple

Tourist information

Viewpoint

Lake Batur
This lake is the main irrigation source for much of the agriculture of Central and East Bali. It is said to be protected by the lake goddess, Ida Betari Dewi Ulun Danu.

VISITORS' CHECKLIST

Road Map D2. from Penelokan & Kintamani.
Jalan Sriwijaya 23, Bangli (0366) 91 537.
Trunyan Bali Aga Village: from Kedisan. Berutuk (Oct).

Shrines on Gunung Abang
In the forest on the peak of Gunung Abang is a temple containing some small, brightly painted shrines.

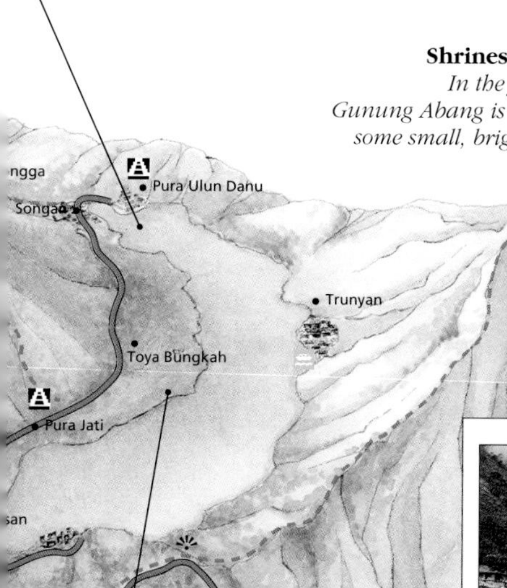

Toya Bungkah
This village near a hot spring has simple restaurants and losmen *accommodation.*

Trunyan, on the eastern shore of Lake Batur, reachable most easily by water

TRUNYAN BALI AGA VILLAGE

One of the culturally isolated Bali Aga villages *(see p46)*, Trunyan is still most easily accessible by boat. Villagers here practise customs found nowhere else in Bali, even in other Bali Aga villages. These include the treatment of their dead bodies, which are placed in pits, and covered by cloth and shabby bamboo canopies. The influence of an ancient tree is said to preserve the corpses from putrefaction. The cemetery is the main feature of interest to visitors. Trunyan is the home of Da Tonta, a 4-m- (13-ft-) high statue of Dewa Ratu Gede Pancering Jagat, patron guardian of the village, which is brought out at the Berutuk festival (usually October). The people here tend to expect "donations" from visitors, whom they now regard as a source of income.

Pura Ulun Danu Batur ㉑

Stone sculpture

THIS TEMPLE IS is one of the most important on Bali because of its association with Lake (*danu*) Batur, which supplies the irrigation system of Gianyar and Bangli through a series of underground springs. From a distance the temple's silhouette can be seen on the rim of the vast Batur caldera. Adjoining this temple are others in the process of enlargement, making up a quite extensive complex.

Temple Flags
Deities and mythical beasts are often depicted in rich colours on temple flags and sculptures.

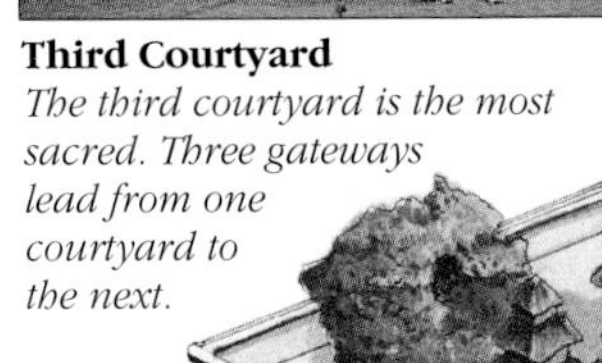

Third Courtyard
The third courtyard is the most sacred. Three gateways lead from one courtyard to the next.

Garuda
The figure of Garuda, a bird from Hindu mythology, is depicted in this stone relief on the courtyard wall.

★ Central Courtyard
The great quadrangle, shown here occupied by a festive structure of bamboo and straw, is the occasional setting for a baris gede *dance* (see p30).

Offerings of fruits and flowers

Offerings to the Lake Goddess

Devotees from all over Bali present elaborate offerings at this temple, which is dedicated to Ida Betari Dewi Ulun Danu, the goddess of Lake Batur. The respect accorded to the goddess is reinforced by events in the temple's history. At its former location closer to the lake, the temple was miraculously saved from destruction in the volcanic eruption of 1917, when the lava flow stopped just short of its walls. Another eruption, in 1926, prompted the villagers to move the temple to its present location.

Visitors' Checklist

Batur. **Road Map** D2.
Penelokan, (0366) 51 370.
7am–6pm daily.
donation. *temple anniversary (Apr & Oct Purnama).*

★ Gold-painted Doors
The great timber doors of the main temple gateway are reserved for the use of priests on important occasions.

Side Gate
This tall, slender gate, built in a combination of brickwork and paras *stone decoration, leads to another temple.*

Entrance

The bale gong is a pavilion housing the temple's set of gamelan instruments, including a great gong believed to have a magical history.

Star Features

★ Central Courtyard

★ Gold-painted Doors

NORTH AND WEST BALI

AT THE HEART OF NORTH AND WEST BALI *is a mountainous, volcanic hinterland. This is ringed by coastal plains where most of the population live. Before the Dutch took over southern Bali in the early 20th century and a harbour was built at Benoa in the 1920s, most contact between the Balinese and the rest of the world took place in this northern and western region of the island.*

North and West Bali corresponds to the regencies of Tabanan, Jembrana and Buleleng, of which the administrative capitals are Tabanan, Negara and Singaraja respectively. To the west of Tabanan regency rice-growing gradually gives way to dry fields and forests. The population is increasingly Muslim as one moves west; the older Muslim settlements were established by Bugis sailors in the 17th century. The landscape of Buleleng regency on the north coast consists of steep mountain slopes plunging down to a narrow stretch of dry land which is generally impervious to irrigation – the exceptions are the relatively fertile hinterland of Singaraja town and the plantation area of Munduk and Busungbiu further inland.

The history of this part of Bali has been influenced as much by the sea as by the traditions of the courts: both Singaraja and Negara have the flavour more of Javanese coastal trading towns than of the Balinese centres of aristocratic power. North Bali is more heavily marked by the Dutch colonial presence than the rest of the island, which was colonized later. Following their brutal takeover of Buleleng in 1849, the Dutch set up a Residentie (prefecture) in Singaraja in 1855. Singaraja shows evidence of its Dutch past in its old offices and mansions and the airy, shady atmosphere of the town. Temples evolved an original, even at times humorous, style of bas-reliefs and sculptures where Europeans, cars, boats and other signs of modernity often appear in the places taken by demons and abstract flower motifs in temples further south.

New converts to Christianity were resettled by the Dutch in the hinterland of Negara. More recently, several settlements have been established along the coast by Madurese migrants.

Ducks being farmed on the coastal plains of western Bali

◁ **Pura Tanah Lot** ***(see p128)*****, a Balinese temple situated on a rocky outcrop by the ocean**

Exploring North and West Bali

WEST BALI HAS areas of great natural beauty. The mountains, black-sand beaches, coconut plantations and ricefields make up some idyllic landscapes. The eastern part is known for its many impressive temples, and for Gunung Batukau, surrounded by Bali's last remaining primary forest. Near the hill-resort area of Bedugul is a string of mountain lakes in an ancient caldera. On the north coast lies Singaraja, once the Dutch colonial capital. A great expanse of territory is occupied by the Taman Nasional Bali Barat (West Bali National Park), and the adjacent area of protected scrub forest.

Clear waters at Pantai Gondol

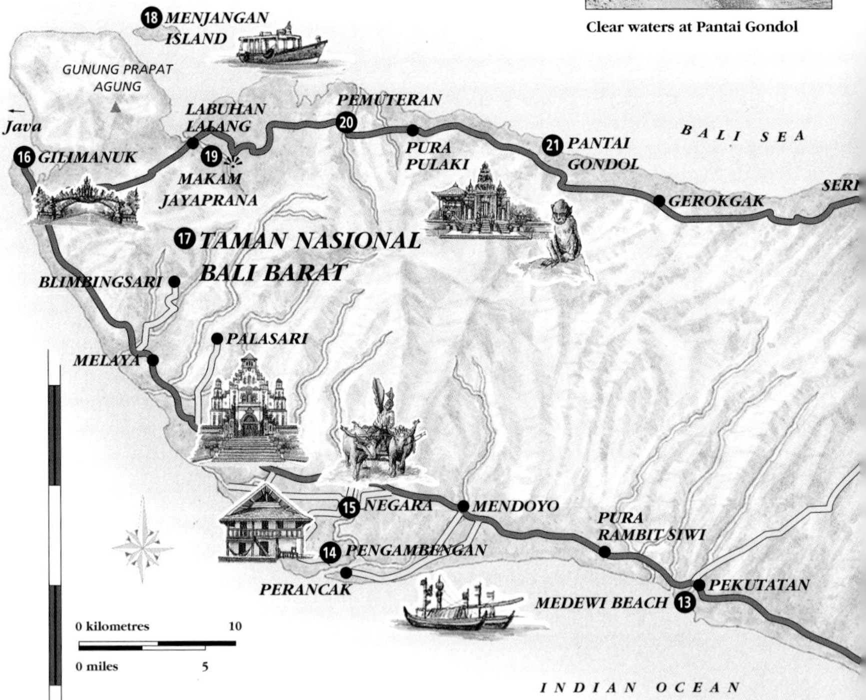

18 MENJANGAN ISLAND
GUNUNG PRAPAT AGUNG
← Java
16 GILIMANUK
LABUHAN LALANG
19 MAKAM JAYAPRANA
PEMUTERAN 20
PURA PULAKI
21 PANTAI GONDOL
BALI SEA
GEROKGAK
SERI
17 TAMAN NASIONAL BALI BARAT
BLIMBINGSARI
PALASARI
MELAYA
15 NEGARA
MENDOYO
PURA RAMBIT SIWI
14 PENGAMBENGAN
PERANCAK
PEKUTATAN
MEDEWI BEACH 13
0 kilometres 10
0 miles 5
INDIAN OCEAN

SIGHTS AT A GLANCE

Banjar 22
Blayu 7
Gilimanuk 16
Gitgit 30
Gunung Batukau 12
Jagaraga 31
Kapal 2
Krambitan 4
Lake Bratan and Bedugul 27
Lake Buyan 26
Lovina 29
Makam Jayaprana 19
Marga 9
Medewi Beach 13
Mengwi pp129–31 6
Menjangan Island 18
Munduk 24
Negara 15
Pantai Gondol 21
Pejaten 3
Pemuteran 20
Pengambengan 14
Pupuan 23
Pura Gangga 11
Pura Meduwe Karang pp148–9 32
Pura Tanah Lot 1
Sangeh 8
Singaraja pp144–6 28
Tabanan 5
Taman Nasional Bali Barat pp136–7 17
Tejakula 33
Yeh Panas 10

Tour

Lake Tamblingan *pp140–41* 25

Ricefield being planted near Tabanan

Getting Around

A car is the ideal means of travelling around North and West Bali, as the distances are relatively great, and public transport is non-existent in remoter places. Along the very busy main road from Denpasar via Mengwi to the port of Gilimanuk, there are branches off to sights including the mountain Gunung Batukau and the coastal temples of Tanah Lot. The main route from Denpasar to Singaraja gives access to sights such as Pura Taman Ayun and Bedugul. Both these major roads are served by *bemo* and public buses, as is the north-coast road from East Bali to Gilimanuk via Singaraja.

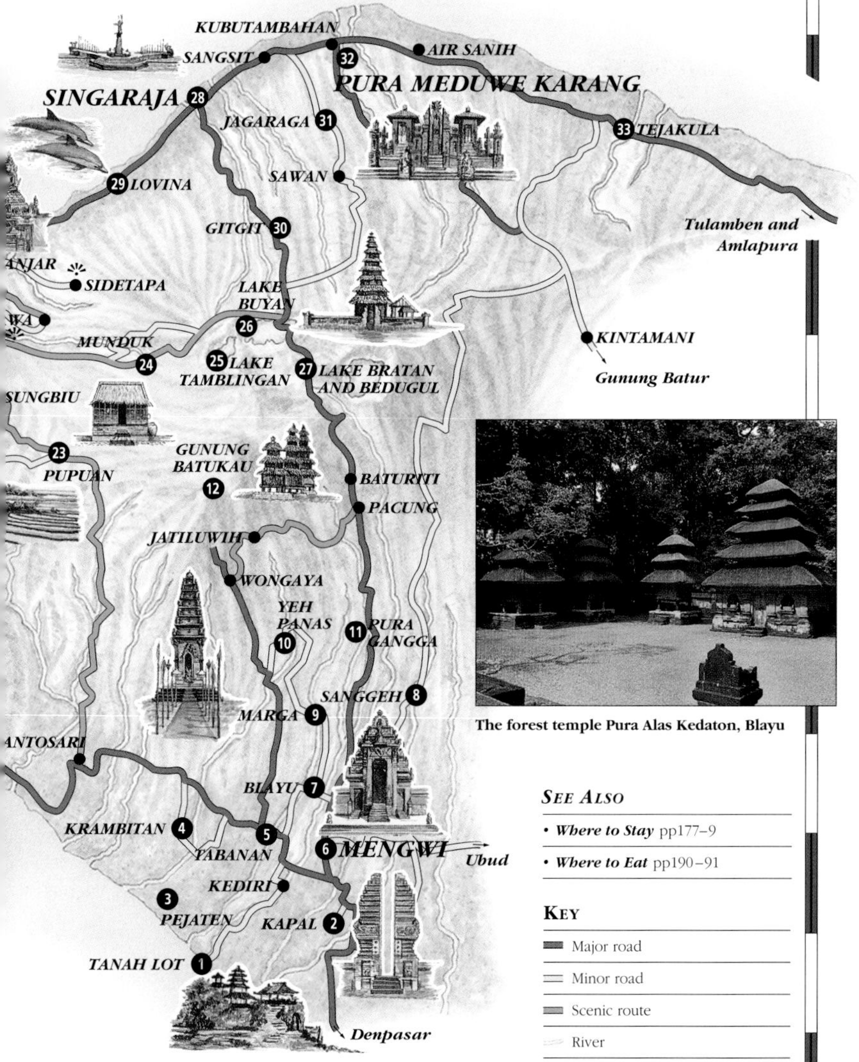

The forest temple Pura Alas Kedaton, Blayu

See Also

- ***Where to Stay*** pp177–9
- ***Where to Eat*** pp190–91

Key

- Major road
- Minor road
- Scenic route
- River
- Viewpoint

Crossing the rocky approach to Pura Tanah Lot at low tide

Pura Tanah Lot ❶

Tanah Lot. **Road Map** B4. *from Denpasar & Kediri.* *Tabanan, (0361) 811 602.* *daily.* *donation.* *temple anniversary.*

One of Bali's most heavily promoted landmarks, Pura Tanah Lot is a temple set dramatically on a small island about 100 m (100 yards) off the coast. It can get very crowded, and to visit the temple proper it is best to arrive well before sunset, when there are not too many visitors around. As the sun goes down, the shrines make a magnificent silhouette against a glowing horizon – a memorable sight despite the throngs of visitors at this time. The many handicraft, souvenir and refreshment stalls at Tanah Lot are a major source of income for the region's women and children.

The islet – a promontory until the beginning of the 20th century – is accessible on foot only at low tide. It is quickly being eroded by the onslaught of the sea. The cliffs around the island have been carefully reinforced with concrete, and tripods have been sunk into the sea to act as breakwaters.

As its name suggests, the temple is situated at the meeting-point of land (*tanah*) and sea (*lot*). The part that faces the sea is dedicated to the Balinese goddess of the sea, Betara Tengah Segara, while the landward side is thought to be the seat of the gods from Gunung Batukau *(see p133)*. The temple is associated with the saint Dang Hyang Nirartha *(see pp46–7)*. He is said to have advised its construction in order to protect Bali against scourges and epidemics; these destructive forces were thought to originate from the sea.

Environs: Along the nearby coast, numerous temples and shrines have been built to protect Tanah Lot. They include **Pura Pekendungan, Pura Jero Kandang, Pura Galuh** and **Pura Batu Bolong**. The latter stands on a small promontory linked to the mainland by a natural bridge.

Kapal ❷

Road Map C4. *from Kediri and Denpasar.* *Tabanan, (0361) 811 602.*

The most conspicuous feature of Kapal is hundreds of shops selling ready-made temple shrines and somewhat "kitsch" cement statues. There is also some attractive earthenware pottery here.

In a quiet street leading off the main road is **Pura Sada**, the temple of origin of the royal house of Mengwi *(see p47)*. Damaged during an earthquake in 1917, it was rebuilt in the 1960s by a team of Indonesian archaeologists based on the 17th-century original. The most interesting part is the 11-tier stone *meru* built in the style of a Javanese *candi*. Such towers are known as *prasada*, and are very rare in Bali. This example is a reminder of the kings' claimed descent from the Majapahit *(see p46)*. The tall, 16-m- (53-ft-) high phallic form emphasizes its dedication to the Hindu god Shiva. Affixed to the sides of the tower are images of the eight lords of the compass directions. Vishnu and Brahma with Shiva, the deities of the Hindu Trimurti (triad), are portrayed on the eastern side. On the lower base of the tower are represented the seven seers of the Hindu-Balinese cosmos. The *candi bentar* (split gate) is decorated with sets of Boma (guardian spirit) heads on the front and back; these are split like the gate itself. The closely packed rows of mini-shrines in the temple yard are said to commemorate the crew of a ship that sank while transporting to Bali the sacred effigy of a Majapahit king.

Statuary for sale at Kapal

Pura Sada
Banjar Pemebetan, near Banjar Celuk, Kapal. *daily.* *donation.*

Cluster of small shrines at Pura Sada in Kapal

Pejaten 3

Road Map B4. *from Denpasar & Tanah Lot.* *Tabanan, (0361) 811 602.*

THE VILLAGE OF PEJATEN is home to a considerable cottage industry that produces terracotta roof tiles, earthenware, pots with coloured glazes, and other decorative objects often attractively naive in character. It is a good place to browse and bargain.

ENVIRONS: About 3 km (2 miles) northeast of Pejaten is the village of **Kediri**, with an ornate white statue marking its centre. Kediri is important locally for its cattle market and colourful fabrics. The road from here south to Tanah Lot crosses enchanting rural landscapes of Bali.

Earthenware pot produced in Pejaten

Krambitan 4

Road Map B4. *from Tabanan.* *Tabanan, (0361) 811 602.*

THE SMALL TOWN OF Krambitan was an old agrarian kingdom until the turn of the 20th century. It still has a village-like atmosphere and some old architecture. Krambitan is an important repository of Balinese classical culture.

Two palaces, **Puri Anyar** and **Puri Agung Wisata**, operate as guesthouses. Occasionally, "royal parties" of Balinese dances take place, complete with torches and *tektekan*, a form of *gamelan* music in which *cengceng* (cymbals) are augmented by bamboo sticks or wooden cowbells.

Puri Anyar and Puri Agung Wisata
(0361) 812 774. *daily.* *public hols.* *donation.*

ENVIRONS: Klating Beach, on the coast 6 km (4 miles) south of Krambitan, is an unspoiled black-sand beach with some simple *losmen* accommodation available nearby.

Tabanan 5

Road Map C4. *from Denpasar.* *Jalan Gunung Agung, (0361) 811 602.*

THIS IS A bustling commercial town. The interesting, if somewhat rundown, **Museum Subak** has mock-ups of the *subak* irrigation systems of Bali *(see pp20–21)*, whereby associations are formed by owners of land irrigated by a common water source. Some traditional farming implements are also displayed.

Museum Subak
Jalan Raya Kediri, Sanggulan.
(0361) 810 315. *daily.* *public holidays.* *donation.*

ENVIRONS: Located in Wanasari, 7 km (4 miles) north on the road to Gunung Batukau, **Taman Kupu Kupu** is a small butterfly park, home to some rare species. Black-sand beaches line the coastal road to Negara *(see p134)*. **Surabrata**, also called Balian Beach, 30 km (19 miles) west of Tabanan, is charming. It has a fishing village set by a cliff, and a small river called "Sacred River" – a name intended to appeal to visitors. The surfing is good and basic accommodation is available.

Taman Kupu Kupu
Jalan Batukau, Sandan Wanasari.
(0361) 814 282. *daily.*

Mengwi 6

Road Map C4. *from Denpasar & Bedugul.* *Tabanan, (0361) 811 602.*

THIS QUIET TOWN was for a long time the seat of the most important kingdom in West Bali. It held sway over the eastern tip of Java for most of the 18th century *(see p47)*. The lanes of the town are a pleasant setting for a stroll. At Mengwi is a temple set in a water-garden, **Pura Taman Ayun** *(see pp130–31)*.

ENVIRONS: The road from Mengwi to Sangeh offers views of ricefields and temples. **Baha**, 5 km (3 miles) north of Mengwi, is a village restored to its traditional state, a good place to see the house compounds and temples typical of a Balinese community.

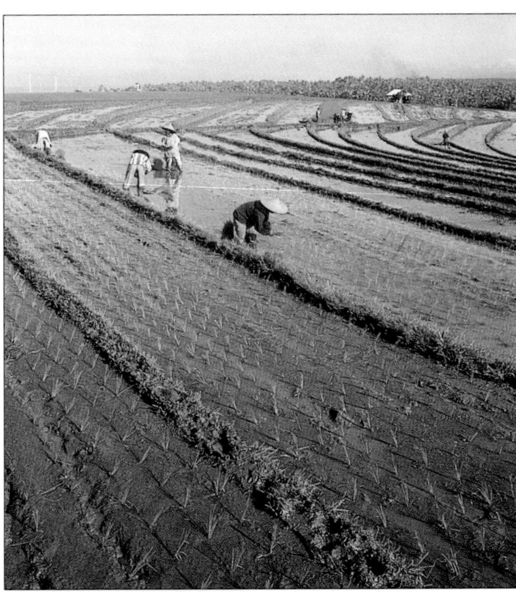

Ricefields in the regency of Tabanan

Mengwi: Pura Taman Ayun

THE TAMAN AYUN ("Vast Garden") temple, in its moated setting, symbolizes the Hindu world set in the cosmic sea. Its *meru* towers represent the mountains, residence of the gods. Located on an axis connecting the mountains with the sea, Pura Taman Ayun is thought to ensure the harmonious circulation of water from the mountains of Bali to the ricefields, then to the sea, and back to the mountains. Originally established in 1740, the temple was restored in 1937. In it there are ancestral shrines of the former ruling Mengwi family and their dependants, as well as shrines dedicated to particular mountains, to the sea and to agricultural deities.

★ Eleven-tiered Meru
The tallest meru *symbolizes the mountain Gunung Batukau* (see p133).

Water from the inner moat is used to cleanse the temple during festivals such as *odalan* (temple anniversaries).

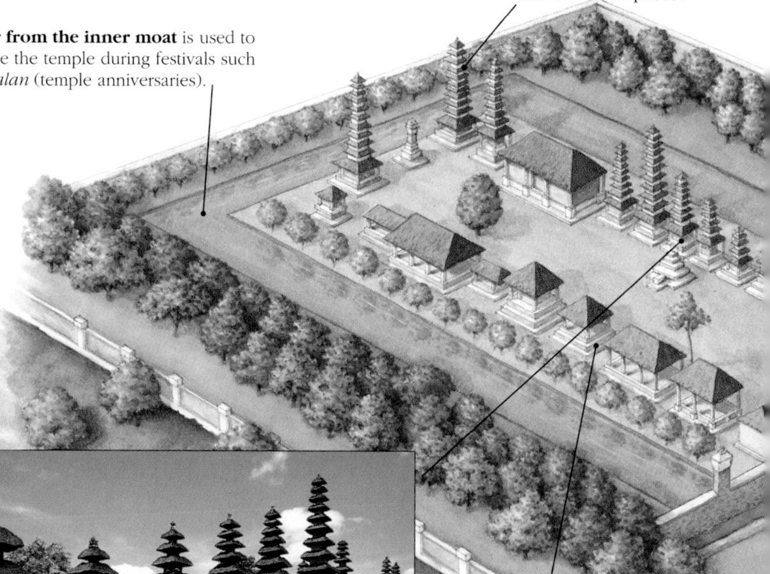

Meru
Some of the meru *towers are shrines to the deities of Bali's mountains, Gunung Batur* (see pp120–21), *Gunung Agung* (see p114) *and Gunung Batukau* (see p133)*; in the courtyard is a Javanese candi (shrine).*

Outer moat

Bale
Several bale *(wooden pavilions) are built on carved stone bases. One contains a lotus throne on which Hindu deities Shiva, Brahma and Vishnu are believed to sit.*

STAR FEATURES

- **★ Eleven-tiered Meru**
- **★ Kori Agung**

Inner Moat
Behind the main gateway, the inner courtyard is surrounded on three sides by a moat, parts of which are filled with lotuses.

Visitors' Checklist

Mengwi. **Road Map** C4. *(0361) 756 175.* *from Denpasar.* *7am – 6pm daily.* *some sections closed to public except during festivals.* *In the courtyards.* *Odalan (temple festival) on Anggarkasih Medangsia of the Balinese calendar.*

Stone Statues
Guardian figures derived from Balinese mythology stand by the main gate.

Footpaths outside the inner moat are accessible to visitors from the outer courtyard and give views of the most sacred part of the temple.

Brick Walls
Lavishly decorated walls delineate the main areas of the temple. They are built the traditional way, without mortar.

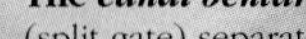

The *candi bentar* (split gate) separates the first courtyard from the grassy areas outside. Visitors may pass through here.

★ Kori Agung
On the lintel of the kori agung *(main gate) is a rare carving of Sai, a guardian figure, with gods and godly seers to each side. The doors are open only during ceremonies.*

Blayu 7

Road Map C3. *from Denpasar & Kediri.* *Tabanan, (0361) 811 602.*

BLAYU, LIKE NEARBY Mambal, is a scenic village on a road lined with beautiful *kori* house gates typical of the area. Near the village is the monkey forest of Alas Kedaton. In the temple, **Pura Alas Kedaton**, is an ancient statue of Ganesha, Hindu god of knowledge

Pura Alas Kedaton
daily. *Anggarkasih Medangsia (29 Mar & 25 Oct 2005, 23 May & 19 Dec 2006, 17 July 2007).*

***Meru* tower at Pura Alas Kedaton, in the monkey forest near Blayu**

Sangeh 8

Road Map C3. *from Denpasar.* *Tabanan, (0361) 811 602.*

MONKEYS ARE FOUND in many gorges and mountains around Bali, and a good place to see them is the monkey forest of Sangeh. It consists of nutmeg trees, some as high as 30–40 m (100–130 ft). Monkeys can be seen around a small temple, **Pura Bukit Sari**, deep in the woods, but signposted on the main road. The monkeys are considered sacred, a tradition deriving from the Hindu *Ramayana* epic, in which Prince Rama allied himself with the monkey kings Subali and Hanoman to attack the evil king Rawana.

The monkeys should be approached with caution. People will be greeted with mischievous grins, but it is not advisable to get too friendly – the monkeys may try to climb up on visitors' shoulders, and will not get down unless given something to eat. Brusque movements can provoke them to bite. The animals may even take spectacles or money, in which case a *pawang* (monkey tamer) will retrieve the stolen object using a banana as an incentive.

A monkey in Sangeh

Pura Bukit Sari
Sangeh. *daily.*

The Battle of Marga

The memorial tower at Margarana

In February 1946, after the Japanese surrendered at the end of World War II, the Dutch strove to reestablish their colonial authority in Bali. Local nationalists led a guerrilla war against them. On 20 November 1946, 94 Balinese fighters under the command of Gusti Ngurah Rai were trapped by Dutch troops west of Marga. Surrounded on the ground and strafed from the air, they fought to the last, in a modern repeat of the ritual *puputan* *(see p51)*. After this bloody defeat, resistance waned and Bali was to remain effectively under Dutch control until the end of 1949.

Marga 9

Road Map C3. *from Denpasar & Mengwi.* *Tabanan, (0361) 811 602.*

THE VILLAGE OF MARGA is the site of a battle between the Dutch and the Balinese guerrillas in 1946. On the western side of the village is the Margarana Monument. Besides the graves of the 94 guerrillas fallen at the battle *(rana)* of Marga, the garden contains monuments to 1,372 heroes of the War of Independence in the 1940s. The graves do not resemble Christian, Muslim or even Hindu graves: they are small, *meru*-shaped structures reminiscent of the ancient temples from the Javanese empire of Majapahit *(see p46)*.

The central monument, not to be mistaken for a Balinese *meru* shrine, is designed as it is to symbolize the day of the proclamation of independence, 17 August 1945. The four steps and five small pillars at its foot represent the year (45); the eight tiers of its roof give the month (August); and the height of 17 m (56 ft) gives the day (17). A statue of Gusti Ngurah Rai *(see p51)* completes the scene.

At Marga, shrines to independence fighters at the Margarana monument

The hot-spring resort and hotel in Yeh Panas

Yeh Panas ⑩

Penatahan, near Penebel. **Road Map** C3. *from Denpasar & Tabanan.* *(0361) 262 356.* *6am–8pm daily.*

IT IS WORTHWHILE dropping by the Yeh Panas hot springs on the road to Gunung Batukau from Tabanan or Penebel. There are several sulphurous springs in this area. The main hot springs have been turned into a spa, which also has a hotel; those which are open to the public are clearly indicated by signs. There is also a spring temple here.

Hot springs are also to be found in the village of Angsri near Apuan. They are in a pleasant, natural setting, but have no modern facilities.

Pura Gangga ⑪

On a small road leading through Perean to Apuan and Baturiti. **Road Map** C3. *Tabanan, (0361) 811 602.* *to visitors.*

PURA GANGGA is a temple on the main highway to Bedugul. It is named after the holy river Ganges (Gangga) in India, and is set on the lush banks of a small river. The temple has a seven-tier *meru* with a stone base. It is unusual in that the base is open at the front, rather than entirely closed in the usual fashion. Although the temple is not open to visitors, its atmospheric compound and architectural features can easily be viewed from outside the precincts.

Gunung Batukau ⑫

Road Map B2. *from Denpasar & Tabanan.* *Tabanan, (0361) 811 602.*

GUNUNG BATUKAU is the second highest peak in Bali (Gunung Agung being the highest). On its slopes is the last remaining true rainforest on the island. The mountain is much revered by the Balinese as the source of irrigation water for areas to the south and west of it.

The temple of **Pura Luhur Batukau** is located among the lofty trees at its foot. It is seen as very important by the Balinese because of its geographical position at Bali's highest western peak. There is a constant stream of worshippers performing rites or requesting holy water from the temple priests.

The charm of the temple's setting lies in a blend of artifice and nature: the spires of its *meru* shrines and other dark-thatched pavilions appear to be engulfed by the forest. Trees, bushes and grass are all in various shades of green, which contrast with the black and reddish profile of the roofs and walls of the temple. Hence the origin of the name given to the central deity of the temple: Sang Hyang Tumuwuh, "The Ultimate Plant Grower".

In the centre of a nearby artificial pool is a small shrine, dedicated to the Lord of Gunung Batukau and the goddess of nearby Lake Tamblingan *(see pp140–41)*.

Pura Luhur Batukau
daily. *donation.* *some areas.*

ENVIRONS: To the east of Pura Luhur Batukau on the road to Baturiti are the famous rice terraces of **Jatiluwih**, stretching down to the sea in the far distance. Rice granaries line the road in the local villages. Other beautiful rice terraces are are to be seen in **Pacung**, at the turn-off to Jatiluwih and Batukau.

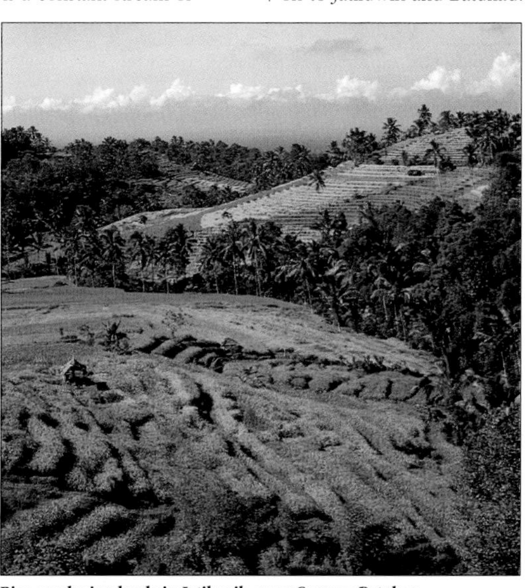

Rice-producing lands in Jatiluwih, near Gunung Batukau

Pura Rambut Siwi, a temple on a promontory west of Medewi Beach

Medewi Beach ⓭

from Denpasar. Negara, (0365) 41 060.

MEDEWI IS A surfers' haunt on the west coast of Bali. The long, rolling breakers can be 7 m (23 ft) high. The beach is composed of black sand, over which are scattered small black stones. The beach is a memorable sight when the stones glitter under the rays of the setting sun. On the horizon is the shape of the Javanese coast. Visitors will find some basic hotels and restaurants here.

ENVIRONS: The **Pura Rambut Siwi** temple complex is built on a promontory, 6 km (4 miles) west of Medewi Beach. The setting offers a fine panorama over the sea. The main temple was established to venerate the priest Dang Hyang Nirartha *(pp46–7)*, after he cured the local villagers of a deadly illness. There is a single, three-tiered *meru*. A lock of hair *(rambut)*, believed to be the priest's, is kept as a relic in the pavilion shrine, or *gedong*. The temple entrance faces the sea and is guarded by a superbly carved statue of the demonic figure, Rangda *(see p25)*. There are other smaller temples in caves along the nearby cliff.

Pura Rambut Siwi
6 km (4 miles) west of Medewi Beach, then 500 m (1,650 ft) south.
daily. *donation.*

Pengambangan ⓮

Negara, (0365) 41 060.

THIS MUSLIM settlement lies on the bank of the Ijo Gading river. Lined up along the shore are brightly painted Bugis boats. Each one has a miniature mosque on top of its mast, a reminder of the Islamic traditions of the Bugis. Not far away is a full-sized mosque, with Islamic arches and a shining dome. Music with a Middle Eastern flavour often blares from the coffee shops here; the place has a particular atmosphere.

ENVIRONS: The village of **Perancak**, on the other side of the river, has a mosque with tiered roof in the traditional Indonesian style.

Negara ⓯

from Denpasar & Gilimanuk.
Jalan Ngurah Rai, (0365) 41 193.

THE REAL CHARM of Negara lies in the Bugis origin of its urban core. On both sides of the Ijo Gading River, south of the central bridge on Jalan Gatot Subroto, is the Bugis community of Loloan. A walk on its streets evokes the atmosphere of Sulawesi, where many early Bugis migrants originated *(see box)*. Wooden houses with elaborately carved balconies line the streets. The most beautiful are at the end of Jalan Gunung Agung and on nearby Jalan Puncak Jaya. Loloan boasts several traditional *pesantren* (Islamic boarding schools); many shipowners' sons were trained as *ulema* (religious scholars) in the holy city of Mecca.

Negara is also known for its *jegog, gamelan* orchestras playing huge bamboo instruments *(see p33)*. A sport which was introduced to West Bali by the descendants of the Madurese of East Java is the *mekepung*. This is a race in which jockeys compete in decorated two-wheeled chariots drawn by a pair of water buffaloes. The most exciting races can be seen from July to October.

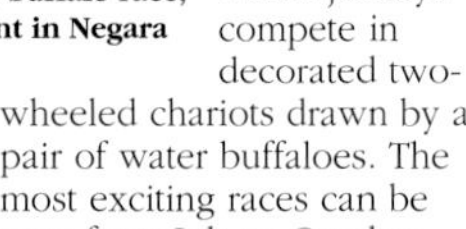

The *mekepung* buffalo race, a regular event in Negara

ENVIRONS: A small road 4 km (2 miles) west of Negara leads to the quiet beach of **Rening**,

The mosque in Perancak, across the river from Pengambangan

North of Negara, the large Catholic church at Palasari

8 km (5 miles) away, where bungalows are available. From the nearby Cape Rening there is a beautiful sunset view over the mountains of eastern Java. Another good beach is Candi Kusuma, 13 km (8 miles) west of Negara.

To the north are two Christian villages: **Palasari** (Catholic) and **Blimbingsari** (Protestant). These were established at the end of the 1930s on State land passed by the Dutch to Balinese converts to Christianity, who were excluded from their own community. The religious architecture in both villages is an interesting mix of Balinese and Dutch-Nordic styles. Near Palasari an irrigation reservoir provides tranquil landscape views.

Gilimanuk ⓰

from Denpasar & Singaraja. *from Ketapang, Java.* *Negara, (0365) 41 193.*

GILIMANUK IS the ferry port to Java. There are many *warung* here catering for travellers who sometimes have to wait hours for a ferry.

The main architectural feature is an enormous arched "gateway to Bali", surmounted by four flaming dragons facing in the cardinal directions, with a throne of heaven in the centre.

ENVIRONS: North of Gilimanuk at Cekik, the **Museum Purbakala** (Archaeological Museum), displays some sarcophagi and neolithic tools excavated from a nearby funerary site. Some promising archaeological discoveries have been made here showing signs of pre-Bronze Age human settlement in this area. Also in Cekik is the headquarters of the Taman Nasional Bali Barat *(see pp136–7)*, the nature reserve covering a substantial area of West Bali.

Museum Purbakala

Jalan Raya. *(0365) 61 328.*
Sun–Fri.

The arched "gateway to Bali" at Gilimanuk

THE BUGIS IN BALI

The Bugis, who are Muslims, are a seafaring people known for their adventurousness. They originated in Sulawesi, one of the Greater Sunda islands north of Bali. After Makasar in Sulawesi fell to the Dutch in 1667, thousands fled, many of them sailing to Java and Bali. East Java was in turmoil at the time. In both Java and Bali the Bugis were often hired as mercenaries. The estuary of the Ijo Gading River in the Balinese kingdom of Jembrana was a good anchorage, and in the 1680s a company of Bugis offered their services to the king. In due course they moved up-river, and settled next to the king's palace at Negara. Other Bugis communities settled on Bali's north coast. Bugis mercenaries helped the king of Buleleng, Panji Sakti, occupy Blambangan, Java, in 1697.

As late as the end of the 19th century, a group of Bugis in South Bali were operating as pirates from Pulau Serangan *(see p72)* near Denpasar.

The Bugis controlled Bali's trade with Java until the mid-20th century, when the opening of the ferry link in Gilimanuk destroyed their economic power. Most of them are now impoverished fishermen.

Bugis boats painted in the traditional bright colours

Taman Nasional Bali Barat ⓱

Heliconia flower

The far west of Bali is occupied by the Taman Nasional Bali Barat ("West Bali National Park"). This is a wildlife preserve established by the Dutch in 1941, bordered by a large area of protected, productive land. The preserve aims to safeguard Bali's remaining wilderness and provides sanctuary for some threatened species. Permits are required for anyone who wants to stay overnight or to penetrate deeply into the park. Only travel on foot is allowed.

★ Mangroves and Wetlands
Mangrove roots protect the coast from erosion; the wetlands are home to fish, mudskippers and crabs.

The Bali Starling Breeding Facility is a haven for the endangered birds.

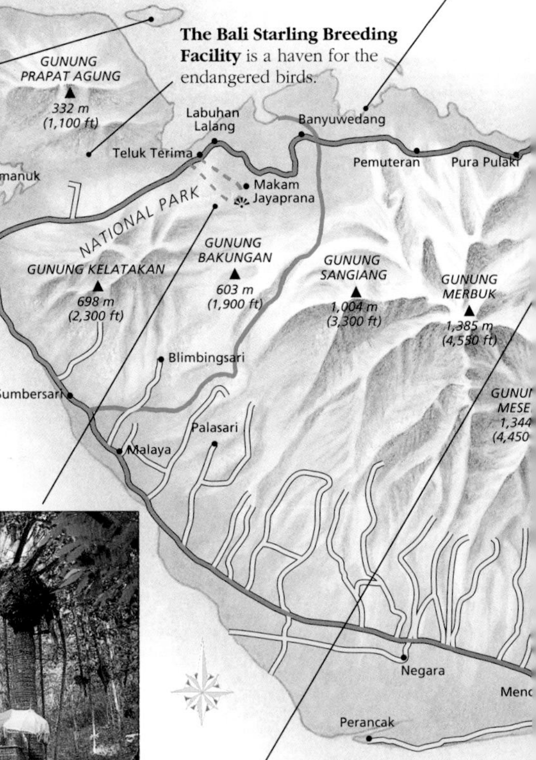

Reefs and Marine Life
The park includes the marine environment around Menjangan Island (see p138)*, a good diving site rich in fish and coral.*

GUNUNG PRAPAT AGUNG 332 m (1,100 ft)
Labuhan Lalang
Banyuwedang
Teluk Terima
Pemuteran
Pura Pulaki
Gilimanuk
Makam Jayaprana
NATIONAL PARK
Cekik
GUNUNG KELATAKAN 698 m (2,300 ft)
GUNUNG BAKUNGAN 603 m (1,900 ft)
GUNUNG SANGIANG 1,004 m (3,300 ft)
GUNUNG MERBUK 1,385 m (4,550 ft)
GUNUNG MESE... 1,344 (4,450...
Blimbingsari
Sumbersari
Palasari
Malaya
Negara
Perancak
Menc...

Nature Walk
A short trek, taken with a guide from the park headquarters, passes by rivers and through rainforest. Close to the route are several forest shrines including one with a hilltop view.

Star Sights

★ **Mangroves and Wetlands**

★ **Savanna**

★ **Sambar Deer**

★ Savanna
Along the north slopes of the central mountain range grow deciduous acacia, palm trees and arid shrubs. Plants live for long periods without rain on this dry savanna grassland.

Grasslands
Fertile grasslands stretch out towards the sea near the quiet beach of Pantai Gondol. A fishery research project is located here.

Visitors' Checklist

Administered by the Indonesian Forestry Service (PHPA). Visitors must apply for permits at these offices. ***City Office:*** *Jalan Suwung 40, Box 329, Denpasar.* ***Park Headquarters:*** *Jalan Raya Gilimanuk, Cekik. (0365) 61 060. 8am–2pm Mon–Thu, 8–11am Fri, 8am–noon Sat.* ***Ranger Station and Branch Office****: Labuhan Lalang. 8am–6pm daily.*

★ Sambar Deer
The forested mountain slopes are the habitat of these deer, which roam freely in the park.

Key

- Major road
- Minor road
- Walking trail
- Wildlife preserve boundary
- Viewpoint

0 kilometres 10

0 miles 5

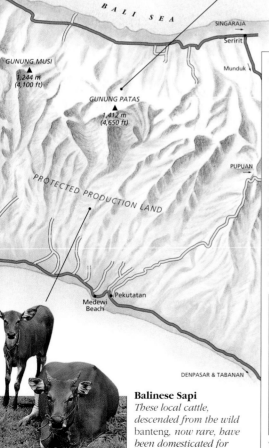

BALI SEA
SINGARAJA
Seririt
Munduk
GUNUNG MUSI
1,244 m (4,100 ft)
GUNUNG PATAS
1,412 m (4,650 ft)
PUPUAN
PROTECTED PRODUCTION LAND
Medewi Beach
Pekutatan
DENPASAR & TABANAN

The Bali Starling

The Bali starling (*Leucopsar rothschildi*), also known as Rothschild's mynah, is the only surviving bird endemic to Bali and one of the world's most endangered bird species. Numbers surviving in the wild have declined to less than ten during the last few years.

The conservation project in the West Bali National Park is an internationally supported attempt to save the species, by breeding the birds in captivity before releasing them to the wild. At the breeding facility, Bali starlings are protected from poaching, the principal cause of their declining numbers in the wild.

The endangered Bali starling

Balinese Sapi
These local cattle, descended from the wild banteng, *now rare, have been domesticated for heavy work in the ricefields.*

Shrine dedicated to a romantic hero at Makam Jayaprana

Menjangan Island ⓲

to Labuhan Lalang from Denpasar & Seririt. *from Labuhan Lalang.* Labuhan Lalang, (0365) 61 060.

FOR DIVING and snorkelling in a pristine environment, Menjangan Island is not to be missed. Technically part of Taman Nasional Bali Barat *(see pp136–7)*, it owes its name to the Java deer *(menjangan)*, which wander across from the mainland at low tide. There are eight main diving points around the island, each with its own marine life. The best is perhaps the Anchor Wreck, named for the encrusted anchor on the reef.

A lionfish and coral off Menjangan Island

Labuhan Lalang, on the bay of Teluk Terima, is Bali's nearest point of access to Menjangan Island. Boat tickets may be bought at the office of the Department of Forestry here. The last boats leave for Menjangan Island at 11am and return at dusk. There is basic accommodation at Labuhan Lalang.

Makam Jayaprana ⓳

Teluk Terima. *from Denpasar & Seririt.* *Singaraja, (0362) 25 141.* *daily.*

THE MAKAM JAYAPRANA ("Jayaprana Mausoleum") is also a temple. It has to be reached by a climb from the road *(see p136)*; however the panoramic view over Gunung Raung in Java, Menjangan Island and Gilimanuk is ample reward for the effort. The shrine was built on the burial site of Jayaprana, a romantic hero of Balinese folklore. According to legend, Jayaprana had married a woman named Layonsari, of such extreme beauty that the Lord of Kalianget decided to get rid of him and marry her. The king pretended that Bugis pirates had landed in Gilimanuk and sent Jayaprana with a body of soldiers to repel them. When they came to their destination the soldiers killed Jayaprana. However, resisting the advances of the king, Layonsari killed herself to rejoin her beloved Jayaprana in death.

Today, suitors ask for favours of love at the grave. It is decorated with statues of Jayaprana and Layonsari.

Pemuteran ⓴

Singaraja, (0362) 25 141.

PEMUTERAN IS a fast-growing coastal resort and fishing village with the best white-sand beach in North Bali. It has beautiful coral reefs with a profusion of tropical fish. There are good diving and snorkelling spots, and a turtle sanctuary. It is a convenient place for visitors to Menjangan Island to stay overnight; a boat can be rented here.

ENVIRONS: A little west of Pemuteran is the small bay of **Banyuwedang**. The name is Balinese for "hot springs". There are many springs along this shore, supposedly with curative powers. They are alternately covered and exposed by the tide. A spa resort, **Mimpi Resort Menjangan** *(see p178)*, has been built over one of them.

Pura Pulaki, about 5 km (3 miles) east of Pemuteran, is a coastal temple near a point where a mountain ridge plunges abruptly into the sea, almost blocking the coastal passage. It is associated with the priest Dang Hyang Nirartha *(see pp46–7)* who is said to have turned the local inhabitants into *gamang* (ghosts). Living around it are monkeys, often mischievous; they are regarded as holy.

Pura Pulaki
Banyu Poh. *daily.* *donation.* *certain areas.*

Pantai Gondol ㉑

6 km (4 miles) west of Grogak, across the field next to the Fisheries Research Project (Perikanan). *Singaraja, (0362) 25 141.*

GONDOL BEACH is located at the foot of a small promontory, the Gondol Cape. With beautiful white sand and coral, it is a good, uncrowded spot for snorkelling and diving. However, there are no visitor facilities here.

The beach at Pantai Gondol, still pleasantly undeveloped

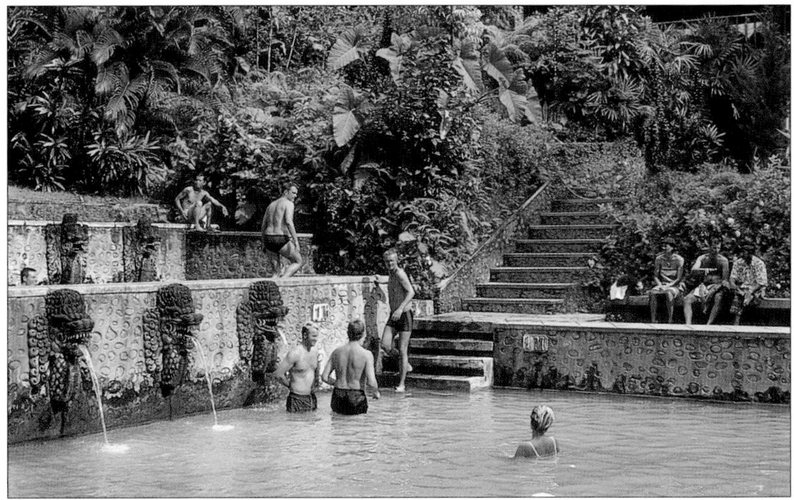

Air Panas at Banjar, a natural hot spring popular with visitors

Banjar ㉒

Road Map A1. *to Seririt, then own transport.* *Singaraja (0362) 25 141.*

BANJAR IS A TOWN of historic significance, set on the coastal plain with the North Bali uplands as a backdrop. In 1871, when still a semi-independent kingdom run by a brahman family, it put up strong resistance to Dutch encroachment. This confrontation is known as the Banjar War. The ruling family was eliminated in one of Bali's first recorded *puputan*, or "fights to the last" *(see p48)*.

The brahmans from Banjar are famous for their literary talents. In the 19th century they adapted texts from classical Kawi (Old Javanese) into common Balinese.

Brahma Vihara Ashrama *(see p23)* is a Buddhist monastery built in 1970 by a powerful local brahman, Bhikku Giri Rakhita, who converted to Theravada Buddhism, the form of Buddhism prevalent in Thailand. The temple contains many Thai iconographic features. There is an impressive view from the monastery over a nearby valley and the shoreline.

Another highlight of Banjar is the **Air Panas** hot spring, popular with both locals and visitors from nearby Lovina. There are three pools; in the highest one the water is hot. Eight carved dragon-heads spurt out greenish-yellow, sulphurous water believed to be therapeutic for complaints of the skin. The hot water is considered sacred by the locals – a temple has been built around the spring, which is set in cool and shady surroundings.

ENVIRONS: From Banjar one can visit **Pedawa**, 10 km (6 miles) inland. This remote place is a Bali Aga village *(see p46)*. It was one of the villages which rebelled against the Javanese occupation of 1343, and has retained Hindu cultural features dating from before that time. Indeed, the Hindu triad of Brahma-Vishnu-Shiva was unknown here until recently. Whereas the Balinese generally build a whole range of shrines for gods and ancestors behind their houses, the people of Pedawa build a single bamboo structure.

There are two routes from Banjar to Pedawa: both run through stunning mountain and plantation landscapes.

In **Sidatapa**, a village on another road running inland from Banjar, there still remain some interesting old houses constructed of bamboo.

Brahma Vihara Ashrama
Between Banjar and Pedawa.
(0362) 92 954. *daily.* *donation.*

Air Panas Banjar
daily. *donation.*

The Buddhist monastery of Brahma Vihara Ashrama at Banjar

A large bunutan tree spanning the road near Pupuan

Pupuan 23

Road Map B2. *from Denpasar & Singaraja.* *Tabanan, (0361) 811 602.*

PUPUAN IS BALI'S vegetable-growing centre, situated in the rainiest part of the whole island. The area around it is cool and mountainous. The road from Seririt to Antosari travels through some of Bali's most beautiful landscape, with excellent coastal views. It climbs steeply via Busungbiu, Pupuan, and through a forested pass 790 m (2,600 ft) high into lush spice-growing countryside. It then winds down to Blimbing and Bajra before passing rice terraces, with rice barns along the road. The road southwest to Pekukatan passes a coffee plantation area, and at one point is arched by the roots of a huge bunutan tree.

ENVIRONS: At **Blimbing**, 12 km (7 miles) to the south, is the nearest accommodation; there are panoramic views and a restaurant.

Munduk 24

Road Map B2. *from Singaraja & Seririt.* *Singaraja, (0362) 25 141.*

MUNDUK IS A highland village amid plantations of coffee and cloves. It is set on a high ridge near the volcanic lakes of Tamblingan, Buyan and Bratan. In the area there are still a few rest-houses from the 1920s, built in a mixed Dutch Colonial-Chinese style. In the village it is possible to visit the workshop of I Made Trip, Bali's most famous maker of bamboo instruments.

Munduk is an ideal base for exploring on rented bicycles, for mountain walks to Pedawa, for ricefield walks to Uma Jero, or for a tour of Lake Tamblingan and Lake Bratan. There are several waterfalls in the area – the most spectacular, 30 m (100 ft) high, can be found 1 km (half a mile) along the road eastwards to Bedugul.

Lake Tamblingan Tour 25

THIS TOUR OF the mountain lakes incorporates a boat trip, a walk and a scenic drive. From Gubug, fishermen take visitors across Lake Tamblingan in a dugout canoe, skirting the north shore where dense forest descends to the edge of the water. The lake is the most unspoiled one on the island and is located in a volcanic caldera. It is surrounded by primary forest with monkeys and many species of birds to discover. The forest resounds with birdsong, especially that of barbets.

Pura Ulun Danu Tamblingan ③
The walk begins with a flight of steps to the temple. From a courtyard the trail leads into the forest.

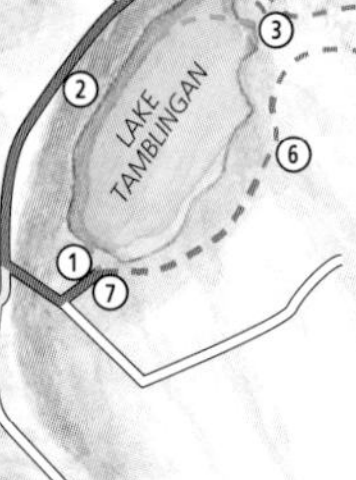

Sacred Spring ②
Inside a cave, marked by parasols and only accessible by water, there is a sacred spring.

Gubug ①
A *warung* in the village of Gubug gives information on the area. There is no trail along the north shore and travel by canoe is necessary to see parts of Lake Tamblingan.

Dugout canoe crossing Lake Tamblingan

Paragliding, one of the water activities available at Lake Bratan

Lake Buyan ㉖

Road Map B2 & C2. *from Singaraja.* *Singaraja, (0362) 25 141.*

THERE ARE GREAT VIEWS over the lake from the mountain road – dense forest scrub vanishes at the shoreline into the water. Boats can be hired from fishermen and treks organized to a cave on the slopes of Gunung Lesong, to Gesing or to Munduk.

Lake Bratan and Bedugul ㉗

Road Map C2. *from Singaraja & Denpasar.* *Tabanan, (0361) 811 602.*

LAKE BRATAN offers a variety of water activities such as parasailing and water-skiing. Visitors can hire boats by the lake and there are guides for treks to the peaks, such as Gunung Puncak Manggu and Gunung Catur. The lake is the setting for the **Pura Ulun Danu Bratan** temple, built on a small island. The 17th-century temple is dedicated to the goddess of the lake, Dewi Danu. There is a small stupa-shaped shrine for Buddhist worshippers, with statues of Buddhas occupying niches that mark the four points of the compass. The panorama includes an 11-tiered *meru* located on the shore across a wooden bridge.

The 155-ha (390-acre) **Eka Karya Botanic Gardens** contains 320 species of orchids, a herbarium, a fern garden and a collection of plants used for making *jamu* (traditional medicines).

To the north of Lake Bratan, the well-manicured Bali Handara Kosaido Country Club *(see p204)* is renowned for having one of the world's best golf courses.

Eka Karya Botanic Gardens

Kebun Raya, west of Candi Kuning. *(0368) 21 273.* *daily.*

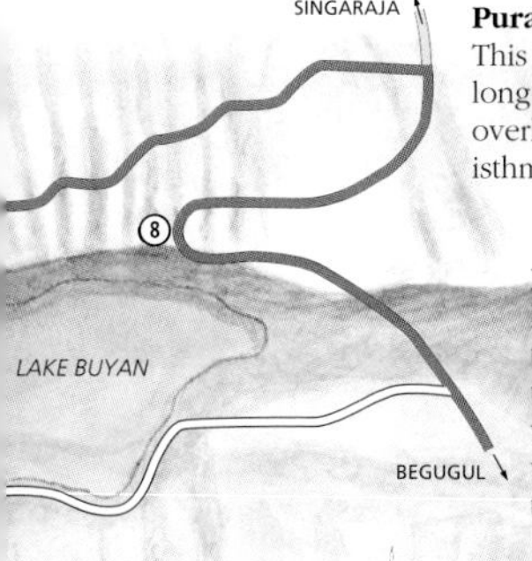

Pura Pekemitan Kangin ④
This temple on the ridge, up a long winding flight of steps, overlooks the narrow forested isthmus separating the two lakes.

Rainforest ⑤
Many trails lead into the dense tropical rainforest extending towards Lake Buyan. The vegetation is characterized by vines, creepers and massive trees with huge buttress roots.

Tips for Walkers

Start point: *Gubug by canoe.*
End point: *Return to Gubug on foot and proceed by pre-arranged vehicle on the scenic road along the top of the ridge, heading west to Bedugul.*
Getting there: *Own transportation via Bedugul or Munduk.*
When to go: *Mornings. Avoid the rainy season when trails are slippery and infested by leeches.*
Tour time: *2–3 hours.*

Pura Dalem Gubug ⑥
A short trail leads to this lakeside temple, which has a tall *meru* on a small promontory.
A path then leads through open pasture back to Gubug.

Gubug ⑦
From here, the tour continues by car on the ridge-top road.

Lake Buyan ⑧
As you travel along the road, you can enjoy views of the lakes from the caldera rim.

0 kilometres 2
0 miles 1

Key

- Boat trip
- Walk route
- Drive route
- Minor road
- Track

Street-by-Street: Singaraja ㉘

Ornament sold in the market

WITH ITS WATERFRONT MOSQUES, temples, market and well-ordered streets, Singaraja is a pleasant place to stroll around. The harbour has not been dredged for 60 years and its business has mostly shifted to Celukang Bawang, 38 km (24 miles) to the west. However, this area is still one of the most interesting parts of the town, occupied by communities of trading minorities – Chinese, Bugis *(see p135)* and other Muslims. The Balinese community lives further east, while the modern commercial centre is near the market, Pasar Anyar, around Jalan Ahmad Yani and Jalan Diponegoro.

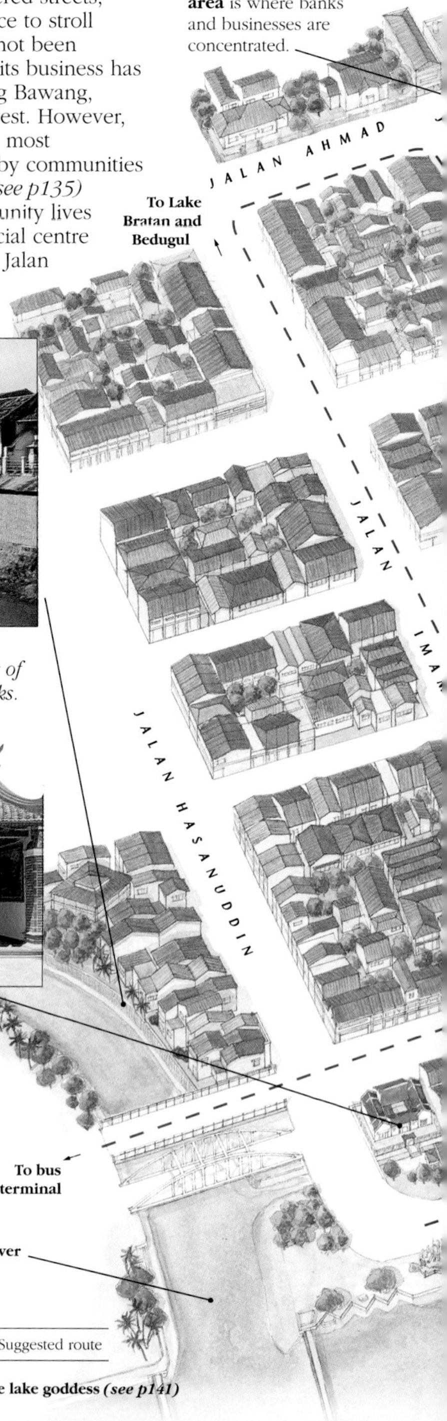

This bustling commercial area is where banks and businesses are concentrated.

JALAN AHMAD

To Lake Bratan and Bedugul

JALAN IMAM

JALAN HASANUDDIN

View of River Buleleng
From the bridge, the old residential houses of Singaraja can be seen along the river banks.

★ Chinese Temple
This temple with its classical red roof tiles, decorated with tablets in gold calligraphy, betokens the presence and influence of the Chinese trading community in this part of Singaraja.

To bus terminal

Buleleng River

STAR SIGHTS

★ Chinese Temple

★ Masjid Nur

★ Independence Monument

KEY

– – – Suggested route

◁ **Pura Ulun Danu Bratan, a temple dedicated to the lake goddess *(see p141)***

Masjid Agung Jamik
The minaret and gleaming dome are prominent features of this mosque set within a large compound.

Visitors' Checklist

Road Map B1. *terminal on Jalan Surapati, Jalan Ahmad Yani & at Sangket.* *Jalan Veteran 2, (0361) 25 141.*

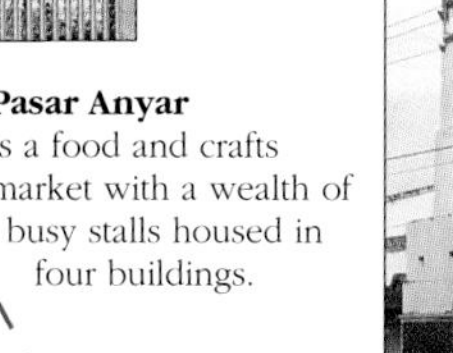

Pasar Anyar is a food and crafts market with a wealth of busy stalls housed in four buildings.

★ **Masjid Nur**
This mosque was built in a style influenced by Indian architecture.

Pabean Harbour
The old harbour attracted settlements of traders from elsewhere in the Indonesian Archipelago; their descendants still live here.

★ **Independence Monument**
The statue commemorates Ketut Merta. During the independence struggle just after World War II, he was shot from a patrol boat as he raised an Indonesian flag in place of the Dutch colours.

Exploring Singaraja

SINGARAJA, NORTH BALI'S main commercial centre, was the administrative capital of Bali in colonial times. Colonial-style architecture remains in streets south of the centre, but buildings erected under the New Order *(see p51)*, such as the Pura Jagat Natha temple, combine monumental scale with traditional style. *Singa* means "lion"; *raja* means "king". The city's identity is expressed in the prominent modern statue of a winged lion where Jalan Veteran meets Jalan Ngurah Rai. The former palace of the kingdom of Buleleng, housing the administrative offices of the regency, was damaged by fire in the brief political disturbances of 1999.

A street scene in Singaraja

Pura Jagat Natha

Jalan Pramuka. *donation.*

Pura Jagat Natha, the territorial Hindu temple of the Buleleng regency, is a large complex of buildings covered in fine stone carvings; its towering *padmasana* shrine *(see p26)* is typical of Balinese temples built from the 1970s on. There are *gamelan* rehearsals in the evenings in one of the courtyards.

Gedong Kertya

Jalan Veteran 20 & 22. *(0362) 22 645.* *Mon–Sat.* *donation.*

Gedong Kertya is a library founded by the Dutch in 1928 for the preservation of Balinese *lontar* manuscripts. These are specially cut palm leaves inscribed with a stylus and rubbed with blacking to make the script legible. The same technique is used to make *prasi*, illustrations of traditional stories. Gedong Kertya, which contains many thousand such manuscripts, is frequented mainly by Balinese in search of their genealogical origins or potent medicinal recipes.

Puri Sinar Nadiputra

Jalan Veteran, next to Gedong Kertya. *Mon–Thu & Sat.*

In a former palace is the Puri Sinar Nadiputra weaving factory, where one can look at the textile-making process, and buy the products. Silk and cotton *ikat* cloth is sold in the adjacent shop.

ENVIRONS: In the village of **Nagasepaha**, 8 km (5 miles) south of Singaraja, glass-painting is practised. Its initiator was a local puppet-master, Jero Dalang Diah. He used to carve the characters for his stories out of buffalo or cow leather before painting them. In 1950, he was inspired by a Japanese glass-painting and from that time he began to paint on glass, using images from Balinese *wayang* stories *(see p30)*. Now, his descendants and several neighbours practise this art-form and sell their works.

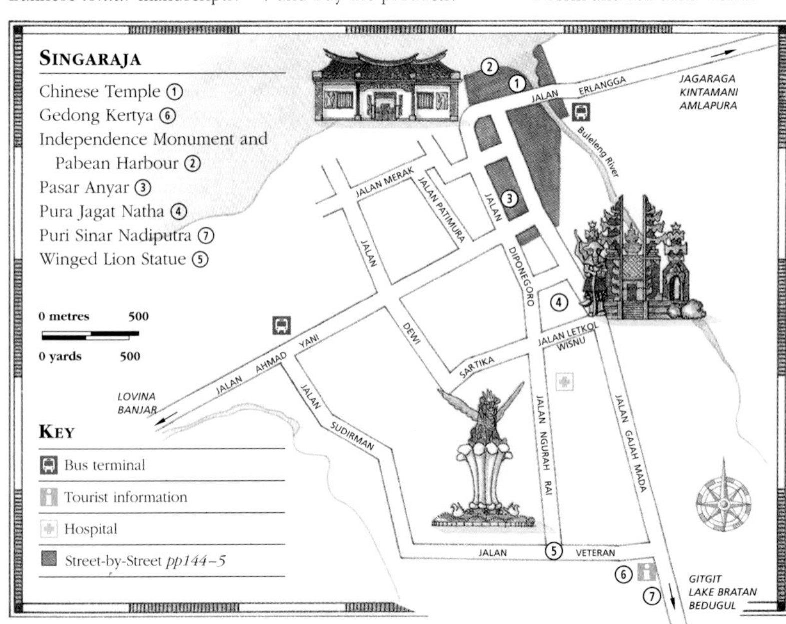

Lovina ㉙

Road Map B1. *Kalibukbuk, (0362) 41 910.*

THE NAME LOVINA means "I love Indonesia", and is often used for a long stretch of the coast encompassing a series of villages, from Tukadmungga in the east to Kaliasem in the west. The beach resort area has quiet, black-sand coves lined with coconut trees. Outriggers add to the nostalgic charm, and dolphins can often be seen in the sea. For snorkellers, there are still pristine coral reefs.

The tourist facilities of Lovina are on Jalan Binaria, which leads to a modern sculpture of dolphins. To the north are ricefields, coconut groves and hotels; to the south, roads lead to small villages with the mountain looming in the background. From the village of Temukus, you can trek to the **Singsing Waterfall**.

Gitgit ㉚

Road Map C1. *from Singaraja & Bedugul.* *Singaraja, (0362) 25 141.* *to waterfall.*

THIS VILLAGE is the location of an impressive waterfall, 45 m (149 ft) high, about 400 m (450 yds) from the main road and surrounded by lush vegetation. Another waterfall, 1 km (half a mile) up the hill, is not quite as high, but there are fewer visitors there.

At Gitgit, Bali's highest waterfall, a refreshing stop for sightseers

Pura Beji, a highly decorated temple in Sangsit, near Jagaraga

ENVIRONS: Pegayaman, 4 km (3 miles) north of Gitgit, maintains some 17th-century Javanese traditions. On the Prophet's birthday *(see p43)*, Muslim villagers parade a *tumpeng* (mountain-shaped offering).

Jagaraga ㉛

Road Map C1. *from Singaraja.* *Singaraja, (0362) 25 141.*

JAGARAGA WAS THE SITE of a battle in 1849, in which the war hero Patih Jelantik held the Dutch to a long stand-off before he was defeated. The relationship between the Balinese and the Dutch is reflected in the lively reliefs of the local temple of the dead, **Pura Dalem**. These were carved in the early decades of the 20th century. The subjects include aircraft, ships and a European in a car being held up by an armed man.

Pura Dalem

Jagaraga. *daily.* *donation.*

ENVIRONS: The central gate of **Pura Beji** in **Sangsit**, 4 km (3 miles) from Jagaraga, is famous for its ornamentation. Garudas (mythical birds) are carved half in the round, half in low relief. The nearby **Pura Dalem** has some grim depictions of the tortures in hell inflicted on those who infringe moral rules.

The country around **Sawan**, 4 km (3 miles) south of Jagaraga, is said to produce some of Bali's best rice. There are impressive river gorges in the area. Sawan is also known for its northern dance and music tradition. **Air Sanih**, 12 km (8 miles) from Sangsit, is a small beach resort named after a spring. There is a pleasant beach restaurant and basic accommodation.

Pura Beji

Sangsit. *daily.*

Relief in the Pura Dalem, Jagaraga, showing a man driving a car

Pura Meduwe Karang ㉜

See pp148–9.

Tejakula ㉝

Road Map D1. *from Singaraja.* *Singaraja, (0362) 25 141.*

THE OLD VILLAGE OF Tejakula is famous for its silver jewellery and its ancient *wayang wong* dance *(see p31)*. This eastern part of the regency of Buleleng is one of the most unspoiled areas of Bali. At Tejakula itself there are some quiet black beaches and idyllic coconut groves.

ENVIRONS: Nearby are several Bali Aga villages *(see p46)*. One of them, **Sembiran** (a short way up the mountain road west of Tejakula), has the characteristic stone-paved roads, some megalithic remains, and good views down to the north coast.

Pura Meduwe Karang ㉜

Frangipani flower

THE LARGE TEMPLE is notable for its statuary and carved panels which can be examined at close quarters. Although not the most extreme example, the temple shows a flowery style of decoration characteristic of North Bali. There are successive split gates and a set of two symmetrical *gedong*, or pavilions. The highest point is the towering, elaborately decorated Betara Luhur Ing Angkasa shrine.

Split Gates
At each level of the temple the ascent to the main shrine passes through a candi bentar *(split gate) decorated with relief carvings.*

★ Ramayana Sculptures
The grand parade of 34 stone figures lined up on the entrance terrace are all characters from the Indian Ramayana *epic.*

Elaborately carved *paduraksa* (stone posts)

The long pavilion at the side of the forecourt is used for gatherings during festival celebrations.

Terraces at different levels are linked by steps.

Entrance

Entrance

STAR FEATURES

- ★ **Ramayana Sculptures**
- ★ **Relief Carvings**
- ★ **Main Shrine**

VISITORS' CHECKLIST

Kubutambahan. **Road Map** C1.
from Singaraja.
8am–5pm daily.
Purnama Sasih Kawulu (Feb).

The Cyclist
On the side of the main shrine is depicted a westerner on a bicycle. He is believed to be the Dutch artist W O J Nieuwenkamp, who came here in 1904.

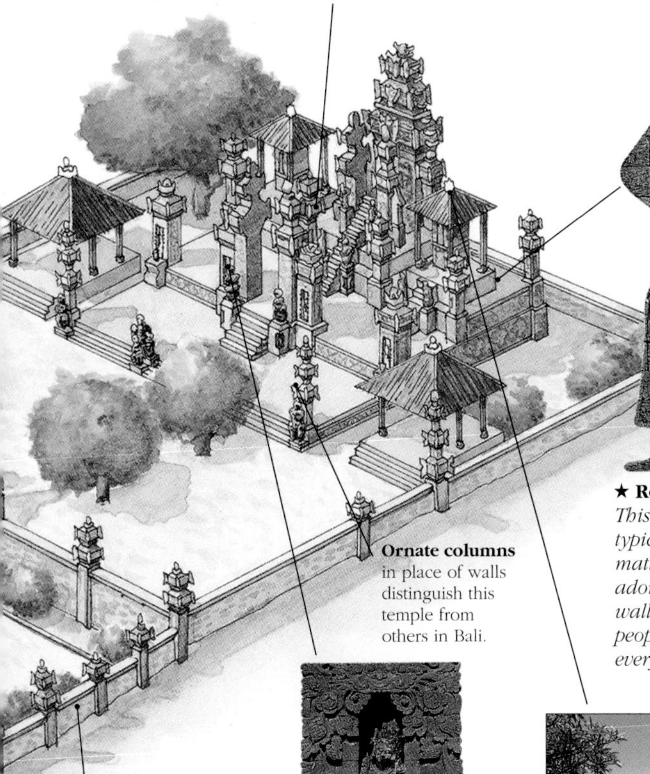

★ Relief Carvings
This local priest is typical of the subject matter of reliefs adorning the courtyard walls, which show people and scenes from everyday life.

Ornate columns in place of walls distinguish this temple from others in Bali.

The walls of the courtyard are reinforced at intervals by pillars topped with carved decorations.

Wall Sculpture
With subjects taken from Balinese legend, these decorate the walls round the central courtyard.

★ Main Shrine
The impressive Betara Luhur Ing Angkasa shrine honours the "Lord possessing the ground". Offerings are also made at the shrine to the sun-god Surya and to Mother Earth for fertility of the agricultural land.

LOMBOK

GLISTENING PADDY FIELDS, *verdant hills, rugged mountains and long stretches of white sandy beach make up the landscape of Lombok. A mix of Muslim Sasaks and Hindu Balinese provides a rich diversity of cultures. In terms of both the local economy and facilities for visitors, Lombok is much less developed than Bali, but easily accessible and rewarding to visit.*

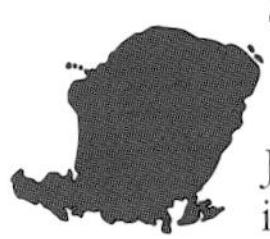

The Sasaks are the indigenous people of Lombok. Numbering about two million, they are thought to be descended from a hilltribe of North India and Myanmar. The minority Balinese population, about 100,000, live mostly near the west coast.

Lombok's identity has been formed by two major influences. Javanese arrivals in the 14th century brought Islam and Middle-Eastern influences, while the Balinese Hindus, who were the colonial masters of the island from the 16th century until the 1890s, have been an important presence.

The Sasaks and the Balinese provide the island with a rich heritage of dialects and languages, traditional dance, music, rituals and crafts. Beautiful pottery is made and cloth woven, using skills passed down through the generations. The influence of Javanese, Hindu and Islamic cultures can be seen in architecture and ceremonies. While Muslim Javanese architectural influences can best be seen in the mosques, the Sasaks provided the distinctive shape of the *lumbung* (rice barn), more rarely seen now than in the past.

Lombok appeals to visitors for its natural beauty more than for its architectural heritage. The island's varied geography provides ideal conditions for trekking, wave- and wind-surfing, diving, snorkelling and game-fishing. A chain of volcanic mountains in the north is dominated by Gunung Rinjani, which offers good trekking country. Sandy beaches punctuated by extinct volcanic peaks and huge cliffs plunging straight into the Indian Ocean make for a spectacular south coast. The east coast is blessed with calm seas, peaceful beaches, sheltered coves and beautiful coral islands.

Sunset over the Lombok Strait seen from Senggigi beach, a resort area on the west coast

◁ **A mosque set in a plantation near Sapit, southeast of Gunung Rinjani**

Exploring Lombok

NOT FAR FROM the ferry terminal at Lembar is Mataram, the provincial capital. From here a road runs from west to east taking in the sights of Narmada, Lingsar, and the hill-station area of Tetebatu. A road to the south coast leads to Kuta, a surfing spot and ideal base for exploring the rugged southern coast, which has many beautiful and remote beaches. Lombok's main resort area is Senggigi beach, north of Mataram. Easily accessible from Senggigi are the Gili Isles, an excellent diving and snorkelling location. North central Lombok is dominated by Gunung Rinjani, a huge volcanic peak surrounded by a national park, with opportunities for trekking in remote areas.

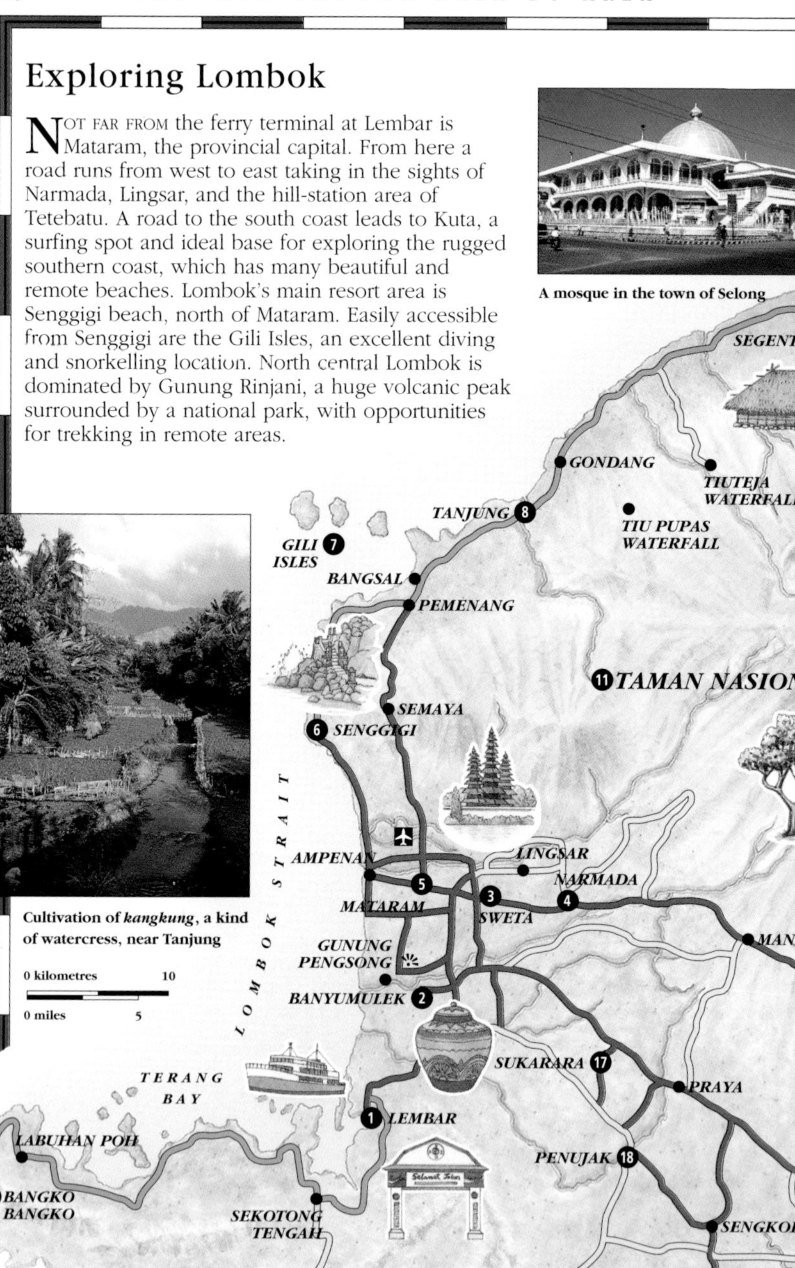

A mosque in the town of Selong

Cultivation of *kangkung*, a kind of watercress, near Tanjung

SEE ALSO

- ***Where to Stay*** p179
- ***Where to Eat*** p191

Getting Around

There are bus and *bemo* services on some main roads in Lombok, particularly the main east-west route from Mataram, and the road to Senggigi. There is little transport elsewhere, even on the road south to Kuta. Independent travellers are strongly recommended to rent their own vehicle, preferably with a driver. Remoter roads can be steep, narrow, or badly surfaced.

The majestic landscape of Taman Nasional Gunung Rinjani

ANYAR
BALI SEA
BAYAN
SENARU
SENDANGGILE WATERFALL
12 SEMBALUN
UNUNG RINJANI
13 SAPIT
14 LABUHAN LOMBOK
TETEBATU 16
AIKMEL
15 PRINGGASELA
LOYOK
MASBAGIK
SELONG
LABUHAN HAJI
ALAS STRAIT
23 TANJUNG LUAR
BATU NAMPAR
TANJUNG RINGGIT

Traditional Sasak dance

Key

- Major road
- Minor road
- Scenic route
- River
- Viewpoint
- Airport

Sights at a Glance

Bangko Bangko 24
Banyumulek 2
Gerupuk 21
Gili Isles 7
Kuta 20
Labuhan Lombok 14
Lembar 1
Mataram p155 5
Narmada 4
Penujak 18
Pringgasela 15
Rembitan and Sade 19
Sapit 13
Segenter 9
Selong Blanak 22
Sembalun 12
Senaru 10
Senggigi 6
Sukarara 17
Sweta 3
Taman Nasional Gunung Rinjani pp158–9 11
Tanjung 8
Tanjung Luar 23
Tetebatu 16

Panoramic view from the hilltop of Gunung Pengsong

Lembar 1

from Padang Bai & Benoa Harbour. ferry terminal.

LOMBOK'S MAIN sea port, in a bay surrounded by hills, is the gateway to the island for passenger car-ferries and a jetfoil from Bali. Crowds of merchants and other travellers mill around Lembar's ferry terminus. Much lively haggling takes place over prices of seats in overloaded buses and vans travelling to other destinations on Lombok. There is a small tourist office, some phones and a few food stalls. At the docks, beautiful Bugis schooners *(see p135)* and small steamers load and unload cargo.

ENVIRONS: The roads around Lembar run through lush, rural scenery. The coast road, skirting the peninsula towards **Sekotong** some 10 km (6 miles) to the south, has good views of the bay and its *bagan*, stationary fishing platforms standing in the sea. Fishermen lower huge nets into which they attract fish with the aid of lanterns. From here skiffs take passengers to the remote coral islands of Gili Gede and Gili Nanggu. Accommodation on the islands is basic, and visitors mostly provide their own entertainment and food.

Banyumulek 2

from Mataram. Mataram, (0370) 634 800.

THIS VILLAGE OF wooden huts with thatched roofs is a centre for the production of handmade terracotta pots. Here, visitors can see how they are made and roam among the displays of pots, some decorated with textiles and rattan. Buyers of pots too large to carry can have them shipped abroad if necessary.

ENVIRONS: About 3 km (2 miles) west of Banyumulek, an easy climb up **Gunung Pengsong** leads to a good view. From the Hindu shrine at the top, Bali's Gunung Agung and Lombok's Gunung Rinjani are visible in opposite directions. On one side the plain of Mataram stretches to the sea and on the other is an arc of rugged mountains.

Sweta 3

Mataram, (0370) 634 800.

ONE OF LOMBOK'S oldest temples, **Pura Lingsar**, is in Sweta. First built in 1714, the large complex has both Balinese Hindu and Sasak Wetu Telu (Muslim) shrines, as well as a pond containing sacred albino eels. At the **Bertais Market**, fruits, vegetables and spices – onions, garlic, bright red chillies in every size imaginable – are displayed in all their colours. One can also bargain for baskets, textiles, bamboo products, and bridles and stirrups.

The bus terminal serving Mataram is at Sweta.

Pura Lingsar
North of Sweta. daily. Perang Topat (Rice Cake War) & Pujawali (Nov–Dec).

Narmada 4

Mataram, (0370) 634 800. daily. Duck Catching Festival (17 Aug).

NARMADA, BUILT IN 1805, was originally a raja's (king's) summer palace. In the gardens is a lake said to represent the crater lake of Gunung Rinjani *(see pp158–9)*. When no longer able to climb the mountain and see the lake, the raja gazed on its likeness. Lotus-filled ponds and terraced gardens recall royal splendours of the past.

Lotus pond in Narmada, a 19th-century royal water palace

LOMBOK'S POTTERY TRADITION

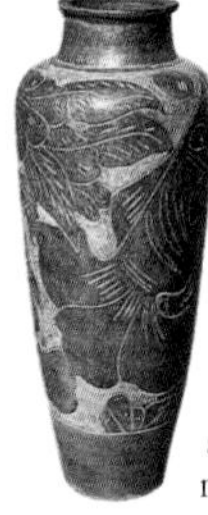
Vase from Penujak

Pottery is the main product of several villages. Traditionally no potter's wheel is used. Some pots are formed by hand using tools known as "stone and paddle", others are built up by coiling lengths of clay. Water decanters, decorated plates and saucers, vases, huge water containers and lamps are all created by hand. Banyumulek's pots are simple in design and devoid of embellishments; Masbagik specializes in distinctive geometric patterns; and Penujak *(see p161)* produces pots decorated with animal motifs.

Mataram 5

MATARAM, AMPENAN AND CAKRANEGARA run together without a break; the whole conurbation is commonly known as Mataram. Mataram proper is the capital of the Indonesian province of West Nusa Tenggara. Its large, white-washed, high-roofed houses hark back to Dutch colonial days. Ampenan, to the west, was once Lombok's main port and a vital link in the spice trade. Cakranegara, to the east, was the royal capital until a century ago; today, it is a bustling commercial centre.

City tourism logo

Visitors' Checklist

Selaparang Airport. Sweta. Department of Tourism, Art & Culture, Jalan Singosari 2, Mataram, (0370) 634 800. Peresean (stick fight) (Aug).

Exploring Mataram

Mataram is characterized by its parks and wide, tree-lined streets with buildings which echo traditional Sasak styles. There are several monuments, such as the Kencana Warga Mahardika, a tribute to outstanding citizenship.

Along the winding streets of Ampenan are homes and businesses of Arab and Chinese merchants. Some of the buildings, now turned into attractive restaurants and cafés, show an Art Deco influence. At sunset, visitors head down to the bustling beach and have a drink in the old colonial bank building.

At the **Lombok Pottery Centre** *(see pp194–5)*, pottery and other handicrafts are sold.

Museum Negeri

Jalan Panji Tilar Negara 6. *(0370) 637 503. Tue–Sun. Mon and public hols.*

The provincial state museum displays local textiles and ceramics, copperwork and woodcarvings, as well as artefacts relating to the history and geography of the islands of West Nusa Tenggara and paintings representing the variety of ethnic cultures.

Mayura Water Palace

Jalan Selaparang, Cakranegara. *(0370) 624 442. daily.*

This complex was built in 1844 under the Balinese Karangasem dynasty. The centrepiece is a lake, surrounded by a park dotted with shrines and fountains.

Pura Meru

Jalan Selaparang, Cakranegara. *daily.*

With its three slender, multi-tiered shrines representing the Hindu Trimurti of Vishnu, Shiva and Brahma, this is Lombok's largest Hindu temple complex.

Pura Meru seen from the Mayura Water Palace

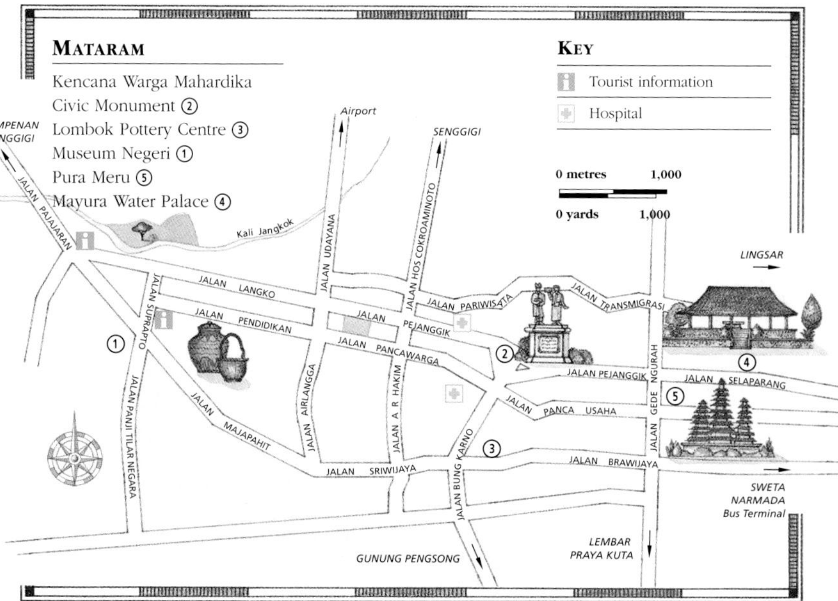

The beach resort area in Senggigi, a major tourist centre of Lombok

Senggigi ❻

from Lembar & Mataram. *Mataram, (0370) 640 691.* *Cultural Appreciation Month (Aug).*

SENGGIGI is the most popular resort in Lombok, attracting visitors with its white sandy beaches and small palm-fringed bays. Although very much less developed than Kuta in Bali, Senggigi has a broad range of accommodation, restaurants and entertainment facilities.

Although Senggigi Beach is strictly speaking two glistening bays, separated by a thrust of white coral jutting out into the ocean, the area now known as Senggigi is a 6-km (4-mile) strip of road and beachfront. Restaurants and small cafés line the colourful main beach road.

The views up and down the coast, and out across the sea to Bali, which can be enjoyed by driving along the coastal road, are majestic. Swimming off the beach is safe; and waves suitable for younger, less experienced wave-riders peel to the left and right off the reef. Many people also enjoy windsurfing here.

Around the reef itself is a variety of marine life and beautiful coral. This is a good spot for relaxed snorkelling.

ENVIRONS: An atmospheric temple shrine stands on a black outcrop of rock reaching out into the sea at **Batu Bolong**, 3 km (2 miles) from central Senggigi. Here, Hindu devotees make their offerings at dusk. The crimson sunsets are beautiful, with the silhouette of Bali's Gunung Agung faintly visible in the distance.

Gili Isles ❼

from Senggigi & Mataram to Bangsal. *from Bangsal.* *Mataram, (0370) 640 691.*

THESE THREE ISLANDS, each no more than 2–3 km (1–2 miles) across, are visited primarily because of the diversity and abundance of colourful marine life in the coral reefs and crystal clear waters around them. They are all accessible from Bangsal by a short boat trip. The best time for diving here is late April to late August.

Gili Air ("ai-year"), closest to the mainland and with the largest resident population, is quiet around the secluded hotels, but elsewhere on the island the local village life is quite lively. A few bars are mixed in with the tropical trees and shrubs, and lodging tends towards the upper end of the range. This is a good place for families.

Gili Meno, which offers a real sense of escape, is the smallest and least developed of the islands. It has fewer accommodation options, but the places to stay are mostly more up-market than those on the other two islands.

Gili Trawangan, the largest and furthest from the mainland, is the party island. A foreshore strip of bars and restaurants tucked in among many simple *losmen* *(see p166)* churn out music till the early hours. The other side of the island is quieter. Except for a few very up-market hotels, prices here are low, a fact reflected in the limited range of creature comforts on offer.

MARINE LIFE IN THE GILI ISLES

Divers *(see pp210–11)* who want to see sharks can generally do so within a day's diving off the Gili Isles. Reef sharks, which have no interest in humans, are often encountered. The coral is fine, despite damage caused by fish-bombing in past years. Over 3,500 species of marine life survive around the Gilis, compared with 1,500 off the Great Barrier Reef. In these waters can be seen the orange-and-white striped clown fish, the brightly coloured parrot fish and the majestic moorish idol. There are two endangered turtle species, the green turtle and the hawksbill, living in these waters. Divers at all levels of ability will find a rich variety of reef fish and other underwater life.

Brightly coloured coral in the waters off the Gili Isles

A drum known as a *kecimol*, at a Muslim wedding in Tanjung

Tanjung 8

from Mataram. Mataram, (0370) 640 691.

TANJUNG'S LIVELIHOOD is based on fishing as well as the agricultural products of the countryside. It is a large village on the road north to the Gunung Rinjani foothills, with a twice-weekly cattle market. It is surrounded by lush country in which coconut groves alternate with ricefields and vegetable gardens. In the river shallows grows *kangkung* (a leafy vegetable rather like watercress), one of Lombok's favourite dishes.

ENVIRONS: The road north runs along the black-sand beach and the terrain becomes distinctly arid. Four km (2 miles) from Tanjung on the coast is **Krakas**, famous for fresh, cool spring water. The spring is located under water 400 m (1,320 ft) offshore at a depth of about 10 m (33 ft). Local fishermen, who will take visitors out in their boats for a small fee, collect the water, which is drinkable. Further north, just past the small town of Gondang, are the **Tiu Pupas** waterfall and seven caves.

Segenter 9

from Mataram. Mataram, (0370) 640 691. 9am–5pm daily. donation.

THE SMALL SETTLEMENT of Segenter is a typical, traditional Lombok community, a good place to wander, and see the people going about their daily lives. The inhabitants are less pushy and commercially minded than those around Senggigi.

In the late morning, many villagers can be seen resting in the "guest huts", open structures with platforms raised above ground level, set between rows of the larger thatched houses which make up the village as a whole.

The people of Segenter lead an almost self-sufficient life; they produce most of the staple food necessary for their daily needs and plant cotton, rice and tobacco to sell at the market.

A house in Segenter, constructed from parts of the coconut palm

Senaru 10

from Sweta & Tanjung. Mataram, (0370) 640 691.

AT A HEIGHT of over 400 m (1,320 ft) on the lower slopes of Gunung Rinjani, Senaru is braced by cool refreshing air. From here one will be rewarded with perfect views of Rinjani to the south and the ocean to the west.

Once a secluded mountain settlement sheltered from the outside world, this village with its traditional-style houses is fast becoming a weekend escape from the heat of the coastal regions.

Senaru has many simple guesthouses and restaurants. It is the most popular departure point for treks and climbs up the mountain *(see pp158–9)*. Arrangements for a trek through the Gunung Rinjani national park and up the volcano can be made: camping equipment, tent and sleeping-bag rental are available, and food and other necessities can be bought. Porters and guides can be engaged here.

ENVIRONS: An easy 30-minute walk to the west of Senaru leads to the dramatic 40-m- (132-ft-) high **Sendanggile Waterfalls**, where water comes straight off one of the highest peaks in Southeast Asia. Here is the chance to wade in what must be the cleanest and freshest water in Indonesia. A little further uphill is the **Tiu Kelep** waterfall, with a lovely pool perfect for swimming.

Another short 30-minute walk from the village centre is **Payan**, with thatched huts and a megalithic appearance: this is one of Lombok's few remaining Wetu Telu villages *(see p23)*. Although somewhat commercialized, it is an example of Lombok's aboriginal village traditions. The women wear traditional sarongs and black shirts for weaving and during Muslim ceremonies. The Muslim practices observed here contain both Balinese and Hindu elements.

The Sendanggile Waterfalls near Senaru

Taman Nasional Gunung Rinjani ⓫

THIS NATIONAL PARK is a magnet for experienced trekkers, and for nature lovers. Gunung Rinjani is a volcano 3,726 m (12,224 ft) high, important in the religions and folklore of both the Hindus and the Sasaks of Lombok. Rinjani itself is not active; the smaller Gunung Baru has erupted several times over the last 100 years. In 1995, the skies rained ash, tremors shook the island, and activities in the National Park were halted. There have been no such problems since. The tourist information office at Mataram can advise on current conditions. Climbs to the caldera rim and to the summit, which are quite challenging, can be arranged in Mataram, Senggigi or Senaru. Sembalun Lawang is another starting point, but there are fewer facilities here.

The ebony leaf-monkey, frequently seen in Lombok

Trekking from Senaru
Climbs can be arranged with many operators working out of local homestays.

BATU KOQ & BAYAN
Batu Koq
Senaru
Sendanggile Waterfall
Base Camp
GUNUNG SENKEREANG JAYA
2,902 m (9,550 ft)
Campsite
Tiuteja Waterfall
Hot Spri
Campsite
GUNUNG PLAWANGAN
2,612 m (8 600 ft)
GUNUN
2,35 (7,75
GUNUNG TANAKLAYUR
2,664 m (8,800 ft)
GUNUNG BUANMANGGE
1,916 m (6,300 ft)
BUKIT KETIMUNAN
1,602 m (5,200 ft)

0 kilometres 5
0 miles 3

★ Danau Segara Anak
The blue-green waters of this lake are surrounded by the steep walls of the volcanic crater. Trails lead down to the small, active volcano of Gunung Baru within the caldera.

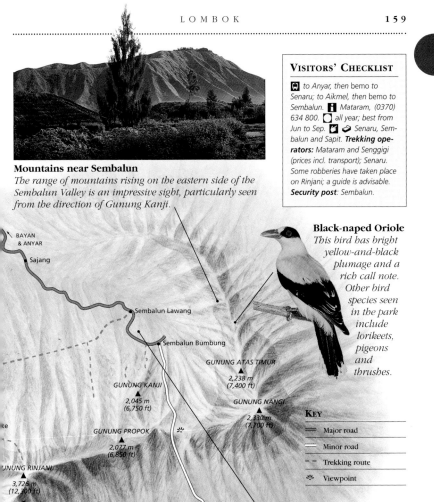

Mountains near Sembalun
The range of mountains rising on the eastern side of the Sembalun Valley is an impressive sight, particularly seen from the direction of Gunung Kanji.

Visitors' Checklist

to Anyar, then bemo to Senaru; to Aikmel, then bemo to Sembalun. *Mataram, (0370) 634 800.* *all year; best from Jun to Sep.* *Senaru, Sembalun and Sapit.* ***Trekking operators:*** *Mataram and Senggigi (prices incl. transport); Senaru. Some robberies have taken place on Rinjani; a guide is advisable.* ***Security post***: *Sembalun.*

Black-naped Oriole
This bird has bright yellow-and-black plumage and a rich call note. Other bird species seen in the park include lorikeets, pigeons and thrushes.

BAYAN & ANYAR
Sajang
Sembalun Lawang
Sembalun Bumbung
GUNUNG ATAS TIMUR 2,238 m (7,400 ft)
GUNUNG KANJI 2,045 m (6,750 ft)
GUNUNG NANGI 2,330 m (7,700 ft)
GUNUNG PROPOK 2,077 m (6,850 ft)
te
UNUNG RINJANI 3,726 m (12,300 ft)
Sapit
AIKMEL & LABUHAN LOMBOK

Key
Major road
Minor road
Trekking route
Viewpoint

Sembalun Valley
Sweeping views of plantations and small villages nestling in the valley can be seen from the mountain pass, 2,000 m (6,600 ft) high, on the road south to Sapit.

★ View from Gunung Rinjani
From the highest point on Lombok, the view stretches beyond the dry volcanic slopes to the coastal plains.

Star Sights

★ Danau Segara Anak

★ View from Gunung Rinjani

Gunung Rinjani towering over plantations near Sapit

Sembalun ⓬

from Mataram & Tanjung. Mataram, (0370) 634 800.

Lying in a valley surrounded by mountains is Sembalun, a village consisting of single-storey wooden buildings. Visitors are few here, and there are only a couple of basic places to stay. However, there is a pleasant sense of remoteness. The air is fresh, and can be quite cold at night. This is a good place for walks in the countryside. The growing of shallots is a major source of income here, and a pungent, but not unpleasant, scent greets the visitor on reaching the valley.

From here the view of Gunung Rinjani is very vivid. The mountain seems to be almost within an arm's reach. Sembalun is the starting point of a Rinjani climb route more direct than that from Senaru *(see pp158–9)*, but the facilities here are not as good.

Environs: The road east to Sapit runs across one of the highest mountain passes in Indonesia. The hairpins and gradients give good views over the Sembalun Valley.

Sapit ⓭

from Sweta. Mataram, (0370) 634 800.

Sapit is situated on the eastern slopes of Gunung Rinjani at about 800 m (2,640 ft) above sea level. It is a refreshingly cool mountain resort commanding views of eastern Lombok, and of Sumbawa across the sea beyond. Blanketing Rinjani's lower slopes around Sapit are emerald-green rice terraces and tobacco plantations.

The village is basic, but gardens and flower-beds make a fresh, orderly impression. There are some inexpensive but clean guest-houses here.

Vessels at a jetty at Labuhan Lombok

Labuhan Lombok ⓮

from Mataram. from Mataram and Sumbawa. in ferry terminal.

The bay around Labuhan Lombok forms a natural harbour. A road runs parallel with the shore, and between it and the waterside are the settlements of Bugis fishermen consisting of houses on stilts. Colourfully painted trawlers are moored nearby. The forebears of this community came from South Sulawesi *(see p135)*. The town's Sunday market sells all

House on stilts in the coastal village of Labuhan Lombok

manner of produce and daily needs. At one end of the bay, 2 km (1 mile) from the town, is the ferry jetty for services running east of Lombok to Sumbawa, the next island in the Lesser Sundas group.

Pringgasela ⓯

from Sweta & Labuhan Lombok. *Mataram, (0370) 634 800.*

IN THE COOL, quiet foothills of Gunung Rinjani is the shady village of Pringgasela. A mountain stream runs through it beside the road. Many villagers here are weavers, and they are happy for visitors to watch them at work. By tradition, girls in the village learn to weave from around the age of ten. Outside many of the houses textiles are displayed for sale, and the overall impression is colourful. The patterns and colours, with blacks and reds predominant, are characteristic of Lombok.

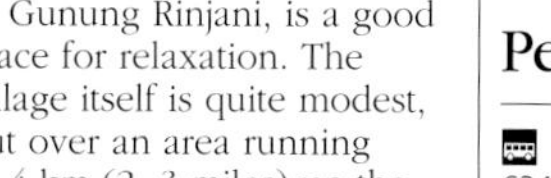

Basket produced in Loyok

ENVIRONS: In the hills south of Pringgasela is another craft centre, **Loyok**, the premier basketware, bamboo and palm-leaf handicraft village in Lombok. The road downhill from Loyok runs parallel to a fast-flowing stream that weaves through a series of beautiful forests and valleys.

Tetebatu ⓰

from Mataram. *Mataram, (0370) 634 800.*

THE HILL-STATION village Tetebatu, with its views of Gunung Rinjani, is a good place for relaxation. The village itself is quite modest, but over an area running 3–4 km (2–3 miles) up the mountain slope there are a number of guesthouses, set among ricefields.

Pleasant walks are to be had in the mountain air, passing large-leaved tobacco plantations. One hike runs to a small river into which flows the Jeruk Manis waterfall – the route is quite strenuous but can be tackled by fit children over ten, as well as adults. Other walks lead to isolated villages and a tropical forest inhabited by monkeys. It is advisable to engage one of the guides who offer their services in the village.

Sukarara ⓱

from Sweta. *Mataram, (0370) 634 800.*

MANY PEOPLE in Sukarara earn their living by weaving *songket* textiles *(see p37)*. The tourist trade is rather evident here. Large numbers of shops display and sell many varieties of cloth from around the region. Village women dressed in black will demonstrate their expertise with the loom and are willing to pose for photographs.

Penujak ⓲

from Sweta. *Mataram, (0370) 634 800.*

ALONG WITH Banyumulek *(see p154)* and Masbagik, Penujak is one of Lombok's main pottery-producing villages, and perhaps the best place to see the process, which the villagers will explain. Traditionally, women made the pots by hand while the men marketed them. Now that export sales have led to increased output, men join in the production process. Each village produces its own distinct pottery decoration and colour, but all the designs are available in all three places.

Traditional earthenware pottery produced in Penujak

TEXTILES IN LOMBOK

A weaver at work on a hand-operated loom in Sukarara

Hand-woven textiles, of very high quality, are produced in Lombok using traditional backstrap looms. The villages which specialize in textile-weaving are Sukarara, Pringgasela, Rembitan and Sade *(see p162)*. There is some larger-scale production around Mataram. In the villages, the entire process of cloth-making can be watched by visitors, from the boiling of barks and roots to make dyes, and the soaking of cotton threads, to the weaving of original patterns on the hand-operated loom. The villagers use only natural plants for the dyes. Yellow dye, for example, is made from an extract of turmeric root, while blue comes from the indigo plant. Roots and bark are pounded and boiled; the cotton threads are immersed for 24 hours, and, when dry, are arranged on the loom in the manner demanded by the pattern of the textile.

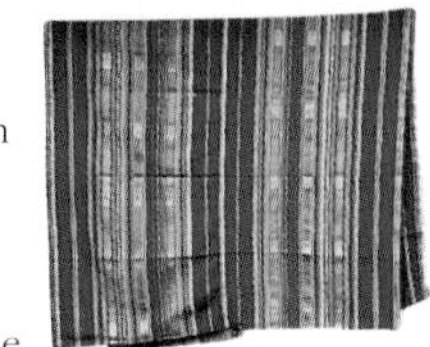

Typical Lombok sarong

Rembitan and Sade ⓳

Mataram, (0370) 634 800. donation.

The farming villages of Rembitan and Sade, about 3 km (2 miles) apart from one another, are both attractively set against the hillside. Despite the fact that many visitors stop here, and therefore sellers of souvenirs abound, Rembitan and Sade remain good places to catch a glimpse of traditional Sasak life, in which weaving textiles, growing rice and rearing goats and cattle are major occupations. A distinctive feature is the *lumbung*, a bonnet-shaped rice barn. Once a symbol of Lombok, these barns are now rare. The walls of the thatch-roofed barns and houses are made of bamboo or palm-leaf ribs.

Kuta ⓴

from Sweta. Mataram, (0370) 634 800. Nyale fishing festival (Feb–Mar).

Lombok's Kuta is mostly undeveloped, in complete contrast to its namesake in Bali. The coastline around it is ruggedly beautiful. Kuta bay has dazzling white sand, and few people. The ocean swells form perfect waves for the surfers who come here.

The village of Kuta consists of a scattered collection of wooden buildings which provide homes for the fishing community and also some visitor accommodation.

A landmark to the east of the village is the Novotel Lombok resort *(see p179)*, which has been designed to fit in with the building style typical of this part of Lombok.

Kuta's rugged coastline, a paradise for surfers and sun-lovers

Environs: There are two other superb beaches not far from Kuta. **Mawun** beach is 8 km (5 miles) west, and attractively isolated. The same distance to the east is **Tanjung Aan**, a wide, sandy bay. Waves crash on rocky outcrops at each end of the bay, but the water on the beach itself is smooth and turquoise.

Gerupuk ㉑

Mataram, (0370) 634 800.

The village of Gerupuk is situated on the edge of a long bay. The village's main income, apart from fishing, comes from seaweed cultivation. The seaweed, used as an ingredient in food products for farm animals, grows on semi-submerged bamboo frames in the waters off the beach. After being harvested it can be seen drying in neat bundles along the roadside.

Gerupuk is home to one of south Lombok's most popular surf breaks. In the bay, swells from the Indian Ocean build up and break on coral reefs, creating fine waves. Surfers hire a small skiff for the short trip to the break; the journey gives breathtaking views of the nearby cliffs and rocky crags. The skiffs anchor a short distance from the break and await the surfers' return.

The waves here are considered more user-friendly and forgiving than others on this coast, where the sea can often be rough. They break on coral deep enough not to cause undue worry to board riders, unlike the shallow breaks and steep take-off points of Maui near Selong Blanak to the west. While the waves mostly break right, left breaks also peel off, although less regularly. The surf is best early in the morning before any wind gets up – usually before 9am; but even later in the day when crosswinds blow offshore, the waves are fine. The surfers are mostly Japanese, Australians and locals from Kuta village itself; there is a smattering of Brazilians and French. They generally find accommodation at Kuta Beach.

The waves at Gerupuk, one of the best surfing spots on Lombok's coast

Selong Blanak ㉒

Mataram, (0370) 634 800.

MARKED AT EACH end by rocky promontories, Selong Blanak is a tranquil bay with a fishing settlement. Lined up on the beach are multi-coloured outrigger canoes. Most people come here to surf at a nearby beach known as **Maui**. The waves are exceptionally fast. Because of the steep take-offs and the fact that the waves are ridden over very shallow coral, this is a place for very experienced surfers only.

Coastal landscape near Selong Blanak

Tanjung Luar ㉓

Mataram, (0370) 634 800.

THE VILLAGE OF Tanjung Luar earns its living from the sea. It is a minor port – travellers from nearby islands land here by means of an inter-island taxi service which uses small outriggers. Many occupations to do with fishing and the sea are represented here. There is a busy fish market. Fishermen return to port after spending several days afloat, and sell their catch beside the water's edge. It is possible to watch huge sharks being brought to shore. Contributing to the lively atmosphere are the salt-sellers, the children fishing off the main jetty, and the people giving their boats a new coat of paint.

Buggy at Tanjung Luar

A short walk from the fish market, lining the beach-front, live some Bugis communities *(see p135)*, their wooden houses raised on stilts. Colourful Bugis schooners, with their distinctive high prows, lie at anchor here.

For many people in Tanjung Luar, *cidomo* are the only form of transport. These are small horse-drawn buggies, brightly painted and often decorated with bright red pompoms and tassels.

Bangko Bangko ㉔

from Lembar. *Mataram, (0370) 634 800.*

A POPULAR place for fishing and surfing, Bangko Bangko lies at the end of a peninsula at the south-west extremity of Lombok. A location rather than a village, it can be reached only along a dirt road. The reward for this trip off the beaten track is some spectacular scenery.

Some surfers have named the area Desert Point. The waves that peel to the left off a coral shelf, before slamming into the base of the cliff-face, provide great conditions for experienced riders. The unpredictable, often dangerous seas are good for game fishing. A fishing trip can be booked through tour-operators in Lembar *(see p154)*.

Harbour scene at Tanjung Luar, with Bugis houses raised on stilts

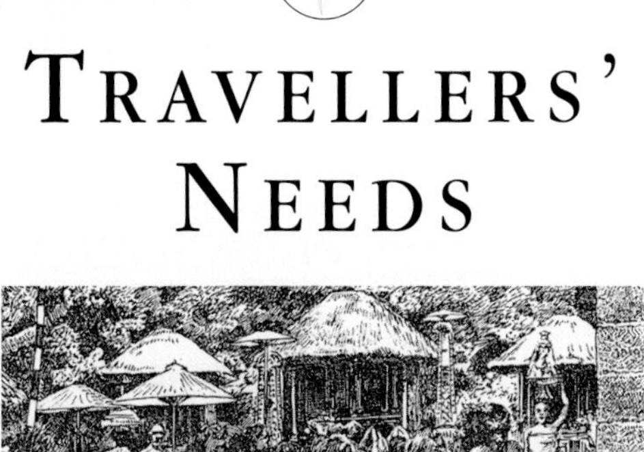

Travellers' Needs

Where to Stay

Set among tropical gardens and gently swaying palm trees, even the largest of Bali's hotels have a Balinese flavour. This is reinforced by the staff and the island's cultural ambience. The range of accommodation has expanded with the emergence of a category of intimate, exclusive hotels known as "boutique hotels", in addition to the resorts that now dot the island. For groups, villas can offer more sense of privacy than hotels. Lombok is less developed than Bali, but offers a good variety of accommodation. There is little provision specifically for the disabled in the hotels of either Bali or Lombok.

Hotel porter

Losmen and Homestays

The most common type of low-budget accommodation in Bali is the *losmen*. The term is derived from the colonial-era word *"logement"* – and once implied little more than a room in a Balinese household. Today the name is applied to a category of small, inexpensive lodgings, in many places the only accommodation available. *Losmen* and true homestays are not formally organized, and are usually not included in hotel listings. You usually cannot reserve, and so you must find a place to stay on reaching your destination.

Losmen generally consist of simple rooms built around a central area. Mosquito nets, a fan, and sometimes a bathroom are provided, but rarely toilet paper. Some *losmen* offer air-conditioning and hot water, but charge more. Breakfast is almost always included. Large numbers of *losmen* are to be found in Kuta (Poppies Lane II), Central Ubud (Jalan Bisma and Jalan Kajeng), the village of Lembongan on Nusa Lembongan and Candi Dasa (the main street); and near the beaches at Lovina, Padang Bai and Amed.

Pool facilities in a resort at Senggigi Beach, Lombok

Hotels and Resorts

Bali's many resorts and hotels tend to be concentrated in the more developed tourist areas of South and Central Bali. They span a broad price range, and in many cases good package deals can be booked in your home country. The choice of hotels and resorts in Lombok is much more limited than in Bali. They are concentrated in the west, around Senggigi and on the Gili Isles.

The dramatically increasing number of resorts in Bali and the growing popularity of boutique hotels and villa vacations are incentives for hotels and resorts to offer good value for money, so it is worth shopping around for the best deal. The large resorts are particularly suitable for families with young children or visitors looking for a complete, all-inclusive holiday. They offer a luxurious experience insulated from the hustle and bustle of the islands' daily life, and usually provide baby-sitting services, or in-house programmes for children.

Nusa Dua, on Bali's southern tip, was conceived as a comprehensive 5-star resort area with a full infrastructure including a magnificent golf course and a large shopping mall *(see p73)*. White sand beaches add to the allure of Nusa Dua, and many visitors find they have no reason to venture further afield.

Elsewhere on the island, large, self-contained resorts offer both privacy and social opportunities. Many of them have been designed and are managed by major operators in the hospitality industry. They offer world-class service and facilities such as tennis courts and gyms, spas, pools, beautiful gardens, first-class restaurants and nightly cultural performances.

Prices vary according to room, region and season. Most hotel rooms will be equipped with fans and bathrooms. However, expect to pay more for hotel rooms with air-conditioning.

The Bali branch of the **PHRI** (Persatuan Hotel dan Restaurant Indonesia, or Indonesian Hotel and Restaurant Association – *see p169)* publishes hotel listings and a star rating, but they

Simple *losmen* accommodation in Lombok

Furnished in Balinese style, a villa with private pool and courtyard

tend to be neither complete nor up-to-date. In theory the association should help with problems, but it is usually more effective to submit any complaints direct to the hotels themselves.

Speciality Hotels and Resorts

Some hotels and resorts cater to visitors interested in certain types of activity, food or cultural experience. For example, those situated on mountains will generally offer trekking. A number of small homestays in Kintamani, and those close to Gunung Agung, offer trekking to the volcanoes.

For snorkelling and diving, excellent choices are the resorts around Amed and Tulamben on the east coast, those on the island of Nusa Lembongan, the North Bali resorts (from which trips can be made to the underwater gardens of Taman Nasional Bali Barat), and those on Gili Trawangan (accessible from Lombok). Cooking courses are offered by several resorts.

For visitors interested in spiritually orientated holidays, Ubud is a popular centre. Some hotels in Ubud and elsewhere offer the opportunity to become involved in local village life, and visitors can try their hand at cooking, weaving, and other local crafts.

Private Villas

For people travelling with children, villas can be a good choice, as they are generally fully staffed with cleaners, babysitters, gardeners and often a cook. They will feature a pool and gardens, satellite television and several bedrooms. For families or groups of friends, they can offer great savings and give opportunities for private relaxation and entertainment that a hotel cannot match. Pool parties, cocktail parties and barbecues can all be a part of a villa holiday.

Some Bali-based agents offer a selection of villas and will work to find something to suit your budget, personal needs and number of guests. The largest operators are **Bali Tropical Villas**, **House of Bali** and **In Touch**.

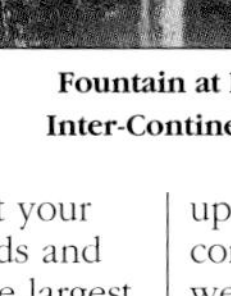

Fountain at Bali Inter-Continental

Travelling with Children

Bali is a wonderland for the young. The Balinese have a particular fondness for children, and hotel staff will take an interest in them. All the large 5-star resorts and many of the smaller ones have good facilities for children, so that parents can sit back and relax. Some of the facilities on offer are babysitting services, organized children's activities, children's clubs and family suites.

Reservations

The internet is a good means of booking direct or investigating a hotel or resort before making a decision. Bypassing the travel agency can mean good discounts, but you may find you have no recourse if all is not as promised.

Many resorts have their own websites, and Bali-based agents have also set up similar services for hotels, private villas and tours. A number of websites are given in the Directory *(see p169)*. Keying in "+accommodation bali" on a search engine will bring up more sites. You can compare prices given on the websites with those quoted by a travel agent, and in some cases even go on a virtual tour of the resorts.

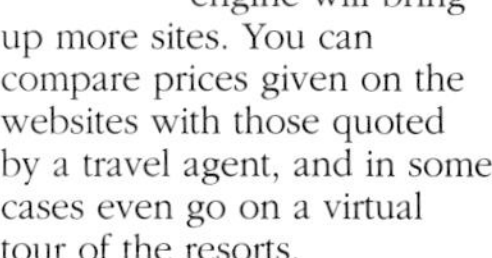

Sheraton Nusa Indah, a large resort with full family facilities at Nusa Dua

Spas and Spa Resorts

Aromatic flowers

Of all the facilities offered to visitors by Bali hotels, the one which has gained most in prominence recently is the spa. Traditional health and beauty treatments derived from local, natural ingredients have been used in Indonesia for many centuries, but it is only in recent years that they have been made widely available to visitors. Some of Bali's top spas have been rated as among the best in the world. Although the smaller salons cannot match the luxury of the most expensive places, some of them offer a range of similar treatments at a fraction of the cost.

Spa and massage room at the Four Seasons Resort, Sayan

Traditional Treatments

Bali's spas aim to provide pleasure and relaxation rather than clinical therapy. They are intended not to treat health problems, but rather to calm the mind and beautify the body. Many of the spas have been designed with couples in mind; with the exception of the local beauty parlours, they offer treatments for both men and women.

A complete treatment will include a full body exfoliation called the *lulur*, an aromatic beauty therapy that has been popular for generations with the Javanese. Other enjoyable experiences include the traditional Balinese massage, a gentle process characterized by long, sweeping hand movements; and the relaxing and therapeutic cream bath, which includes an hour-long head-and-shoulder massage and a natural hair treatment. These are popular with both men and women.

Western influence has made itself felt, particularly through the addition of aromatherapy. Indonesia has an abundance of natural herbs and flowers, and an industry has grown up dedicated to creating high-quality natural oils. Even during a simple massage you will be offered a choice of oils designed to create a variety of moods.

Choosing a Spa

There is an extensive range of spas in Bali. They cater for a wide variety of budgets and preferences. It is worth shopping around. Most spa resorts offer combination packages – these are particularly suitable for first-time visitors, who would like to sample the range of treatments available.

The **Four Seasons Resort** in Jimbaran has a multi-million-dollar spa facility that has won many international awards. A full menu of local and Western treatments is available in its private rooms, many of which have outdoor areas bursting with tropical colour. One of its specialities is a massage in which water is sprinkled from above, simulating a calming, warm rainshower. Another is a *jamu* (natural remedies) bar where local herbal recipes are prepared. Natural ingredients from the sea are featured in most of the treatments.

The **Nusa Dua Spa**, at the Nusa Dua Beach Hotel, was one of the first spas to be established on Bali. It is still one of the biggest. Simple beauty treatments and massages are offered in private rooms, and residents at the hotel who want the full package may enjoy treatments in their villas. Eastern and Western treatments are

Javanese Lulur Treatment

The *lulur* treatment is a traditional beauty ritual which originated in the royal palaces of Central Java. It is the most popular therapy among the many offered by Balinese spas. It usually lasts two-and-a-half hours. A yellow paste is made from a fragrant blend of powdered turmeric, herbs, nuts, grains and other ingredients: this is first spread over the body and then rubbed off to remove dead skin. The skin is then moisturized with splashes of cool yoghurt. This stage is followed by a shower and a scented bath before a long, slow, relaxing massage is performed. There are a number of variations to this treatment, with ingredients ranging from coffee to ginger and spices.

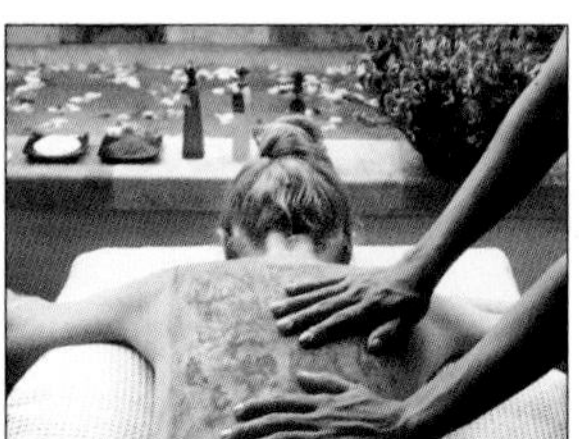

The Javanese *lulur* treatment – a rejuvenating treat for the skin

available, with one of the best ranges of spa products.

Thalasso, located at the Grand Mirage Resort, is a French treatment centre. Natural sea water is used in many of its therapies.

A particular attraction of the small spa at **Tjampuhan Hotel and Spa** is its unusual setting. It is carved out of a cave beside the river that runs through Ubud. Stone features and other artistic touches add to the ambience. Quite different in style, the spa at the luxurious **Four Seasons Resort** in Sayan is modern and air-conditioned. The **Bali Hyatt** in Sanur has a beautiful new outdoor facility in a setting constructed of stone. A full range of traditional Balinese treatments is available here. Also recommended is the **Bali Inter-Continental Resort** in Jimbaran. Treatment pools are among the facilities here. Eastern and Western massage techniques and spa products are offered in beautifully appointed private rooms.

Bodyworks in Seminyak is a small, privately run spa with comfortable rooms and a full range of treatments, ranging from hair colouring to manicures, pedicures and facials. Bodyworks has another salon, larger and more luxurious, in Peti Tenget.

Mandara Spas has taken over the management of some of the best spas on Bali and Lombok, mostly within hotels and resorts. Their signature treatment is performed by two masseuses who work harmoniously together. A full range of scrubs and aromatherapy oils is available, and many of the rooms are specially designed for couples. Some Mandara locations are: **Hotel Padma**, **Novotel Lombok**, **The Alila** and **The Legian**.

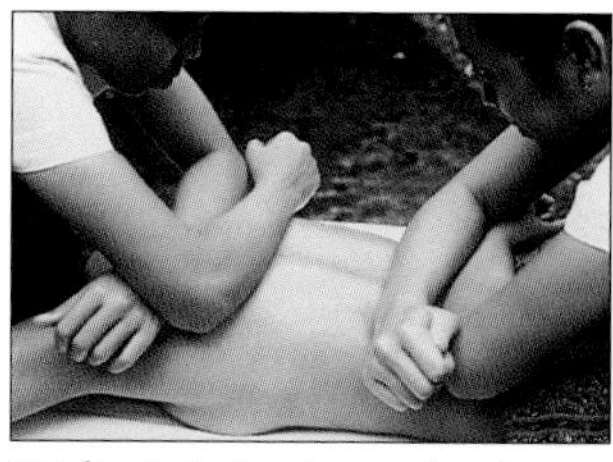

Mandara Spa's signature treatment performed by two therapists

Nur Salon was one of the first salons to operate in Ubud; it is still traditional in style and very inexpensive. **Bali Hati** boasts pristine massage rooms with a steam room and outdoor jacuzzi. Prices are quite reasonable, and profits go towards charitable works in Bali.

DIRECTORY

GENERAL INFORMATION

PHRI (Bali branch)
Villa Rumah Manis, Jalan Nakula, Seminyak.
(0361) 730 606.

YOGA

Bali Spirit
Jalan Hanoman 44, Padang Tegal, Ubud.
(0361) 973361.
W www.balispirit.com

Prana Spa
The Villas, Jalan Kunti 118x, Seminyak, Kuta.
(0361) 730 840.
@ spa@thevillas.net

VILLA AGENCIES

Bali Hati
Jalan Raya Andong, Ubud.
(0361) 977 578.
W www.balihati.com

Bali Tropical Villas
Gang Lalu 7, Seminyak.
(0361) 732 083.
W www.bali-tropical-villas.com @ anita@bali-tropical-villas.com

House of Bali
Jalan Raya Banjar Semer 23, Kerobokan.
(0361) 739 541.
FAX (0361) 412 804.
W www.houseofbali.com
@ krobokan@houseofbali.com

In Touch
Jalan Raya Seminyak 22, Seminyak.
(0361) 731 047.
W www.intouchbali.com
@ intouch@dps.centrin.net.id

SPAS AND SPA RESORTS

Grand Hyatt
Nusa Dua.
(0361) 771 234.
W www.bali.grand.hyatt.com
@ baligh.inquiries@hyattintt.com

Bali Inter-Continental Resort
Jalan Uluwatu 45, Jimbaran.
(0361) 701 888.
FAX (0361) 701 777.
W www.bali.intercontinental.com

Bodyworks
Kayu Jati 2, Peti Tenget.
(0361) 733 317.

Four Seasons Resort, Jimbaran
Jimbaran Bay.
(0361) 701 010.
FAX (0361) 701 020.
@ fsrb.jimbaran@fourseasons.com

Four Seasons Resort, Sayan
Sayan, Ubud.
(0361) 977 577.
FAX (0361) 977 588.
@ fsrb.sayan@fourseasons.com

Mandara Spa at Hotel Padma
Jalan Padma 1, Kuta.
(0361) 752 111.
FAX (0361) 752 140.
@ operator@hotelpadma.com

Mandara Spa at Novotel Lombok
Pantai Putri Nyale Pujut, Lombok Tengah, Lombok.
(0370) 653 555.
W www.novotellombok.com

Mandara Spa at The Alila
Melinggih Kelod, Payangan, Ubud.
(0361) 975 963.
W www.alilahotels.com
@ ubud@alilahotels.com

Mandara Spa at The Legian
Jalan Laksmana, Seminyak.
(0361) 730 622.
FAX (0361) 730 623.
W www.ghmhotels.com

Mandara Spa at The Alila
Buitan, Banjar Manggis.
(0363) 41 011.
FAX (0363) 41 015.
W www.alilahotels.com

Nur Salon
Jalan Hanoman 29, Padang Tegal, Ubud.
(0361) 975 352.
FAX (0361) 974 622.

Nusa Dua Spa
Nusa Dua Beach Hotel, Nusa Dua.
(0361) 771 210.
FAX (0361) 771 229.
@ ndbh@indosat.net.id

Thalasso
Grand Mirage Resort, Jalan Pratama 74, Tanjung Benoa.
(0361) 771 888.
FAX (0361) 772 148.

Tjampuhan Hotel and Spa
Jalan Raya Campuhan, Ubud.
(0361) 975 368.

Choosing a Hotel

Bali and Lombok's hotels cover the spectrum from luxurious resorts to simple *losmen*. Most *losmen (see p166)* do not take advance bookings, and are best chosen on arrival. They are not listed here. During high seasons (mid-December to mid-January, July and August), hotel rates may be hiked up. Discounts can often be negotiated during low seasons.

South Bali

Hotel	Credit Cards	Children's Programmes	Pool	Restaurants	Business Facilities
Canggu: *Bolare Beach Bungalows* $$$ Banjar Berawa. (0361) 730 258. FAX (0361) 731 663. @ bolare@indosat.net.id These bungalows by the beach are in contemporary Balinese style – clean, quiet and small. A good range of facilities and excellent sports activities are available. TV **Rooms:** 20 ▤ 20	AE DC MC V		■	●	
Canggu: *Le Meridien* $$$$ Tanah Lot. (0361) 815 900. FAX (0361) 815 904. W www.bali.lemeridien.com An enormous, beautiful hotel with villas, beside Pura Tanah Lot and next to one of Bali's three main golf courses. TV **Rooms:** 278 ▤ 278	AE DC JCB MC V	●	■	●	■
Canggu: *Hotel Tugu Bali* $$$$$ Jalan Panti Batu Bolong. (0361) 731 701. FAX (0361) 731 704. W www.tuguhotel.com This lovely hotel, designed by an Indonesian collector to house his many artworks, is well appointed and has beautifully designed common areas. It is situated next to the ricefields. TV **Rooms:** 22 ▤ 22	AE DC MC V		■	●	
Jimbaran: *Bali Inter-Continental Resort* $$$$$ Jalan Uluwatu 45. (0361) 701 888. W www.baliintercontinental.com Seven swimming pools, all with different themes, are dotted around this resort located on Jimbaran Beach. TV **Rooms:** 425 ▤ 425	AE DC JCB MC V	●	■	●	■
Jimbaran: *Four Seasons Resort* $$$$$ Jimbaran Bay. (0361) 701 010. FAX (0361) 701 020. W www.fourseasons.com A superb resort with 147 villas all beautifully appointed, with private plunge pools, separate living/dining pavilions and spectacular gardens. The spa is one of the best in Bali. TV **Rooms:** 147 ▤ 147	AE DC JCB MC V	●	■	●	■
Jimbaran: *Pansea Puri Bali* $$$$$ Jl Yoga Perkunti-Uluwatu. (0361) 701 605. FAX (0361) 701 320. W www.pansea.com A charming beach-side atmosphere, pleasant rooms and a peaceful location on Jimbaran Beach make this a good choice for a relaxing holiday. TV **Rooms:** 41 ▤ 41	AE DC MC V	●	■	●	■
Jimbaran: *Ritz Carlton* $$$$$ Jalan Karang Mas Sejahtera. (0361) 702 222. FAX (0361) 702 758. W www.ritzcarlton.com Situated on a promontory overlooking the ocean. Excellent dining and entertainment. TV **Rooms:** 388 ▤ 388	AE DC MC V	●	■	●	■
Kuta: *Bounty Hotel* $$ Jalan Segara Batu Bulong. (0361) 753 030. FAX (0361) 752 121. W www.bountyhotel.com A pleasant hotel with gardens and a pool. Close to the beach. It belongs to a group that owns the island's biggest nightclubs and several restaurants, for which you will receive vouchers. A good choice for younger travellers. TV **Rooms:** 166 ▤ 166	AE DC JCB MC V		■	●	
Kuta: *Poppies Cottages* $$$ Jalan Pantai. (0361) 751 059. FAX (0361) 752 364. W www.poppiesbali.com A very pretty small hotel located in a busy area, and run by the owners of Poppies Restaurant. Good value for money. TV **Rooms:** 20 ▤ 20	AE DC MC V		■	●	■
Kuta: *Un's* $$$ Jalan Benesari 16. (0361) 758 411. FAX (0361) 758 414. W www.unshotel.com A Western-run hotel in a convenient location close to the heart of Kuta. Good value. TV **Rooms:** 30 ▤ 12	MC V		■	●	■
Kuta: *Alam Kul Kul* $$$$ Jalan Pantai. (0361) 752 520. FAX (0361) 752 519. W www.alamkulkul.com This resort has recently had a complete renovation and the results are striking and modern. Opposite the main beach in Kuta and a short walk from Hard Rock Café and Kuta Square. TV **Rooms:** 80 ▤ 80	AE DC JCB MC V	●	■	●	■

Price categories for a standard double room per night, inclusive of breakfast, service charges and any additional taxes.
$ under US$25
$$ US$25–50
$$$ US$50–100
$$$$ US$100–200
$$$$$ over US$200

CREDIT CARDS
Credit cards accepted: *AE* American Express; *DC* Diners Club; *JCB* Japan Credit Bureau; *MC* MasterCard; *V* Visa.
CHILDREN'S PROGRAMMES
Planned children's activities with supervision.
POOL
Pool facilities for guests.
RESTAURANTS
At least one restaurant; open to non-guests.
BUSINESS FACILITIES
Message service; fax; meeting room; internet access.

Hotel	Credit Cards	Children's Programmes	Pool	Restaurants	Business Facilities
KUTA: *Hard Rock Hotel* $$$$ Jalan Pantai. *(0361) 761 869.* FAX *(0361) 761 868.* W *www.hardrockhotels.net* Wings with different themes are set around elaborate grounds and big swimming pools. Bungalows around the pools are available for hire daily and the music never stops. The Hard Rock Café is out front on the beach side. TV **Rooms:** *418* *418*	*AE DC JCB MC V*	●	■	●	■
LEGIAN: *Sari Beach Inn* $$ Jalan Padma Utara. *(0361) 751 635.* FAX *(0361) 751 735.* @ *sbi@indo.net.id* This small, affordable hotel is located right on the beach, and is set in beautiful gardens. **Rooms:** *24* *24*	*MC V*		■	●	
LEGIAN: *Three Brothers* $$ Jalan Legian, Three Brothers Lane. *(0361) 751 566.* FAX *(0361) 756 082.* A pretty, ramshackle kind of property with various styles of accommodation located in the centre of Legian. **Rooms:** *90* *90*			■	●	
LEGIAN: *Bali Padma* $$$$$ Jalan Padma 1. *(0361) 752 111.* FAX *(0361) 752 140.* W *www.hotelpadma.com* A 5-star resort in a central location, with good amenities, beautiful swimming pool and spa. TV **Rooms:** *405* *405*	*AE DC JCB MC V*	●	■	●	■
NUSA DUA: *Hotel Bualu* $$$ Nusa Dua. *(0361) 771 310.* FAX *(0361) 771 313.* W *www.balinusa2.com* One of the older resorts in the area, and not as glamorous as its neighbours, Hotel Bualu is a comfortable and clean hotel with a friendly atmosphere and a competitive price. TV **Rooms:** *50* *50*	*AE DC JCB MC V*	●	■	●	■
NUSA DUA: *Bali Hilton* $$$$ Nusa Dua. *(0361) 771 102.* FAX *(0361) 771 616.* W *www.balihilton.com* This resort has an ostentatious entrance, in authentic Balinese style, with a great deal of carved stone and wood. An impressive range of facilities. **Rooms:** *537* *537*	*AE DC JCB MC V*	●	■	●	■
NUSA DUA: *Nusa Dua Beach Hotel & Spa* $$$$ Nusa Dua. *(0361) 771 210.* FAX *(0361) 772 617.* W *www.nusaduahotel.com* A resort in old raja style, richly decorated in gold and purples with lots of wood. Facilities include a lagoon pool, a VIP wing and an award-winning spa and health club. TV **Rooms:** *381* *381*	*AE DC JCB MC V*	●	■	●	■
NUSA DUA: *Amanusa* $$$$$ Nusa Dua. *(0361) 772 333.* FAX *(0361) 772 335.* W *www.amanrersorts.com* The 33 beautifully appointed suites are situated high above the golf course and overlook the sea. Offers quiet, tasteful service and excellent restaurants, beach club and bar. TV **Rooms:** *33* *33*	*AE DC MC V*		■	●	■
NUSA DUA: *Grand Hyatt* $$$$$ Nusa Dua. *(0361) 771 234.* FAX *(0361) 772 038.* W *www.bali.grand.hyatt.com* The largest resort on the island, superbly landscaped with dining and recreational options including water sports at the beach, extensive swimming pools and water slides. TV **Rooms:** *750* *750*	*AE DC JCB MC V*	●	■	●	■
NUSA DUA: *Nikko Bali Resort & Spa* $$$$$ Jalan Raya Nusa Dua Selatan. *(0361) 773 377.* FAX *(0361) 773 388.* W *www.nikkobali.com* An imposing resort that scales 14 storeys up the cliff-side. Commanding ocean views, swimming pools, a wealth of dining options, spa facilities and a breezy beach make up for the isolated location. TV **Rooms:** *390* *390*	*AE DC JCB MC V*	●	■	●	■
NUSA DUA: *Sheraton Laguna Nusa Dua* $$$$$ Nusa Dua. *(0361) 771 327.* FAX *(0361) 771 326.* W *www.starwood.com/bali* A beautiful lagoon-theme resort. Ground-floor rooms lead directly to the pools. TV **Rooms:** *270* *270*	*AE DC JCB MC V*	●	■	●	■

Price categories for a standard double room per night, inclusive of breakfast, service charges and any additional taxes.
$ under US$25
$$ US$25–50
$$$ US$50–100
$$$$ US$100–200
$$$$$ over US$200

Credit Cards
Credit cards accepted: *AE* American Express; *DC* Diners Club; *JCB* Japan Credit Bureau; *MC* MasterCard; *V* Visa.
Children's Programmes
Planned children's activities with supervision.
Pool
Pool facilities for guests.
Restaurants
At least one restaurant; open to non-guests.
Business Facilities
Message service; fax; meeting room; internet access.

Nusa Dua: *Westin Resort* $$$$$
Nusa Dua. *(0361) 771 906.* FAX *(0361) 771 908.* W *www.westin.com/bali*
This resort has excellent facilities for families including two-bedroom suites with stuffed toys, play stations and one of the best children's clubs on the island. ***Rooms:** 355* *355*

Nusa Lembongan: *Hai Tide Huts* $$$$
Nusa Lembongan. *(0361) 720 331.* FAX *(0361) 720 334.* W *www.balihaicruises.com*
Situated on a beach, the traditional thatched-roof huts are set around a large pool. Busy by day, quiet by night. ***Rooms:** 15* *15*

Nusa Lembongan: *Nusa Lembongan Resort* $$$$
Nusa Lembongan. *(0361) 725 864.* FAX *(0361) 725 866.*
W *www.nusa.lembongan.com* This up-market resort has luxurious accommodation and perfect views, with a lovely restaurant, a games room and a pool. ***Rooms:** 12* *12*

Nusa Lembongan: *Waka Nusa Resort* $$$$
Mushroom Beach, Nusa Lembongan. *(0361) 723 629.* FAX *(0361) 722 077.*
W *www.wakaexperience.com* The stylish, round houses built on sand are separate from the day resort with its pool, activities and buffet lunch. Offers romantic dinners under the stars. ***Rooms:** 10* *10*

Sanur: *Hotel Santai* $
Jalan Danau Tamblingan. *(0361) 281 684 or 281 685.* FAX *(0361) 287 314.*
W *www.pplhbali.or.id* Basic clean rooms on two floors surround a pool. There is an internet café and vegetarian restaurant on the premises. Hotel Santai is run by an environmentally-friendly NGO. ***Rooms:** 17* *17*

Sanur: *Puri Kelapa Garden Cottages* $$
Jalan Segara Ayu 1. *(0361) 286 135.* FAX *(0361) 287 417.*
@ *purikelapa@denpasar.wasantara.net.id* This friendly and relaxed resort has thatched-roof bungalows, a pool and beach access. ***Rooms:** 46* *46*

Sanur: *Gazebo Cottages* $$$
Jalan Danau Tamblingan 35. *(0361) 288 212.* FAX *(0361) 288 300.*
Tiny split-level bungalows with air-conditioning and modern brick rooms. Beach-side location at the centre of Sanur. ***Rooms:** 77* *77*

Sanur: *Laghawa Beach Inn* $$$
Jalan Danau Tamblingan 57. *(0361) 288 494.* FAX *(0361) 289 353.*
W *www.laghawahotel.com* This hotel is located right on the beach. The recently-renovated rooms are basic and clean. There is also an internet café. ***Rooms:** 38* *38*

Sanur: *Segara Village Hotel* $$$
Jalan Segara Ayu. *(0361) 288 407.* FAX *(0361) 287 242.*
W *www.segaravillage.com* This elegant hotel is divided into small "villages" that derive their architecture from different parts of Indonesia. ***Rooms:** 127* *127*

Sanur: *Bali Hyatt* $$$$
Jalan Danau Tamblingan. *(0361) 281 234.* FAX *(0361) 287 826.*
W *www.bali.resort.hyatt.com* This is an attractive resort with wonderful food, famous gardens, a clean beach, excellent children's club and spa. ***Rooms:** 390* *390*

Sanur: *Griya Santrian* $$$$
Jalan Danau Tamblingan 47. *(0361) 288 181.* FAX *(0361) 288 185.*
W *www.santrian.com* Two seaside resorts within walking distance of each other with a full range of facilities including thoughtful touches for children. Large, spacious rooms. The Puri Santrian is slightly more up-market. ***Rooms:** 90* *90*

	Credit Cards	Children's Programmes	Pool	Restaurant	Business Facilities
Westin Resort	AE DC JCB MC V	●	■	●	■
Hai Tide Huts	AE DC JCB MC V	●	■	●	
Nusa Lembongan Resort	AE DC JCB MC V		■	●	■
Waka Nusa Resort	AE DC JCB MC V		■	●	
Hotel Santai			■	●	■
Puri Kelapa Garden Cottages	MC V		■	●	
Gazebo Cottages	AE MC V		■	●	■
Laghawa Beach Inn	AE MC V		■	●	■
Segara Village Hotel	AE DC MC V	●	■	●	■
Bali Hyatt	AE DC MC V	●	■	●	■
Griya Santrian	AE DC MC V		■	●	■

Hotel	Price	Cards	1	2	3	4
SANUR: *Tandjung Sari* Jalan Danau Tamblingan 41. *(0361) 288 441.* FAX *(0361) 287 930.* W *www.tandjungsarihotel.com* This elegant hotel maintains an old-world charm and has a good location. It has an excellent restaurant and bar, and accommodation is in bungalows. ***Rooms:** 26* *26*	$$$$	AE DC JCB MC V		■	●	■
SANUR: *Waka Maya Resort* Jalan Tanjung. *(0361) 289 912.* FAX *(0361) 270 761.* W *www.wakaexperience.com* A well-priced, sophisticated mini-resort with bungalow-style accommodation amid graceful gardens. Very quiet. ***Rooms:** 12* *12*	$$$$	AE DC MC V		■	●	
SEMINYAK: *Sing Ken Ken Hotel* Jalan Double Six. *(0361) 730 980.* FAX *(0361) 730 535.* @ *skk_hotel@indo.net.id* This hotel is near the beach and has a 24-hour restaurant/bar. Negotiate for about half the published rate. ***Rooms:** 25* *25*	$$	MC V		■	●	
SEMINYAK: *Dhyana Pura Beach Hotel* Jalan Abimanyu. *(0361) 730 442.* FAX *(0361) 730 980.* W *www.indo.com/dhyana/pura* A hotel situated on the beach, close to nightlife and restaurants. It also has a nice pool for children. TV ***Rooms:** 120* *100*	$$$	MC V		■	●	■
SEMINYAK: *Villa Kendil* Jalan Raya Kerobokan 107. *(0361) 731 467.* FAX *(0361) 731 470.* W *www.villakendil.com* Pretty and self-contained two-storey villas with private pools and full hotel facilities. TV ***Rooms:** 15* *15*	$$$$	AE DC JCB MC V		■	●	■
SEMINYAK: *Villa Lumbung* Jalan Raya Peti Tenget 100. *(0361) 730 204.* FAX *(0361) 731 106.* W *www.hotellumbung.com* These stylish villas offer privacy, full hotel facilities, a freeform swimming pool and a restaurant. TV ***Rooms:** 30* *30*	$$$$	AE MC V		■	●	■
SEMINYAK: *Villa Seri* Banjar Umalas Kauh. *(0361) 730 262.* FAX *(0361) 730 784.* W *www.villaseri.com* A quiet mini-resort with spacious two-storey villas, full facilities, comfortable rooms with television, stereos and outdoor relaxation areas. A pretty pool overlooks the ricefields. ***Rooms:** 22* *22*	$$$$	AE DC MC V		■		■
SEMINYAK: *Oberoi* Jalan Kayu Aya. *(0361) 730 361.* FAX *(0361) 730 791.* W *www.oberoihotels.com* One of the first luxury hotels on the island, the Oberoi offers stylish indulgence. Excellent food, great garden and beach-side location just a little out of the way of the crowds. TV ***Rooms:** 75* *75*	$$$$$	AE DC JCB MC V		■	●	■
SEMINYAK: *Rumah Manis* Jalan Nakula 18. *(0361) 730 606.* FAX *(0361) 730 505.* W *www.balibountygroup.com* A boutique resort offering single rooms with outdoor entertaining areas and duplexes with private plunge pools. TV ***Rooms:** 40* *40*	$$$$$	AE DC MC		■	●	
SEMINYAK: *The Legian* Jalan Laksmana. *(0361) 730 622.* FAX *(0361) 730 623.* W *www.ghmhotels.com* The Legian is the ultimate in style. This all-suite hotel offers studios, or one- and two-bedroom suites. Other attractions include a French-run restaurant, a two-tiered pool, an attractive bar and a beautiful spa. TV ***Rooms:** 70* *70*	$$$$$	AE DC JCB MC V		■	●	■
SEMINYAK: *The Villas Hotel* Jalan Kunti 118X. *(0361) 730 840.* FAX *(0361) 733 751.* W *www.thevillas.net* Elegant and well-priced one- and three-bedroom villas with fully-equipped kitchens and full-time staff. The hotel also has a Moroccan spa, art gallery, bar and amphitheatre. TV ***Rooms:** 50* *50*	$$$$$	AE DC MC V		■	●	
TANJUNG BENOA: *Novotel Benoa Bali* Jalan Pratama. *(0361) 772 239.* FAX *(0361) 772 237.* W *www.novotelbali.com* This quirky little resort sits on both sides of the road and offers spacious rooms, two swimming pools, an excellent French restaurant and al fresco dining. TV ***Rooms:** 186* *186*	$$$$	AE DC JCB MC V	●	■	●	■
TANJUNG BENOA: *Conrad Hotel* Jalan Pratama Raya 168. *(0361) 778 788.* FAX *(0361) 773 888.* W *www.conradhotels.com* The newest 5-star hotel in Bali offers every luxury in beautiful surroundings. TV ***Rooms:** 313*	$$$$$	AE DC JCB MC V		■	●	■

Price categories for a standard double room per night, inclusive of breakfast, service charges and any additional taxes.
$ under US$25
$$ US$25–50
$$$ US$50–100
$$$$ US$100–200
$$$$$ over US$200

CREDIT CARDS
Credit cards accepted: *AE* American Express; *DC* Diners Club; *JCB* Japan Credit Bureau; *MC* MasterCard; *V* Visa.
CHILDREN'S PROGRAMMES
Planned children's activities with supervision.
POOL
Pool facilities for guests.
RESTAURANTS
At least one restaurant; open to non-guests.
BUSINESS FACILITIES
Message service; fax; meeting room; internet access.

	Credit Cards	Children's Programmes	Pool	Restaurants	Business Facilities
TANJUNG BENOA: *Grand Mirage Resort* $$$$$ Jalan Pratama 74. *(0361) 771 888.* FAX *(0361) 772 148.* *www.grandmirage.com* A large beachside resort suitable for families and package holiday-makers. The Thalasso Spa facility is a big draw. Personable and friendly. TV ***Rooms:** 310 310*	AE DC JCB MC V	●	■	●	■
TUBAN: *Kuta Paradiso* $$ Jalan Kartika Plaza. *(0361) 761 414.* FAX *(0361) 756 944.* *www.kutaparadisohotel.com* A nicely decorated hotel with an impressive entrance beside Kuta Square. TV ***Rooms:** 243 243*	AE DC JCB MC V	●	■	●	■
TUBAN: *Bali Hai Resort* $$$ Jalan Wanasegara 33. *(0361) 753 035.* FAX *(0361) 754 548.* *www.balihai-resort.com* This is a pleasant resort with a great rooftop bar and family suites with colourful bunk beds and computer play stations for children. TV ***Rooms:** 200 200*	AE DC JCB MC V	●	■	●	■
ULUWATU: *Bali Cliff Hotel* $$ Jalan Pura Batu Pageh. *(0361) 771 992.* FAX *(0361) 771 993.* *www.balicliffresort.com* This hotel has a spectacular swimming pool and good food, although the isolated location does not suit all. TV ***Rooms:** 143 143*	AE DC JCB MC V	●	■	●	■
ULUWATU: *Udayana Lodge* $$ Uluwatu. *(0361) 261 204.* FAX *(0361) 701 098.* *www.ecolodgesindonesia.com* An eco-friendly resort situated in sprawling bushland with fairly basic accommodation in brick buildings, but the quiet surroundings are a positive feature. Close to the university. ***Rooms:** 10 10*	MC V		■	●	
CENTRAL BALI					
AYUNG RIVER GORGE: *Alila Ubud* $$$$ Melinggih Kelod, Payangan. *(0361) 975 963.* FAX *(0361) 975 968.* *www.alilahotels.com* This very stylish hotel is up the mountain ridge past Ubud. Its restaurant is excellent, the views are stunning and the pool is beautiful. It also has a good spa. ***Rooms:** 54 54*	AE DC JCB MC V	●	■	●	■
AYUNG RIVER GORGE: *Sayan Terrace Resort* $$$$ Sayan. *(0361) 974 384.* FAX *(0361) 975 384.* *www.sayanterrace.com* *Losmen*-style rooms on the ridge overlooking the Ayung River. Rooms in the White Lotus Annexe have been upgraded. Good for long-term stays. ***Rooms:** 8*	MC V		■	●	■
AYUNG RIVER GORGE: *Taman Bebek Villas* $$$$ Sayan. *(0361) 975 385.* FAX *(0361) 976 532.* *www.baliwww.com/tamanbebek* Simple, gracefully aged cottages with interesting features set this place apart. Each has a small kitchen and leafy verandahs. ***Rooms:** 9 2*	AE MC V		■	●	
AYUNG RIVER GORGE: *Amandari* $$$$$ Kedewatan. *(0361) 975 333.* FAX *(0361) 975 335.* *www.amanresorts.com* A boutique resort and one of the most exclusive places on the island. Discreet service, excellent restaurant, beautifully designed rooms, and an award-winning spa. ***Rooms:** 30 30*	AE DC MC V	●	■	●	■
AYUNG RIVER GORGE: *Four Seasons Resort* $$$$$ Sayan. *(0361) 977 577.* FAX *(0361) 977 588.* *www.fourseasons.com* One of the most talked about resorts on the island owing to its unusual modern construction, luxurious facilities, impeccable service and stunning views of the river gorge. TV ***Rooms:** 60 60*	AE DC JCB MC V		■	●	■

SANGGINGAN: *Pita Maha Resort and Spa* $$$$$
Jalan Raya Sanggingan. Tel *(0361) 974 330.* FAX *(0361) 974 329.* W *www.pitamaha-bali.com* A boutique hotel perched on the edge of a valley overlooking the river. Traditional, but spacious and luxurious. TV **Rooms:** *24* *24*

AE DC JCB MC V | ● | ■ | ● | ■

TEGALLALANG: *Alam Sari Keliki* $$$
Keliki, Tegallalang. Tel *(0361) 240 308.* FAX *(0361) 981 420.* @ *alamsari@indo.net.id* A laid-back cottage-style resort with beautiful gardens that emphasizes the environment and is excellent for families or small groups. Good value. **Rooms:** *10* *10*

AE DC MC V | ● | ■ | ● | ■

UBUD: *Alam Indah* $$$
Nyuh Funing Village. Tel *(0361) 974 629.* FAX *(0361) 974 629.* W *www.alamindahbali.com* One of the most serene boutique hotels in this area, the staff here will pamper and please. The traditional Balinese-style rooms with modern bathrooms have views over rice fields and lush gardens. **Rooms:** *10* *10*

MC V | | ■ | ● |

UBUD: *Murni's House* $$$
Jalan Setra. Tel *(0361) 975 165.* FAX *(0361) 975 282.* @ *murnishouses@yahoo.com* Murni's House is located next to Ubud's cemetery and is a short walk from the shops and restaurants. This quiet and idyllic hotel is ideal for those looking for an authentic and relaxed stay. **Rooms:** *4* *4*

AE MC V | | | |

UBUD: *Tjampuhan Hotel and Spa* $$$$
Jalan Raya Campuhan. Tel *(0361) 975 368.* FAX *(0361) 975 137.* W *www.tjampuhan.com* This hotel stands on the site of what was once Walter Spies' home *(see p88)*. It has been nicely renovated and features a pool carved from rock and surrounded by lush vegetation. Accommodation is in bungalows. Above-average prices. **Rooms:** *67* *25*

AE DC MC V | ● | ■ | ● | ■

UBUD: *Waka Di Ume Resort* $$$$
Jalan Suweta. Tel *(0361) 973 178.* FAX *(0361) 973 179.* W *www.wakaexperience.com* Waka Di Ume is a small resort that offers stylish luxury. This hotel is quiet and spacious, with an emphasis on relaxation. There is even a meditation room. The location is beautiful, and the resort overlooks ricefields. **Rooms:** *16* *8*

AE DC JCB MC V | | ■ | ● | ■

UBUD: *Begawan Giri Estate* $$$$$
Banjar Begawan. Tel *(0361) 978 888.* FAX *(0361) 978 889.* W *www.begawan.com* One of Bali's most luxurious accommodations and magnificently situated. Its five villas can be rented whole or as rooms. TV **Rooms:** *25* *25*

AE DC JCB MC V | ● | ■ | ● | ■

UBUD: *Ibah Resort* $$$$$
Jalan Raya Ubud, Campuhan. Tel *(0361) 974 466.* FAX *(0361) 974 467.* W *www.ibahbali.com* A very stylish mini-resort built along traditional Balinese lines, sporting modern, polished interiors. Good value. TV **Rooms:** *15* *15*

AE DC JCB MC V | | ■ | ● | ■

UBUD: *Kamandalu Resort and Spa* $$$$$
Jalan Tegallalang, Banjar Nagi. Tel *(0361) 975 825.* FAX *(0361) 975 851.* W *www.kamandalu-resort.com* Laid out like a Balinese village so that it blends in with the surrounding area, this resort provides very luxurious accommodation. Each villa is uniquely designed and includes a sunken bathtub, a private courtyard with outdoor shower and satellite television. TV **Rooms:** *58* *58*

AE DC JCB MC V | | ■ | ● | ■

UBUD: *Kayumanis Villas and Spa* $$$$$
Sayan. Tel *(0361) 972 777.* FAX *(0361) 972 680.* W *www.baliprivatevilla.com* Built in 2002, the majority of this hotel's guests are honeymooners, perhaps because it does not permit children under 16 to stay. Each stylish villa boasts a private pool, and guests can use the free limousine service to travel into Ubud. TV **Rooms:** *9* *9*

AE DC JCB MC V | | ■ | ● | ■

UBUD: *Komaneka Resort* $$$$$
Jalan Br. Tanggayuda, Kedewatan. Tel *(0361) 978 123.* FAX *(0361) 973 084.* W *www.komaneka.com* This boutique hotel near Ubud is surrounded by lush, tropical vegetation and rice terraces. The beautifully-designed rooms all feature marble sunken baths, and villas have their own plunge pools. The resort contains a spa and can organise a variety of activities. TV **Rooms:** *20* *20*

AE DC JCB MC V | | ■ | ● |

For key to symbols see back flap

Price categories for a standard double room per night, inclusive of breakfast, service charges and any additional taxes.
$ under US$25
$$ US$25–50
$$$ US$50–100
$$$$ US$100–200
$$$$$ over US$200

CREDIT CARDS
Credit cards accepted: *AE* American Express; *DC* Diners Club; *JCB* Japan Credit Bureau; *MC* MasterCard; *V* Visa.
CHILDREN'S PROGRAMMES
Planned children's activities with supervision.
POOL
Pool facilities for guests.
RESTAURANTS
At least one restaurant; open to non-guests.
BUSINESS FACILITIES
Message service; fax; meeting room; internet access.

	Credit Cards	Children's Programmes	Pool	Restaurants	Business Facilities
UBUD: *Kori* $$$$$ Jalan Raya Sanggihan. *(0361) 972 487.* FAX *(0361) 972 486.* W *www.koriubud.com* Located outside of town, this recently developed hotel has an excellent Mediterranean and Balinese restaurant attached. The environmentally-friendly hotel is quiet and spacious and attracts couples on a romantic getaway. TV ***Rooms:*** *12* *12*	AE DC JCB MC V		■	●	
UBUD: *Maya Ubud* $$$$$ Jalan Gunung Sari. *(0361) 977 888.* FAX *(0361) 978 844.* W *www.mayaubud.com* Set in 10 hectares of hillside garden, Maya Ubud overlooks two river valleys and paddy fields. This stylish hotel offers poolside dining, and deluxe villas have private pools. TV ***Rooms:*** *108* *108*	AE DC JCB MC V		■	●	■
UBUD: *Natura Resort and Spa* $$$$$ Banjar Laplapan. *(0361) 978 666.* FAX *(0361) 978 222.* @ *natura@indosat.net.id* Designed by a well-regarded Indonesian architect, the 14 private, luxurious villas blend beautifully with their natural surroundings. Excellent riverside spa and restaurant. TV ***Rooms:*** *14* *14*	AE DC MC V		■	●	■
UBUD: *Uma* $$$$$ Jalan Raya Sanggihan. *(0361) 972 448.* FAX *(0361) 972 449.* W *www.uma.como.bz* This boutique hotel is located in a quiet location next to the Neka Museum. Built in 2004 in modern Balinese style, the hotel also has an excellent restaurant and all modern facilities. TV ***Rooms:*** *29* *29*	AE DC JCB MC V		■	●	■
EAST BALI					
AMED: *Coral View* $$$ Amed. W *www.bali-travelnet.com/hotels/coralview_villas/* This mid-range hotel is quiet and remote. Like most places in Amed, there is still no phone. Located right on the beach, Coral View has a spring-fed pool, children's playground and it rents out snorkelling and diving equipment. ***Rooms:*** *35* *35*	MC V		■	●	
AMED: *Indra Udhyana* $$$ Jalan Raya. *(0363) 22 348.* FAX *(0363) 22 348.* A beautifully located place that features up-market, quite luxurious cottages. A little overpriced. TV ***Rooms:*** *35* *35*	AE MC V		■	●	
CANDI DASA: *Ayodya Seaside Cottages* $ Jalan Raya. *(0363) 41 629.* FAX *(0363) 41 629.* These unusual cottages feature bathtubs offering an ocean view, beach frontage, and a laid-back atmosphere. ***Rooms:*** *15*				●	
CANDI DASA: *Hotel Fajar Candi Dasa* $$ Jalan Raya. *(0363) 41 539.* FAX *(0363) 41 538.* An older hotel with tasteful but slightly overpriced rooms in a central location. Negotiate for a good discount. ***Rooms:*** *19* *19*	AE MC V		■	●	■
CANDI DASA: *The Water Garden* $$$ Jalan Raya. *(0363) 41 540.* FAX *(0363) 41 164.* Across the road from the beach, this resort offers tastefully decorated rooms with private verandahs set around peaceful water gardens. ***Rooms:*** *14* *9*	AE MC V		■	●	
CANDI DASA: *Puri Bagus Candi Dasa* $$$$ Jalan Raya. *(0363) 41 131.* FAX *(0363) 41 290.* W *www.candidasa.puribagus.net.id* Luxurious resort at the quiet end of the beach offering excellent food and service, and beautiful rooms and villas. TV ***Rooms:*** *48* *48*	AE DC MC V		■	●	■

GUNUNG BATUR: *Hotel Puri Bening* $
Toya Bungkah. *(0366) 51 234.* FAX *(0366) 51 248.*
One of the few places with up-market accommodation in this area, the hotel is modern and the rooms have sweeping views. TV ***Rooms:** 33*
MC V

GUNUNG BATUR: *Under The Volcano* $
Toya Bungkah. *(0366) 51 166.*
Not the most luxurious, but the rooms are clean. ***Rooms:** 5* *5*

MANGGIS: *Ida Beach Village Hotel* $$
Jalan Puri Bagus, Candi Dasa. *(0363) 41 118.* FAX *(0363) 41 041.*
A quirky beach-side resort with traditional Balinese architecture and a lovely, small swimming pool. ***Rooms:** 17* *8*
MC V

MANGGIS: *Puri Bagus Manggis* $$$$
Manggis. *(0363) 41 304.* FAX *(0363) 41 305.*
@ *pbmanggis@denpasar.wasantara.net.id* Overlooks hills and terraced ricefields, and has exquisite teak furniture. TV ***Rooms:** 7* *7*
AE DC MC V

MANGGIS: *Alila Manggis* $$$$$
Jalan Raya Buitan. *(0363) 41 011.* FAX *(0363) 41 015.*
W *www.alilahotels.com* The rooms in the resort all face a central pool set in a large garden edged with coconut palms. This secluded and quiet hotel is a perfect retreat and a great place to explore the east coast of the island. There is also a lovely spa. TV ***Rooms:** 55* *55*
AE DC JCB MC V

MANGGIS: *Amankila* $$$$$
Manggis. *(0363) 41 333.* FAX *(0363) 41 555.* W *www.amanresorts.com*
Spectacularly set on a hillside, this exclusive hotel looks out over the bay and has a breathtaking three-tiered swimming pool and a beach club.
TV ***Rooms:** 33* *33*
AE DC JCB MC V

PADANG BAI: *Pantai Ayu Homestay* $
Jalan Silayukti. *(0363) 41 396.* FAX *none.*
Slightly away from the beach, this friendly place has great views of the bay. Good value. ***Rooms:** 10*

PADANG BAI: *Hotel Puri Rai* $$
Jalan Silayukti. *(0363) 41 385.* FAX *(0363) 41 386.*
A collection of basic two-storey cottages at the end of the bay, with a swimming pool opposite the beach. ***Rooms:** 30* *10*

SIDEMAN: *Sacred Mountain Sanctuary* $$$
Sidemen Karangasem. *(0366) 24 330.* FAX *(0366) 23 456.*
W *www.sacredmountainresort.com*
Popular with spiritual groups and trekkers planning to scale Gunung Agung and bask in the clear mountain air. ***Rooms:** 20*
MC V

TULAMBEN: *Mimpi Resort* $$$
Tulamben. *(0363) 21 642.* FAX *(0361) 435 424.* W *www.mimpi.com*
Luxurious villa-type accommodation popular with divers and their families. ***Rooms:** 30* *30*
AE JCB MC V

NORTH AND WEST BALI

GUNUNG BATUKAU: *Puri Lumbung* $$$
Munduk. *(0362) 925 14.* W *www.travelideas.net/bali.hotels/lumbung.html*
Located in a small village, this hotel overlooks fields and gorges. Various classes are offered, including yoga, dance and music. ***Rooms:** 16*
AE DC MC V

LAKE BRATAN & BEDUGUL: *Bali Handara Koshaido Country Club* $$$
Pancasari. *(0362) 22 646.* FAX *(0362) 23 048.* W *www.balihandarakoshaido.com*
This world-class golf club offers comfortable, modern accommodation from standard rooms to cottages. TV ***Rooms:** 77*
AE DC JCB MC V

LAKE BUYAN: *Lake Buyan Resort* $$$
Jalan Raya Bedugul, Pancasari. *(0362) 21 351.* FAX *(0362) 21 388.*
The two-bedroom cottages have kitchens, audio-visual equipment, living/dining areas, fireplaces and outdoor terraces. The lake and golf course are close by. TV ***Rooms:** 18* *18*
JCB MC V

LOVINA: *Hotel Angsoka* $
Kalibukbuk. *(0362) 41 841.* FAX *(0362) 41 023.* @ *angsoka@singaraja.wasantara.net.id*
Fan-cooled rooms with thatched roofs and air-conditioned brick double rooms with bathrooms. Excellent prices. ***Rooms:** 44* *15*
MC V

For key to symbols see back flap

Price categories for a standard double room per night, inclusive of breakfast, service charges and any additional taxes.
$ under US$25
$$ US$25–50
$$$ US$50–100
$$$$ US$100–200
$$$$$ over US$200

CREDIT CARDS
Credit cards accepted: *AE* American Express; *DC* Diners Club; *JCB* Japan Credit Bureau; *MC* MasterCard; *V* Visa.
CHILDREN'S PROGRAMMES
Planned children's activities with supervision.
POOL
Pool facilities for guests.
RESTAURANTS
At least one restaurant; open to non-guests.
BUSINESS FACILITIES
Message service; fax; meeting room; internet access.

Hotel	Credit Cards	Children's Programmes	Pool	Restaurants	Business Facilities
LOVINA: *Melka Hotel* $ Kalibukbuk. *(0362) 41 552.* FAX *(0362) 41 543.* *melka@telkom.net* A small, reasonably priced, German-run resort that is perfect for families and budget travellers. Comfortable and clean. ***Rooms:*** *30* *30*	MC V		■	●	■
LOVINA: *Susila Backpackers Hotel* $ Kalibukbuk. *(0362) 41 080.* FAX *(0362) 41 023.* This cheap and clean hotel claims to be the only backpackers' hotel in Lovina to supply toilet paper. Guests can get discounted rates for the Angsoka Hotel pool. ***Rooms:*** *6*			■		
LOVINA : *Banyualit Hotel* $$ Jalan Lovina Kalibukbuk. *(0362) 412 43.* FAX *(0362) 415 63.* *www.banyualit.com* This restful hotel offers a variety of rooms, some with TVs and balconies. Beautiful beachside gardens. ***Rooms:*** *22*	MC V		■	●	■
LOVINA: *Damai Lovina Villas* $$$$ Lovina. *(0362) 41 008.* FAX *(0362) 41 009.* *www.damai.com* Owned by an award-winning Danish chef, this has lovely cottages and sweeping views. Offers cookery classes. ***Rooms:*** *8* *8*	AE DC JCB MC V		■	●	
LOVINA: *Puri Bagus Lovina* $$$$ Jalan Raya Lovina. *(0362) 21 430.* FAX *(0362) 22 627.* *www.bagus-discovery.com* A hotel with beautiful rooms and villas, a spring-fed swimming pool, library, reading and relaxation areas, a stylish bar and an excellent restaurant. ***Rooms:*** *40* *40*	AE DC JCB MC V		■	●	■
MENJANGAN ISLAND: *Mimpi Resort* $$$$ Banyuwedang, Taman Nasional Bali Barat. *(0362) 944 97.* FAX *(0361) 435 424.* *www.mimpi.com* Luxurious and stylish boutique resort within the National Park, with pools fed by natural hot springs. ***Rooms:*** *54* *54*	AE DC JCB MC V		■	●	■
MENJANGAN ISLAND: *Waka Shorea* $$$$ Labuhan Lalang, Taman Nasional Bali Barat. *(0361) 484 085.* FAX *(0362) 484 767.* *www.wakaexperience.com* Accessible only by boat, this luxurious resort located in the National Park has a safari theme, with individual bungalows conceived as tents. ***Rooms:*** *16*	AE DC JCB MC V		■	●	
PEMUTERAN: *Taman Sari Bali Cottages* $$ Desa Pemuteran. *(0362) 947 55.* FAX *(0362) 93 264.* *www.balitamansari.com* Offers old-style rooms and villas set in gardens beside a beach. Meditation areas and water activities are available. ***Rooms:*** *29* *13*	MC V			●	■
PEMUTERAN: *Taman Selini Bali* $$$ Pemuteran. *(0362) 947 46.* FAX *(0362) 93 449.* *www.tamanselini.com* Each cottage has its own roomy verandah with day bed and outdoor bathroom. The beach-side restaurant offers excellent Greek specialities and the chef is happy to cater to special requests. ***Rooms:*** *11* *11*	MC V		■	●	■
PEMUTERAN: *Matahari Beach Resort and Spa* $$$$$ Pemuteran. *(0362) 92 835.* FAX *(0362) 92 313.* *www.matahari_beach_resort.com* A very popular hotel for those who want to take it easy or enjoy good diving facilities and restaurant dining. ***Rooms:*** *32* *32*	AE DC JCB MC V	●	■	●	■
PEMUTERAN: *Puri Ganesha Villas* $$$$$ Pemuteran. *(0361) 947 66.* FAX *(0361) 93 433.* *www.puriganesha.com* Very stylishly appointed, all four villas have two bedrooms, living areas and a pool. Cookery courses offered. ***Rooms:*** *4* *4*	AE MC V		■	●	■
PUPUAN: *Cempaka Belimbing Guest Villas* $$$$ Banjar Suradadi-Belimbing, Pupuan. *(0361) 754 897.* FAX *(0361) 752 777.* Charming, spacious, cottage-style villas with good views. Staff will take guests trekking in the locality at no extra charge. ***Rooms:*** *16*	JCB MC V		■	●	■

SINGARAJA: *Kala Spa Living* $$$$ Banjar Asah Panji, Wanagiri Sukasada. *(0361) 419 606.* FAX *(0361) 419 607.* W *www.kalaspa.com* Isolated resort with a contemporary mountain-cottage theme. The views are magnificent. ***Rooms:*** *18*	AE DC MC V		■	●	
TABANAN: *Waka Gangga* $$$$ Yeh Gangga, Banjar Sudimare. *(0361) 416 256.* FAX *(0361) 416 353.* W *www.wakaexperience.com* This stylishly simple place is set among the famously green rice terraces of Tabanan, near the black-sand surfing beaches. ***Rooms:*** *10* *2*	AE DC JCB MC V		■	●	
LOMBOK					
GILI ISLES: *Hotel Gili Air* $ Gili Air. *(0361) 634 435.* FAX *(0370) 634 435.* Facing a superb beach, a hotel with lovely bungalows set amid lush gardens. Good value. ***Rooms:*** *35* *16*	AE MC V		■	●	
GILI ISLES: *Hotel Salobai* $ Gili Trawangan. *(0370) 643 152.* FAX *(0370) 643 151.* An up-market resort offering ocean views. The restaurant, Dino, is one of the best on the island. ***Rooms:*** *14* *14*	MC V			●	
GILI ISLES: *Gazebo Hotel* $$ Gili Meno. *(0370) 635 795.* FAX *(0370) 635 795.* A hotel with clean and spacious rooms, set in gardens just off the beach. ***Rooms:*** *10* *10*	MC		■	●	
GILI ISLES: *Hotel Vila Ombak* $$$ Gili Trawangan. *(0370) 642 337.* FAX *(0370) 642 337.* W *www.hotelombak.com* A stylish, comfortable hotel in partnership with a reputable dive school. Good value. ***Rooms:*** *36* *36*	MC V		■	●	
KUTA: *Novotel Lombok* $$$ Pantai Putri Nyale, Pujut-Lombok Tengah. *(0370) 653 333.* FAX *(0370) 653 555.* W *www.accorhotels.com/asia* A stylish, quirky resort, part Moroccan, part French and part local. Good facilities. ***Rooms:*** *100* *100*	AE DC JCB MC V	●	■	●	
SENGGIGI: *Café Wayan Homestay* $ Jalan Raya Senggigi. *0370 693 098.* This tiny hotel is big on service and is located right on the beach. The rooms are basic and surround a private garden. ***Rooms:*** *4* *4*				●	
SENGGIGI: *Pondok Damai* $ Jalan Raya Mangsit. *(0370) 693 019.* FAX *(0370) 693 019.* Cheap and cheerful bungalows situated on the beach front, with friendly staff. ***Rooms:*** *14*	AE DC JCB MC V			●	
SENGGIGI: *Pacific Beach Hotel* $$ Jalan Raya Senggigi. *(0370) 693 006.* FAX *(0370) 693 027.* @ *pacificdiamond@yahoo.com* A great place for the family. Attractions include a 24-hour bar and restaurant, and wonderful sunset views. ***Rooms:*** *26* *26*	MC V		■	●	
SENGGIGI: *Puri Mas Hotel* $$ Jalan Raya Mangsit. *(0370) 693 831.* FAX *(0370) 693 023.* A medium-range hotel with well-established gardens offering good value and beach frontage. ***Rooms:*** *21* *21*	MC V		■	●	■
SENGGIGI: *Holiday Inn Resort Lombok* $$$ Jalan Raya Mangsit. *0370 693 444.* FAX *0370 693 092.* W *www.bluebirdgroup.com* A large resort with a collection of houses, apartments and beach bungalows set in extensive landscaped gardens. ***Rooms:*** *159* *159*	AE DC MC V	●	■	●	■
SENGGIGI: *Sheraton Senggigi Lombok* $$$$ Jalan Raya Senggigi km 8. *0370 693 333.* FAX *0370 693 140.* W *www.sheraton.com/senggigi* Sheraton offers 5-star comfort in the centre of town and a great range of facilities for adults and children. ***Rooms:*** *156* *156*	AE DC JCB MC V	●	■	●	■
TANJUNG: *The Oberoi Lombok* $$$$$ Medana Beach. *0370 638 444.* FAX *0370 632 486.* @ *obroil@indosat.net.id* A luxury hotel with views of the ocean and the Gili Isles, and an excellent sports programme. ***Rooms:*** *50* *50*	AE DC JCB MC V		■	●	■

For key to symbols see back flap

Where to Eat

From local food at *warung* and *rumah makan* to international restaurant cuisines, Bali and Lombok cater for all tastes. Good food is available over a wide price range. As the number of visitors has increased, many new establishments have opened, and generally they show a high level of skill and confidence. The range is particularly wide in the more developed parts of Bali – the options in remoter parts of the island, and in Lombok, are more limited. Credit cards are accepted in more sophisticated restaurants and cafés. Prices on menus may be expressed in US dollars, although payment in rupiah is accepted. Restaurants will accommodate disabled visitors, although most do not make any specific provisions.

Chilli, a spice often used in local food

Barbecued seafood being prepared in a hotel kitchen

Eating Hours

The Balinese have no set meal times and most places will be happy to serve guests throughout the day. However, there are not many dining options before 7am or after midnight.

Local Food

The everyday Balinese diet consists of a couple of meals based on rice with a little meat, vegetables and the occasional egg. The combination is known as *nasi campur (see p182)*. This and other Balinese dishes are served in most restaurants.

For the "genuine" – and often tastier – article, try the *warung* (food stalls) or *rumah makan* (eating houses) where locals eat when away from home. The food here is cheap, fresh and spicier than in restaurants. Lining the streets and parked at night markets are *kaki lima* (food carts), which are not recommended as the standard of hygiene is often questionable.

International Restaurants

Bali offers the world on a plate, from the entire complement of Asian cuisines to traditional Western food. A large number of foreign chefs have been attracted to Bali by the hotel chains, and some have started up their own operations. In turn they have trained many local chefs in foreign food preparation. French, Italian and other Mediterranean cuisines are all part of the enormous range offered in the island's restaurants, and standards are generally high. The prices are very reasonable by international standards. Some very good Japanese food can be enjoyed in Bali for a fraction of what it would cost in most other places.

Hotel Dining

Many hotels in Bali offer excellent meals in surroundings more luxurious than those encountered in most other tourist destinations. The best are often featured in international food and travel magazines and deservedly so. The Aman resorts have an excellent reputation for hiring young chefs with signature styles, as do the Four Seasons Resorts and the GHM hotels – the Legian, Chedi and Serai *(see pp173–7)*. The major chain hotels all offer the full range of dining styles from coffee shops to cafés and restaurants. It is often possible to eat in the open air. Hotel bars and restaurants are open to the public as well as to hotel guests *(see pp170–79 and pp184–91)*.

Eating in hotels will generally be more expensive than in restaurants outside, and menus in hotel restaurants are often priced in US dollars.

***Warung* selling rice and a variety of Indonesian dishes**

Cafés and Coffee Shops

Since the 1970s when surfers and independent travellers put Bali on the tourist map, the island has embraced the idea of casual eating. Bars and beach-side eateries serving fairly simple fare are common sights. They serve

Al fresco dining at Senggigi Beach, on the west coast of Lombok

nasi goreng (fried rice), the ubiquitous banana pancake, fresh local fruit juices and grainy Bali coffee. However, growing demand from visitors and increased awareness among locals have fired up the café scene. Particularly in the artistic village of Ubud, European-style cafés with espresso machines are now common, as are, increasingly, up-market coffee houses serving gourmet blends of freshly-roasted Indonesian coffee varieties. Accompaniments include everything from tiramisu to the delicious *bubur hitam* (black rice pudding). In fashionable Seminyak, north of Kuta, many new establishments have opened. Here the modern coffee house can be seen in all its varieties from French patisseries to espresso bars offering Italian-style sandwiches and fresh salads.

Fast Food and Takeaways

Bali has seen the rapid establishment of fast-food chains, and McDonald's, Pizza Hut, Kentucky Fried Chicken, Starbuck's, Burger King and Wendy's can be found in tourist and city areas. Most restaurants will do *bungkus* (takeaways) and some will deliver.

Alcohol

It would be a pity to visit Bali and Lombok without sampling the local alcohol, especially since imported alcohol attracts high duties and is expensive. Bintang is a popular, refreshing lager; Bali Hai, while cheaper, is not as good. A local rosé wine called Hatten's is being produced – this is light, dry, inexpensive and fairly drinkable. *Arak* cocktails, made with palm brandy, are a popular choice.

Alcohol is available almost everywhere in Bali, even in small *warung* outside tourist areas. In Muslim Lombok, alcohol is available only in tourist areas and up-market hotels, and should be consumed within the premises.

Children

The restaurant scenes in Bali and Lombok do not generally cater specifically to children, but it is easy to find something children will eat. Some restaurants will serve a half-portion, and have high-chairs available on request; others will not. The larger hotels often offer buffet breakfast free to children under 12.

View of Jimbaran Bay from PJ's at Four Seasons Resort

Vegetarian Food

There is a wonderful range of tasty and nutritious vegetarian dishes in Bali and Lombok. *Tahu* (tofu) and *tempe* (cakes made of compressed, fermented soy beans) are popular and plentiful, as is *bubur sayur bayam* (rice porridge with spinach leaves, chilli, coconut shavings and coconut milk).

Many restaurants include a variety of vegetarian dishes on their menus. Those with Chinese-style dishes usually offer a wider range. It is possible to get vegetarian versions of non-vegetarian dishes on request. Just make sure your order is stated clearly.

Dining in the courtyard of the Hard Rock Hotel in Kuta

Restaurant Etiquette

Many Balinese still eat with the right hand and no cutlery (the left hand is never used), and well-dressed locals can often be seen eating in this traditional way even in Western restaurants.

Food will often appear in random order. It is best simply to start rather than wait until everyone is served.

Casual clothing is accepted everywhere, but people tend to be more smartly dressed in up-market restaurants. Most restaurants are open-air, so smoking is generally allowed; only the most exclusive places will have a non-smoking area.

Tipping is more common than it once was; expensive places tend to add a service charge anyway. Staff in cheaper local restaurants will be happy with a token tip.

What to Eat in Bali and Lombok

***Sapi rendang* (beef curry)**

AUTHENTIC BALINESE FOOD, of the kind served at places catering for the local population, consists mostly of rice dishes (*nasi campur* is the most common) and simple snacks. The fresh seafood is good. Coconut milk is a favourite ingredient in many Balinese recipes. It gives fragrance and a rich texture to curries and sauces. Commonly used ingredients include ginger, turmeric, coriander seeds, onion, garlic and tamarind; red chillies and pepper are often added. The fresh fruit is varied and delicious. The simplicity of the everyday cuisine contrasts with the lavish presentation of dishes for festivals and ceremonies.

Nasi goreng *(fried rice) is usually served with a fried egg. This dish is eaten for breakfast and throughout the day.*

Mie goreng *(fried noodles) is a mix of vegetables, tofu and sometimes seafood. It is most often eaten for lunch.*

Ayam bakar *(grilled chicken) is a simple meal, served with* sambal *and sometimes with french fries.*

Bebek betutu *(spicy duck) is crispy and cooked with chilli. It is usually served with a tangy lemon sauce.*

Satay *(grilled meat slices on a stick) is pork, chicken, beef and sometimes seafood, grilled and served with a sweet, peanut dipping sauce.*

Nasi campur *(mixed rice) is a combination of steamed rice with a range of accompaniments varying according to the occasion.*

Babi guling *(roast pig) is a very succulent pork dish for special occasions.*

Rujak *(tropical salad) is a mix of fruit and vegetables with peanut or chilli sauce.*

Kerupuk *(fried crackers) is a snack served with a sweet, peanut dipping sauce.*

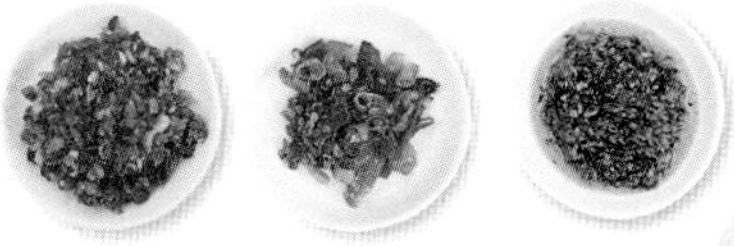

Sambal *are pastes made with chilli or spices, tasty sauces to accompany rice-based dishes and snacks.*

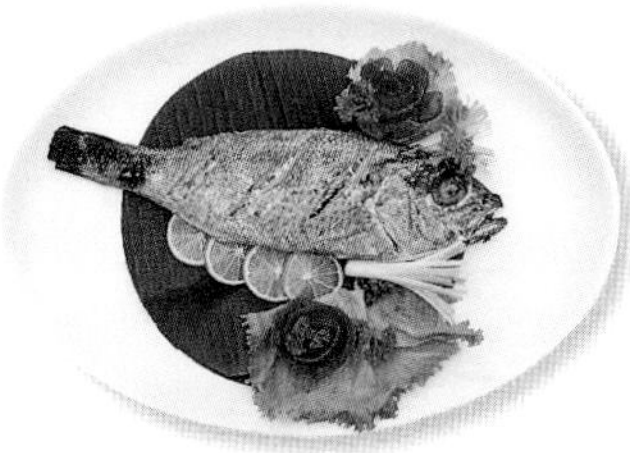

Ikan bakar *(grilled fish) is often eaten with slices of lime,* sambal *and rice dishes.*

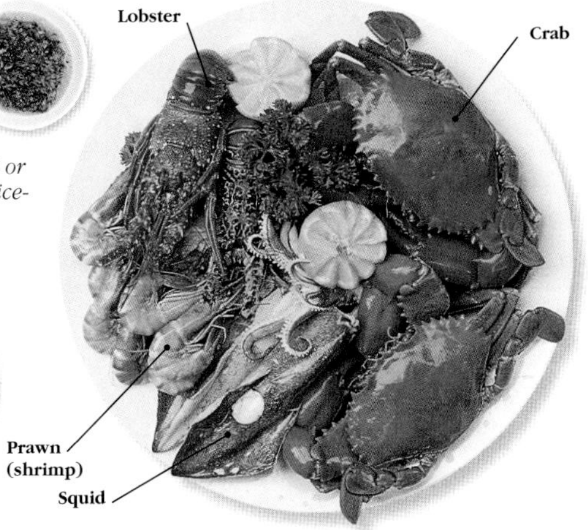

A seafood platter *has local lobster, crayfish, prawn (shrimp), squid and crab. Platters are sometimes deep-fried, but more often barbecued and served with simple sauces.*

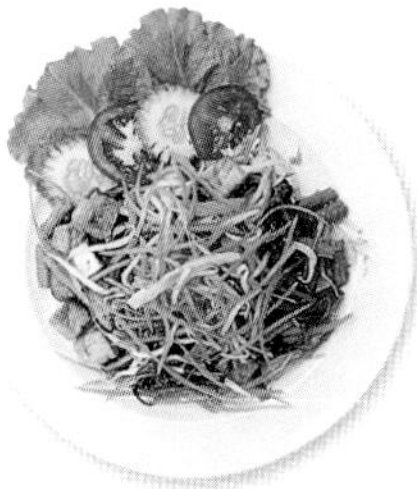

Urab *is a dish of salad vegetables, mixed with coconut milk and spices.*

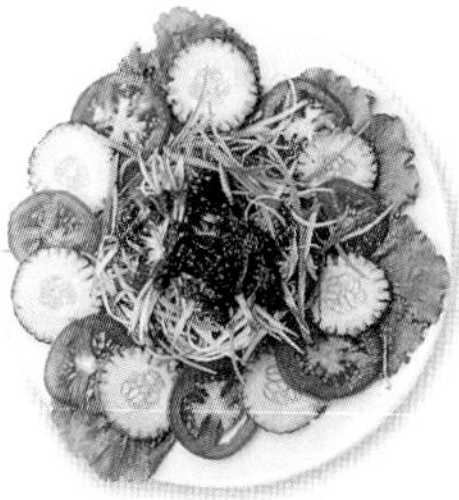

Tahu telur *is deep-fried beancurd, coated in egg and served with a sweet sauce.*

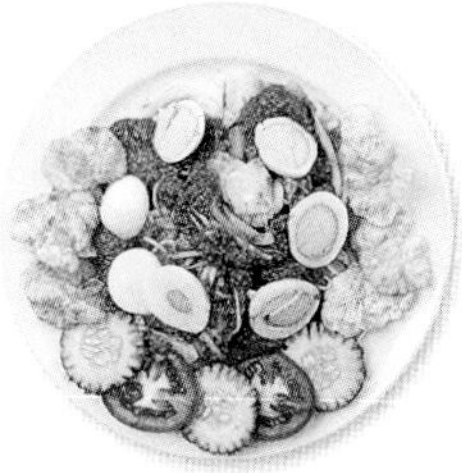

Gado gado *is blanched mixed vegetables, served with a sweet peanut sauce.*

Banana pancakes *are usually drizzled with honey.*

Jajan *are colourful steamed cakes that are coconut-based.*

Bubur hitam *(black rice pudding) is served hot or cold.*

Es campur *(fruits, nuts and jellies) is served with shaved ice.*

Tropical Fruits

Fruits are eaten at all times of the day and are often sold from small carts at the side of the street. Peeled and skewered fresh fruit can be bought cheaply as a snack, and restaurants serve cut fruit selections on top of crushed ice.

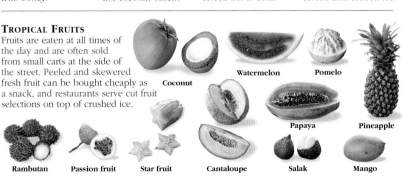

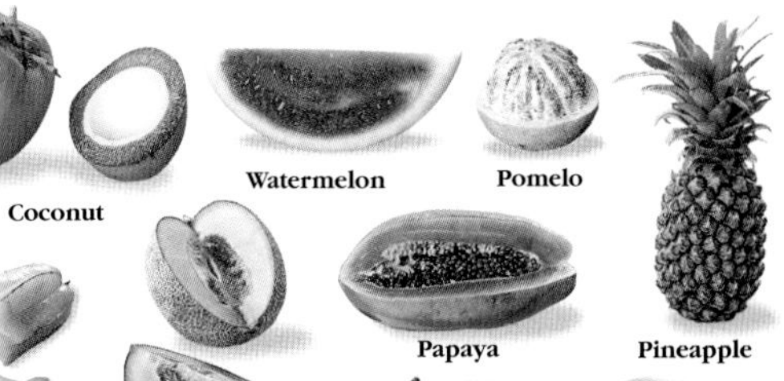

Coconut

Watermelon

Pomelo

Papaya

Pineapple

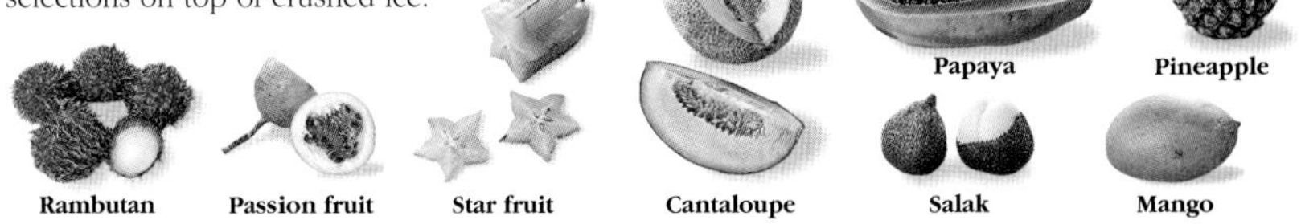

Rambutan

Passion fruit

Star fruit

Cantaloupe

Salak

Mango

Choosing a Restaurant

Bali and Lombok's restaurants serve a wide range of cuisines generally at reasonable prices. Several hotels *(see pp170–79)* have good restaurants, although these are often a little more expensive. The recommendations in this guide have been chosen for their value, exceptional food and interesting location. Many places serving international food also serve some local dishes.

	Price	Credit Cards	Wine List	Vegetarian Cuisine	Indonesian Cuisine	Outdoor Dining
South Bali						
Denpasar: *Warung Wardani* Jalan Yudistira. *(0361) 224 398.* Good, authentic Indonesian food. Popular with the locals, especially for lunch.	Rp			●	●	
Denpasar: *Rasa Sayang* Jalan Teuku Umar. *(0362) 262 006.* An excellent and very popular Chinese restaurant, scrupulously clean, with white tablecloths and crisp service.	RpRpRp	MC V		●		
Jimbaran: *Jimbaran Seafood Markets* Jimbaran Beach. The Markets comprise small bamboo huts run by the families of local fishermen. Choose your own seafood and they will grill it over coconut husks and serve it up with rice, a simple salad, baked potato and cold beer. Good value and delicious.	RpRp		●			●
Jimbaran: *La Indonesie* Jalan Raya Uluwatu 108. *(0361) 701 763.* Located on the beach, this restaurant has been recently renovated and offers authentic Indonesian cuisine.	RpRpRp			●	●	●
Jimbaran: *The Cliff* Bali Cliff Resort, Jalan Pura Batu Pageh Unggasan. *(0361) 771 992.* The Sunday brunch at the Bali Cliff's coffee shop is extensive, and the price includes the use of the resort's pool.	RpRpRpRp	AE DC MC V		●	●	●
Jimbaran: *PJ's* Four Season Resort Bali, Jimbaran Bay. *(0361) 701 010.* A casual bistro on the Jimbaran beach. The fresh food, great cocktails and desserts are hard to resist.	RpRpRpRpRp	AE JCB MC V	●	●		●
Kerobokan: *Khaima* Jalan Laksmana Oberoi. *(0361) 742 3925.* This Moroccan restaurant serves excellent cous-cous and tajin curry with all the trimmings. The room is decorated with colourful fabrics.	RpRp		●	●		●
Kuta: *Café Warna* Jalan Pantai Arjuna. *(0361) 737 138.* The menu here offers a variety of international dishes, including burritos, Thai chicken curry, cheeseburgers and satays. Diners can request to eat in a tree house overlooking the ocean.	RpRpRp	AE MC V	●	●	●	●
Kuta: *Kafe Batan Waru* Bali Garden Hotel, Jalan Kartika Plaza. Located across the street from Waterbom Park *(see p67)*, this upmarket café dishes up traditional Indonesian food and Western favourites.	RpRpRp	AE MC V		●	●	●
Kuta: *Papa's Café* Jalan Pantai. Located in the centre of Kuta, this restaurant serves authentic Italian food.	RpRpRp	AE JCB MC V	●	●		●
Kuta: *The Balcony* Jalan Bensari 16. *(0361) 757 409.* *balcony@balihotelsandvillas.com* The balcony serves a variety of cuisines, including mediterranean, Spanish and Australian dishes. The servings are generous.	RpRpRpRp	MC V	●			
Kuta: *Hard Rock Café* Jalan Pantai. *(0361) 755 661.* The famous café at this Kuta Beach location has great Western food, good bands and lots of fun every night.	RpRpRpRp	AE DC JCB MC V	●	●		●

Price categories are for a two-course meal for one, including service charges, excluding drinks.
(Rp) under Rp25,000
(Rp)(Rp) Rp25,000–50,000
(Rp)(Rp)(Rp) Rp50,000–100,000
(Rp)(Rp)(Rp)(Rp) Rp100,000–250,000
(Rp)(Rp)(Rp)(Rp)(Rp) over Rp250,000

CREDIT CARDS
Credit cards accepted: *AE* American Express; *DC* Diners Club; *JCB* Japan Credit Bureau; *MC* MasterCard; *V* Visa.
WINE LIST
An extensive range of good quality wines.
VEGETARIAN CUISINE
A good selection of vegetarian dishes.
INDONESIAN CUISINE
Indonesian cuisine on the menu.
OUTDOOR DINING
Garden, courtyard or terrace with outside tables.

Restaurant	Price	Credit Cards	Wine List	Vegetarian Cuisine	Indonesian Cuisine	Outdoor Dining
KUTA: *Kori Restaurant & Bar* Poppies Lane II. (0361) 758 605. www.korirestaurant.com Kori offers excellent variety and good value in a lovely indoor/outdoor setting. The bar is popular in its own right.	(Rp)(Rp)(Rp)(Rp)	AE MC V	●	●	●	●
KUTA: *Kunyit* Hotel Sautika Beach, Jalan Kartika Plaza. (0361) 751 267. One of the best restaurants in the area for sampling fresh Balinese food.	(Rp)(Rp)(Rp)(Rp)	AE DC MC V		●	●	
KUTA: *Made's Warung 1* Jalan Pantai. (0361) 755 297. warmade@indo.net.id Kuta's oldest-established *warung* has had a beautiful face lift. Excellent Indonesian, Asian and Western choices for breakfast, lunch and dinner. One of the most popular restaurants in Kuta.	(Rp)(Rp)(Rp)(Rp)	AE MC V	●	●	●	
KUTA: *TJ's Tex-Mex* Poppies Lane I. (0361) 751 093. A long-established place serving up some of the best authentic Mexican food on the island. Laid-back atmosphere, gardens and good music.	(Rp)(Rp)(Rp)(Rp)	AE MC V	●	●		
LEGIAN: *Aroma's* Jalan Legian 341. (0361) 751 003. Purely vegetarian but not short on indulgence, Aroma's is a popular choice for snacks, main meals, coffees and their famous desserts.	(Rp)(Rp)(Rp)	AE JCB MC V	●	●	●	●
LEGIAN: *Ketupat* Jalan Legian 109. (0361) 754 209. This restaurant is named after a traditional Indonesian dish which consists of a packet of steamed rice served with various condiments.	(Rp)(Rp)(Rp)	AE DC MC V	●	●	●	●
LEGIAN: *Macaroni Club* Jalan Legian 52X. (0361) 754 662. The striking modern decor is a perfect setting for the light Italian menu. Great for people-watching. Features live bands occasionally.	(Rp)(Rp)(Rp)	AE MC V	●	●		●
LEGIAN: *Teras* Jalan Legian 494. (0361) 730 492. An indoor/outdoor terrace restaurant with a lively atmosphere and a good Italian menu. A seafood and meat grill, brick pizza oven and a separate vegetarian kitchen provide lots of variety.	(Rp)(Rp)(Rp)	JCB MC V	●	●		●
LEGIAN: *Fuel* Jalan Legian 62. Located in the heart of Legian, this upmarket bar and restaurant serves a bistro menu with many dishes cooked on an outdoor grill. The stylish interior is comfortable and there is also a patio. A DJ mixes tunes six nights a week.	(Rp)(Rp)(Rp)(Rp)	AE MC V	●	●		●
NUSA DUA: *Pasar Senggol* Nusa Dua. (0361) 771 234. inquiries@grandhyattbali.com For a single price, guests wander from stall to stall sampling food from around the world, then relax at candle-lit tables to watch traditional entertainment.	(Rp)(Rp)	AE DC JCB MC V	●	●		●
NUSA DUA: *The Restaurant* Amanusa, Nusa Dua. (0361) 772 333. www.amannusa.com This restaurant at the Amanusa resort offers a modern, mainly Italian menu. Indoor and poolside dining available.	(Rp)(Rp)(Rp)(Rp)	AE DC MC V	●	●	●	●
NUSA DUA: *The Terrace* Amanusa, Nusa Dua. (0361) 772 333. amanusa@indosat.net.id A well-regarded restaurant overlooking Nusa Dua's golf course and sandy beaches. Serves Thai-inspired, Pacific Rim cuisine.	(Rp)(Rp)(Rp)(Rp)(Rp)	AE DC JCB MC V	●	●	●	●

For key to symbols see back flap

Price categories are for a two-course meal for one, including service charges, excluding drinks.
Rp under Rp25,000
RpRp Rp25,000–50,000
RpRpRp Rp50,000–100,000
RpRpRpRp Rp100,000–250,000
RpRpRpRpRp over Rp250,000

CREDIT CARDS
Credit cards accepted: *AE* American Express; *DC* Diners Club; *JCB* Japan Credit Bureau; *MC* MasterCard; *V* Visa.
WINE LIST
An extensive range of good quality wines.
VEGETARIAN CUISINE
A good selection of vegetarian dishes.
INDONESIAN CUISINE
Indonesian cuisine on the menu.
OUTDOOR DINING
Garden, courtyard or terrace with outside tables.

Restaurant	Price	Credit Cards	Wine List	Vegetarian Cuisine	Indonesian Cuisine	Outdoor Dining
NUSA LEMBONGAN: *Jojo's Restaurant* Nusa Lembongan Resort. *(0366) 245 38.* Beautifully situated. Serves Western and Southeast Asian food with a French twist. The speciality is seafood grilled in banana leaves.	RpRpRp	AE DC JCB MC V	●	■	●	■
SANUR: *Ketut's Warung* Jalan Danau Poso 78, Blanjong. *(0361) 289 757.* Serves simple, good local dishes in a relaxed, traditional atmosphere.	Rp			■	●	
SANUR: *Sanur Deli* Jalan Danau Poso 46. *(0361) 270 544.* This tiny gem sells a tasty range of homecooked food, including quiches, sandwiches, breads, desserts and fresh juices.	Rp			■		■
SANUR: *Jazz Bar and Grille* Jalan Bypass Ngurah Rai. *(0361) 285 892.* The international menu here has an emphasis on Mexican, but the Hawaiian dishes are also worth trying. There is nightly jazz music.	RpRp	AE JCB MC V	●	■		
SANUR: *Massimo's* Jalan Danau Tamblingan 206. *(0361) 288 942.* W *www.balimassimo.com* This reasonably-priced Italian restaurant prepares delicious pizzas and traditional dishes. There is also a huge wine cellar, stocking a large collection of bottles from all over the globe.	RpRp	MC V	●	■		■
SANUR: *The Village* Jalan Danau Tamblingan. *(0361) 285 892.* An American-style restaurant that dishes up the usual fare of pizza, steak and seafood. Prices are reasonable.	RpRp	AE MC V	●	■		■
SANUR: *Café Batujimbar* Jalan Danau Tamblingan 152. *(0361) 287 374.* This café by the pavement serves up Western and Indonesian dishes and features fresh, healthy ingredients, juices and some indulgent desserts. Excellent vegetarian selection.	RpRpRp	AE JCB MC V	●	■	●	■
SANUR: *Café Wayang* Komplek Sanur Raya 12–14. *(0361) 287 591.* This café has a wide following for its Asian-Mediterranean fusion cuisine. Friday night entertainment is a popular draw.	RpRpRp	MC V	●	■	●	
SANUR: *Pergola* Jalan Danua Toba 2. *(0361) 288 462.* Pergola serves a variety of international dishes, including duck á l'orange, beef stroganoff and flambées. The restaurant also doubles as a cooking school for adults and children.	RpRpRp	MC V	●	■		■
SANUR: *Telaga Naga* Bali Hyatt, Jalan Danau Tamblingan. *(0361) 281 234.* This Chinese restaurant specialises in Cantonese and Szechwan cuisine. Ideal for a romantic evening meal, the tables are surrounded by a tranquil lotus pond.	RpRpRp	AE JCB MC V	●	■		■
SEMINYAK: *Warung Batavia* Jalan Raya Kerobokan. *(0361) 731 641.* A popular *warung* serving excellent *nasi campur* *(see p182)*.	Rp			■	●	
SEMINYAK: *Puri Seafood Bintang Lima* Jalan Lasmana 5. *(0361) 733 038.* A unique Balinese restaurant offering unusual seafood specials in an intimate, comfortable atmosphere.	RpRp		●	■	●	

SEMINYAK: *Zula* (Rp)(Rp)
Jalan Dhyana Pura 5. *(0361) 732 723.*
This popular vegetarian café is a rare find along this stretch of beach. The menu is predominantly Middle Eastern, but the Planet Platter includes seaweed, tempura, tofu and brown rice.

SEMINYAK: *Hana Restaurant* (Rp)(Rp)(Rp)
Jalan Raya Seminyak. *(0361) 732 778.*
An intimate, high-quality Japanese restaurant serving both raw and grilled Japanese food. Very reasonably priced.

SEMINYAK: *Made's Warung 2* (Rp)(Rp)(Rp)
Jalan Raya Seminyak. *(0361) 732 985.*
A sister to the famous Made's Warung of Kuta *(see p185)*, with lovely modern Balinese decor and themed shops. Good food and service. Booking is highly recommended for dinner.

SEMINYAK: *Paul's Place* (Rp)(Rp)(Rp)
Jalan Laksmana 4A. *(0361) 736 715.*
Located on the famous "Eat Street", Paul's Place is renowned for its Thai curries. Its open-air, third floor café overlooks rice fields. There is also a shop selling Asian arts and crafts.

SEMINYAK: *Ryoshi* (Rp)(Rp)(Rp)
Jalan Raya Seminyak. *(0361) 731 152.*
Ryoshi's reputation for reliable, quality Japanese food at very reasonable prices is well deserved.

SEMINYAK: *Santa Fe Restaurant* (Rp)(Rp)(Rp)
Jalan Abimanyu 11A. *(0361) 731 147.*
This 24-hour eatery is popular with the locals and great for a late night bite. Pizzas, Mexican and lots more in this hip roadside eatery.

SEMINYAK: *Axiom* (Rp)(Rp)(Rp)(Rp)
Jalan Raya Seminyak 18a. *(0361) 738 820.*
This excellent restaurant is located on the main street in Seminyak. The menu specialises in modern Australian and European cuisine with a twist. A meat-eaters heaven.

SEMINYAK: *Fabio's* (Rp)(Rp)(Rp)(Rp)
Jalan Raya Seminyak 66. *(0361) 261 232.* *fabiobali@yahoo.com*
Lobster thermidor is the speciality at this Italian restaurant with a garden setting. The homemade ice cream is also excellent.

SEMINYAK: *La Lucciola Restaurant Bar Beach Club* (Rp)(Rp)(Rp)(Rp)
Jalan Kayu Aya, Kayu Aya Beach. *(0361) 730 838.*
Superbly located on the beach, La Lucciola is very popular. Offers a brasserie-style menu and delicious desserts. Book ahead for dinner.

SEMINYAK: *Kafe Warisan* (Rp)(Rp)(Rp)(Rp)(Rp)
Jalan Raya Kerobokan, Banjar Taman. *(0361) 731 175.*
www.kafewarisan.com A popular restaurant overlooking the ricefields, serving delicious, authentic French food.

SEMINYAK: *Ku De Ta* (Rp)(Rp)(Rp)(Rp)(Rp)
Jalan Laksmana 9. *(0361) 736 969.* *www.kudeta.net*
This popular restaurant and cigar bar serves excellent Australian food. The large, modern dining area is open air.

SEMINYAK: *The Legian* (Rp)(Rp)(Rp)(Rp)(Rp)
Jalan Laksmana 9. *(0361) 730 622.* *www.ghmhotel.com*
Another popular, open-air restaurant located on the beach front. The international cuisine here is prepared by award-winning chefs. Live piano jazz is played in the evenings.

TANJUNG BENOA: *Bumbu Bali* (Rp)(Rp)(Rp)
Jalan Pratama. *www.balifoods.com*
For authentic Balinese cuisine, Bumbu Bali is a must. Order the set menu.

TANJUNG BENOA: *Coco's Beach Club* (Rp)(Rp)(Rp)(Rp)
Novotel Benoa. *(0361) 772 239.*
A beach-side bistro offering breakfast, lunch and dinner. It has a good, lively, Robinson Crusoe-style bar.

Restaurant	Cards	Col 2	Col 3	Col 4	Col 5
Zula			■		
Hana Restaurant	MC V	●	■		■
Made's Warung 2	AE JCB MC V	●	■	●	■
Paul's Place	AE JCB MC V	●	■		■
Ryoshi	AE DC JCB MC V	●	■		■
Santa Fe Restaurant	MC V	●	■	●	
Axiom	AE MC V	●			■
Fabio's	AE MC V	●	■		■
La Lucciola Restaurant Bar Beach Club	AE MC V	●	■		■
Kafe Warisan	AE MC V	●	■		■
Ku De Ta	AE JCB MC V	●	■		■
The Legian	AE DC JCB MC V	●	■		■
Bumbu Bali	AE MC V	●	■	●	
Coco's Beach Club	AE DC JCB MC V	●	■		■

For key to symbols see back flap

Price categories are for a two-course meal for one, including service charges, excluding drinks.
Ⓡ under Rp25,000
ⓇⓇ Rp25,000–50,000
ⓇⓇⓇ Rp50,000–100,000
ⓇⓇⓇⓇ Rp100,000–250,000
ⓇⓇⓇⓇⓇ over Rp250,000

Credit Cards
Credit cards accepted: *AE* American Express; *DC* Diners Club; *JCB* Japan Credit Bureau; *MC* MasterCard; *V* Visa.
Wine List
An extensive range of good quality wines.
Vegetarian Cuisine
A good selection of vegetarian dishes.
Indonesian Cuisine
Indonesian cuisine on the menu.
Outdoor Dining
Garden, courtyard or terrace with outside tables.

Restaurant	Price	Credit Cards	Wine List	Vegetarian Cuisine	Indonesian Cuisine	Outdoor Dining
Tuban: *All Star's Surf Café* Jalan Kartika Plaza 8x. *(0361) 757 933.* This themed café features surf memorabilia, an accessories shop, international beers and an American-style menu.	ⓇⓇ	AE MC V	●	■		■
Tuban: *Khin Khao Thai Restaurant* Jalan Kartika Plaza 170. *(0361) 757 808.* The barbecue is a signature meal here. Everyone chooses from a variety of fresh ingredients and the food is cooked on a hot grill at the table.	ⓇⓇⓇ	AE MC V	●	■		
Tuban: *Golden Lotus* Bali Dynasti Resort, Jalan Kartika Plaza. *(0361) 752 403.* At the Sunday *yum-cha*, steaming trolleys are wheeled around, from which guests can choose their food. The rest of the week the restaurant serves first-class Chinese *dim sum* and à la carte.	ⓇⓇⓇⓇ	AE DC JCB MC V	●	■	●	
Tuban: *Ma Joly* Jalan Wana Segara. *(0361) 753 708.* One of the new, fashionable eateries, Ma Joly's serves exquisite French food. Located right on the beach, specials include fish jubilee and lobster with mustard sauce.	ⓇⓇⓇⓇ	AE DC MC V	●	■		■
Central Bali						
Ayung River Gorge: *Ayung Terrace Restaurant* Four Seasons Resort, Sayan. *(0361) 977 577.* This restaurant has a spectacular location in the Four Seasons. An excellent choice of Asian and fusion dishes for special occasions.	ⓇⓇⓇⓇ	AE JCB MC V	●	■	●	■
Ayung River Gorge: *The Restaurant* Alila Hotel, Payangan. *(0361) 975 963.* Recommended for its great views, delicious food, excellent service and sense of style. The Sunday brunch is very popular.	ⓇⓇⓇⓇ	AE DC JCB MC V	●		●	■
Ayung River Gorge: *Amandari Restaurant* Amandari Resort, Kedewatan. *(0361) 975 333.* A good place for a special celebration. This restaurant features a top-quality menu full of inspiring suggestions for a meal and a good (but costly) wine list. The atmosphere is peaceful and stylish.	ⓇⓇⓇⓇⓇ	AE DC JCB MC V	●	■		
Sanggingan: *Indus* Jalan Raya Sanggingan. *(0361) 977 684.* Owned by the group that runs Casa Luna in Ubud, Indus is the more stylish cousin with plenty of tempting items on the menu. Beautifully decorated, great views.	ⓇⓇ	MC V	●	■	●	■
Tegallalang: *Blue Yogi* Tegallalang. *(0361) 901 368.* The Blue Yogi offers some surprising French and English specials along with more traditional fare and home-made wine. Great views.	Ⓡ					
Tegallalang: *Kampung Café* Tegallalang. *(0361) 901 201.* A little off the beaten track, this café is well worth a visit. Offers a delicious menu, and is known for its vegetarian dishes and fresh salads. Reasonable prices.	ⓇⓇⓇ	MC V	●	■	●	■
Ubud: *Bali Spirit Yoga Studio and Café* Jalan Hanoman 44. *(0361) 973 381.* *www.balispirit.com* One of the newer eateries in Ubud that serves delicious baked desserts and an assortment of coffees, teas and juices. There is a yoga studio upstairs.	Ⓡ	MC V		■		■

UBUD: *Dirty Duck (Bebek Bengil)* Rp Rp

Jalan Hanoman and Monkey Forest Road. *(0361) 975 489.*

A local institution, the Dirty Duck serves up traditional Indonesian dishes, and European home-style cooking such as bratwurst and mash, and old-fashioned apple crumble. It also has a great bar.

AE JCB MC V

UBUD: *Ary's Warung* Rp Rp Rp

Jalan Raya Ubud. *(0361) 975 053.* *www.dekco.com*

An elegant restaurant suited for people watching and sampling a variety of Asian dishes. The small portions are artfully presented – try the "Tasting Menu" for a bit of everthing.

AE JCB MC V

UBUD: *Café Lotus* Rp Rp Rp

Jalan Raya Ubud. *(0361) 975 660.*

This café gets its name from the lotus pond at its front. It serves Italian and Indonesian cuisine, and is famous for its delicious *bebek betutu* (spicy duck) and *babi kecap* (pork in sweet sauce).

AE MC V

UBUD: *Terazo Bar and Restaurant* Rp Rp Rp

Jalan Suweta. *(0361) 978 941.*

This restaurant–bistro serves Mediterranean and Asian cuisine. Specials include fresh mud crabs and lamb shank.

AE MC V

UBUD: *Tut Mak* Rp Rp Rp

Jalan Dewi Sita. *(0361) 975 754.*

This place was one of the first to offer gourmet coffee in Ubud. There is also a full selection of light, delicious meals on the menu. Good place for an afternoon snack.

AE MC V

UBUD: *Batan Waru* Rp Rp Rp Rp

Jalan Dewi Sita. *(0361) 977 528.*

Billed as Ubud's answer to Made's Warung in Kuta *(see p185)*, Batan Waru is clean and efficient, dishing up great Indonesian and Western dishes made with quality ingredients.

AE JCB MC V

UBUD: *Café Wayan* Rp Rp Rp Rp

Monkey Forest Road. *(0361) 975 447.*

Delicious home-style cooking and an unbeatable chocolate cake make this a popular café.

MC V

UBUD: *Casa Luna* Rp Rp Rp Rp

Jalan Raya Ubud. *(0361) 973 283.*

A laid-back café-style restaurant famous for its cakes and Sunday brunch. Good for a healthy lunch or snack. Films are screened nightly.

AE MC V

UBUD: *Ryoshi* Rp Rp Rp Rp

Jalan Raya Ubud. *(0361) 972 192.*

Ryoshi serves sushi, grilled selections, noodles and rice dishes in a cheerful yet traditional atmosphere. Excellent prices.

AE DC JCB MC V

UBUD: *Three Monkeys Cuisine and Art Café* Rp Rp Rp Rp

Monkey Forest Road. *(0361) 975 554.*

This stylish restaurant specialises in modern Mediterranean and Asian cuisine. The delicious homemade ice creams, cakes and desserts are worth leaving room for. The cappuccino bar sells organic teas and fresh juices, and paintings by contemporary Indonesian artists are on display.

MC V

UBUD: *Wunderbar* Rp Rp Rp Rp

Jalan Pengosekan. *(0361) 978 339.* *www.wunderbar-bali.com*

This bright yellow and orange German-style café is one of the few in town with air conditioning. Meat-lovers will adore the rib-eye steaks and beef tenderloin. There is a pool table and large screen TV.

MC V

UBUD: *biji* Rp Rp Rp Rp Rp

Begawan Giri Estate, Banjar Begawan. *(0361) 978 888.*

Secluded restaurant with a spectacular setting, featuring a Thai-style menu. Champagne brunch on Sundays is delicious.

AE JCB MC V

EAST BALI

CANDI DASA: *TJ's Water Garden* Rp Rp Rp

Jalan Raya. *(0363) 41 540.*

This restaurant on the main road at Candi Dasa offers simple, healthy sandwiches, salads, Mexican dishes and tempting desserts.

AE JCB MC V

Price categories are for a two-course meal for one, including service charges, excluding drinks.
(Rp) under Rp25,000
(Rp)(Rp) Rp25,000–50,000
(Rp)(Rp)(Rp) Rp50,000–100,000
(Rp)(Rp)(Rp)(Rp) Rp100,000–250,000
(Rp)(Rp)(Rp)(Rp)(Rp) over Rp250,000

Credit Cards
Credit cards accepted: *AE* American Express; *DC* Diners Club; *JCB* Japan Credit Bureau; *MC* MasterCard; *V* Visa.
Wine List
An extensive range of good quality wines.
Vegetarian Cuisine
A good selection of vegetarian dishes.
Indonesian Cuisine
Indonesian cuisine on the menu.
Outdoor Dining
Garden, courtyard or terrace with outside tables.

Restaurant	Credit Cards	Wine List	Vegetarian Cuisine	Indonesian Cuisine	Outdoor Dining
Manggis: *Sea Salt Restaurant* (Rp)(Rp)(Rp)(Rp) The Serai Resort. (0363) 41 041. Well respected for its cooking school, this excellent restaurant offers local cuisine as well as inventive Pacific Rim selections.	AE DC JCB MC V	●	●	●	●
Manggis: *Amankila Beach Club* (Rp)(Rp)(Rp)(Rp)(Rp) Amankila. (0363) 41 333. The more casual and reasonably priced of Amankila's two restaurants offers world-class modern cuisine in a stylish tranquil setting.	AE DC JCB MC V	●	●	●	●
Padang Bai: *Pantai Ayu* (Rp)(Rp) Jalan Silayukti. (0363) 41 396. A popular hangout offering a wide variety of dishes at excellent prices. Good choice of Indonesian snacks.			●	●	●
Padang Bai: *Puri Rai Restaurant and Bar* (Rp)(Rp) Jalan Silayukti. (0363) 41 187. One of the best restaurants in Padang Bai. The vegetarian dishes and pizzas are good value. Interesting drinks list, including *arak* coffee.			●	●	●
Sideman: *Sacred Mountain* (Rp)(Rp)(Rp)(Rp) Banjar Budamanis. (0366) 24 330. The Thai-based menu offers healthy choices and a good selection of vegetarian meals in a tranquil atmosphere.	MC V	●	●		●
Tulamben: *Tunjung Restaurant* (Rp)(Rp)(Rp)(Rp) Mimpi Resort. (0366) 21 642. 24-hour room service One of a few options in the locality, Tunjung's food is of good quality, tasty and varied.	AE JCB MC V		●	●	●
North and West Bali					
Lovina: *Warung Bamboo* (Rp) Pantai Anturan. (0362) 41 882. Accessible by beach only, so park nearby and walk. Serves good Western and Indonesian basics, cold beer and a must-try chocolate cake.			●	●	●
Lovina: *Khi Khi Restaurant* (Rp)(Rp) Kalibukbuk. (0362) 41 548. Khi Khi offers Japanese and Indonesian specialities such as sushi, noodles and grilled food in a pleasant environment.			●	●	
Lovina: *Sea Breeze* (Rp)(Rp)(Rp) Jalan Binaria. (0362) 41 138. A beach-side eatery featuring tempting English and Indonesian café-style food. Healthy selections, fresh juices and good desserts.			●	●	●
Lovina: *Saraswati Restaurant* (Rp)(Rp)(Rp)(Rp) Puri Bagus Hotel. (0362) 21 403. This elegant 24-hour restaurant overlooks the hotel's gardens and pool. Authentic Balinese and Western dishes with an Asian influence.	AE DC JCB MC V	●	●	●	●
Lovina: *Damai's Restaurant* (Rp)(Rp)(Rp)(Rp)(Rp) Damai Lovina Villas. (0362) 41 008. A small, tasteful restaurant on top of a mountain and rated as one of the top restaurants in Southeast Asia. Lunch includes a selection; dinner is a set menu. Cookery courses available by prior arrangement.	AE DC JCB MC V	●	●	●	●
Pemuteran: *Puri Ganesha* (Rp)(Rp) Pemuteran. (0362) 94 766. This small restaurant, located in a simple villa complex, serves delicious food. An ayurvedic menu has fish and chicken but no red meat, they will prepare a special menu if you phone in advance. Cookery classes.	AE MC V	●	●		●

PEMUTERAN: *Taman Selini Restaurant* RpRpRpRp
Pemuteran. ☎ *(0362) 93 449.*
The menu reflects the chef's vast experience with Greek cooking. Set in a beautiful position overlooking the beach, this restaurant serves well-prepared food at reasonable prices.
MC V

PUPUAN: *Star Fruit Café* RpRp
Banjar Suradadi, Blimbing.
The quality of the food is excellent and the setting is wonderful. The fresh salads are superb, and the daily specials are worth trying. Scenic walks nearby.
MC V

LOMBOK

GILI ISLES: *Big Chili* Rp
Pantai Gili Trawangan.
Small beach restaurant with a great view and Indonesian food. The *nasi campur (see p182)* is excellent.

GILI ISLES: *Borneo Café* Rp
Pantai Gili Trawangan. A good place to sample traditional seafood, *nasi kuning* (yellow rice) and *kangkung goreng* (fried watercress leaves), and wash it all down with cold beer.

GILI ISLES: *Borobudur* Rp
Pantai Gili Trawangan. ☎ *(0370) 634 893.*
One of the best beach restaurants, clean and with internet facilities. Serves delicious grilled seafood.
MC V

GILI ISLES: *Dino Restaurant* Rp
Salobai Hotel, Gili Trawangan. ☎ *(0370) 643 152.*
Great menu featuring Chinese, Western and Indonesian food. The bar is in a boat and the restaurant overlooks the ocean. Weekly parties.

GILI ISLES: *Rudy's Pub & Restaurant* Rp
Pantai Gili Trawangan. ☎ *(0370) 642 311.*
It's party time every Friday night at Rudy's, where there is good Western food, great views and the dancing goes on until 3 am.

GILI ISLES: *Waves Restaurant* RpRp
Hotel Vila Ombak, Gili Trawangan. ☎ *(0370) 642 336.*
An open-air restaurant with ocean views. Waves' nightly entertainment includes live bands, acoustic guitar and traditional dancing.
MC V

SENGGIGI: *Asmara Restaurant* RpRp
Jalan Raya. ☎ *(0370) 693 619.*
Asmara specializes in steaks and seafood. It has a children's pool and play area. Pool and billiards are available.
MC V

SENGGIGI: *Café Wayan* RpRp
Jalan Raya, Batubulan. ☎ *(0370) 693 098.*
Well worth the trip up the hill from Senggigi for its delicious Indonesian and Italian dishes. Its fresh bread and chocolate cake are famous.

SENGGIGI: *Papaya Restaurant* RpRp
Jalan Raya. ☎ *(0370) 693 616.*
Strategically located in the heart of Senggigi, Bayan is a place where East meets West in a blend of traditional and modern.
MC V

SENGGIGI: *Sun Shine Restaurant* RpRp
Jalan Raya. ☎ *(0370) 693 232.*
A busy beachfront restaurant specializing in authentic Chinese food. The seafood is recommended.
MC V

TANJUNG: *Lumbung Restaurant* RpRpRpRpRp
Oberoi Hotel, Mendana Beach. ☎ *(0370) 638 444.*
An exclusive and beautiful place for a special meal, looking over the water towards the Gili Isles. The seafood is particularly good.
AE DC JCB MC V

For key to symbols see back flap

Shopping in Bali and Lombok

Visitors unused to bargaining may find shopping in Bali and Lombok a frustrating experience, but the temptations can be quite irresistible – in fact, many people travel to the islands just to buy goods for export. Many things easily available in Bali are fashionable elsewhere, and purchasing these direct at the source can be very rewarding. There are many products with "designer" labels on sale. Some are copies, hard to distinguish from the real thing. Others are genuine, produced under licence in Indonesia. Almost everything produced in Bali and Lombok is available in the busier shopping areas of Kuta, Sanur and Ubud and at the Galleria shopping centre in Nusa Dua. In general, the better presented the shop, the more one pays. Shops with similar goods, for example basketware, fabrics, furniture, jewellery and paintings, will often be grouped together, useful for comparing prices.

Bamboo and timber table lamp

Kuta Square – a popular shopping destination for visitors

Shopping Hours

Shopping hours vary from area to area, but most shops are open from around 10am until at least 6pm (10pm in Kuta). Markets generally start very early and close before the shops – the stalls usually begin to pack up around 3pm. Shopping in Bali and Lombok can be tiring – it is best to avoid the heat in the middle of the day.

How to Pay

Many shops catering to tourists price their goods in US dollars, but rupiah will be accepted. Major international credit cards, such as American Express, Visa and MasterCard, can be used in most upscale shops and major department stores. Some shops will add a surcharge (usually 3–5 per cent) for credit card payments. Cash is preferred in smaller shops.

Bargaining

Except in more expensive shops, where prices are clearly marked, bargaining is the normal practice. Begin by asking the shopkeeper for his price, then make an initial offer, usually a third to two-thirds of the asking price, before then moving towards a sensible compromise.

Hawkers

The hawkers on the streets can be aggressive and aggravating. Many of the goods they sell are of poor quality, and not always cheap. Unless you are interested, avoid eye contact and ignore them completely. In some areas of Bali hawkers are now required to wear coloured shirts with serial numbers. If they are causing trouble, take down their number and report them to the police. Just telling them you will do this is often enough to send them away.

Street hawkers selling goods to a tourist

Entrance to Matahari, the biggest chain store in Bali

Department Stores and Shopping Centres

Department stores and shopping centres are air-conditioned and comfortable, and sell both local and imported goods at excellent prices. Shoes, cosmetics and clothes are popular buys. The biggest chain is **Matahari**, with four stores located in Legian, Denpasar and Kuta.

Ramayana, also in Denpasar, is around the corner from Matahari, and has a variety of speciality shops. Bali Galleria at Simpang Siur in Kuta has two bookshops and numerous clothing and music shops. Bali's two major shopping centres are: Kuta Centre, with its sports shops, designer boutiques, shoe stores and "duty-free"; and Discovery Mall in front of Discovery Kartika Plaza in Kuta.

Bamboo and cane products on display at Pasar Ubud

Markets

Markets are crowded and sometimes airless, but it is worth searching in them for local handicrafts. **Kumbasari Market** in Denpasar is a dense warren of small shops selling goods sourced from around Indonesia. **Pasar Ubud** in Ubud *(see p89)* sells traditional fabrics, clothes, homewares and all manner of bric-à-brac. **Sukawati Art Market** in Gianyar is loud and claustrophobic, but an excellent source of locally produced crafts. In Lombok, the **Sweta Market**, located at the busy bus station on the eastern side of Sweta *(see p154)* is well worth a visit. It is packed with colourful stalls selling all kinds of handicrafts made on the island, including beautiful *ikat* and *songket* fabrics, baskets and pottery.

Supermarkets

The biggest supermarket on the islands is **Makro** between Benoa and Kuta. Besides local products, it also sells a full range of Western food. **Bintang Supermarket** and **Alas Arum** in Seminyak have fresh produce and a large range of local and imported food. In Lombok, **Pacific Supermarket** in Mataram has a wide-ranging stock.

Delis and Bakeries

For visitors in need of a change from local cuisine, there are a number of excellent delis. The following patisseries are recommended for their excellent breads, cakes and deli items: **Bali Deli** in Seminyak; **Le Bake, Bali Bakery** and **Dijon Deli** in Kuta; **Sanur Deli** in Sanur; and **Casa Luna** and **Kakiang Bakery** in Ubud.

Textiles

There are numerous tailors in Bali, and many visitors rush to have clothes custom-made. For textiles, the main centre is **Jalan Sulawesi** in Denpasar *(see p60)*. Here you will find everything from traditional fabrics to saris, silks, cottons, velvet, lace, wools and rayon in every colour. For fine silks, lace and linens, **Duta Silk**, located beside Matahari in Denpasar, though small, is very popular. **Klungkung** textile market is the best place for traditional textiles. **Threads of Life** in Ubud supports a weaving cooperative.

Clothes

Boutiques in Kuta Square and along the main road in Legian and Seminyak are among the best places for women's fashion. Recommended shops are **Paul Ropp** and **Body & Soul** in Kuta and Seminyak, and **Mama and Leon** in Nusa Dua. Also worth visiting are the boutiques in the Sheraton Nusa Indah in Nusa Dua and the Novotel in Tanjung Benoa. Balinese garments such as finely embroidered *kebaya* and silk sarongs can be found at **Wira's** in Kuta.

Children's Wear

Children's wear in depart ment stores is often very good value. **Kuta Kids** sells printed lycra outfits, surf styles and swimwear for "under tens"; **Rascals** has a good range of colourful kids' clothing and batiks. **Kahuna Kids** in Legian stocks top-label surf clothing made for younger girls and boys.

Teenage girls will love the casual and surf clothes at **Surfer Girl**, Kuta, while teenage boys can get authentic surf labels at **Billabong** and **Rip Curl**, also in Kuta.

Individualistic shop-front at a designer boutique in South Bali

Casual wear and surfing gear for sale in a shop in Kuta

Jewellery

Silver jewellery comes mainly from Celuk *(see p82)*. **Suarti**, which offers a large range and up-to-date styles, has outlets around the island and a large factory in Celuk. In Kuta, **Jonathan Silver** and **Yusuf Silver** offer a good selection. In Seminyak, **Talismans of Power** has an unusual range of silver set with gemstones, and in Ubud, **Treasures** at Ary's Warung has a large range of designer jewellery, although at high prices.

Gold jewellery with intricate designs created from very bright, 24-carat gold is favoured by the Balinese. Gold is generally priced by weight, with a premuim added if a lot of work has gone into the piece. The place to go is **Jalan Hasanudin** in Denpasar, where there are many outlets and designs can be compared. Prices are good.

Leather Goods

Handmade leather clothing and shoes are popular and inexpensive buys in Bali. The many shops along **Jalan Padma** and the intersecting **Jalan Menu** in Legian are good places for leather jackets, skirts, shoes and boots.

Puppets

Puppets used in *wayang kulit* (shadow puppet) performances are skilfully fashioned from leather which is painstakingly cut into intricate lacy panels.

The best place to purchase puppets is the Babakan neighbourhood near the Pasar Seni markets in Sukawati, or in art and antique shops. Try **Wayan Mardika** and **Wayan Narta** in Sukawati, where it is possible to see puppets being made. Javanese *wayang golek* puppets, which perform in front of the screen and are used in Java to enact old folktales, are popular with visitors. **Wayan Wija** in Peliatan specializes in animal puppets.

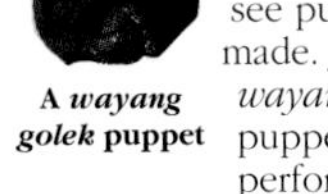

A *wayang golek* puppet

Basketware

Two main types of basketware are available: those from the Balinese village of Tenganan *(see pp110-11)*, and those from Lombok *(see p37)*. Baskets from Tenganan, made of rattan, are intricately and tightly woven. Prices can be high, and visitors should consider buying direct from the village. Rattan baskets made in Lombok are mostly cheaper. A good place to buy them is **Sweta Market**.

Wood and Stone Carvings

The village of Mas is the traditional centre of woodcarving in Bali and here the streets are lined with the carvers' workshops.

The greatest concentration of soft stone carving is in the village of Batubulan and the villages around Singapadu. Elsewhere, the shops lining Jalan Bypass Ngurah Rai in South Bali are worth visiting and **Jimbaran Gallery** is an excellent source of stone works from all over the island.

Workshop in Seminyak selling furniture made mostly from teak

Pottery

Lombok's pottery is still formed the traditional way and fired in pits in the earth to a strong brick-red *(see p37)*. The use of paints and various other finishes is a quite recent innovation. The **Lombok Pottery Centre** has branches in Kuta (South Bali) and in Mataram (Lombok).

In Jimbaran, South Bali, **Jenggala Keramik** makes an attractive range of stoneware and porcelain. Here, visitors can test their own skills at making and painting pots.

Paintings

There are many highly gifted painters at work in Bali. Much of their output is produced for visitors, but the standard is high. Paintings in many styles can be bought in the small galleries lining the streets of Ubud. Paintings are also sold in the galleries at the **Neka Art Museum, ARMA,** and Pendet Museum in Nyuh Kuning village. The monthly exhibitions at **Ganesha Gallery**, at the Four Seasons, Jimbaran, and the Alila in Kedewaten, are worth visiting.

Balinese painting with a floral theme

Furniture

Indonesian teak furniture is internationally fashionable. There are not many genuine antiques. Sometimes old wood is combined with new pieces to replace those which have been lost or broken. The result can be good, but close inspection is needed. If buying new furniture ensure the wood is sustainably produced and carries a Forest Stewardship Council certificate.

Along the main road north of Seminyak is a busy furniture centre with many shops offering a full range of new and old furniture and home accessories. **Warisan** is one of the best – and most expensive. You can see a wider range at their Sempidi factory. **Tarita and Tops** on Jalan Seminyak in north Kuta offers excellent value for money. The other main area for furniture is Jalan Bypass Ngurah Rai, between Sanur and Kuta; the most popular places here are **Nostalgia** and **Victory**.

Changes in moisture, such as exposure to a drier climate or an air-conditioned room, affects wood. Newly manufactured furniture made from wood which has not been properly dried may crack later. Buy from a reputable dealer and be prepared to pay extra for a quality product that will last. Use a good shipping company, such as **MSA**, **CSA** or **PAL** to ensure furniture arrives in good condition.

Directory

Department Stores

Macro
Jalan Bypass Ngurah Rai 222x, Sesetan, Denpasar.
(0361) 723 222.

Matahari
Jalan Dewi Sartika, Denpasar.

Jalan Legian Kuta, Legian.

Kuta Square, Kuta.

Simpung Siur, Jalan Bypass, Kuta.

Ramayana
Mal Bali, Jalan Diponegoro, Denpasar.
(0361) 246 306.

Markets

Klungkung Market
Main crossroads Semarapura, Klungkung.

Kumbasari Market
Jalan Gajah Mada, Denpasar.

Pasar Ubud
Jalan Raya Ubud, Ubud.

Sukawati Art Market
Sukawati, Gianyar.

Sweta Market
Jalan Sandubaya, Sweta, Lombok.

Supermarkets

Alas Arum
Jalan Raya Seminyak, Seminyak.
(0361) 730 914.

Bintang Supermarket
Jalan Raya Seminyak, Seminyak.
(0361) 730 552.

Jalan Raya Sangginen 45, Ubud. (0361) 972 972.

Hero Supermarket
Jalan Teuku Umar, Denpasar.
(0361) 262 038.

Pacific Supermarket
Jalan Langko, Mataram.
(0370) 623 477.

Pepito's
Jalan Kediri 36A, Tuban, Kuta. (0361) 763 957.

Delis and Bakeries

Bali Bakery
Jalan Iman Bonjol, Kuta.
(0361) 755 149.

Bali Deli
Jalan Kunti 117x, Seminyak.
(0361) 733 555.

Casa Luna
Jalan Raya Ubud, Ubud.
(0361) 977 409.

Dijon Deli
Kuta Ploeng Art and Antique Mall, Blok A1–A2, Jalan Setiabudi, Kuta.
(0361) 759 636.

Kakiang Bakery
Jalan Pengosekan, Pengosekan.
(0361) 978 984.

Le Bake
Jalan Griya Anyari, Kuta.
(0361) 753 979.

Sanur Deli
Jalan Danau Poso, Sanur.
(0361) 270 544.

Textiles

Duta Silk
Next to Matahari, Denpasar.
(0361) 232 818.

Jalan Sulawesi
Denpasar. Shops on street.

Threads of Life
Jalan Kajeng 24, Ubud.
(0361) 972 187.

Wardani's
Monkey Forest Road, Ubud.
(0361) 975 538.

Wira's
Jalan Raya Kuta, Kuta.
(0361) 751 727.

Clothes

Biasa
Jalan Raya Seminyak 36.
(0361) 730 308.

Body & Soul
Kuta Square and Jalan Legian 162, Kuta.
(0361) 756 297.

Mama and Leon
Nusa Dua Galleria.
(0361) 288 044.

Paul Ropp
Jalan Raya Seminyak 39, Seminyak.
(0361) 731208.

Children's Wear

Billabong
Kuta Square, Kuta.
(0361) 756 296.

Kahuna Kids
Jalan Legian, Kuta.
(0361) 755 927.

Kuta Kids
Bemo Corner, Kuta.
(0361) 755 810.

Rascals
Kuta Square, Kuta.
(0361) 754 253.

Rip Curl
Jalan Legian, Kuta.
(0361) 757 404.

Surfer Girl
Jalan Legian, Kuta.
(0361) 752 693.

Jewellery

Jalan Hasanuddin
Denpasar. Shops on street.

Jonathan Silver
Jalan Legian 109, Kuta.
(0361) 754 209.

Suarti
Jalan Raya Celuk 100X, Celuk. (0361) 751 660.

Talismans of Power
Jalan Seminyak 30, Seminyak.
(0361) 732 959.

Treasures
Ary's Warung, Ubud.
(0361) 976 697.

Yusuf Silver
Jalan Legian, Kuta.
(0361) 758 441.

Leather Goods

Jalan Padma & Jalan Menu
Legian. Shops on street.

Puppets

Wayan Mardika
Banjar Babakan, Sukawati.
(0361) 299 646.

Wayan Nartha
Banjar Babakan, Sukawati.
(0361) 299 080.

Wayan Wija
Banjar Kalah, Peliatan.
(0361) 973 367.

Wood and Stone Carvings

Jimbaran Gallery
Jalan Bypass Ngurah Rai, Jimbaran.
(0361) 774 957.

Pottery

Jenggala Keramik
Jalan Uluwatu II, Jimbaran.
(0361) 703 310.

Lombok Pottery Centre
Jalan Kartika Plaza 8X, Kuta.
(0361) 753 184.

Jalan Sriwijaya 111A, Mataram, Lombok.
(0370) 640 351.

Paintings

Ganesha Gallery
Four Seasons, Sayan.
(0361) 977 577.

Neka Art Museum
Jalan Raya Campuhan, Ubud. (0361) 975 074.

Furniture and Shipping

CAS
Jalan Ngurah Rai 109x, Suwung Kauh, Denpasar.
(0361) 720525.

MSA Cargo
Jalan Hayam Wuruk 238, Denpasar.

Nostalgia
Jalan Bypass Ngurah Rai, Sanur. (0811) 395 082.

PAL
Jalan Sekar Jepun 5, Gatsu Timor, Tohpati.
(0361) 466 999.

Victory
Jalan Bypass Ngurah Rai, Sanur. (0361) 722 319.

Warisan
Jalan Kerobokan, Seminyak.
(0361) 731 175.

What To Buy in Bali and Lombok

Batik shoes

DECORATIVE ART AND CRAFT products are probably the best buys in Bali and Lombok. They are sold in all the major tourist centres. More adventurous visitors may choose to buy products in the villages where they are made. Woven textiles, including *songket* and *ikat*, are produced chiefly in East Bali. Jewellery is made in Celuk, south of Ubud. Good basketware, pottery and textiles can be bought in Lombok. Surfwear and other casual clothing is widely available, particularly in the resort areas of South Bali.

Masks
Characters from Balinese mythology are skilfully represented by woodcarvers; the masks are used in theatrical performances.

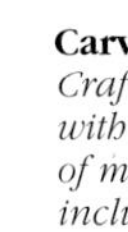

Carvings
Craftsmen work with a variety of materials including paras *(a soft, volcanic stone), ceramics, wood and silver. Small figurines include Garudas and Buddhas.*

Woodcarving

***Paras* carving**

Lombok Pottery
This distinctive, brick-red or black pottery, widely available in Bali and Lombok, is exported all over the world. Most retailers will pack fragile items and arrange shipping.

Puppets from Bali and Java
Many attractive puppets are made or sold in Bali, including the hand-painted puppets made of tanned hide used in Balinese wayang kulit (see p31), *and these Javanese-style puppets.*

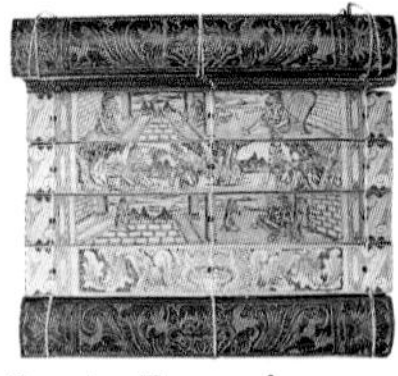

Lontar Engravings
The village of Tenganan (see pp110–11) *is known for these engravings on the leaves of lontar palms.*

Furniture
Modern and reproduction pieces are made from teak and mahogany. Dutch colonial-style furniture is popular though there are few antiques. Not all new furniture is made with materials from sustainable harvests, but some shops use recycled timber.

Teak chair

Bamboo table

Carved wood panel

Kites

During kite season in Bali (see p41), *local communities collaborate in making kites by hand. Mass-produced kites, made of bamboo and nylon, are also attractive.*

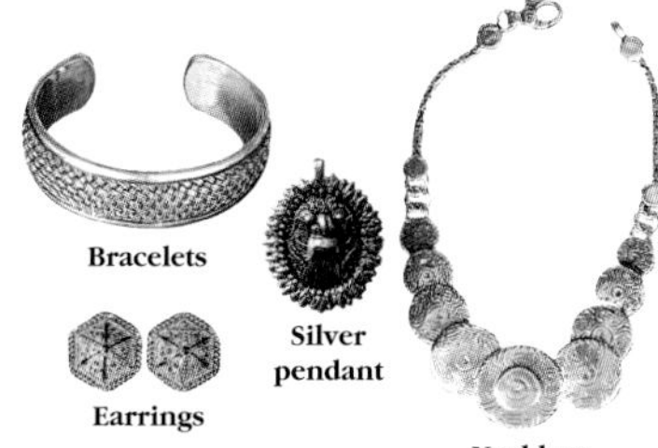

Bracelets

Silver pendant

Earrings

Necklace

Jewellery

Celuk is the jewellery centre of Bali. Gold and silver pieces are designed, made and sold here and the level of craftsmanship is high. Designs are contemporary and traditional.

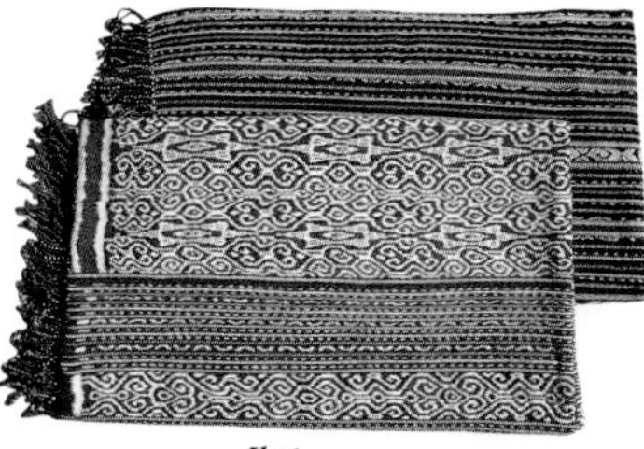

Ikat

Textiles

The most commonly produced cloth is endek, *for which a single* ikat *dye process is used.* Ikat *in earthy tones can be found in the markets. Double-*ikat geringsing, *made in Tenganan, is unique to Bali.* Songket *is embellished with gold and silver thread.*

Sash

Child's outfit

Fabrics and Custom-made Clothes

Made-to-measure clothes are very affordable – there are many tailors in Bali. Fabrics are mostly rayon but there are imported cottons. The best place to buy fabrics is Jalan Sulawesi in Denpasar.

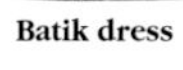

Batik dress

Lombok Basketware

Rattan baskets can be purchased directly in the villages where they are made or at many local markets.

Luggage

Bali produces finely woven rattan bags and handmade, durable leather goods which are sold in shops and markets. The decoration is usually geometrical.

Leather bag

Woven bag

Star fruit

Nutmeg

Mango

Papaya

Pineapple

Salak

Preserved Fruits and Nuts

Dried fruits and nuts are inexpensive and palatable local snacks that can be bought ready-packaged at supermarkets. The local markets and some warung *sell strips made up of more than one fruit such as mango, papaya and pineapple. Flavours range from sweet to spicy or tart.*

ENTERTAINMENT

ENTERTAINMENT for the Balinese has traditionally been associated with religious festivals and ceremonies, a major component of which is the performance of dances accompanied by music. While most traditional dances and music are associated with religious ceremonies, in recent decades some have entered the secular arena, and are regularly staged for tourists. Western-style nightlife is concentrated in the tourist areas, especially in South Bali, which is packed with discos and bars catering to all age groups, musical tastes and budgets. Seminyak's scene is more fashionable than Kuta's. Sanur is more laid back, as is Nusa Dua, and Ubud has good live music and theatre.

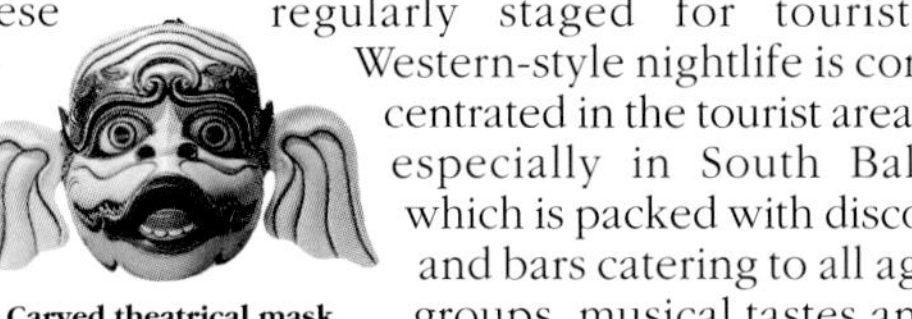

Carved theatrical mask

INFORMATION SOURCES

EXCELLENT ENTERTAINMENT listings can be found in *Hello Bali*, *The Beat* and *Bali Advertiser*. The *Bali Echo* and the English-language daily *Jakarta Post* provide good information, and so do the hotels and notices outside various establishments.

BUYING TICKETS

IT IS NOT DIFFICULT to find Balinese dances, as there are performances nearly every night at almost all the tourist centres. Prices start at around Rp50,000. Trips to these performances booked through agents will cost much more, although the price will usually include transport.

The best places to purchase tickets for performances on the public stages are the hotel tour desks, and the tour-operators and moneychangers to be found throughout Bali's tourist centres. Payment is usually made by cash in rupiah, although US dollars are also accepted.

Dancers with elaborate costumes and masks in Denpasar

TRADITIONAL DANCE

MOST OF THE Balinese dances staged for tourists are not entirely authentic. Many offer a smorgasbord of extracts and highlights of a variety of traditional dances. Standards, however, are generally very high, and visitors are given an explanatory leaflet which usually comes in a several languages, including English, Japanese, French and German. There are no seat reservations, so it pays to turn up early.

Ubud, generally regarded as the artistic heartland of Bali, is the place to go for dance, and most visitors to Ubud spend a good part of their evenings at one of the numerous shows staged every night. One of the best venues is **Puri Saren** *(see p90)*, where the outer courtyard makes a spectacular backdrop. The main dances performed are the *Ramayana* ballet and the *legong*; the latter is a highly stylized dance performed by two young girls. Tickets at Puri Saren can be purchased through a tour operator or at the door. Nightly performances begin at 7:30pm.

The village of Batubulan *(see p82)* has several stages on which dances are performed. Daily Barong and Keris performances *(see p25)* by the celebrated Denjalan troupe are staged at 9:30am at the **Pura Puseh**. The Stage Sila Budaya at the **Puri Anom Tegehe Batubulan** is an outdoor theatre that features Barong and Keris dances daily at 9:30am, and the *kecak* *(see p30)* and fire dances nightly at 6:30pm. It is generally not necessary to buy tickets in advance.

The **Taman Werdhi Budaya** *(see p61)* in Denpasar has numerous events scheduled throughout the year; its programme can be found in the *Bali Post*. There are often special events on Saturday nights. The Taman Werdhi Budaya is the main venue for the Bali Arts Festival, Bali's premier cultural event, which takes place in June and July.

Legong dancers in gold-painted *prada* costumes

A *gamelan* orchestra accompanying a dance in Ubud

Traditional Music

Every traditional Balinese dance is accompanied by music, but the *gamelan* orchestra *(see pp32–3)* is now heard more widely. Many hotels engage musicians for *gamelan* performances. The music is loud, percussive and intriguing, and it is generally enjoyed by foreigners as much for its showmanship as for the music itself.

A temple is one of the best places to see a *gamelan* orchestra perform; visitors are always welcome to watch and listen. Local tourist offices, hotels and guides can provide details of places and dates.

In Ubud, performances by **Semara Ratih** in Kutuh and **Cudamani** in Pengosekan demonstrate superb musicality. The latter also provide classes for local children and visitors.

Puppet Theatre

The shadow puppet play, or *wayang kulit*, is prominent in Balinese life. Delicately cared for and finely gilded leather figures are one-dimensional representations of the gods and myriad characters in the ancient Hindu epics, the *Ramayana* and the *Mahabharata*. Performed behind a screen by a *dalang* or puppeteer, and illuminated by a flickering candle, the *wayang kulit* is loved by the Balinese. It is rarely staged in its entirety for tourists as these full performances regularly last for hours. Neither is it staged for tourists in traditional authentic form, as this is difficult to follow. However, the *wayang kulit* is sometimes staged at hotels with an emphasis on its dramatic aspects. A more authentic *wayang kulit* performance can be seen at **Oka Kartini's** in Ubud on Wednesdays and Saturdays at 8pm. *Wayang kulit* is performed at Balinese family and temple celebrations. Special performances by **Wayan Mardika**, **Wayan Wija** and **Nyoman Sumandhi** can be arranged.

A relatively new although very dramatic innovation is *wayang listrik* (named for its use of lighting and giant shadow images).

An elaborately painted puppet

Entertainment for Children

Children can be easily occupied in Bali. The larger resorts often have very good in-house children's programmes, and some will accept children of non-guests for a fee. The **Westin Resort Nusa Dua**'s facilities, which are open to non-guests, are highly recommended. **Bali Cliff** welcomes non-guests to its pools. The price for a day's admission is quite high, but on Sundays the price of the vast brunch includes use of the pool and the playground.

Children will love the colour and pageantry of the more dramatic Balinese dances. Hotels sometimes have classes and opportunities for children to dress up, and there are performances around the island where children are welcome. Two of the more spectacular venues are **Bali Cliff**'s Cave, where an enchanting *kecak* dance is performed on the beach and the characters scale the cliffs; and the **Grand Hyatt**'s Pasar Senggol, where for an all-in price you choose your meal from the many food stalls and enjoy the show over dinner.

Rafting, trekking and cycling tours are well supervised, safe and fun for older children. Camel rides beside the Nikko in Nusa Dua and elephant rides north of Ubud *(see p206)* are popular choices. **Bali Adventure Tours** and **Sobek** are excellent operators. At **Pemuteran Stables** and **Umalas Stables**, horse-riding lessons for children and supervised riding tours are available. Children will enjoy the white-water rafting trips organized by **Bali Adventure Tours**.

A number of water and nature parks are designed for families. The most popular is the **Waterbom Park & Spa**. The park is well-managed, and safety is a major consideration. South of Ubud, the **Bali Bird Park** *(see pp84–5)*, with over a thousand birds, and the **Bali Reptile Park** *(see p82)*, are good family attractions.

Fun for people of all ages at the Waterbom Park & Spa in Tuban

NIGHTLIFE

Bali has been a party island since the first surfers arrived in the early 1970s, and the large resorts all offer some kind of in-house entertainment. Outside of the resorts, however, organized nightlife is found only in the major tourist areas.

Each area's character is reflected in its entertainment. Some of Kuta's oldest night-clubs are still doing great business selling jam-jars full of the local *arak* (distilled palm brandy) to revellers. More sophisticated and elegant night spots have emerged to meet the demands of 5-star travellers. Nightlife is concentrated mainly in the tourist areas of Kuta, Sanur, Seminyak, Ubud and Nusa Dua.

In Kuta, **Kori**, **Peanuts**, **The Bounty**, **TJ's** and **Un's** are popular places for a drink or chat. **Macaroni Club** has a jazz band and serves sophisticated cocktails. Along Poppies Lanes I and II are bars that are simple hang-outs for relaxation, offering cheap beer, videos and the like. Most are catering to budget travellers.

The **Hard Rock Beach Hotel** has a good cocktail bar with acoustic bands while **Hard Rock Café** offers an excellent line-up of local and foreign bands after 11pm; there is always a good crowd, and its bar upstairs is a lively meeting place. **Holiday Inn Bali Hai** has a secluded, romantic rooftop bar. **Ku Dé Ta** has an air-conditioned cigar bar overlooking the beach and a full cocktail list.

The Bounty, one of the many large clubs in South Bali

In Tuban, **All Stars Surf Café** has interesting theme music nights and a live band.

The best nightclub in Sanur is **Koki Bar**, which attracts a young, local crowd. **The Jazz Bar and Grill** and **I'm Jazz** host live music every evening; **Kafe Wayang** is at its busiest on Friday nights.

In Seminyak, along the beach from **Hotel Padma** to **La Lucciola**, sunset is a great time for volleyball, snacks and cold beers. Visitors then head back to the hotel for a shower and move on to one of Seminyak's many restaurants for dinner.

Some long-established places such as **Warisan** and the **Jaya Pub** have a relaxed, casual atmosphere. **Q Bar** is where the late night gay scene is. **Double Six** is the most popular dance club on the island and has a full-size bungy-jump. Most of the action in Seminyak now happens on Jalan Dhyana Pura in places such as **A-Bar**, the most popular cocktail bar, **Gado Gado** and **Santa Fe**.

There are no real late-night haunts in Ubud – everything closes around 1am. **Jazz Café**, with live music from Tuesdays to Saturdays, is the place to head for in Ubud. **Exiles** is renowned for its Saturday night dance music, and **Tegale Lounge** has regular rock and reggae nights. **Wunderbar** is the place to head to for jazz and blues on Monday nights.

Lovina has locally run bars with passable reggae and standard cover bands. The strip leading down to the beach is the setting for the happy-hour wars – choose a bar you like the look of, sit back and enjoy a cold Bintang beer.

The **Four Seasons Resort** at Sayan, near Ubud, has a spectacularly located bar, well worth the price of a drink. For those in search of a little luxury, the **Alila** and **Amankila** at Manggis are great places to spend an evening.

Nusa Dua's resorts have cocktail bars, beach bars where the sunset can be enjoyed, and often in-house nightclubs. There are usually beach parties at full moon – late at night, and tending to trance dance music best suited to the young.

Peanuts, one of Kuta's most popular bars

DIRECTORY

TRADITIONAL DANCE

Pura Puseh
Jalan Raya, Batubulan, Gianyar.
(0361) 298 038.

Puri Anom Tegehe Batubulan
Jalan Raya Batubulan, Gianyar.
(0361) 298 505 or (0361) 298 092.

Puri Saren
Jalan Raya Ubud, Ubud.
(0361) 975 957.

Taman Werdhi Budaya
Jalan Nusa Indah, Denpasar.
(0361) 222 776.

TRADITIONAL MUSIC

Cudamani
Jalan Raya Pengosekan, Ubud.
(0361) 977 068.

Semara Ratih
Banjar Kutuh, Ubud.
(0361) 973 277.

PUPPET THEATRE

Nyoman Sumandhi, M. A.
Jalan Katrangan Lane 5B/6, Denpasar.
(0361) 246 216.

Oka Kartini's
Jalan Raya Ubud, Ubud.
(0361) 975 193.

Wayan Mardika
Banjar Babakan, Sukawati.
(0361) 299 646.

Wayan Wija
Banjar Kalah, Peliatan.
(0361) 973 367.

ENTERTAINMENT FOR CHILDREN

Bali Adventure Tours
Adventure House, Jalan Bypass Ngurah Rai, Pessanggaran.
(0361) 721 480.
FAX *(0361) 721 481.*

Bali Bird Park
Jalan Serma Cok Ngurah Gambir, Singapadu, Batubulan, Gianyar.
(0361) 299 352.

Bali Cliff
Jalan Pura Batu Pageh, Uluwatu.
(0361) 771 992.

Bali Reptile Park
Jalan Serma Cok Ngurah Gambir, Singapadu, Batubulan, Gianyar.
(0361) 299 344.

Grand Hyatt
Nusa Dua.
(0361) 771 234.

Pemuteran Stables
Jalan Singaraja, Gilimanuk.
(0362) 92 339.
FAX *(0362) 92 339.*

Sobek
Jalan Tirta Ening 9, Sanur.
(0361) 287 059.
FAX *(0361) 289 448.*

Umalas Stables
Banjar Umalas, Kerobokan.
(0361) 731 402.

Waterbom Park & Spa
Jalan Kartika Plaza, Tuban.
(0361) 755 676.

Westin Resort Nusa Dua
Nusa Dua, Bali.
(0361) 771 906.
W www.westin.com/bali

NIGHTLIFE

A-Bar
Jalan Dhyana Pura 10, Seminyak.
(0361) 733 270.

Alila
Manggis.
@ manggis@alilahotels.com

All Stars Surf Café
Kuta Centre, Jalan Kartika Plaza, Tuban.
(0361) 757 933.

Amankila
Manggis, near Candi Dasa.
(0363) 41 333.

Double Six
Jalan Double Six, Seminyak.
(0361) 731 266.

Exiles
Jalan Bima, Peliatan.
(0361) 974 842.

Four Seasons Resort
Sayan, Ubud.
(0361) 977 577.

Gado Gado
Jalan Dhyana Pura, Seminyak.
(0361) 730 955.

Hard Rock Beach Hotel and Café
Jalan Pantai, Kuta.
(0361) 731 869.

Holiday Inn Bali Hai
Jalan Wanasegara 33, Tuban.
(0361) 753 035.

Hotel Padma
Jalan Padma 1, Legian.
(0361) 752 111.

I'm Jazz
Jalan Danau Tamlingan 27, Sanur.
(081) 835 7005.

Jaya Pub
Jalan Raya Seminyak 1, Seminyak.
(0361) 730 973.

Jazz Café
Jalan Sukma 2, Tebesaya, Ubud.
(0361) 976 594.

Kafe Wayang
Lippo Plaza, Sanur.
(0361) 287 591.

Koki Bar
Jalan Bypass Ngurah Rai 9X, Sanur.
(0361) 287 503.

Kori
Poppies Lane II, Kuta.
(0361) 758 605.

Ku Dé Ta
Jalan Kayu Aya 9, Seminyak.
(081) 1388 801.

La Lucciola
Jalan Kayu Aya, Kayu Aya Beach, Seminyak.
(0361) 261 047.

Macaroni Club
Jalan Raya Kuta, Kuta.

Peanuts
Jalan Raya Kuta, Kuta.
(0361) 752 364.

Q Bar and Café
Abimanyu Arcade, 1–2 Jalan Dhyana Pura, Seminyak.
(0361) 730 927.

Santa Fe
Jalan Dhyana Pura, Seminyak.
(0361) 731 147.

Tegale Lounge
Jalan Bima, Peliatan.

The Bounty
Jalan Legian Kelod, Kuta.
(0361) 754 040.

The Jazz Bar and Grill
Jalan Bypass Ngurah Rai 15–16, Sanur.
(0361) 285 892.

T. J.'s
Poppies Lane I, Kuta.
(0361) 751 093.

Un's
Poppies Lane I, Kuta.
(0361) 752 607.

Warisan
Jalan Raya Seminyak.
(0361) 731 175.

Wunderbar
Jalan Raya Pengosekan, Pengosekan, Ubud.
(0361) 978 339.

Outdoor Activities

The range and quality of outdoor activities available in Bali and Lombok are exceptional; they are among the best in the world. In addition to the established favourites, such as surfing, fishing, sailing, snorkelling, trekking and diving, there are "adrenalin" sports such as bungy-jumping, skydiving, paragliding, kayaking and ocean and white-water rafting. The energetic visitor can ride surfboards on the waves, horses along the beach, elephants in the jungle and motorbikes into the unknown. Reptiles and birds are there to be observed; there are dolphin cruises, cycling trips into the hills and adventure tours off the beaten track. Tennis and golf are both available in luxurious, 5-star surroundings in Bali's Nusa Dua resort area. In this respect as in others, Lombok is much less developed and more informal than Bali. Its main outdoor attractions are surfing, snorkelling and trekking.

Windsurfing, a popular water sport in Bali

Surfboards available for rent on the beach at Legian

Surfing

Bali is a very popular centre for surfing, offering almost perfect year-round conditions for both beginners and more experienced veterans. Boards and gear can be bought or rented at most beaches. Well-managed surf schools in Sanur and Kuta, such as the popular **Cheyne Horan School of Surf**, charge by the day or by the hour for private instruction. There is also a women-only group, **Surf Goddesses**. The liveliest scenes are around Kuta. For more on the best surfing sites see pp208–209.

Diving and Snorkelling

Organized tours with experienced guides are a good way to explore the waters off Bali and Lombok. Besides day trips, there are tours that cover a wider range of dive spots. Live-aboard trips that include diving off nearby islands, such as Komodo and Sumbawa, are popular. A valid licence must be produced for dive trips; PADI (Professional Association of Diving Instructors) certification is generally recognized. Most dive operations are professionally run. Good rental equipment is available. **Bali Marine Sports**, **Dream Divers**, **Geko Dive** and the 5-star **Reefseekers Dive Centre** offer a range of trips. For more detailed information on diving sites, see pp210–11.

Windsurfing and Water-skiing

Sanur is the place in Bali to go for windsurfing; the lagoon *(see pp64–5)* offers good protection from the ocean swells. Here, as elsewhere in Bali and Lombok, most beach-front hotels will have boards for rent.

The facilities of the **Blue Oasis Beach Club** in Sanur are the best on the island. In addition to windsurfing, it also offers water-skiing. Trick skis and wakeboards are available for rent. All staff are professional and qualified.

A number of windsurfing courses, conducted by Asian windsurfing champions, are available for all ability levels. Courses last 4–6 hours.

Fishing

Several tour operators such as **Indonusa Segara Marine** and **Moggy Offshore Cruising Catamaran** specialize in deep-sea fishing trips; they have offices in the Kuta-Legian area *(see pp68–9)*, in the east around Padang Bai and Candi Dasa *(see p108)* and in the north at Singaraja *(see p146)*. There are boats from Padang Bai, Candi Dasa, Amed, Tulamben, Singaraja and Sanur, but most leave from Benoa Harbour *(see p72)*, and trips usually take all day.

Some companies offer yachts and fishing boats with guides for game fishing charters; the aim is to catch tuna, *mai-mai*, mackerel and marlin. Cod, snapper and coral trout can be found on reef-fishing trips.

Depending on your budget, you can choose to go fishing in an outrigger, a small boat or a state-of-the-art Black Watch fishing vessel with experienced crew, full insurance and all electronics and safety gear. Extended charters to the waters off Lombok and islands further east can be arranged.

Outriggers offering game fishing trips off Lombok

Benoa Harbour, the best-equipped marina in the area

Cruises

There is a range of sailing and yachting options off Bali and Lombok. Cruise options include day trips to offshore islands and remote reefs, or sunset dinners aboard a modern cruise liner, a traditional Bugis schooner or a yacht.

Scheduled sailing cruises ranging from 3 to 14 days depart from Benoa Harbour, the main port of call, and here it is also easy to book daily cruises. Major sailing and yachting companies use this as a home base; it is an interesting place for the boat-lover to explore and a well-stocked bar overlooks the pontoons. From Benoa, it is possible to sail by tall ship to the west coast of Lombok to explore the Gili Isles *(see p156)* and the waters off Senggigi *(see p156)*, or charter a luxury yacht for a once-in-a-lifetime wedding cruise. Most people, however, prefer to spend a day sailing to the islands of Nusa Lembongan or Nusa Penida *(see p75)*.

Island Explorer Cruises organizes day trips to Nusa Lembongan on a choice of yachts or on the speed boat *Quick Cat*. **Bali Hai** offers sailing trips to Nusa Lembongan aboard luxury catamarans fully equipped for snorkelling. On the islands, a full holiday experience is provided, with beach clubs, restaurants, pools and diving and snorkelling equipment (the latter at extra cost). They also have a sailing boat that goes to Lembongan. **Island Explorer Cruises** offers kayaking, snorkelling and banana boat rides on its trip to Lembongan. **The Bounty** has dinner sunset cruises around Nusa Dua, as well as journeys to Lembongan. On most cruises, children under 14 receive a 50 per cent discount.

If you prefer to be in charge of your own craft, dinghy rentals are available from Sanur, Nusa Dua and Jimbaran. Alternatively, charter a yacht or schooner with 2–16 cabins, an experienced crew and a tour guide.

White-water Rafting, Ocean Rafting and Kayaking

There is a number of white-water rafting companies offering trips through rapids ranging over Grades 2–4 (from fairly easy to rigorous). Standards are generally high. **Sobek Bali Utama**, one of the best, offers world-class guides and Grade 3 rapids, while **Bali Safari Rafting** offers Grade 4 rapids. The excitement and the stunning scenery make a thrilling experience. The Ayung River, northwest of Ubud *(see pp96–7)*, and the Unda River, north of Klungkung *(see p105)*, are the most popular starting points. Trips organized by **Ayung River Rafting** last from 3 to 4 hours. The Telaga Waja River in East Bali near Muncan and Sidemen *(see p105)* is also becoming popular. When planning, allow for transfer time from and back to your hotel. **Bali Adventure Tours**' package includes changing rooms, hot showers, towels and food and drinks. Bring a change of clothes, a hat and sun-screen. The price for a rafting trip should include hotel transfers, full instruction, qualified guides, lunch and insurance.

The more adventurous can try ocean rafting aboard a large inflatable raft with qualified instructors. Trips include snorkelling, exploring off-shore islands, drinks and light snacks. **Captain Zodiac Ocean Rafting** offers full- and half-day island cruises.

River kayaking, also offered by **Ayung River Rafting**, is a more recent and exciting development. Hurtling through the rapids in a two-person inflatable kayak is a much more intense experience than rafting.

Lake kayaking, a more relaxed option, is offered by **Sobek Bali Utama** at Lake Tamblingan *(see pp140–41)*.

White-water rafting on the Ayung River

A ride on a banana boat in South Bali

Swimming

Beaches in Bali and Lombok can be superb for swimming, with secluded bays and crystal-clear seas. However, it is important to take note of any warnings posted regarding bad rips and strong currents as the waters, especially along the south coasts, can be very dangerous. A safer option for swimming is the hotel pool.

Many of the major international hotels and luxury resorts located in Nusa Dua in Bali *(see p73)* and Senggigi in Lombok *(see p156)* have good swimming facilities.

Club Med in Nusa Dua offers an all-day guest ticket (valid until 5pm) which includes access not only to the pool itself, but also to a whole range of other sports activities. It also includes an Asian and Western lunch buffet with unlimited wine, beer and soft drinks.

Kuta's **Waterbom Park & Spa** has a range of top-quality water slides.

Golf and Tennis

There are four spectacular golf courses in Bali, all open to non-members for a fee, where you can play a round or two against a backdrop of ocean views or misty mountain scenery. Nusa Dua is home to the 18-hole **Bali Golf and Country Club**, and close by in Sanur is a 9-hole course at the Grand Bali Beach Hotel. Near the shores of Lake Bratan, high in the hills near Bedugul *(see p141)*, is **Bali Handara Kosaido Country Club**, an award-winning 18-hole golf-resort. The most dramatic golf course in Bali is the 18-hole **Nirwana Bali Golf Club** near Tanah Lot in Tabanan.

Most of the larger hotels provide excellent tennis facilities with floodlit courts, expert coaching, playing partners and racket rental.

Wreathed hornbill

Eco-tours

Eco-tourism is catching on in Bali and Lombok, and a number of operators are now starting to cater to visitors who prefer ecologically based holidays and activities.

Dolphin-watching has become popular for a day out, and involves four-hour trips into the waters off South Bali. **Bali Hai Cruises** provides early morning high-speed cruises along the Nusa Dua and Uluwatu coastline to see dolphins at play, while **Ena Dive Centre** offers dolphin-watching tours and water sports.

Off the shores of Lovina in the north of Bali *(see p147)*, small, traditional fishing boats, known as outriggers, are used for dolphin-watching. As dolphins are wild animals, the certainty of actually seeing one on a trip can never be guaranteed.

Bird-watching is a little more predictable. The **Bali Bird Park** *(see pp84–5)*, near Singapadu, gives an excellent view of bird life in Bali and elsewhere in the tropics in a well-managed garden setting. The **Bali Reptile Park** *(see p82)*, just next to the Bali Bird Park, is equally worth a visit, to see the range of reptile life that lives on the islands.

For visitors looking for birds in the wild, organized bird-watching trips can be arranged to the **Taman Nasional Bali Barat** *(see*

A boat trip at Lake Bratan near the Bali Handara Kosaido Country Club

pp136–7). The slopes of Gunung Batukau *(see p133)* are also rich in bird life. Experienced guides for birdwatching and mountain trekking are available in nearby villages.

Guided tours to other parts of Bali and Lombok are available by prior arrangement. Morning bird walks around Ubud can be arranged with the Bali Bird Club (through **Sobek Bali Utama**). Birdwatching and trekking around Lake Tamblingan *(see pp140–41)* and the adjacent high forest can be arranged through **Nyoman Witama**.

Another nature tour worth considering include a trip to **Taman Kupu Kupu** (Butterfly Park) in Wanasari near Tabanan *(see p129)*, which is home to some rare species of butterflies.

Bottlenose dolphins frolicking in the waters off South Bali

Walking and Camping

Sightseeing on foot reveals the unspoilt Bali and Lombok, with mountains, rolling hills, ricefields, jungles, traditional villages, volcanoes and national parks to explore. Trips range from full- and half-day visits to overnight trips to the top of Gunung Rinjani in Lombok *(see pp158–9)*.

Guides are important in remote areas; but well-worn hill paths such as those around Manggis *(see p108)* and north of Tenganan in East Bali *(see p109)*, Ubud *(see pp94–5)*, and the Ayung River Gorge *(see pp96–7)* are safe enough to explore unaccompanied. There are some pleasant short walks on Lombok's outlying Gili Isles *(see p156)*.

Traditional villages such as the Bali Aga villages of Tenganan *(see pp110–11)*, and Trunyan on the shores of Lake Batur *(see p121)*, can also be interesting.

Exploring rural Bali on foot, one of the most rewarding ways

Try camping in North Bali at Air Sanih *(see p147)* or the national parks, such as Taman Nasional Bali Barat or Gunung Rinjani *(see pp136–7 and 158–9)*.

Mountain Trekking

Lovers of mountains, and particularly of volcanoes, can undertake treks on Bali's Gunung Agung *(see p114)* and Gunung Batur *(see pp120–21)*, as well as on Lombok's Gunung Rinjani *(see pp158–9)*. During the wet season from October to April, mountains can be very dangerous places and not suitable for climbing. Personal security can be a problem, and all trips to volcanoes should be accompanied by professional guides. A few very reliable tour operators, such as **Mandalika Tours**, organize an interesting variety of trips including walks through the rainforest around Gunung Batukau *(see p133)*. **Bali Sunshine Tours** offers a sunrise trek over the volcanic caldera of Gunung Batur.

Car and Bike Tours

Organized four-wheel-drive tours are ideal ways to escape from more developed areas. The price for these day-trips should cover lunch, drinks and transfers. **Waka Land Cruise** offers tours by Land Rover to the Waka Louka rainforest camp high in the mountains. If you prefer to be in charge, you can rent your own car and explore at your leisure. Check out **Bali Car Rentals** for details. Maps are easy to buy (although not always very detailed or reliable) and roads are generally good. However, driving in Indonesia can be dangerous. Pavements are rarely used by pedestrians; people and animals walk into traffic with apparent lack of concern. Always check you are fully insured.

Exploring by motorcycle is enjoyable, although accidents are common. Always inspect the bike for road-worthiness, insist on insurance and check your helmet. Watch out for potholes and gravel on the road, especially on corners and near large towns.

Bali Adventure Tours organizes off-road trail-bike trips. This is an exciting, and safer, alternative to battling with the island's traffic.

Touring by bike along the scenic route beside Lake Batur

Cycling

Organized cycling trips on mountain bikes are great for seeing the spectacular scenery in Bali around Ubud, Gunung Batur *(see pp120–21)* and Sangeh *(see p132)*. **Bali Adventure Tours** offers mountain cycling through Bali's central highlands. Safety equipment is provided as well as towels, drinks, picnic boxes, transfers and insurance. This activity is not suitable for children under ten.

Horse Riding

In Bali you can ride a horse along a deserted beach, through the surf at sunset, or through lush, green paddy fields in the central hills. **Jaran Jaran**, **Umalas Stables** and **Pemuteran Stables** offer idyllic horse-riding experiences for beginners as well as for experienced riders.

The horses come in various heights – from small ponies to large horses. You can ride with a guide leading your horse, or ride unassisted. Wear long trousers and a pair of shoes (not sandals), and bring lots of sunblock.

Ride on an elephant in the Elephant Safari Park

Elephant Safaris

The ultimate in tropical outdoor activities has to be an elephant safari in the hills and jungles of central Bali. The **Elephant Safari Park** *(see p99)* is located about 20 minutes north of Ubud in beautifully landscaped gardens at Desa Taro. It offers the opportunity to hand-feed, touch, and interact with these amazing animals. The park's reception centre has a full-size mammoth skeleton, and an extensive graphic display explaining the elephant's natural history.

Elephant rides are available, and there are special rides for children. Prices usually include entrance fees, lunch, hotel transfers and insurance. Bookings can be made through their parent company **Bali Adventure Tours**.

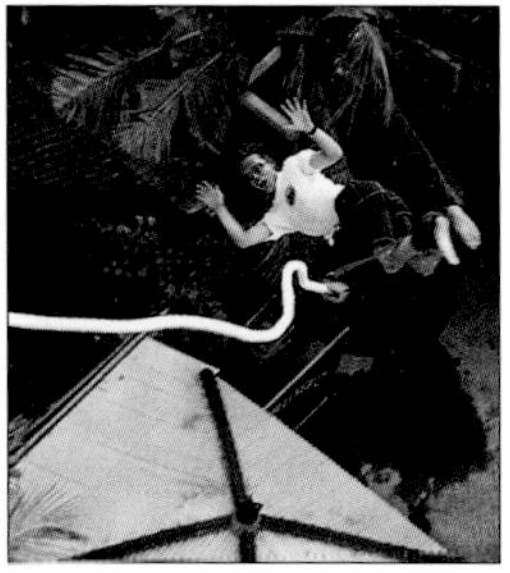

Thrill in mid-air at Bali Bungy Company in Kuta

Bungy-jumping

Over recent years, extreme sports have established themselves in Bali with world-famous New Zealander A J Hackett bringing the sport of bungy-jumping into the public eye. **A J Hackett Company** has a spectacular jump off an Australian-manufactured tower that is 44 m (145 ft) high. On Saturdays you can even jump at night.

There are now several companies offering a variety of bungy-linked thrills including one at 3am that involves jumping from the top of a tower that is 30 m (105 ft) high and situated in one of Kuta's busiest nightclubs. Variations on the same theme include **Bali Bungy Company**'s Sky Surfer and Bali Slingshot, both in the Kuta-Legian area.

A bungy-jump package usually includes a souvenir photo and a T-shirt; the Sky Surfer and Slingshot experiences are at around half the price of a bungy-jump. Some companies will capture your jump on a videotape which you can then purchase.

The best-of-all-worlds extreme is at **Adrenalin Park** in the heart of Kuta, which offers bungy-jumping, with optional water touches (dips into the pool) from a tower (Bali's tallest) that is 50 metres (160 feet) high, the new slingshot experience, a climbing wall, restaurants, a bar and a swimming pool.

Paragliding and Parasailing

Paragliding off the windy cliffs at Uluwatu in the south of Bali *(see p76)* is a spectacular experience available only in the afternoons, subject to weather conditions. All instructors are fully trained and experienced, and will accompany first-time fliers on a 20-minute tandem ride. **Bali Adventure Tours**' prices include hotel transfers and insurance. Paragliding is not suitable for children under ten.

Tanjung Benoa *(see p72)* is the best place for parasailing. **Bali Hai Cruises** offers 10-minute parasailing trips.

Skydiving

For an unforgettable view of Bali and Lombok, try skydiving. **Skydive Bali** is suitable for beginners and experienced skydivers alike. Fully qualified and professional instructors give thorough briefings and safety checks before each jump. Tandem jumps, where instructors accompany skydivers on their jumps, may appeal to beginners. Skydiving is not suitable for children under ten.

Parasailing over the scenic Lake Bratan in the central mountains

DIRECTORY

SURFING

Cheyne Horan School of Surf
Jalan Legian 406, Kuta.
(0361) 735 868.

Surf Goddess Retreats
(08133) 870 5553.
W www.surfgoddessretreats.com

DIVING AND SNORKELLING

Bali Marine Sports
Jalan Bypass Ngurah Rai 90, Sanur.
(0361) 289 308.

Dream Divers
PT Samudra Indah Diving, Lombok.
(0370) 692 047.
W www.dreamdivers.com

Geko Dive
Jalan Silayukti, Padang Bai.
(0363) 41 516.

Reefseekers Dive Centre
Gili Air Harbour, Lombok.
(0370) 641 008.

WINDSURFING & WATER-SKIING

Blue Oasis Beach Club
Sanur Beach Hotel, Sanur.
(0361) 288 011.

FISHING

Indonusa Segara Marine
Benoa Harbour.
(0361) 282 080.

Moggy Offshore Cruising Catamaran
Bali International Marina, Jalan Pelabuhan Benoa, Benoa Harbour, Denpasar.
(0361) 723 601.

CRUISES

Bali Hai Cruises
Benoa Harbour.
(0361) 720 331.

Bounty Cruises
Benoa Harbour.
(0361) 726 666.
FAX (0361) 730 404.

Quick Silver Cruises
Jalan Kerta Dalem 96, Sidhakarya, Denpasar.
(0361) 727 946.

WHITE-WATER RAFTING, OCEAN RAFTING AND KAYAKING

Ayung River Rafting
Jalan Diponegoro 150B-29, Denpasar.
(0361) 238 759.
W www.ayungriverrafting.com

Bali Adventure Tours
Adventure House, Jalan Bypass Ngurah Rai, Pesanggaran.
(0361) 721 480.

Bali Safari Rafting
(0361) 221 315.
W www.balisafaris.com

Captain Zodiac Ocean Rafting
Jalan Majapahit 54, Kuta.
(0361) 761 660.

Sobek Bali Utama
Jalan Tirta Ening 9, Sanur.
(0361) 287 059.

SWIMMING

Club Med
Lot N-6, Nusa Dua.
(0361) 771 521.

Waterbom Park & Spa
Jalan Kartika Plaza, Tuban.
(0361) 755 676.
W www.waterbom.com

GOLF

Bali Golf & Country Club
Nusa Dua.
(0361) 771 791.

Bali Handara Kosaido Country Club
Pancasari Village, Bedugul.
(0361) 288 954.

Nirwana Bali Golf Club
Jalan Raya Tanah Lot, Kediri, Tabanan.
(0361) 815 970.

ECO-TOURS

Bali Bird Park
Jalan Serma Cok Ngurah Gambir, Gianyar.
(0361) 299 552.

Bali Reptile Park
Jalan Serma Cok Ngurah Gambir, Gianyar.
(0361) 299 344.

Ena Dive Centre
Jalan Tirta Ening 1, Sanur.
(0361) 288 829.

Nyoman Witama
Puri Lumbung Cottages, Munduk.
(0362) 92 514.

Taman Kupu Kupu
Wanasari, Tabanan.
(0361) 814 282.

Taman Nasional Bali Barat
Jalan Raya Gilimanuk, Cekik.
(0361) 720 063.

CAMPING AND TREKKING

Bali Sunshine Tours
Jalan Pondok Indah Raya III/1, Gatot Subroto Barat, Denpasar.
(0361) 414 057.

Keep Walking Tours
Jalan Hanoman 44, Ubud.
(0361) 970 581.

Mandalika Tours
Jalan Hang Tuah Raya 11, Sanur.
(0361) 287 450.

CAR, CYCLING AND BIKE TOURS

Bali Adventure Tours
Adventure House, Jalan Bypass, Pesanggaran.
(0361) 721 408.
W www.baliadventuretours.com

Bali Car Rentals
(0361) 418 381.

Waka Land Cruise
Jalan Pulau Moyo 25x, Pedungan.
(0361) 723 629.

HORSE RIDING

Pemuteran Stables
Jalan Singaraja, Pemuteran.
(0362) 92 339.
FAX (0362) 92 339.

Umalas Stables
Banjar Umalas Kauh, Kerobokan.
(0361) 739 821.

ELEPHANT SAFARI

Elephant Safari Park
Taro, Tegallalang, Gianyar.
(0361) 721 480.

BUNGY-JUMPING

Adrenalin Park
Jalan Benesa 69, Kuta.
(0361) 757 841.

A J Hackett Company
Jalan Double Six, Legian, Kuta.
(0361) 731 144.

Bali Bungy Company
Jalan Pura Puseh, Kuta.
(0361) 752 658.

PARAGLIDING AND PARASAILING

Bali Adventure Tours
Adventure House, Jalan Bypass Ngurah Rai, Pesanggaran.
(0361) 721 480.

Bali Hai Cruises
Benoa Harbour.
(0361) 720 331.
FAX (0361) 720 334.

SKYDIVING

Skydive Bali
(0361) 736 830.
FAX (0361) 733 031.

Surfing and Beach Culture

Sea shell

Bali and, to a lesser extent, Lombok, have a vibrant beach culture. Surfers made Bali a popular destination from the 1960s onwards, and for many visitors the beaches are still the most alluring features of both islands. The whole range of beach activities is available – from surfing, windsurfing and water-skiing to less energetic options such as sunbathing and a beach massage. Conditions for beach life, including surfing, are best during the months from May to September. For those who cannot take their own gear, watersports equipment can be rented on all the more popular beaches, particularly those of South Bali.

Surfboards for rent on Kuta Beach

Canggu Beach *offers high-performance surfing popular with locals and visitors. Best before midday, the swells roll in over the rock-bottom forming peaks that split left and right.*

Windsurfing

Bali offers good surf on many of its beaches, with Sanur and Tanjung Benoa considered the best places for windsurfing with world-class waves and fast, good-sized breaks.

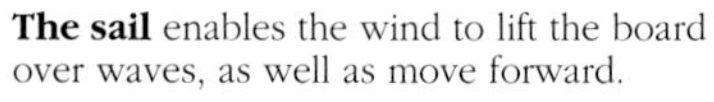

The sail enables the wind to lift the board over waves, as well as move forward.

The windsurfing board, made of fibreglass, has a mast and a sail.

Top Surfing Areas

Surfers off Bali and Lombok make most use of the south-facing beaches. These catch the ocean swells arriving from the directions of southern Africa and western Australia. Tide charts are available at surf shops and a local magazine, *Surf Time*, provides information on surfing competitions and other events.

BALI SEA
BALI
LOMBOK
Canggu
Sanur
Kuta
Pulau Serangan
Desert Point
Padang-padang
Maui
Gerupuk
INDIAN OCEAN
0 kilometres 75
0 miles 50

Beach massage services *are common to most of Bali's popular beaches. Prices are generally low and negotiated by the hour.*

Parasailing*, seen here at Tanjung Benoa, has become a very popular activity. Other options include paragliding, jet-skiing, banana boating and ocean rafting.*

Bali's wave breaks give opportunities for acrobatics.

Kuta Beach *is the birthplace of Bali's surfing tradition. The sand-bottom beach wave breaks with thin lips attract surfers of all levels of skill – this is a good place for beginners. Watch out for rip tides.*

Safety Precautions

Not all beaches have visitor or medical facilities.

- *Remember that lifeguards are found only on popular beaches such as Kuta and Nusa Dua.*
- *Keep between the safety flags, if there are any.*
- *Use high-protection sunscreen.*
- *Wear sunglasses and a hat.*
- *Pack a first-aid kit.*

On Sanur Beach*, sailing boats can be rented. Shown here is a hobie cat, a small catamaran notable for its speed. Boats of this kind flip easily, so caution needs to be exercised in high winds or lively seas, conditions sometimes encountered here.*

Diving in Bali and Lombok

Butterfly fish

BALI'S DIVE SITES are rich in marine life, lush coral gardens and reef walls. There are several shipwrecks. Top sites include Menjangan Island *(see p138)* for its variety of soft and hard coral; Tulamben, site of the *Liberty* wreck; and Nusa Penida and Nusa Lembongan *(see pp74–5)* for sightings of the ocean sunfish. Lombok offers good diving and snorkelling off the Gili Isles. The PADI (Professional Association of Dive Instructors) system of certification is generally recognized. The greatest concentration of diving-trip operators is in the South Bali resort areas *(see p57)*.

Diving instruction *off Pemuteran, where the current is minimal, and visibility is good. There are many such diving schools on Bali where PADI certification can be obtained.*

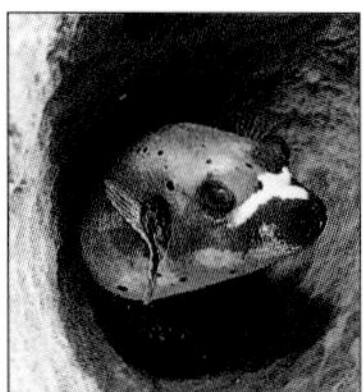

The black spotted puffer fish *can be found in the coral gardens off Menjangan Island, where walls dominate the reef structure.*

The reef wall is a haven for many forms of marine life.

Apparatus can be rented from the many PADI-certified organizers of diving trips.

Dive Site Ratings

There is a good variety of sites around these islands. Divers should know the level of experience required in any dive site before braving the waters.

	Snorkelling	Novice Diving	Advanced Diving	Expert Diving
Candi Dasa ④	●		●	■
Gili Isles ⑧	●	■	●	■
Menjangan Island ①	●	■	●	■
Nusa Dua ⑦	●	■	●	■
Nusa Penida ⑤			●	■
Pemuteran ②	●	■	●	■
Sanur ⑥	●	■	●	■
Tulamben ③	●	■	●	■

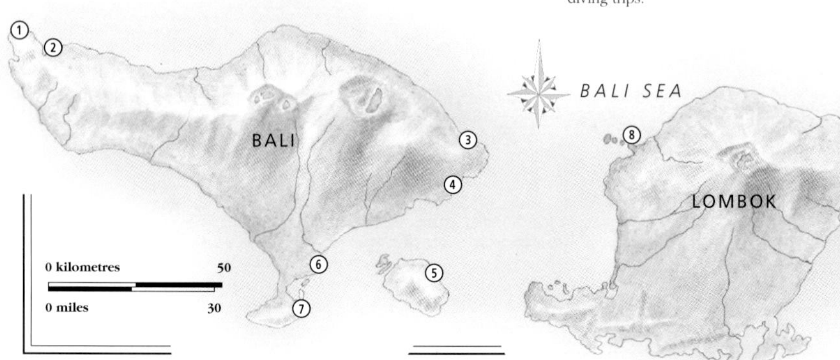

A diver's platform *is attached to the rear of a boat. It is often used to facilitate the training of novice divers, who can explore shallow depths of around 15 m (50 ft) at the most.*

Getting to the Remoter Dive Sites

Most organized diving trips include transport and there are some live-aboard trips available through hotels. For those travelling independently, ***Menjangan Island*** *and* ***Pemuteran*** *are best reached by car or motorcycle.* ***Tulamben*** *and* ***Candi Dasa*** *are closer to South Bali and a bemo is an option. The* ***Gili Isles****, off Lombok, are reached most easily from* ***Senggigi****.*

The coral hawkfish *can sometimes be seen in the waters off Nusa Penida, where marine life includes jacks, tuna, manta rays, reef sharks and, on rare occasions, whale sharks.*

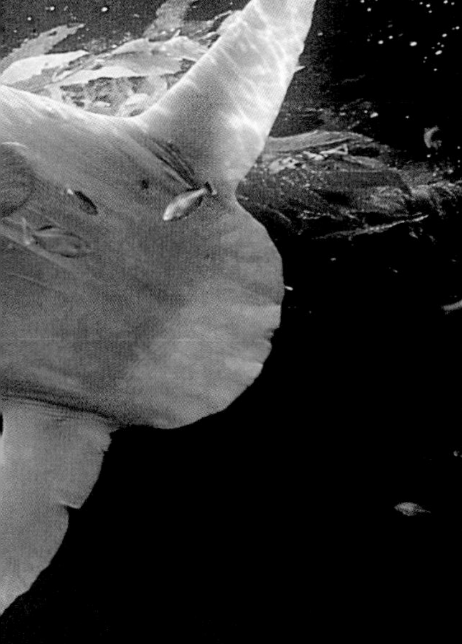

Marine Life

The rare ocean sunfish, known in Bali as the "mola mola", migrates through Balinese waters in great numbers from November to February. It is a memorable sight. The absence of a distinct tail fin gives the fish a "chopped off" appearance.

A correctly equipped diver *can explore marine and coral life in safety provided due regard is given to strong currents in some areas.*

Fish of the Gobiidae family *dwell in the crevices and branches of coral. There are many hundreds of species of these fish living in the Indo-Pacific region and they are easily observed by divers in the waters of Bali and Lombok.*

Survival Guide

Practical Information

Bali and Lombok, like the rest of Indonesia, have been undergoing profound and rapid changes since the end of the Suharto regime in 1998. The furious pace of development exerts continuous pressure on the social and physical landscape. Visitors should be prepared for unexpected changes in prices, regulations, facilities, phone numbers, office hours, street names, and even attitudes. Check websites *(see p217)* for the latest information.

Tourism Development Project logo

Bali is generally more developed than Lombok. There is an international airport at Denpasar. The tourism infrastructure is most developed in the beach resorts of South Bali, in Ubud, the "cultural heartland" of Bali, and increasingly in the north and east. Tourism in Lombok is concentrated on the north-west coast around Senggigi; outside this area, tourism services are scarce. Most visitors go to Bali first, to savour its busy nightlife, absorb its charming culture and get accustomed to the warm climate. They then move on by sea or air to Lombok, to enjoy its quieter pace and unspoiled natural beauty.

When to Go

High seasons in Bali and Lombok, with attendant crowds and higher prices, are from mid-December to mid-January (Christmas–New Year period), and in July and August. The weather is most pleasant from May to September *(see pp40–43)*.

Visas and Passports

To enter Indonesia, your passport must be valid for at least six months after the date of departure. Airport immigration officials may ask to see a ticket out of Indonesia, or proof of funds for the duration of your stay and for onward travel, without which you may be refused entry.

A visa ruling in 2004 decreed that tourist visas are only good for 30 days and are non-extendable. Visitors coming from most south-east Asian countries do not need a visa, and those from 21 other countries (including USA, UK, Australia and Japan) may purchase a visa on arrival. Visitors should check with their local Indonesian consulate or embassy.

Tourist pass on passport

Be sure to keep the white immigration card (attached to your passport upon entering the country), as you will need to return it to immigration officials when you leave.

Driving Permits

If you plan on driving in Indonesia, you must have an International Driving Permit, which can best be obtained in your own country if you already have a valid driver's licence.

If you plan to drive a motorcycle, ensure that your International Driving Permit includes a motorcycle permit – this is better than going through the laborious process of obtaining a motorcycle permit in Bali.

Immunization and Health Precautions

While there are no legal medical requirements for visitors from most countries, cholera, hepatitis A, typhoid and polio inoculations are recommended and tetanus shots should be up-to-date. Dengue fever has been reported in Bali and Lombok, and malaria is a real risk in Lombok, so consult your physician about preventive and emergency medication before you begin your trip.

What to Take

Casual clothes in lightweight natural materials are recommended, with at least one set of conservative dress clothes *(see pp218–19)*, should you need to visit a government office. A wide range of sports equipment for diving, golf, surfing, snorkelling and tennis can easily be rented or bought at most sports locations.

Surfboards available for rent on the beach at Sanur

Most medicines are available in the major towns, but if you require special medication, bring a full supply in the original packaging. You may also wish to bring some first-aid items such as antiseptic

Casual clothes are acceptable in resorts and tourist areas

cream, aspirin, sticking plaster, diarrhoea medication and insect repellent. If you wear prescription spectacles, bring a spare set.

It is possible to exchange rupiah in and outside Indonesia. Visitors are advised to purchase some rupiah before entering the country, at least enough for taxi fare from the airport and spending for the first day.

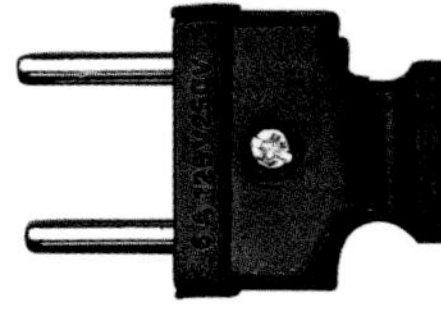

Two-pin plug of the type used in Bali and Lombok

Electricity and Electrical Appliances

Electricity generally runs at 220V–240V AC. In some rural areas, the system still runs on 110V, and some remote areas do not have electricity at all. Power supplies may be unstable.

You may need a plug adaptor with two-pronged, parallel pins. You should buy an adaptor if necessary before you travel.

Customs and Duty-free

Indonesian customs regulations allow foreign nationals to import 200 cigarettes (or 50 cigars or 100 grams of tobacco) and 2 litres of alcohol. Visitors may be asked to declare photographic and electronic equipment. There are restrictions on the import and export of products such as ivory and turtle shell, on things made from endangered species, and on the export of antiquities and certain cultural objects. Check with an Indonesian embassy or consulate for details. There are duty-free shops in Bali and in the departure area of the airport. Import or export of rupiah is limited to Rp50,000,000 per person.

Duty-free shop logo

Facilities for Disabled Travellers

Provisions for disabled people are, as in much of Asia, inadequate. Facilities for the disabled that are available are not as sophisticated as they are in the United States and in Europe.

The terrain is often hilly, and there are stairs and steps everywhere. Wheelchair access is very rare. Pavements rarely have slopes to aid getting on or off them; most are high and uneven. Many public places are accessed by steps; very few have ramps, and wheelchair users will find public transport inaccessible.

The more up-market hotels, however, are slowly becoming increasingly aware of the needs of disabled travellers. Some recently built 5-star hotels have wheelchair access, and villas usually have spacious bathrooms and extensive grounds, suitable for wheelchair users.

Steps to temple hindering wheelchair access

Facilities for Children

In Bali and Lombok, children are treated with great respect and appreciation. In fact, small children are likely to be greeted (in some places) with far more enthusiasm by hotel staff than by fellow guests. Some hotels have special rates, facilities and activities for children of various ages, so ask your hotel. Because Indonesian children are constantly attended and included in general society, no special safety measures are taken for them, and there are few facilities outside of resorts specifically for children. Parents of small children need therefore to be especially alert to environmental hazards such as stairs, unguarded edges and traffic.

Child enjoying herself in a pool with a rubber ring

Paraphernalia for infant care are available in department stores and most pharmacies.

Children will find much to keep themselves happily occupied in Bali and Lombok. There is an enormous range of activities available: water-based activities in beaches, pools and water parks; jungle rides, trekking, rafting and mountain-biking; and music and dance performances. For more information on activities suitable for children, see p199 and pp202–7.

The Law

For drivers, motor insurance is both obligatory and highly recommended. You must tell the police *(see p220)* if you intend to spend more than 24 hours in a private home. Notify your consulate if you are arrested for a crime. Inform the police and your consulate if you are in an accident where someone is injured or there is property damage; if your passport is lost or stolen; if you are the victim of any other crime; if you give birth; or if someone in your party dies.

Warning

Indonesian law prescribes the death penalty for trafficking in illegal drugs, and heavy penalties for possession of weapons.

Tourist Information and Service Centres

There are government-run tourist information offices (*Dinas Pariwisata Pemerintah Propinsi Daerah Tingkat I Bali*) in each regional capital, in some cases there are several in one town. These offices offer a range of brochures on major tourist sites. Tourist areas also have information centres. Opening hours are normally 7:30am–3pm from Mondays to Thursdays and 7:30am–2pm on Fridays. Offices in major tourist sites such as those in Kuta, Sanur and Ubud have longer opening hours.

Tourist brochure

A good source of local information is the many small businesses in tourist areas which also offer some or all of the following services: telephone, fax, e-mail, tours, car and bicycle rentals, airline bookings, cargo packing and shipping, currency exchange, video rental, film processing, postal service and *post restante*, and sale of tickets for cultural performances.

A tourist information centre offering a variety of services

Locals starting their day early at the morning market at Sidemen

Time

Bali and Lombok are eight hours ahead of Greenwich Mean Time (GMT), the same as Perth, while Jakarta is seven hours ahead. Because of the proximity to the equator, days and nights are of almost equal length and vary little throughout the year. Night falls very quickly, at around 6–7pm.

Opening Hours

For farmers and market vendors, the day begins before dawn – in Muslim Lombok, with prayers amplified from the mosques. By two in the afternoon, it is time to rest. Banks, government offices and many small businesses generally follow this pattern. Businesses catering to tourists keep hours more like their guests, opening mid-morning and closing mid-evening, every day except major public holidays *(see p43)*.

BUKA
OPEN
TUTUP
CLOSED

Open (*buka*) and closed (*tutup*) signs

Tourist sites, such as temples, are open during daylight hours every day. Museum hours and opening days vary. Government office hours are 8am–4pm, although some places may close earlier, especially on Fridays. Banks are generally open from 8am to 3pm from Mondays to Fridays.

Christian Worship for Visitors

The dominant religion in Bali is Hinduism, while that in Lombok is Islam. However, there are several Christian churches offering services in English, such as **Legian Church**. Some hotels, such as the **Nusa Dua Beach Hotel** and the **Grand Bali Beach Hotel** in Sanur also offer services on Sundays at which both hotel guests and non-residents are welcome.

Cagar Budaya Nasional (National Heritage Site)

Keep an eye out for small white signs with black lettering marked "Cagar Budaya Nasional"; they indicate a national heritage site. In Bali, some of these are historic sites, but many are temples. Until the 1990s, most temples were open to anyone as long as you wore a temple sash. That is no longer the case. Except for very important temples, those not designated as "Cagar Budaya Nasional" are likely to be closed, except during their anniversary festivals, when anyone who is correctly dressed and not in a taboo condition *(see p219)* may visit. Cagar Budaya Nasional sites generally have a visitors' kiosk with a guest book and donation box – a few thousand rupiah is enough – and there are sarongs and sashes which you may borrow to fulfil temple dress requirements. Some sites may charge an admission fee.

A Cagar Budaya Nasional sign marking a national heritage site

Balinese-style toilet signs in a restaurant

Public Toilets

Public toilets are scarce in Bali and Lombok, except at major tourist stops. Hygiene is poor and toilet paper rare. Toilets (*kamar kecil*) consist of a "squat" toilet and a large bin of water (*bak mandi*), with which you flush the toilet and cleanse yourself. Toilet signs – *"wanita"* (female) or *"pria"* (male) – are often elaborate woodcarvings at tourist areas.

Conversion Chart

Imperial to Metric
1 inch = 2.54 centimetres
1 foot = 30 centimetres
1 yard = 0.9 metres
1 mile = 1.6 kilometres
1 ounce = 28 grams
1 pound = 454 grams

Metric to Imperial
1 centimetre = 0.4 inches
1 metre = 3 feet 3 inches
1 metre = 1.11 yards
1 kilometre = 0.6 miles
1 gram = 0.04 ounces
1 kilogram = 2.2 pounds
1 litre = 0.22 gallons
1 litre = 1.8 pints

Fabric sold by length in a textile shop

Directory

Useful Phone Numbers

Ngurah Rai International Airport Information
Tel (0361) 751 011.

Useful Websites

W www.baliblog.com
W www.bali.com
W www.balidiscovery.org
W www.baliguide.com
W www.balitravelforum.com
W www.geocities.com/bali-info_4u
W www.lombok-network.com

Tourist Information Services

Badung
Badung Tourism Authority (South Bali, Java, West Nusantara and Lombok), Jalan Raya Kuta 2, Kuta.
Tel (0361) 756 175.
FAX (0361) 756 176.
W www.badung.go.id

Denpasar
Regional Office of Tourism, Art and Culture, Jalan Raya Puputan Niti Mandala, Denpasar.
Tel (0361) 225 649.
FAX (0361) 233 474.
W www.bali.go.id/tourism

Denpasar
Bali Toursim Authority (DIPARDA), Jalan S Parman Niti Mandala, Denpasar.
Tel (0361) 222 387.
FAX (0361) 226 313.
W www.balitourism authority.net

West Nusa Tenggara
Provincial Tourist Service, Jalam Langko 70, Ampenan, Lombok.
Tel (0364) 21 730.

Regional Office of Tourism, Art and Culture, West Nusa Tenggara, Jalan Singosari 2, Mataram, Lombok.
Tel (0370) 632 723 or (0370) 634 800.
FAX (0370) 637 233.

Foreign Consulates

Australia
(also represents Canada, New Zealand, and other Commonwealth countries in emergencies.)
Tel (0361) 283 011 or (0361) 283 241.
FAX (0361) 282 281.
W www.dfat.gov.au/bali
@ bali.congen@dfat.gov.au

Great Britain
Jalan Mertasari 2, Sanar.
Tel (0361) 270 601.
FAX (0361) 270 572.

United States
Jalan Hayam Wuruk 188, Renon, Denpasar.
Tel (0361) 233 605.
FAX (0361) 222 426.

Immigration Offices

Airport
Kantor Imigrasi Ngurah Rai Tuban, Jalan Raya I Gusti Ngurah Rai, Tuban.
Tel (0361) 751 038.

Denpasar
Kantor Imigrasi Denpasar, Jalan Di Panjaitan, Niti Mandala, Renon.
Tel (0361) 227 828.

Lombok
Kantor Imigrasi Lombok, Jalan Udayana 2, Mataram, Lombok.
Tel (0370) 632 520.

Christian Worship

(English-language services.)

Bali Legian Church
(Interdenominational.) Jalan Patimura.
Tel (0361) 754 255.

Christian City Church
Jalan Diponegoro 148, Denpasar.
Tel (0361) 281 319.

Eastern Orthodox Church Service
(Divine liturgy.) Mykonos Restaurant, Jalan Laksmana 52.
Tel (0813) 3874 3782.

MSIC
(Morning Star International Church.) Hilton Hotel, Samudera Room.
Tel (0361) 776 212.

Sanur
(Interdenominational.) Grand Bali Beach Hotel, Sanur.
Tel (0361) 703 342.

St Joseph Church
(Catholic holy mass.) Jalan Kepundung, Denpasar.
Tel (0361) 233 729.

Etiquette

Visitors behaving with due courtesy will generally be made welcome in Bali and Lombok. Indeed the greatest pleasure of travelling in Indonesia is getting to know its very hospitable and gracious people. The Balinese are an extroverted, cheerfully self-confident people; the Sasaks of Lombok are more reserved. The inhabitants of both islands will treat tourists well, especially those with a little knowlege of local manners.

Balinese dressed up in formal attire for a ceremony

What to Wear

The dress code at resorts is very relaxed, and shorts and bare arms and shoulders are generally accepted. Upper-end hotels may require "smart casual" dress in the evenings. However, most Indonesians may be offended by immodest attire and visitors should be sensitive to this when entering towns and villages.

Within tourist enclaves, dress is very casual. A hat or cap and comfortable shoes that slip off easily are best for touring – Indonesians generally remove their shoes before entering a home.

When visiting a government office, conservative dress is obligatory: for men, long trousers and long-sleeved shirt, shoes and socks; and for women, a knee-length dress or skirt, a blouse that covers the upper arms, and shoes. Rubber flip-flops are considered "not polite" by Indonesians in general.

Outside tourist areas, especially in Lombok, conservative dress is a sign of courtesy. Ubud's dress code is more conservative than that of beach resort areas. Some Ubud visitors adopt the sarong.

Languages

Most locals who deal with tourists speak some English, and there are guides trained in Japanese and major European languages.

Bahasa Indonesia is the national language of Indonesia. It is based largely on Malay, for centuries the trading language of the archipelago, and uses the Latin alphabet. Verbs take suffixes and prefixes, making it difficult to look up a word in a phrasebook without knowing its root form. It is easy to master a simplified form of Bahasa Indonesia that is widely used with visitors.

The Balinese and the Sasaks of Lombok maintain their indigenous languages which share a common base with Javanese, and are written with a Sanskrit-based alphabet. There is a complex system of parallel vocabularies to reflect status rankings, and mistakes can cause offence.

Tourists at a temple wearing the required sarong and waist sash

The lotus, a symbol of grace in Bali

Social Behaviour

In Bali and Lombok, certain social rules are observed, which, if followed by visitors, will open up a warm exchange; and if ignored, may cause embarrassment or even seriously offend.

Always give and receive things with the right hand, never the left. Avoid pointing with the index finger, especially at a person: this gesture may be taken as a physical challenge. If you must point at something, only use the thumb of your right hand. To be very polite, do so while cupping your right elbow. Never point to anyone or anything with your foot.

Avoid touching anyone's head, even a child's – a person's head is considered the most sacred part of the body – and do not stand next to someone who is sitting down. If you need to walk past someone who is sitting on the ground, it is best to bend from the waist and murmur something apologetic (*"Maaf"* or *"Sorry, sorry"*).

In a social situation with Indonesians where refreshments are served, wait until you are invited before you begin drinking or eating. (Indonesians wait until they are bidden several times before they do so.) Similarly, do not sit down until you are directed to a place; spatial placement holds a significant social code for Indonesians.

As far as possible, do not express anger or behave in a confrontational manner. Any extravagant displays of emotion will make you look foolish. As in much of Asia, it is considered coarse to call attention to oneself unnecessarily, especially while in public. Gracious behaviour is much appreciated by Indonesians and will get better results than an angry outburst.

Indonesians frown on public displays of private affection – these are considered embarrassing to others and therefore rude.

Social Encounters

It is usual to greet people whether you know them or not, and to acknowledge those nearby with a smile and a nod when you arrive or leave a place. Polite conversation often takes the form of an exchange of questions. Westerners may find these intrusive – the best solution is to ask questions in return.

Visitor taking off his shoes before entering a Balinese home

Places of Worship

Hindus in Bali and Lombok observe strict rules in regard to their temples, which they believe must be observed by everyone, including visitors, for safeguarding the spiritual hygiene of sacred places. These rules mainly concern dress requirements and conditions of *sebel* (taboo).

A waist sash, and in many places a sarong, is the dress required of anyone entering a temple or other holy ground, whether or not there is a ceremony in progress. These may be borrowed at temples that regularly accept tourists, but it is easy to buy your own almost anywhere.

There is no moral censure attached to being in a state of *sebel*; on the contrary, to acknowledge this state is a mark of self-awareness. These rules should be observed, even if they conflict with your religious beliefs.

Conditions of *sebel* are: menstruation or having an open wound – this relates to a prohibition on shedding blood in a temple; bringing food into a temple as it clashes with offerings; being physically or mentally ill, or in a state of psychic disturbance; being in a state of bereavement (for the Balinese, up to 42 days from the date of the death of a close relative); and having given birth within the past 42 days (thought to attract attention from spirits).

There are other rules that should be observed when entering temples, especially during festivals.

Ask permission before entering a courtyard, as some gates are reserved for priests and holy objects. It is best to stay quietly at the back of a courtyard until invited. Do not walk in front of anyone who is praying, or a priest performing a ritual.

Photography is restricted in some temples, so check with temple attendants before using a camera.

Temple offerings should also not be touched, and temple walls and shrines must never be climbed. It is considered sacrilegious to do so unless one is a priest.

There are rules that should be observed when entering mosques: visitors should take off their shoes before going into a mosque, and cover up shoulders, arms and legs; women should cover their heads with a scarf, and must not enter when menstruating.

Bargaining for a straw bag at a market

Bargaining

Except for up-market shops and department stores, most shops do not have fixed prices and shopkeepers expect customers to bargain before finalizing a sale. Indonesians consider it fair that tourists pay higher prices than the (usually much poorer) locals. Be realistic. To get a good price, learn the prices of goods elsewhere before making a purchase, then disarm the vendor by being polite.

Unwelcome Attention

If you do not wish to buy something from a street or beach peddler, or accept the offer of "transport", it is usually enough to say quietly "No, thank you".

Avoid giving money to children. If you have a small gift for them, give it to their parents instead.

Women are regarded with respect in Indonesia, and it is rare for foreigners to be bothered by sexual harassment. However, dressing modestly helps.

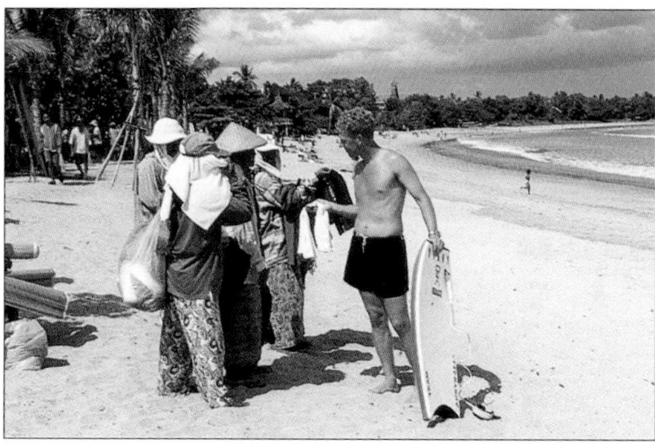

Hawkers peddling their wares to a potential buyer

Personal Security and Health

VISITORS TO BALI AND LOMBOK generally face no greater personal danger than sunburn and perhaps a day or two of digestive upset. It is important, however, to bear in mind that visitors are operating in a "parallel economy" which is conspicuously richer than that of the largely poor, local population; that it takes some time for visitors from temperate areas to adjust to the tropical climate; and that the sanitation and medical infrastructure is not yet as complete as in developed countries. In general, tourists should follow the same precautions they take when visiting their own local cities.

Bicycles are convenient, as here on a one-way street in Kuta

Looking After Your Property

VIOLENT CRIME in Bali and Lombok is rare; but tourist areas attract delinquents, and you should treat your belongings with care.

Most hotels offer some form of lock-up storage. Use it. To leave valuables lying around unattended is to invite theft. Put valuables and important documents in your hotel safe. Lock the doors and windows of your hotel room when you are not there. Be on guard against pickpockets, who usually operate in crowded places such as public transport vehicles and airport terminals. At banks and especially at moneychangers, count cash carefully at the counter and put it immediately in your wallet before leaving the premises. Do not let the moneychanger handle the money after you have counted it.

Make a note of the serial numbers of your camera, computer or other equipment, and keep photocopies of documents such as your passport data and visa pages, credit cards and driving licence – these will come in useful in the event of a police report or an insurance claim.

Personal Safety

TOURISTS IN BALI and Lombok are generally treated as valued guests. If you travel alone late at night off the beaten track, you will certainly attract attention from local people, but probably in the form of concern for your welfare. Women travelling alone should exercise the usual precautions.

In places such as Kuta where there is a developed nightlife, be alert, as you would in any other country.

Some cases of armed robbery have been reported in the remoter parts of Lombok, especially around Gunung Rinjani. You should seek local advice before travelling in this area alone.

If you are pestered by someone, immediately seek out a crowded place. Be aware that if you are robbed and you call out for help, this may arouse an entire village, who could well enact "street justice" on the spot, with tragic consequences for any person accused, so be cautious about accusing anyone.

The recent terrorist attacks in Indonesia resulted in travel warnings from some countries. Check your government's travel advice for most recent information. It is also advised not to get involved in political demonstrations while in Bali.

A police patrol car

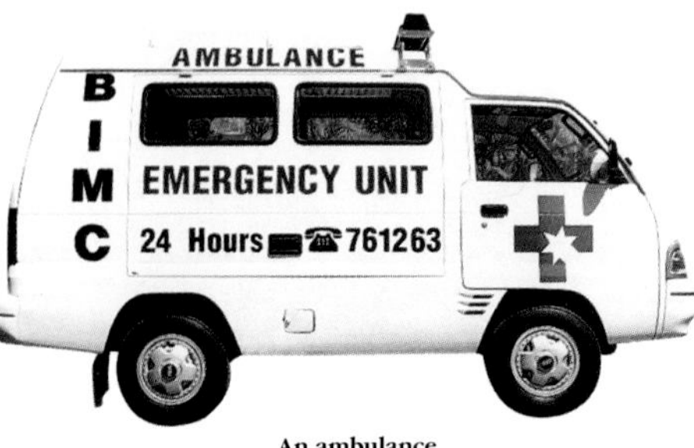

An ambulance

Medical Facilities

THERE ARE 24-HOUR CLINICS in the major tourist areas for minor illnesses and first-aid. The fact that they cater mainly to tourists is reflected in their prices. The clinics include the **Bali International Medical Centre**, the **Bali Nusa Dua Emergency Clinic**, the **SOS Clinic,** the **General Hospital** and the **Ubud Clinic**. There is an extra charge for house calls.

The local equivalents to these clinics are the Puskesmas, not always staffed round the clock, and not as well equipped. Major hotels have doctors on call. There are public hospitals (*rumah sakit umum*) in every regional capital – the best is in Sanglah, Denpasar. There are a few private hospitals. Visitors are strongly advised to take out medical evacuation insurance before travelling.

Common Ailments

The most common health problems for visitors are over-exposure to sun, digestive troubles, infections arising from untreated surface cuts and motorcycle mishaps.

Use a sunblock and renew it after you swim; avoid the beach (sunny or not) between 11am and 2pm; and wear a hat. Resist the temptation to make a motorcycle tour in your bathing suit – not only will you look silly (crash helmets are obligatory), your skin will be scorched by both sun and wind. Wear protective clothing, and beware of the exhaust pipe, which can give your leg a deep, slow-to-heal burn.

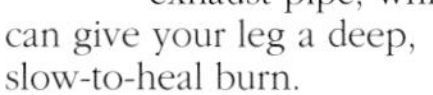

Bottled water

Tropical ulcers are infections that can arise when surface wounds such as cuts, blisters or scratched mosquito bites go unattended. Even very minor wounds should be washed with soap and water and treated with antiseptic powder or cream.

Treat stomach upsets with a mild diet (boiled rice and black tea is an effective remedy). Severe diarrhoea must be followed with a rehydration treatment; neglect of this can be fatal for infants. The water of a young coconut is also effective. If you suspect cholera, see a doctor.

Hats and shades offer sun protection

To minimize digestive problems, avoid fresh fruit that you do not peel yourself. Drink only bottled water, checking first that the seal is intact. Food at local food stalls is always fresh, but it is highly spiced and hygiene is questionable. In some tourist places, on the other hand, excessive faith in refrigeration can result in food being stored too long. In cases of serious doubt, plain rice with a little salt is generally safe.

APOTIK
ANGKASA
(NO. SIA PO 00.02. SIA-RA.VII.98.2915)
JL. KEMAYORAN. BANDARA NGURAH RAI
TELP. 763102

Pharmacies *(apotik)* usually stock a wide range of medicines

Pharmacies

Pharmacies are known as *"apotik"* and are well signposted as such. They are privately run businesses and are abundant in towns. There is usually a qualified pharmacist on hand who speaks some English and can advise you on medications. Imported, branded medications are relatively expensive; cheaper, generic equivalents are often easily available.

Snakes and Insects

Snakes (*ular* in Bahasa Indonesia, *lelipi* in Balinese) can sometimes be seen – Bali still has field and water snakes. Most are harmless. The brilliantly coloured green tree viper has a poisonous bite which can be fatal to small children and the physically weak. It inhabits ricefields and trees. Do not go into thick vegetation without adequate protection, and make warning noises. Cobras have been sighted in gardens in South Bali.

Scorpions and centipedes sometimes lurk in quiet corners; their bite is not generally dangerous, but can be very painful. Mosquitoes are prevalent in coastal areas. Use repellents and protective clothing, and burn mosquito coils (*obat nyamuk*), available in most hotels and restaurants.

Directory

Emergency Services

Ambulance ☎ *118.*
Fire ☎ *113.*
Police ☎ *110.*
Red Cross ☎ *(0361) 225 465.*
Rescue ☎ *115, 111 or 151.*

Clinics

Bali International Medical Centre (BIMC)
Jalan Bypass Ngurah Rai 100X, Kuta.
☎ *(0361) 761 263.*
FAX *(0361) 764 345.*
@ info@bimcbali.com
W www.bimcbali.com
24 hours.

Bali Nusa Dua Emergency Clinic
BTDC Complex, Nusa Dua.
☎ *(0361) 772 392.* *24 hours.*

General Hospital
Jalan Pejanggik, Mataram, Lombok.
☎ *(0370) 22 254.* *24 hours.*

SOS Clinic
Jalan Bypass Ngurah rai 505x, Kuta.
☎ *(0361) 710 544.* *24 hours.*

Ubud Clinic
Jalan Raya Campuhan 36, Ubud.
☎ *(0361) 974 911.* *24 hours.*

Emergency dental care is available at the 24-hour clinics.

Environmental Hazards

The tropical sun is deceptively strong; so too are the currents of the Indian Ocean on the south coasts of Bali and Lombok. Not all beaches have lifeguards or markers. Drownings are common. Rivers which cross beaches and empty into the sea have traversed towns where sanitation can be poor or even non-existent. For this reason, and because of mudslides, avoid even upstream rivers for bathing.

Banking and Local Currency

An old *kepeng* coin from the past

SINCE THE 1997 FINANCIAL CRISIS, exchange rates between Indonesian and other currencies have fluctuated wildly, as have prices encountered by visitors. Modern banking and exchange facilities are available in the bigger towns and tourist centres. Major international credit cards are widely accepted. Although cash and traveller's cheques in other major currencies can be exchanged, US dollars are most widely welcomed. Many tourist services are priced in US dollars. Local currency will often be used for giving change.

A branch of BCA, an Indonesian bank, in Kuta

Banking Services

THE ONLY foreign banks in Bali are **ABN Amro** and **Citibank**. In Bali, the main offices of the major Indonesian banks are in Denpasar, with branch offices in the regional capitals, as well as in Kuta, Sanur and Ubud, and in major hotels. Major banks in Lombok are in Mataram. Most banks in tourism areas have facilities for exchanging foreign currency. It is possible to wire money directly to a bank in Indonesia.

Traveller's Cheques and Moneychangers

TRAVELLER'S CHEQUES, not normally accepted in place of cash in Bali and Lombok, may be cashed at most banks and moneychangers, usually for less favourable rates than currency. Bring your passport for identification. Exchange facilities are widely available in Bali and in major tourist areas in Lombok. Elsewhere, visitors should carry cash. Authorized moneychangers are found in abundance in tourist centres. Elsewhere, rates may be disadvantageous. Abuses have been reported, so exercise normal precautions.

An automatic teller machine or ATM at a bank

Automatic Teller Machines (ATMs)

ELECTRONIC BANKING has grown rapidly and ATMs can be found at banks in tourist areas such as Sanur, Kuta, Denpasar and Ubud, and at the airport's international and domestic arrival halls. Major international credit cards are widely accepted.

A 24-hour moneychanger in Seminyak

Directory

Credit Cards

American Express
c/o Pacto, Ltd, Grand Bali Beach Hotel, Sanur.
(0361) 288 449 or (0361) 288 511, ext. 1111 (for traveller's cheques).

BCA Card Centre
(for BCA, Visa, MasterCard and JCB Cards)
Jalan Raya Kuta 55XX, Kuta.
(0361) 759 010 or (0361) 759 011 (for lost or stolen Visa cards).
(001) 803 65 6576 (toll-free).

Banking Services

The major banks in Indonesia are used to dealing with foreign exchange, credit card advances and telegraphic transfers. Normal weekday banking hours are 8am–3pm and on Saturdays 8–11am.

ABN Amro
Jalan Diponegoro, Kompleks Kerta Wijaya ID1A1, Denpasar.
(0361) 244 277.

Bank Danamon
Jalan Raya Legian 87, Kuta.
(0361) 761 620.

Bank Lippo
Jalan M.H. Thamrin 59, Denpasar.
(0361) 436 047.

Bank Mandiri
Jalan Danau Tamblingan 59, Sanur.
(0361) 288 271.

Bank Negara Indonesia
Grand Bali Beach Hotel, Sanur.
(0361) 288 511.

Jalan Gajah Mada 30, Denpasar.
(0361) 263 304.

Jalan Langko 64, Mataram, Lombok.
(0370) 636 046.

Jalan Legian 359, Kuta.
(0361) 751 914.

Jalan Raya Ubud, Ubud.
(0361) 975 986.

Jalan Surapati 52A, Singaraja.
(0362) 22 648.

Nusa Dua Beach Hotel, Nusa Dua.
(0361) 771 906.

Citibank
Jalan Teuku Umar 208, Denpasar.
(0361) 269 999.

Credit Cards

Major international credit cards (such as American Express, Visa and MasterCard) are accepted at most establishments which cater for visitors in Bali and Lombok, and they are becoming more widely used by Indonesians. Cash advances on credit cards are available at most banks, although this is usually subject to a commission fee and a maximum withdrawal.

Local Currency

The Indonesian currency unit is the rupiah. In 2004, it was valued at around 9,000 to the US dollar, with a meal at a local food stall costing about Rp7,000. Carry an adequate amount of currency in small denominations: people may often not be able to give change for large notes. Some old notes are still in circulation. Be cautious when receiving badly soiled or damaged notes. Current import and export limit is Rp50,000 per person.

Banknotes

Notes come in denominations of Rp100, Rp500, Rp1,000, Rp5,000, Rp10,000, Rp20,000, Rp50,000 and Rp100,000.

1,000 rupiah

5,000 rupiah

10,000 rupiah

20,000 rupiah

50,000 rupiah

100,000 rupiah

Coins

Coins come in the following denominations: Rp25 (rare and virtually worthless), Rp50, Rp100, Rp500 and Rp 1,000. Some coins from earlier designs are still in circulation.

50 rupiah

100 rupiah

100 rupiah

500 rupiah

1,000 rupiah

Communications

hellobali
BALI'S BEST RESTAURANT AWARDS

***Hello Bali*, a tourist magazine**

Communications with the rest of the world are good in the major tourism centres, and steadily improving throughout Bali and Lombok. Telkom is the government-owned telephone utility, and offers Internet service; Indosat is a major telecom service-provider. *Wartel* (from "*warung telkom*", or "telecom shops") are public telecom service outlets run by local businesses. International phone rates are among the highest in the world, especially if you make calls chargeable to your hotel bill.

Using Bali and Lombok's Telephones

Public phones use either coins or phonecards. Phonecards are more economical and may be purchased at many shops and *wartel*. Some coin-operated phones may take only the largest of the several forms of Rp100 coins *(see p223)*.

Payphone charges are calculated according to time and distance. Local calls are subject to time charges. Rates are usually posted at a *wartel*. Mobile phones are becoming common among most Indonesians. Visitors can buy cheap phonecards to put in their mobile phones while here.

Fax services are available at *wartel*, business centres and internet cafés. Charges are made for sending and receiving faxes, and are based on phone rates, plus page number. The rates vary widely. Both Bali and Lombok have phone directories, with information given in both Indonesian and English, and English-language *Yellow Pages*. There is no standard system for alphabetizing Balinese names – a person named "Ida Bagus Made Gunung" may well be listed in the directory as "I B Md Gunung" under "I" or "G".

Gunung Bromo
200 unit
BANK TABUNGAN NEGARA
Pelopor KPR untuk semua masyarakat

Phonecards

WARTEL

Wartels providing phone services

Postal Services

The Indonesian post office provides all the services you would normally expect. International delivery normally takes 8–10 days. There are many informal postal-service outlets at tourist shops where you may buy stamps and post letters. The central post office is on the main road in Renon in Denpasar. Post offices in Ubud, Kuta and Singaraja have *poste restante* services.

Using a Card-operated Phone

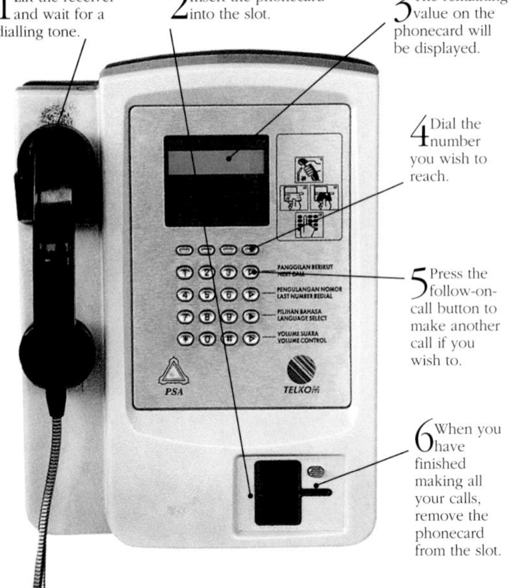
1 Lift the receiver and wait for a dialling tone.
2 Insert the phonecard into the slot.
3 The remaining value on the phonecard will be displayed.
4 Dial the number you wish to reach.
5 Press the follow-on-call button to make another call if you wish to.
6 When you have finished making all your calls, remove the phonecard from the slot.
PSA
TELKOM

Reaching the Right Number

Indonesian telephone numbers are composed of the country code (62), an area code, and a 5- or 6-digit number. When making an *interlokal* call to other places within Indonesia, a zero is added before the area code.

Area Codes

South Bali
Badung regency: **361**
Central Bali
Gianyar regency: **361**
East Bali
Bangli regency: **366**
Klungkung regency: **366**
Karangasem regency: **363**
North Bali
Buleleng regency: **362**
West Bali
Tabanan regency: **361**
Jembrana regency: **365**
Lombok: **370**

Courier

Major international courier services have offices in Bali and Lombok. Most are based in Denpasar, although **FedEx** and **DHL** have branch offices in Ubud. All promise door-to-door service, but in reality some will ask you to deliver to their office.

Internet

Indonesia has more than 50 Internet Service Providers (ISPs). Users should check with their services for international access numbers. The simplest way to access the Internet is through **Telkom's** dial-up number, which offers free access with no registration.

Internet cafés can be found throughout Bali and Lombok, and a few even offer satellite or broadband connections. However, the majority are still quite slow so ask about the type of connection first.

Recommended internet cafés include **Legian Cyber**, **Roda Internet Café**, **Bali 3000**, **Hello Internet Café** and **Wi Fi Connection**.

Television

Satellite television is increasingly widespread in urban Indonesia and is found in all major hotels on both Bali and Lombok. Indonesia has ten private TV channels and the government-run TVRI. Bali TV has numerous cultural programmes with lots of music and traditional dancing. All the channels are in the Indonesian languages, although they offer some American programmes and foreign films.

Newspapers and Magazines

English-language daily newspapers – primarily the American *International Herald Tribune* and the well-respected *Jakarta Post* – are available in tourist outlets and (at slightly higher prices) from many of the street vendors.

Several English-language magazines are available. *Hello Bali* is a free monthly magazine for tourists obtainable at hotels and dining outlets. The bimonthly *Bali Echo* and *Bali and Beyond* are tourism, art and culture magazines that cover events and happenings in Bali and Lombok. The bimonthly *Yak* and *Bud* are specifically focused on the Seminyak and Ubad areas.

The biweekly newspaper *Bali Advertiser*, also free, is aimed at the expatriate community, but has information about restaurants, tours, and activities that may be of interest to short-term visitors. *The Poleng* is an audacious new magazine on art, culture and society in Bali.

Directory

Telephone

Local
Tel 108.

National
Tel 0809 108 108.

International
Tel 102.

Operator-assisted Local Calls
Tel 100.

Operator-assisted International Calls
Tel 101.

International Direct Dialing
Tel 001, 017 or 008.

Courier

DHL
Jalan Bypass Ngurah Rai, Tuban.
Tel *(0361) 768 282.*

Jalan Bypass Ngurah Rai 155, Sanur.
Tel *(0361) 282 818.*

Jalan Legian Kaja 451, Kuta.
Tel *(0361) 762 138.*

Jalan Raya Ubud 16, Ubud.
Tel *(0361) 972 195.*

Eltheha Lombok
Jalan Koperasi 8, Mataram, Lombok.
Tel *(0370) 631 820.*

FedEx
Jalan Bypass Ngurah Rai 72, Jimbaran.
Tel *(0361) 701 727.*

Jalan Raya Ubud 44, Ubud.
Tel *(0361) 977 575.*

United Parcel Service (UPS)
Jalan Bypass Ngurah Rai 2005.
Tel *(0361) 764 439 or (0361) 766 676.*

Internet Connection

Telkom
Free internet access with no registration.
Tel 0809 89 999.
In dialogue box, key in username "telkomnet@instan" and password "telkom".
Tel *162 (Information).*

Internet Cafés

Bali 3000
Jalan Raya Ubud.
Tel *(0361) 978 538.*

Dana Makmur Wartel Internet
Jalan Pantai, Kuta.
Tel *(0361) 753 376.*

Hello Internet Café
Ramayana Bali Mall, 3rd Floor, Denpasar.
Tel *(0361) 246 001.*

@ Highway
Jalan Raya Ubud.
Tel *(0361) 972 107.*
W www.highwaybali.com

Legian Cyber
Legian Village Hotel, Jalan Sahadewa 21, Legian.
Tel *(0361) 761 804.*

Legian Village Hotel, Jalan Yudhistira.
W www.legiancyber.com

Putra Internet
Jalan Hang Tuah, Sanur.
Tel *(0361) 284 104.*

Roda Internet Café
Jalan Bisma 3, Ubud.
Tel *(0361) 973 325.*

Wi Fi Connection
Bali Deli, Jalan Kunti 117x, Seminyak.
Tel *(0361) 738 686.*

Computer Sales & Rental

Adi Computer
Jalan Tukad Yeh Penet 2, Renon, Denpasar.
Tel *(0361) 236 531 or (0361) 238 430.*

Harry's Computer
Jalan Teuku Umar 173, Denpasar.
Tel *(0361) 232 470 or (0361) 266 773.*

PC Mac
Jalan Iman Bonjol 266D, Denpasar.
Tel *(0361) 489 747.*
@ *pcmac@indosat.net.id*

Travel Information

Bali is one of the main gateways into Indonesia. Its international airport, Ngurah Rai Airport, serves many airlines from around the world, and its harbour is equipped with customs and immigration officers to handle international arrivals. Lombok's airport handles international arrivals only from Singapore, on Silkair. It is also possible to reach Bali and Lombok from within Indonesia by bus and ferry. Transport from the airport is handled by airport taxis and hotel shuttle buses. An airport tax is levied upon departure.

Logos of Indonesian airlines

Aircraft arriving at Ngurah Rai Airport in Bali

Flying to Bali

The Ngurah Rai International Airport in Bali is located in Tuban, south of Kuta, but the destination is referred to as Denpasar. There are frequent direct flights from Europe (especially from London), North America, Australia, New Zealand and countries in East Asia, such as Singapore, Thailand and Japan.

Flights from Europe generally make a stop at Jakarta's excellent airport. Some carriers go no further, but make onward connections to Denpasar via **Garuda Indonesia**, Indonesia's national carrier.

There are numerous flights between Jakarta and Denpasar every day. Many travellers from Europe fly to Singapore, from where there are several daily direct flights to Denpasar on Garuda and **Singapore Airlines**. **Malaysia Airlines** and **Qantas** both fly to Denpasar.

Most flights from North America leave by way of Los Angeles (although some go by San Francisco, Seattle or Vancouver), with stops in the Pacific or at Tokyo. Carriers from Taiwan (**China Airlines**) and Hongkong (**Cathay Pacific Airways**) stop in their own capital cities.

Airfares and Taxes

Fares are highest during high season; but the definition of "high season" varies according to the airline. For instance, "high season" for **Ansett Australia** and **Air New Zealand** includes the summer holidays in December. Flights from London are generally cheaper than those from other European capitals. **Air Paradise** offers excellent value for money if you are flying from Australia.

The airport levies a nominal departure tax on domestic flights. Taxes on international flights are higher.

Getting to and from the Airport

The Ngurah Rai airport is about a 30-minute drive on a major road from Kuta, Nusa Dua and Sanur, and about an hour from Ubud. Traffic moves well once you get outside the centres.

Transport from the airport is restricted to special airport taxis, hotel shuttle buses and private vehicles. Several car-rental companies *(see p229)* have facilities at the airport.

To get a taxi, go to the taxi kiosk located just outside the airport building exit. Fares are posted and vary according to the destination – they range from about Rp30,000 (for Kuta Beach) up to Rp115,000 (for Ubud). Purchase a voucher at the kiosk and you will be guided to your assigned taxi. This system was devised to eliminate touting and confusion, and to give all drivers an equal opportunity to obtain fares. When you arrive at your destination, give the driver your voucher.

An airport taxi

Fares are in rupiah. There are moneychangers just inside the exit door, and exchange rates are usually quite favourable at the airport. There are ATMs in the international and domestic terminal buildings which accept major credit cards.

For transport to the airport, there are, apart from taxis, cheap shuttles from the main tourist centres.

A tourist information outlet offering tickets and reservations

Travelling to Islands off Bali

Nusa Penida is not usually considered a tourist destination except for the most rugged of travellers. It can be reached by small boats from Sanur Beach, from

Kusamba Beach or Padang Bai. Nusa Lembongan off the northwest coast of Nusa Penida is developing as a destination for day-trips and overnight trips. **Bali Hai Cruises**, **Bounty Cruises** and **Island Explorer Cruises** offer daytrips to the island. **Ombak Putin** goes to the eastern islands in a schooner.

Flying to Lombok

Bali's airport is a major terminal for Indonesian domestic flights, served by a number of domestic airlines. Air travel between Bali and Lombok's airport at Mataram is handled by **Merpati Nusantara Airlines**. Schedules are subject to change depending on demand, but currently there are about ten daily flights. Flight time is about 25 minutes, and there is a departure tax for each leg of the trip.

Travelling to Lombok by Sea

The cheapest way to cross the Lombok Straits is by ferry, although the voyage takes nearly a whole day. Ferries travel from Padang Bai in East Bali to Pelabuhan Lembar (Lembar Harbour) in Lombok at 60- to 90-minute intervals. The crossing takes four hours (or more, depending on conditions). Seasoned travellers get to Padang Bai well in advance in order to choose one of the newer and safer ferries. A first-class ticket buys a seat in an air-conditioned saloon, but this is not as pleasant as being on the deck. There is an extra charge for bicycles, motorcycles and cars. Tickets are purchased at the harbour.

Ferries at Pelabuhan Lembar (Lembar Harbour)

There are alternatives to the ferry. **Bounty Cruises** has daily trips to Lombok. There is also a flight to Mataram from Denpasar which will get you door to door in under 30 minutes. Perama Shuttle offers a bus and boat ride to Lembar daily at 6am for about $15. The bus leaves Kuta for Padang Bai and the passage is on Perama's own boat. An alternative is to take their bus from either Kuta or Ubud at 10am to catch the 1pm regular ferry to Lembar.

Travelling to Islands off Lombok

The most convenient way to get to the Gili Isles from Senggigi is by a shuttle boat. This can be arranged in advance from Bali. You can also negotiate the charter of an outrigger boat from Senggigi or Bangsal. Cruise options are also available. **Bounty Cruises** offers daily excursions to the Gili Isles.

The jet-powered Mabua Express ferry service leaving for Lombok

Directory

International Airlines

Air New Zealand
(0361) 768 255.

Ansett Australia
(0361) 289 637.

Cathay Pacific Airways
(0361) 766 931.

China Airlines
(0361) 757 298.

Eva Air
(0361) 751 011.

Garuda Indonesia
(0361) 254 747 (Denpasar).
(0361) 270 535 (Sanur).
(0361) 751 361 (Kuta).
(0361) 287 915 (Sanur Beach Hotel).

Malaysia Airlines
(0361) 757 299.

Qantas Airways
(0361) 288 331 (Grand Bali Beach Hotel, Sanur).

Singapore Airlines
(0361) 768 388.

Domestic Airlines

Air Paradise
Jalan Bypass Ngurah Rai, Megah Blok 1, Kuta.
(0361) 756 666.

Merpati Nusantara Airlines
Jalan Melati 51, Denpasar.
(0361) 235 358.

Jalan Selaparang, Mataram, Lombok.
(0370) 36 745.

Cruise Services

Bali Hai Cruises
Benoa Harbour, Bali.
(0361) 720 331.

Bounty Cruises
Jalan Pelabuhan, Benoa Harbour.
(0361) 726 666.

Jalan Raya Senggigi, Senggigi.
(0370) 693 567.

Island Explorer Cruises
Jalan Bypass Ngurah Rai 622, Suwung, Badung.
(0361) 728 088.

Ombak Putin
Kuta Poleng D7, Kuta.
(0361) 766 269.

Travelling by Road

A road map of Bali

The only means of land travel within Bali or Lombok is by road. Getting around Bali, especially in the south and in Ubud, is becoming increasingly hectic as cars and motorcycles become more numerous. Inexpensive public transport, such as *bemo* and buses, is available throughout Bali and Lombok. However, many people prefer to rent a car with a driver. Tourist shuttles are also good alternatives.

Public Transport

Public transport in Bali and Lombok is cheap, but not always convenient for visitors, since it becomes scarce after dark, and the routes are designed to serve the needs of the local population rather than tourists.

Bemo are minivans that drive along pre-determined routes. Small *bemo* service a town while large *bemo* travel between towns, such as from Denpasar to Ubud or Kuta. Fares are low (less than Rp1,600 within a town and less than Rp4,000 between towns), but it may take several hours to cover a distance of 15 km (10 miles), and tourists are sometimes overcharged. *Bemo* are often very crowded.

Buses, used mainly by locals, operate long-distance inter-city and inter-island routes. With fewer stops, buses generally have shorter journey times than *bemo*. Main routes are from Denpasar to Singaraja, Denpasar to Amlapura and Sweta to Labuhan Lombok. Fares (less than Rp8,000 and non-negotiable) are paid to the driver or the conductor. Tickets cannot be bought in advance except for inter-island trips.

The main terminals in South Bali are around Denpasar: at Batubulan in the north; at Kereneng in central Denpasar; and at Ubung in the west.

Taxis

In South Bali, metered taxis with air-conditioning can be flagged down or called by phone. Sometimes drivers will try to negotiate a flat fee; it is usually better to use the meter. Some drivers are reluctant to go to Ubud at night because it is hard for them to find a fare for the return trip. Usually a 20% surcharge is added to the fare.

Bahasa Indonesia and Balinese road signs

Tourist Shuttles

A recent innovation which is very useful is tourist shuttles – minivans or minibuses that travel between tourist destinations at regular intervals. They are popular with backpackers and a good way to meet other travellers. Several companies run services between the major tourist destinations on a regular schedule for reasonable, posted fares (Rp30,000–75,000). It may be necessary to book in advance.

Car and Motorcycle Rental

Car rental is popular in Bali and Lombok, and many international agencies are represented. Good self-drive rates can be negotiated with local agencies. As road conditions become more crowded, it is well worth paying a little extra to have the services of a driver, who will act as a guide as well.

Rental options range from the charter of a minivan to the rental of a luxury car, complete with a chauffeur and multi-lingual guide.

The major tourism centres are lined with local agencies that rent cars and motorcycles. Vehicles for rent range from a Volkswagen Safari to a BMW. The most popular are the Suzuki Jimny (ideal for two people) and the Toyota Kijang (good for up to eight people).

You may negotiate directly yourself, or ask your hotel to arrange a rental for you. Be sure to clarify whether the price includes fuel and insurance. Insurance is obligatory, and helmets are compulsory for motorcyclists. Check that the vehicle's lights, brakes, signals and horn are in good working order before you drive off.

You should obtain your International Driving Permit in your home country before your arrival in Bali or Lombok *(see p214)*.

Motorcycle was once the most popular way of getting around and motorcycle hire is still widely available in tourist

A taxi

A *bemo*

A tourist shuttle

centres, but traffic conditions make biking increasingly hazardous. It is not recommended in crowded South or Central Bali or in towns.

Driving in Bali and Lombok

Indonesians drive on the left-hand side of the road. Traffic rules and regulations and driving conventions in practice do not always coincide: motorbikes overtake on either side; drivers pull out into traffic without looking – they expect you to avoid them. Right of way belongs to whoever is bigger or flashes his lights first. As the pavements (sidewalks) are scarce and narrow, pedestrian traffic flows onto the roads including livestock, pushcarts, religious processions and cyclists going the wrong way.

Motorcycles in Singaraja – the most popular form of transport for locals

Rice drying on the road – an obstacle to watch out for

In Lombok, traffic is much lighter, but you must watch out for pony carts.

It is the general practice to sound the horn briefly before overtaking. Traffic lights are scarce: at intersections where you are going straight ahead rather than turning, hazard lights should be used. In towns, one-way systems are increasingly common.

Parking in towns and at markets is supervised by a parking attendant who collects a small fee (generally Rp500–1,000 depending on the vehicle) and helps you get back on to the road.

Driving just after dark is generally inadvisable because of poor visibility and, in particular, the inadequate lighting on bicycles and motorcycles. Drivers should watch out for piles of black sand on the road (dumped there for the next day's building activities). Motorcyclists in particular should avoid driving at dusk because of the number of flying insects.

Indonesians are generally glad to help anyone in trouble on the road. It is customary in such circumstances to offer some small compensation in return.

Pony carts, a hazard for drivers in rural areas

Directory

Terminals

Batubulan Terminal
Batubulan.
(0361) 298 526.

Kereneng Terminal
Jalan Hayam Wuruk, Denpasar.
(0361) 226 906.

Tegal Terminal
Jalan Imam Bonjol, Denpasar.

Ubung Terminal
Jalan Cokroaminoto, Denpasar.
(0361) 237 172.

Mandalika Terminal
Sweta, Lombok.

Taxi Service

Bali Taxi
(0361) 701 111.

Ngurah Rai Taxi
(0361) 724 724.

Praja Taxi
(0361) 289 090.

Tourist Shuttles and Services

Danasari
Poppies Lane 1, Kuta.
(0361) 755 125.

Perama
Jalan Legian 39, Kuta.
(0361) 751 551.

Jalan Hanoman, Ubud.
(0361) 974 722.

Vehicle Rental

Avis Rent-a-Car
Denpasar Airport, Jalan Raya Uluwatu 8A, Jimbaran.
(0361) 701 770.

Bali Bayus Rent Car
Jalan Raya Kerobokan Kelod Br 55, Kuta.
(0361) 735 364.
www.balibayusrentcar.com

Bali Car Rentals
(0361) 418381.
24-hour reservation hotline: (081) 138 0699.
www.balicarrentals.com

Bali Limousine
Banjar Nyuh Kuning, Dusun Mas, Gianyar.
(0361) 978 144.
www.balilimousine.com

Hertz
Grand Bali Beach Hotel, Area Cottage 50, Sanur.
(0361) 281 180.

General Index

Page numbers in **bold** type refer to main entries.

A

B

E

F

G

H

I

J

N

O

P

R

Acknowledgments

Dorling Kindersley would like to thank the following people whose contributions and assistance have made the preparation of this book possible.

Main Contributors

Andy Barski is a motorcycle enthusiast and writer who has written extensively on travelling around the Indonesian archipelago, where he has been based since 1987.

Bruce Carpenter first came to Bali in 1974. He has written numerous books and articles on Balinese art and culture.

John Cooke taught zoology at Oxford University before becoming a wildlife filmmaker, photographer and writer.

Jean Couteau settled in Bali in 1979. He writes short stories and art criticism in French, English and Indonesian.

Diana Darling is a freelance writer and editor who has lived in Bali since 1981. She is the author of *The Painted Alphabet: a Novel* (1992), based on a Balinese tale.

Sarah Dougherty arrived in Bali in 1993 to become editor of *Bali Echo* magazine. She contributes to many international publications and is working on a cookbook.

Tim Stuart is a travel writer, photographer and teacher of business communication. With his wife Rosa, he publishes Lombok's only English-language travel magazine, *Inilah!*.

Tony Tilford is a wildlife photographer and writer with wide experience of Indonesian flora and fauna. An avid traveller, he is in search of common and exotic subjects.

For Dorling Kindersley

Managing Editor Anna Streiffert
Publishing Manager Kate Poole
Senior Publishing Manager Louise Lang
Director of Publishing Gillian Allan
Publisher Douglas Amrine
Production Marie Ingledew, Michelle Thomas
Map Co-ordinators Dave Pugh, Casper Morris

Design and Editorial Assistance

Helle Amin, Christine Chua, Victoria Heyworth-Dunne, Hoo Khuen Hin, Kok Kum Fai, Patricia Rozario, Karen Villabona.

Additional Photography

Luis Ascui.

Fact Checking

Rucina Ballinger, Anak Agung Gede Putra Rangki, Anak Agung Oka Dwiputra.

Proof Reading and Indexing

Kay Lyons.

Special Assistance

Edi Swoboda of Bali Bird Park; Ketty Barski; Steve Bolton; Georges Breguet; Georjina Chia and Kal Muller; Lalu Ruspanudin of DIPARDA, Mataram; Justin Eeles; Peter Hoe of evolution; Ganesha Bookshop; David Harnish; Chris Hill; Jean Howe and William Ingram; Rio Helmi of Image Network Indonesia; I Wayan Kicen; Lagun Sari Indonesia Seafood Pte Ltd; Peter and Made of Made's Warung; M Y Narima of Marintur; Rosemarie F Oei of Museum Puri Lukisan; Jim Parks; David Stone; The Vines Restaurant; Bayu Wirayudha, Made Widana and Luh Nyoman Diah Prihartini.

Photography Permissions

The publisher would like to thank all the parks, temples, museums, hotels, restaurants, shops, galleries and sights too numerous to thank individually, for their co-operation and kind permission to photograph at their premises.

Picture Credits

t = top; tl = top left; tlc = top left centre; tc = top centre; tr = top right; cla = centre left above; ca = centre above; cra = centre right above; cl = centre left; c = centre; cr = centre right; clb = centre left below; cb = centre below; crb = centre right below; bl = bottom left; b = bottom; bc = bottom centre; bcl = bottom centre left; br = bottom right; d = detail.

Every effort has been made to trace the copyright holders and we apologize in advance for any unintentional omissions. We would be pleased to insert the appropriate acknowledgements in any subsequent edition of this publication.

The publisher would like to thank the following individuals, companies and picture libraries for permission to reproduce their photographs and drawings:

Bes Stock: 208cla, 208–209c, 210tl, 210–211c, 211bl, 212–213; © Alain Evrard 12, 43cla, 209tl; © Globe Press 24cr; Blue Marlin Dive Center, Lombok: © Clive Riddington 156bc.

Editions Didier Millet: 3c, 17tr, 20br, 22cl, 25tl, 28tr, 30tl, 32tr, 45bc, 45bcl, 46bl, 47clb, 48cb, 51tl, 64br, 83tr, 88bl, 165c, 167tl, 167crb, 167br, 194tl, 199tr, 202cla, 203t; © Gil Marais 23bl; © Tara Sosrowardoyo 45ca, 46bc, 46br.

Four Seasons Resort: 168cl, 181bl.

A.A. Gede Ariawan: 88cl.

Hard Rock Hotel: 181cr.

Photo and Print Collection of the Koninklijk Instituut voor Taal-, Land- en Volkenkunde (KITLV), Leiden: Woodbury & Page, Batavia 48br, Neeb 49tl, 50tc.

Mandara Spa: 169tr; Kal Muller: 19crb, 19br, 210tr, 210cla, 211tl, 211cra, 211crb; Museum Puri Lukisan: 14c, 24br, 34cla, 34bcl, 34br, 34–35c, 35cr, 35bl, 35br, 87br, *Bubuk Sah and Gagak Aking* I Cokot (1935) 88tr, 92tr, 92cla, 92bl, 92bc, 93tc, 93cr, 93bl, 97tr.

NASA: Image STS068-160-53 11br; Neka Art Museum: 34tr, 35tr, 44, 96cr, 115tl; The Nieuwenkamp Foundation, Vleuten: 9c, 49br, 213c; Novotel Benoa Bali: 168bc.

Jim Parks: 16tl; © Photobank/Tettoni, Cassio and Associates Pte Ltd: 1, 2–3, 8–9, 18cla, 18cra, 18bl, 18crb, 22tr, 22c, 27br, 30tr, 30cl, 30bcl, 30br, 31tr, 31cla, 31cra, 31clb, 31crb, 31bl, 32–33c, 33tl, 33cr, 33bl, 33br, 36tr, 37cra, 37clb, 37br, 38cl, 38bl, 38–39c, 48tc, 49crb, 52–53, 56, 57b, 65tl, 70–71, 78, 79b, 89tl, 91tr, 100, 106cl, 118–119, 124, 125b, 153tr, 153cr, 159bl, 164–165, 198tc, 198c, 198bl, 199tl, 200tr, 200bl, 202br, 209tr, 209br; Prima Foto: 30cra, 205cl; PT Media Wisata Dewata: 224tl.

Reefseekers Dive Centre: 136cla; Robert Harding Picture Library: © Gavin Hellier 142–143.

© Morten Strange/Flying Colours: 17bl, 136br.

© TC Nature: 18tr, 19bl, 81br, 84tl, 84tr, 84cl, 84c, 84cr, 84bl, 84br, 85tl, 85bc, 85br, 94tl, 94tr, 94clb, 94bc, 95tr, 95crb, 109cla, 109crb, 109bc, 110bl, 136tl, 136tr, 136clb, 137ca, 137bl, 138tl, 140crb, 140bl, 141br, 148tl, 204c, 205tc; © John Cooke 16tr, 16bl, 16br, 19cra, 54tl, 109tc, 121tl; © Tony Tilford 19clb, 54tl, 85bl, 137br.

Adrian Vickers: 50bl.

Front Endpaper: All special photography except © Photobank: tl, tlc, cra, bl.

Jacket Front - A1 Pix: HAGA c; DK Picture Library: Richard Watson cl; Robert Harding Picture Library: Gavin Hellier b; Powerstock Photolibrary: David Ball main image. Back: - DK Picture Library: Richard Watson tl; Getty Images: D.R. Austen br. Spine: - Powerstock Photolibrary: David Ball t.

Further Reading

History

Bali in the 19th Century Ide Anak Agung Gde Agung (Jakarta: Yayasan Obor Indonesia, 1991)

Bali Profile: People, Events, Circumstances (1001–1976) Willard A Hanna (American Universities Field Staff, 1976)

Bali at War: a History of the Dutch-Balinese Conflict of 1846–49 Alfons van der Kraan (Monash Asia Institute, 1995)

In Praise of Kuta: From Slave Port to Fishing Village to the Most Popular Resort in Bali Hugh Mabbett (January Books, 1987)

Lombok: Conquest, Colonization, and Underdevelopment, 1870–1940 Alfons van der Kraan (Heinemann Educational Books, 1980)

Negara: the Theater State in 19th Century Bali Clifford Geertz (Princeton University Press, 1981)

Society and Culture

Adat and Dinas: Balinese Communities in the Indonesian State Carol Warren (Oxford University Press, 1993)

Bali: A Paradise Created Adrian Vickers (Tuttle, 1997; first published 1989)

Bali: Cultural Tourism and Touristic Culture Michel Picard (Archipelago Press, 1998)

Bali, Morning of the World Luca Invernizzi Tettoni and Nigel Simmonds (Periplus, 1997)

Bali: Rangda and Barong Jane Belo (University of Washington Press, 1949)

Bali: Sekala and Niskala F B Eiseman (Periplus, 1989)

Bali: Studies in Life, Thought, and Ritual (Foris Publications, 1984)

Bali Today: Real Balinese Stories Jean Couteau with Usadi Wiratnaya et al (Spektra Communications, 1999)

The Balinese Hugh Mabbett (January Books, 1985)

Being Modern in Bali: Image and Change ed Adrian Vickers (Yale University Southeast Asia Studies, 1996)

The Food of Bali ed Wendy Hutton (Periplus World Food Series, 1999)

Island of Bali Miguel Covarrubias (Periplus, 1999; first published 1937)

The Peoples of Bali Angela Hobart, Urs Ramseyer and Albert Leeman (Blackwell, 1997)

Priests and Programmers J Stephen Lansing (Princeton University Press, 1991)

A Sacred Cloth Religion: Ceremonies of the Big Feast Among Wetu Telu Sasak Sven Cederroth (Nordic Institute of Asian Studies, 1991)

Staying Local in the Global Village: Bali in the Twentieth Century eds Raechelle Rubinstein and Linda H Connor (University of Hawaii Press, 1999)

Arts and Architecture

The Art And Culture of Bali Urs Ramseyer (Oxford University Press, 1977/1987)

At Home in Bali Made Wijaya, photography Isabella Ginannesch (Abbeville Press, 1999)

Bali: the Imaginary Museum Michael Hitchcock and Lucy Norris (Oxford University Press, 1996)

Bali Modern: The Art of Tropical Living Gianni Francione, photography Luca Invernizzi Tettoni (Tuttle, 1999)

Bali Sketchbook watercolours Graham Byfield, text Diana Darling (Archipelago Press, 1998)

Bali Style Rio Helmi and Barbara Walker (Times Editions, 1995; Thames & Hudson, 1995; Vendome Press, 1996)

Balinese Dance in Transition: Kaja and Kelod I Made Bandem, Frederik Eugene Deboer (Oxford University Press, 1995)

Balinese Dance, Music and Drama I Wayan Dibia, Rucina Ballinger (Periplus Press, 2004)

Balinese Gardens photography Luca Invernizzi Tettoni, text William Warren et al (Periplus/Thames and Hudson, 1996/2000)

Balinese Music Michael Tenzer (Periplus, 1991/1994)

Balinese Textiles Brigitta Hauser-Schublin, Marie-Louise Nabholz-Kartaschoff and Urs Ramseyer (Periplus, 1991/1997)

The Epic Of Life: A Balinese Journey Of The Soul Idanna Pucci (Alfred van der Marck Editions, 1985)

The Folk Art of Bali Joseph Fischer and Thomas Cooper (Oxford University Press, 1998)

Kecak: The Vocal Chant Of Bali I Wayan Dibia (Hartanto Art Books, 1996)

The Language of Balinese Shadow Theater Mary Sabine Zurbuchen (Princeton University Press, 1987)

Masks of Bali: Spirits of An Ancient Drama Judy Slattum, photography Paul Schraub (Chronicle, 1992)

Monumental Bali A J Bernet Kempers (Periplus, 1991/1997; first published 1977)

Museum Puri Lukisan Jean Couteau (Ratna Wartha Foundation, 2000)

Music in Bali Colin McPhee (Da Capo Press, 1976; first published 1966)

W O J Nieuwenkamp: First European Artist in Bali Bruce W Carpenter (Archipelago Press, 1998)

Perceptions of Paradise: Images of Bali in the Arts Garrett Kam (Dharma Seni Museum Neka, 1993)

Pre-War Balinese Modernists 1928–1942 Dr F Haks et al (Ars et Amimatio, Haarlem, the Netherlands)

Ulat-ulatan, Traditional Basketry in Bali Fred B Eiseman Jr (White Lotus, 1999)

Vessels Of Life: Lombok Earthenware Jean McKinnon (Saritaksu, 1996)

Nature

Bali – Periplus Action Guide Wally Singian, David Pickel (Periplus, 2000)

Birds of Bali Victor Mason and Frank Jarvis (Tuttle, 1994)

The Birds of Java and Bali Derek Holmes, illustrations Stephen Nash (Oxford University Press, 1989)

Diving and Snorkeling Guide to Bali and the Komodo Region Tim Rock (Pisces, 1996)

The Ecology of Java and Bali Tony Whitten et al (Oxford University Press, 1997)

Flowers of Bali Fred Eiseman (Periplus, 1994)

Fruits of Bali Fred Eiseman and Margaret Eiseman (Periplus, 1994)

Travelogues and Memoirs

Bali: the Last Paradise Hickman Powell, photography André Roosevelt (Oxford University Press, 1930/1989; Dodd, Mead, 1936)

Bali: People and Art Gregor Krause (White Lotus, 2000; first published in German 1926)

The Birthmark: Memoirs of a Balinese Prince A A M Djelantik (Periplus, 1998)

A House in Bali Colin McPhee (Tuttle/Periplus, 2000; first published 1946)

A Little Bit One O'Clock William Ingram (Ersania Books, 1998)

The Night of Purnama Anna Matthews (Jonathan Cape, 1965)

Our Hotel In Bali: ... A Story Of The 1930s Louise G Koke (January Books, 1987)

Stranger In Paradise: the Diary of an Expatriate in Bali 1979–80 Made Wijaya (Wijaya Words, 1984)

Travelling to Bali: Four Hundred Years of Journeys Adrian Vickers (Oxford University Press, 1995)

Fiction

Bali Behind the Seen: Recent Fiction From Bali trans and ed Vern Cork (Darma Printing, 1996)

The Edge of Bali Inez Baranay (Angus & Robertson, 1992)

The Painted Alphabet: a Novel Based on a Balinese Tale Diana Darling (Tuttle, 2001; Graywolf, 1994; Houghton Mifflin, 1992)

The Sweat of Pearls: Short Stories About Women of Bali Putu Oka Sukanta, trans Vern Cork (Darma Printing, 1999)

A Tale from Bali Vicki Baum (Tuttle/Periplus, 2000; first published 1937)

Books for Children

Bye, Bye, Bali Kai Harriett Luger (Browndeer, 1996)

The Dancing Pig Judy Sierra (Gulliver, 1999)

The Haughty Toad, And Other Tales From Bali Victor Mason, illustrations by artists Of Pengosekan (Bali Art Print/Hamlyn, 1975).

Rice Is Life Rita Golden Gelman (Henry Holt, 2000)

Glossary

Architecture

atap: palm-leaf thatched roof
bale: pavilion
candi bentar: split gate
gedong: enclosed pavilion
kori: roofed gate
kori agung: grand gate
kulkul: drum tower
meru: multi-tiered shrine
padmasana: tall shrine to the Supreme Deity
pelinggih: shrine, spirit house
pura: temple
puri: palace, house of nobility
rumah: house
wantilan: public pavilion with double roof
warung: coffee stall, small shop

Arts and Crafts

geringsing: warp- and weft-dyed textile, "double ikat"
ikat: warp resist-dyed textile
kayu: wood
lontar: type of palm; palm-leaf book
lukisan: painting
mas: gold
pande: metalsmith
paras: volcanic stone used for building and statuary
patung: statue
perak: silver
prada: gilt-painted cloth
songket: textile with supplementary weft thread, often gold or silver
tapel: mask
tenunan: weaving

Music and Dance

arja: Balinese opera
baris: classical solo male dance
baris gede: a sacred dance for rows of male dancers
Barong: large sacred effigy danced by two men
belaganjur: processional percussion orchestra
gambuh: ancient court dance
gamelan: percussion orchestra
gangsa: bronze-keyed instrument
kebyar: vigorous style of gamelan music; vigorous solo dance
kendang: drum
keris: sacred wavy-bladed dagger
legong: classical dance for three females
prembon: mixed programme
Rangda: sacred demonic effigy, consort of the Barong
rejang: sacred dance for rows of female dancers
suling: bamboo flute
tari: dance
topeng: masked dance based on geneological tales
trompong: bronze instrument with 8 to 12 kettle gongs
wayang kulit: shadow puppet theatre
wayang wong: masked dance based on Hindu epics

Dress

baju: shirt, dress
baju kaus: T-shirt
destar: head cloth for Balinese males
gelungan: ornate headdress
jilbab: head cloth for Muslim females
kain: cloth; long hip cloth, unsewn
kebaya: traditional jacket for females
peci: hat for Muslim males
sarong: sewn long hip cloth
selendang: ceremonial temple sash
sepatu: shoes

Religions and Community

banjar: village association
hari raya: any religious holiday
karya: work, especially collective ritual work
mesjid: mosque
odalan: temple festival
pedanda: high priest
pemangku: temple priest
penjor: festooned bamboo pole
pura dalem: temple of the netherworld
pura desa: village temple
pura puseh: temple of origins
sebel: taboo
sunat: Islamic ritual circumcision
tirta: holy water
yadnya: Hindu ritual (generic)

Food

air minum: drinking water
ayam: chicken
babi guling: roast pig
babi: pork
bakar: grilled
bebek tutu: smoked spicy duck
buah-buahan: fruit
cumi-cumi: squid
daging: meat
gado-gado: vegetarian dish with peanut sauce
garam: salt
goreng: fried
gula: sugar
ikan laut: fish
jeruk nyepis: lime
jeruk: orange; citrus
kelapa: coconut
kopi: coffee
makan: eat
mie: noodles
minum: drink
nasi: food; rice; rice meal
pedas: hot (spicy)
pisang: banana
roti: bread
sambal: spicy condiment
sapi: beef
sate, sate lilit: small skewers of barbecued meat
susu: milk
teh: tea
telur: egg
udang: prawn, shrimp

Nature and Landscape

bukit: hill
burung: bird
danau: lake
gunung: mountain
hujan: rain
jalan: road
laut: sea
mata hari: sun
pantai: beach
pohon: tree
sawah: ricefield
subak: irrigation co-operative
sungai: river, stream
taman: garden, park
tanah: ground, earth, soil

Travel and Transport

bemo: public minibus
cidomo: rubber-tyred pony cart (in Lombok)
dokar: pony cart
jukung: outrigger sailing canoe
mobil: car
sepeda motor: motorcycle

Miscellaneous

adat: customary law
bagus: good, handsome
baik: good
Bapak: polite term of address for a man
bayar: pay
cantik: pretty
dingin: cold
Ibu: polite term of address for a woman
mahal: expensive
murah: inexpensive
panas: hot, warm
pariwisata: tourism
puputan: suicidal fight-to-the-end
roko: cigarette
sakit: hurt; sick
selamat jalan: farewell ("on your journey")
terima kasih: thank you
tidak: no, not
tidur: sleep
uang: money

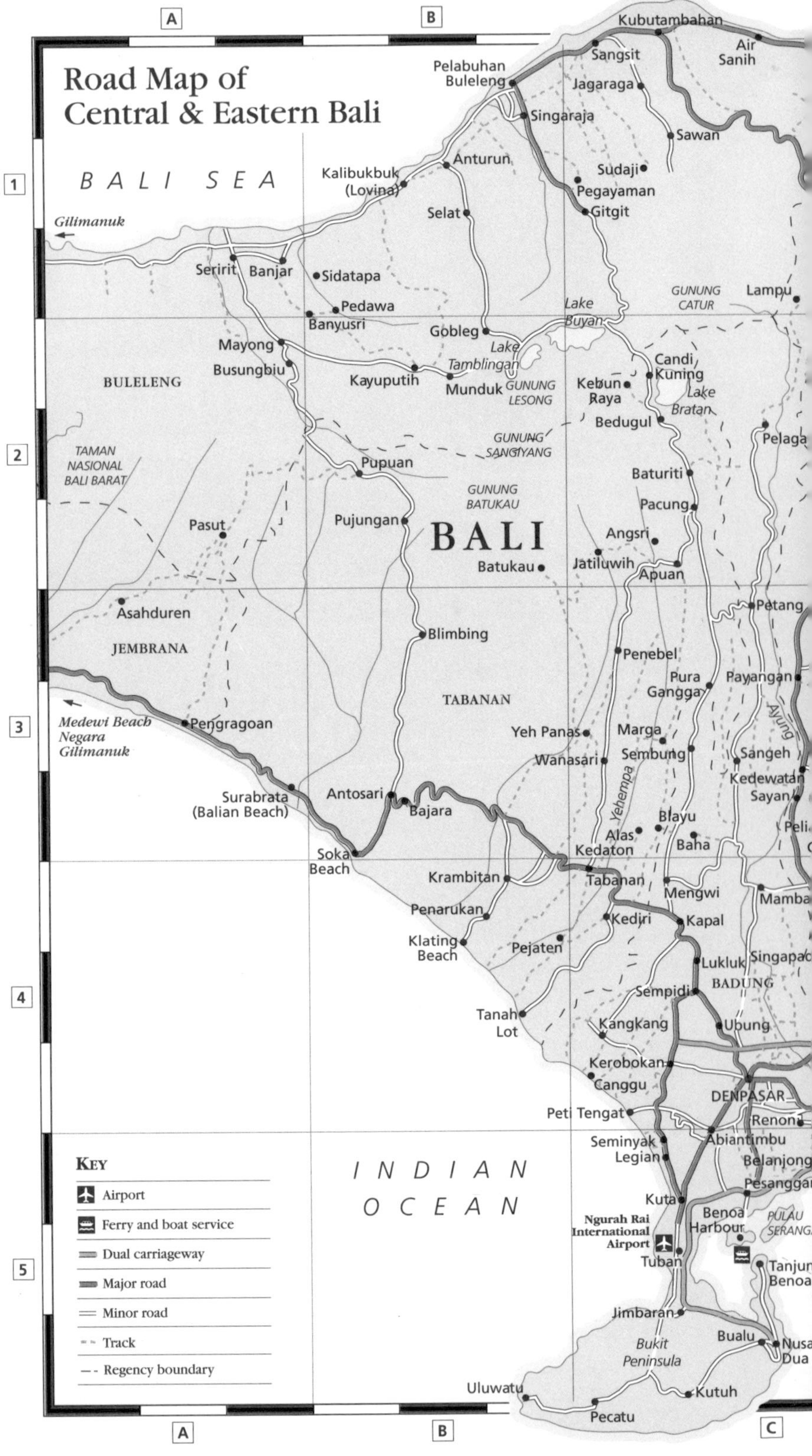
Road Map of Central & Eastern Bali
A
B
C
1
2
3
4
5
BALI SEA
INDIAN OCEAN
BALI
Gilimanuk
Medewi Beach
Negara
Gilimanuk
BULELENG
JEMBRANA
TABANAN
BADUNG
DENPASAR
TAMAN NASIONAL BALI BARAT
GUNUNG LESONG
GUNUNG SANGIYANG
GUNUNG BATUKAU
GUNUNG CATUR
Lake Buyan
Lake Tamblingan
Lake Bratan
Yehempa
Ayung
PULAU SERANGAN
Bukit Peninsula
Kubutambahan
Air Sanih
Sangsit
Jagaraga
Pelabuhan Buleleng
Singaraja
Sawan
Sudaji
Pegayaman
Gitgit
Anturun
Kalibukbuk (Lovina)
Selat
Seririt
Banjar
Sidatapa
Pedawa
Banyusri
Gobleg
Lampu
Mayong
Busungbiu
Kayuputih
Munduk
Candi Kuning
Kebun Raya
Bedugul
Pelaga
Pupuan
Baturiti
Pacung
Pujungan
Pasut
Angsri
Batukau
Jatiluwih
Apuan
Asahduren
Petang
Blimbing
Penebel
Pura Gangga
Payangan
Pengragoan
Yeh Panas
Marga
Wanasari
Sembung
Sangeh
Kedewatan
Sayan
Surabrata (Balian Beach)
Antosari
Bajara
Blayu
Alas Kedaton
Baha
Soka Beach
Krambitan
Tabanan
Mengwi
Mamba
Penarukan
Kediri
Kapal
Klating Beach
Pejaten
Lukluk
Singapad
Sempidi
Tanah Lot
Kangkang
Ubung
Kerobokan
Canggu
Peti Tengat
Renon
Seminyak
Legian
Abiantimbu
Belanjong
Kuta
Pesanggar
Ngurah Rai International Airport
Benoa Harbour
Tuban
Tanjung Benoa
Jimbaran
Bualu
Nusa Dua
Uluwatu
Kutuh
Pecatu
KEY
Airport
Ferry and boat service
Dual carriageway
Major road
Minor road
Track
Regency boundary